Days of Awe

Days of Awe

Reimagining Jewishness in
Solidarity with Palestinians

ATALIA OMER

The University of Chicago Press
Chicago and London

The University of Chicago Press, Chicago 60637
The University of Chicago Press, Ltd., London
© 2019 by The University of Chicago
Published 2019
Printed in the United States of America

28 27 26 25 24 23 22 21 20 19   1 2 3 4 5

ISBN-13: 978-0-226-61591-2 (cloth)
ISBN-13: 978-0-226-61607-0 (paper)
ISBN-13: 978-0-226-61610-0 (e-book)
DOI: https://doi.org/10.7208/chicago/9780226616100.001.0001

This book is made possible in part by support from the Institute for Scholarship in
the Liberal Arts, College of Arts and Letters, University of Notre Dame.

Library of Congress Cataloging-in-Publication Data

Names: Omer, Atalia, author.
Title: Days of awe : reimagining Jewishness in solidarity with Palestinians /
   Atalia Omer.
Description: Chicago ; London : The University of Chicago Press, 2019. | Includes
   bibliographical references and index.
Identifiers: LCCN 2018043422 | ISBN 9780226615912 (cloth : alk. paper) |
   ISBN 9780226616070 (pbk. : alk. paper) | ISBN 9780226616100 (e-book)
Subjects: LCSH: Palestinian Arabs—Government policy—Israel. | Arab-Israeli
   conflict—1993- —Peace. | Jews—Political activity—United States. | Jews—
   United States—Religion.
Classification: LCC DS128.2.O547 2019 | DDC 956.7405/5—dc23
LC record available at https://lccn.loc.gov/2018043422

♾ This paper meets the requirements of ANSI/NISO Z39.48–1992
(Permanence of Paper).

To Jason and our children Yonatan and Pnei'el Alois Omer-Springs
and with hope for a world beyond the occupation

Contents

Acknowledgments

This book took shape over more than five years. I benefited from the generosity of the University of Notre Dame's Institute for Scholarship in the Liberal Arts and the Kroc Institute for International Peace Studies. Both institutes enabled me to conduct research with Jewish Palestine solidarity activists in the US and the West Bank, Palestine/Israel, and facilitate the editing and production processes of the book. Over these long years, I accrued personal debt to the many activists and other critical Jews who agreed to share their stories with me and invest the time in responding to my queries. Many of them became friends. In some cases, I felt as if I had known them my entire life. In the course of research, my family and I have found a home in a synagogue in Chicago that has embodied the process of rescripting Jewishness that the book captures and analyzes. We will continue to be members there long after the book is printed and distributed. The synagogue, Tzedek Chicago, does not occupy an actual physical space but rather roams around Chicago borrowing spaces from other establishments (union halls, churches, heritage centers, and community organizer facilities) in order to perform its innovative liturgy and events, and plan its social justice interventions. This nomadic condition befits the process of reimagining American Jewish identity and values. I was also personally challenged and transformed by the many young people I encountered along the way, whether in Chicago or Boston or those Millennials—but also by veteran activists—who partook in a Jewish Palestine solidarity delegation to the West Bank in May 2017. Their ethical commitments and moral outrage reinforced my own, as well as the tools I employ to interrogate these commitments and emotions.

I am also in debt to the colleagues at the University of Notre Dame (and elsewhere), Ann Mische, Jason Springs, Cecelia Lynch, Ernesto Verdeja,

Shanna Corner, Ruth Carmi, Hamid Dabashi, Thomas Tweed, Christian Smith, Aline Kalbian, and Shaul Magid. They all offered conceptual feedback to specific chapters or the manuscript as a whole. I am also thankful to Marc Dollinger, who shared the proofs for his forthcoming book with me, and the three anonymous readers who offered important interventions and constructive feedback. I likewise remain in debt to friends and mentors who continue to inspire and support me. They include Robert Orsi, Slavica Jakelic, Asher Kaufman, Martin Kavka, John Kelsay, David Little, Harvey Cox, Scott Appleby, Loren Lybarger, David Cortright, Ruth Abbey, John Paul Lederach, Robert Johansen, Mary Ellen O'Connell, Richard Hecht, Santiago Slabodsky, Peter and Lena Wallensteen, Diane Moore, Karen Jacob, Barbara Lockwood, Lyn Spillman, David and Gayle Hachen, Amir Hussain, Brant Rosen, Michael Davis, Lynn Gottlieb, Lesley Williams, Lynn Pollack, Lisa Kosowski, Julie Kosowski, Jay Stanton, Scout Bratt, Carla Singer, and Mary Ellen Konieczny (of blessed memory). I am grateful for the excellent editorial assistance from Ben Dillon and Emily Gravett and the superb shepherding, by Kyle Adam Wagner and Douglas Mitchell of the University of Chicago Press, of the manuscript through the review and publication process. I am likewise grateful for the wonderful research assistance I received from Kelly McGee and Madeleine Paulsen, my former undergraduate students at the University of Notre Dame, and the generosity of the photographers Gili Getz, Ethan Miller, and Christopher Hazou. I also offer thanks to Madeline Foley, Anna Johnson, and Anna Fett for their help in proofreading the book and to Derek Gottlieb for indexing.

The chapters constitute original contributions. However, seeds of the conceptual framing of the book are already found in an earlier published article (Atalia Omer, "Nationalism and the Comparative Study of Religious Ethics: Future Trajectories," *Sounding* 98, no. 3 [2015]: 322–53) and the chapter "Religion, Nationalism, and Solidarity Activism," in *The Oxford Handbook of Religion, Conflict, and Peacebuilding*, ed. Omer, R. Scott Appleby, and David Little (Oxford: Oxford University Press, 2015), 613–58. Additionally, chapter 7 developed out of my contribution to a 2015 conference on People's Peace at Arizona State University's Center for the Study of Religion and Conflict. Similarly, portions of chapters 8 and 9 that specifically address Mizrahi critique emerge from and substantially revise some of my earlier engagement with mizrahiness in Atalia Omer, "Hitmazrehut or Becoming of the East: Re-Orienting Israeli Social Mapping," *Critical Sociology* 43, no. 6 (2017): 949–76. The concept of "critical caretaking" that features especially in chapter 4 but is threaded throughout the book was also developed in my *When Peace Is Not Enough: How the Israeli Peace Camp Thinks about Religion, Nationalism, and Justice* (Chicago: University of Chicago Press, 2013), and in Atalia Omer, "Can a Critic Be a Caretaker Too? Religion, Conflict, and Conflict Transformation," *Journal of the American Academy of Religion* 79, no. 2 (2011): 459–96. Critical caretaking in the present book takes different forms and draws on different scholarly conversations than my earlier engagement with this concept. I also benefited widely from presenting my ideas to colleagues at Harvard Divinity School's Center for the Study of World Religions, University of California–Los Angeles, and the University of Alberta's Chester Ronning Centre, among other places.

The support of my family has been indispensable in bringing this work to fruition. I am especially grateful to Nurit Manne Adizes for her relentless support and to Dani Omer whose memory and prophetic courage continue to ignite me. I am likewise in debt to Kathy and Lance Springs, Alois Lewis, and James B. Lewis (of blessed memory). Of course, the greatest debt I owe is to my partner in life and scholarship, Jason Springs, who enabled me on my journey with Jewish Palestine solidarity, and our children Yonatan Daniele and Pnei'el Alois Omer-Springs, for whom, I hope, this book and this adventure will one day be significant. At the same time, I hope that the occupation will rescind into a mere chapter in the books of history. It is to them and this aspiration that I dedicate this book.

A Note about Spelling and Acronyms

One word receives an unconventional spelling throughout the book. I chose to spell *antisemitism* and *antisemitic* without hyphen or capitalization in order to delegitimize "Semitism," a pseudo-scientific category central to race theories.[1] Likewise, the word "occupation" is spelled with a lowercase "o," reflecting the fluidity with which different people define the occupation, its boundaries, and its normative scope. When quoting other authors, however, I have left their spelling of these words unchanged.

Acronyms and non-English terms are ubiquitous throughout the book. They include the following:

BDS = Boycott, Divestment, Sanctions campaign
hasbarah = the Hebrew for Israel's global public relations mechanisms (literally "explanation")
INN = IfNotNow
JFREJ = Jews for Racial & Economic Justice
JOC = Jews of Color
JOCSM = Sephardi, Mizrahi, and Jews of Color
JVP = Jewish Voice for Peace
MBL = Movement for Black Lives
NAI = Network Against Islamophobia
Nakba = the Palestinian catastrophe of 1948
OH = Open Hillel
POC = People of Color
RPB = religion and peacebuilding
RVP = religion, violence, and peacebuilding
SJP = Students for Justice in Palestine
sumud = the Palestinian concept of steadfastness
teshuvah = the Jewish liturgical concept of atonement or return

Living the Days of Awe, Relentlessly:
An Introduction

Sure, on Rosh Hashanah our fate is—according to some—written in one of those two books-of-the-binary, but it isn't until tonight, until Yom Kippur, that our fate is actually sealed. We have, in fact, been living in the in-between, a time when, according to our liturgy, we could actually change what was written for us on Rosh Hashanah.

If we have done the work of repentance and reflection, we may have been doing the work of rewriting. Our traditions actively encourage us to use this time as if we are in between the Books of Life and Death. Most notably, we don't actually know which book we were written into on Rosh Hashanah. We don't actually know how necessary it is for us to rewrite our fate. We may never know—we have been acting out of uncertainty, occupying the uncertain space.

. . . It is in this liminal space that I believe creation happens and transformation occurs. Out of our comfort zones, out of our privileged standpoints of knowing, that we create new understandings. In expanding upon that oh-so-binary story of creation, Pirkei Avot inside the Mishnah describes ten things created at twilight, created precisely during the in-between of the sixth day of creation's end and restful Shabbat's beginning. Twilight yielded us the rainbow. The manna we ate in the desert. Moses's staff. The tablets and writing of the Ten Commandments. I like those.

This twilight is seen as possibility: possibly day, possibly night, neither wholly one nor the other. And, yet, it is time for creation. This is the active non-binary . . .

I want us to courageously acknowledge how our comfort, our safety, our security lie in the binary and in the reliance of us vs. them. On the reliance of separation. I want us to speak to the unspoken binaries in order to find the twilights. Twilights like rewriting our inscription in the Book of Life or the Book of Death. Twilights like being gender non-binary that maybe other people don't understand, that may be confusing. Twilights that seem unthinkable, seem irrational, seem impossible . . .

Naming and confronting the separations take waking up every day as if it is one of the ten days of awe. It means not avoiding the unknown, not ignoring the nagging questions. It means relentlessly and humbly giving up our certainty. Maybe it seems unfair to ask us to sustain the intensity and vulnerability of these past ten days. I would argue that we've been working a lot harder, for a lot longer, all year round, to sustain the binaries in our world. I think we can do this.[1]

These are the words of Scout Bratt, a member of Tzedek Chicago (established in 2014), a values-based Jewish community or "congregation" that explicitly defines itself in terms of nonviolence, solidarity, equality, and non-Zionism. Bratt's Kol Nidrei sermon, on the eve of Yom Kippur, captures an insight that broadly animates American Jewish Palestine solidarity activists and other Jewish critics of Israel's occupation of Palestine. I focus on their process of reimagining Jewishness as they grapple relentlessly with communal sins, especially the suffering inflicted on Palestinians in the name of Jews, effected through a specific narration of Jewish identity. The book, in other words, investigates a continuous "Days of Awe" where, as Bratt says, we inhabit "the in-between" or a "liminal space" where "creation happens and transformation occurs." In Bratt's words, "the work of repentance and reflection" entails "rewriting" our stories through a space of uncertainty rather than the one of either-or certainty, the hallmark of binary thinking.

In conducting research for this book, I often experienced the kind of pain generated from unsettling certainties and destabilizing narratives. Even though I am a product of the Israeli peace camp, my sustained engagement with American Jewish critics and anti-occupation activists as well as the analytical tools they employ in their solidarity work, and in their courageous collective look in the mirror, was excruciating. It was excruciating because I grew up in Jerusalem, because my family carries the traumatic sadness of loss and displacement from Europe, and because the Israeli friends I love so much pour their hearts and souls into fighting the occupation and Israeli policies against asylum seekers, as well as advocating for increased pluralistic practices. Unlike many of my American Jewish interviewees, I could never turn my back on them and tell them that they constitute a "perversion" of Jewish history. They are so very real and layered with complexities that defy simply categorizing them as perpetrators of violence, full stop. The deep pain I experienced as I followed anti-occupation American Jews in their journeys is rooted in that unbearable collective look in the mirror. Despite examining illusions and ideological constructs, I remained unable to turn my back on my Israeliness and my friends who are in both Israel and Palestine. For them, the prospect of peacebuilding and cohabitation necessitates cultivating constructive and Jewishly meaningful alternative national imaginations, which cannot bracket Israel or Zionism as "un-Jewish" or a departure from the supposedly more authentic Jewishness of the diasporas. While challenging a binary outlook in general, Bratt and others in the movement often fail to recognize the immobility and lack of a fluid self-reflexivity regarding the one binary of Zion versus diasporas. I inhabit this entanglement, and thus understand and anticipate where the potential critics of this book may be coming from. Such critics may categorize the anti-occupation Jewish activists as misled, naïve, self-hating, and as posing actual danger to Israel's security. The new battlefields, as we will see in chapter 1, are university campuses and the arena of public opinion and branding, where departures from controlled narratives justifying Israeli policies constitute apparent threats to the Jewish community. The activists I engaged refuse this logic, persist in exposing the ligaments underpinning the narratives they have inherited, disrupt the mechanisms of social reproduction, and force the Jewish community to look in the mirror, grapple with its sinfulness, and reimagine alternative communal meanings and ethics that draw upon the lessons of the Holocaust, pluralistically rather than tribally. Indeed, they exhibit enhanced levels of self-approval and self-love, celebrating their reclaimed sense of Jewishness as joyful and diasporic and their role as the generation that will end the moral catastrophe of the occupation. Hence, even while recognizing where the potential detractors of American Jewish Palestine solidarity and anti-occupation activists are coming from in terms of fears, interests, and outlooks, it is important to listen to what their internal Jewish critics are telling them louder and louder and how they articulate their arguments through interrogating Jewish histories, meanings, narratives, symbols, and texts. In researching for this book, I listened to them and learned in ways that challenged me profoundly, both as a scholar of religion, violence, and peacebuilding as well as personally, in terms of my own positionality.

I am an Israeli-born, cisgender, Ashkenazi woman who has spent over two decades in the US. My spouse is Christian, but we chose to raise our two children Jewish. As a critic of the Israeli occupation, I have struggled for years with precisely how to raise our children as Jews in an American Jewish landscape that so strongly and uncritically accepts the occupation, its routine violation of human dignity, episodic massacres of Palestinian civilians, and overwhelming disregard for Palestinian lives. Through my engagement with Jewish Palestine solidarity in the US, I found a space for my family in Tzedek Chicago (not an easy commute from South Bend, Indiana). My research and immersion in the conversations unfolding in activist circles have also enhanced my own embrace of a relentless engagement with the Days of Awe in ways I had not anticipated. In particular, the interconnections among sites of politicization such as gender, feminism, antimilitarism, and racism became clear to me only through listening to the mostly young Jews for whom resistance to the occupation, which demanded putting their (mostly privileged and white) bodies on the line, became an urgent necessity. Prior to immersing myself in the movement, I did not realize that my identity and privilege as a cisgender woman was of any relevance to the discussion of the Israeli occupation of Palestinians. But it is, I have learned, relevant to the broader interrogation of privilege so pivotal for an intersectional analysis that connects multiple sites of oppression, as the Jewish Palestine solidarity movement does. I emerged, on the other side of this research, with a deeper understanding of gender and race and how they intersect with the study of religion as well as religion's relevance to sociopolitical and cultural change and vice versa.

Even while struggling with the pain I discuss above, I myself was transformed over the course of my research. In particular, the Days of Awe continue to haunt me as I recall my experience, as a part of the Center for Jewish Nonviolence's (CJNV) solidarity delegation in May 2017, in the Palestinian village of Susiya in the Southern Hills of Hebron. Under constant threats of total demolition, with drones monitoring every move, the village barely exists anymore. Yet the Rural Women Association and the children with whom we worked hosted us with warmth, enthusiasm, and a steadfastness that capture the Palestinian experience of *sumud*, or existence as resistance. I looked up at the mountaintop illegal outposts and settlements surrounding us and examined their lavishness in contrast to the poverty and lack of infrastructure in the Palestinian Susiya and felt, more profoundly than ever, the ugliness of the communal sin of the occupation. Back in Chicago on the eve of Yom Kippur 5778/2017, as I finished writing this book, I listened to Bratt's Kol Nidrei sermon before partaking in the reinterpreted liturgy. I was deeply moved during the reinterpreted ritual of communal *vidui* or confession for the sins of militarization, occupation, dehumanization, and so forth. The point is not only to name such sins but also to act from a place of repentance to transform the terms of the conversation through discursive critique and by standing in solidarity and alliance with the marginalized, and in the process to reimagine one's own script. This is what this book is about.

The Days of Awe unsettle comfort and privilege. They facilitate "new understandings" by challenging the binary logic underpinning the status quo, the ordinary time outside the creativity of twilight. These liminal days constitute a site of terrible anxiety and self-interrogation, but Jewish Palestine solidarity embraces the terrible and, in the process of denaturalizing what appears natural and self-evident, reimagines Jewishness itself. *Days of Awe* tells this story of reimagining. Along the way, it highlights the experiences of ethical outrage, ideological unlearning, and grassroots meaning-making. Its emphasis on decolonization shifts the disciplinary boundaries of religion, violence, and peacebuilding (RVP) studies in ways that elucidate and chart new paths for thinking about religion's role in sociocultural and political transformative processes.

What I mean by "decolonization" will become clearer in later chapters as I show what it entails for Jewish Palestine solidarity activists to inhabit relentlessly the Days of Awe. They do so when they protest in front of the institutions of the American Jewish establishment to express shame at the sinfulness of complicity with the occupation, or put their bodies on the line in the

West Bank. They also engage the Days of Awe relentlessly when they rescript Jewishness. They do so by reclaiming the secular Jewish socialist Bundist tradition—founded in 1897 in Lithuania, Poland, and Russia—or by reinterpreting rituals and liturgy. Inhabiting the twilight as a space for creation leads activists, through their participation in a broader social movement against all forms of oppression and racism, to progressively scrutinize the construction of Jews as "white" and the enduring orientalism that animates the history of Zionism, including the marginalization of Mizrahi, Sephardi, and Jews of Color (JOCSM) from normative Jewish life. It demands interrogating the relevance of concepts such as "settler colonialism" and "white supremacy" to the processes of self-critique and self-refashioning.

Reimagining Jewishness entails interrupting certainties by contending with race history, including the racializing of religion and the production of narratives where some people are "civilized" and others are "barbarians." This history is deeply entrenched in modernity's colonial roots, which in turn entrenched (white) Jews in a civilizational identity in ways that precluded a multiperspectival view of interconnections among the genocides of modernity—those in colonial Africa, for example, and elsewhere and in the Holocaust—as well as the interconnections among systems of domination that continuously ghettoize and dehumanize marginalized communities. Hence, Palestine solidarity—in both its Jewish and non-explicitly Jewish forms—is enhanced through an alliance with a wide array of causes in the US, as a way of reclaiming *doikayt*, or "hereness," signaling the Bundist commitment to fight in solidarity with all of one's neighbors, thereby rejecting Zionism and diasporic enclave practices. This reclamation of *doikayt* also entails fighting globally against military occupations, neoliberal policies, and other forms of oppression. Most critically, however, it traverses ethical indignation and solidarity with the Palestinian struggle. "It is *their* [Palestinians'] struggle you are here to support,"[2] a veteran Jewish activist from the Student Nonviolent Coordinating Committee of the US civil rights movement in the 1960s reminded us in a hotel conference room in Bethlehem, which was filled with Jewish Palestine solidarity and anti-occupation activists. Reimagining Jewishness through Palestine solidarity involves not only a struggle with the legacy of antisemitism, but also an interlinking of this struggle with struggles against racism, white supremacy, economic exploitation, and bigotry in all its forms and shapes.

As I learned over the course of my research, reimagining Jewishness also involves sensitization to gender and feminist critiques. When Bratt described the Days of Awe as a time "to break binaries, to break the power inequity inherent within them," and a time of "naming and confronting the separations" the binaries produce, Bratt spoke from their own comprehension of what it means to inhabit a non-binary gender identity and to inhabit it actively. Bratt, like many young people I interacted with throughout this research, used their non-binary lived experiences to unlearn Zionism's reliance on a host of binaries. Jewish Palestine solidarity, through processes of politicization on gender, race, and other sites of injustice, challenges the binaries informing exclusivist modes of solidarity that rely on binarizing "Jews" and "Arabs" and posit one side as more worthy of "grievability," in the words of Judith Butler.[3] When one destabilizes a narrative that justifies the valuing of one kind of blood (life) over another, it opens up the possibility, as Bratt stressed, of "relentlessly and humbly giving up our certainty." Giving up one's certainty about Israeli violence and the Zionist teleological narration of Jewish history, devaluing and negating the diasporic, precipitated reconfiguration of Jewishness that cannot only be explained through the lens of Palestine solidarity.

If we take Butler's view of religion as "a matrix for subject formation whose final form is not determined in advance, a discursive matrix for the articulation and disputation of values, and a field of contestation,"[4] we can trace, as I do in this book, the discursivity of the matrix of Jewishness. The reimagined community is not predetermined, but a product of contention and introspection. As such, it is deeply influenced by (and informed by) the analytic frameworks and categories of a broader social justice movement that also revolts against the hold of coloniality and its foundational distinction between those who deserve grief and those who do not. Reimagining Jewishness, therefore, involves not only the tools of extra-traditional critical theory, but intra-traditional literacy in history and hermeneutics. The emphasis on gender and race as critical sites for interrogation and renarration in the twilight of ethical outrage, in the face of collective sinfulness and empathy with Palestinians' experiences of injustice, conveys the intersectional and relational dynamics of American Jewish Palestine solidarity and processes of new communal creation, where the "new" is often framed hermeneutically as a recovery of what was lost, perverted, or derailed.

The analysis thus suggests that the processes of refiguring American Jewish identity are both *relational* (confronted by Palestinian narratives) and *intersectional* (influenced by multiple social justice issues). It thus complements and expands upon recent scholarship[5] that identifies how socioeconomic and cultural comfort has led many Americans, especially young American Jews, to embrace cosmopolitanism and global humanitarianism. Such "do-goodism," however, is not the same as a grassroots prophetic critique, which grapples with communal sin and privilege.[6] The examination here moves beyond introspective structural and cultural analyses of Israel's transformation from a locus of consensus to the epicenter of internal conflict within the American Jewish community.[7] It also expands explanatory accounts that attribute this change to intra-Jewish intellectual currents.[8] Instead, I focus on the agentic meaning-making capacity of activists in social movements. In doing so, I foreground how ethical outrage, solidarity with Palestinians, and struggles for social justice in other areas motivate activists to reimagine Jewishness through liturgical and hermeneutical innovation and social protest. The "ethical outrage" or "cognitive dissonance" many activists express does not arise automatically; my interviews and other methods of investigation show how processes of prior politicization—especially on questions of gender, feminism, militarization, and race—generate ethical outrage, spur unlearning, and refashion identity. This refashioning of Jewishness requires hermeneutical work with cultural and traditional resources, but it is not only backward-looking. It is also forward-looking and innovative because of its historical embeddedness.

Hence, my examination of American Jewish Palestine solidarity activists interweaves religious studies and social movement theory as well as insights from the study of RVP, a field often driven by the real moral urgencies of our world. The focus on relationality, intersectionality, and social movement dynamics illumines grassroots religious innovation, leadership and authority, and resources for reframing narratives and inspiring collective action. The intersectional lens looks in from the margins, accounting for multiple and constitutive forms of discrimination and marginality.[9] This method for producing oppositional knowledge, Patricia Hill Collins argues, avoids a facile containment within a politics of identity that ignores a critique of capitalism in its neoliberal moment.[10] Black feminists' modalities of oppositional knowledge, critical inquiry, and political praxis offer, Collins contends, resources for solidarity, ethical commitment, and political action of broad-based coalitions. The focus on black feminism, the locus from which intersectional analysis emerged, does not suggest parochialism. On the contrary, this mode of critique and political praxis is, by definition, broad in scope: it recognizes how various forms of oppression relate to one another and offers an intricate analysis of how systems of power interrelate. The creativity of twilight, as Bratt put it, unfolds through activist non-binary and intersectional epistemology from the margins. This is where "creation happens and transformation occurs." To this extent, *Days of Awe* intervenes in and expands the subfield of RVP by focusing on sites of discursive violence intersectionally, thereby decolonizing the modernist abstraction of "religion" from "ethnicity," "nationality," "culture," and "race" as well as examining the refiguring of communal boundaries and identities through activist prophetic and discursive interventions. The turn to intersectionality does not entail a mere focus on the *negative* experiences of oppression, but also involves a multiplicity of *positive* aspirations, values, and forms of subjectivity[11] that, in the case of anti-occupation American Jews, are often rewritten from the margins and the grassroots through fluid and elastic participation in social movement work.

Organization and Argument

First, let me offer a word on my mixed methodology. In this study, I employed participant observations, interviews,[12] and analyses of social and other media. To investigate differences and similarities between Jewish and non-Jewish distant issue activists, I interviewed both Jewish and non-Jewish American Palestine solidarity activists. My study also involved participant observation in a Jewish solidarity trip to the West Bank, Jewish Voice for Peace (JVP) activism in Chicago and nationally, and as a member at Tzedek Chicago. Many members of this Jewish community are Palestine solidarity activists, or explicit critics of Zionism and Israel. My choice to study the American Jewish community of critics and activists is not intended to diminish the significance of comparable groups in other diasporic contexts. Instead, the choice relates to the obvious fact that American Jews' influence on Israel and American foreign policy is critical, and to the belief that addressing subterranean challenges and transformations could carry profound ramifications for Israel and Palestine on the ground.

This book is about the reimagining of American Jewishness in the nexus of anti-occupation critique and social justice activism. Throughout, I remain descriptively close to the processes, critiques, and reframing of Jewishness that the activists themselves articulate and embody. As I mentioned above, I anticipate that detractors will employ the labels of "self-hating," "anti-semitic," or "hopelessly naïve" to characterize this book—the same labels that are used to classify and dismiss the Jewish critics of the occupation. In response, I underscore that I examine how the activists and critics themselves challenge such labels. Indeed, for the Jewish activists, challenging Zionist norms is not a matter of mere debate. Rather, it has become a pivotal mechanism for their process of reimagining their identity as Jews through solidarity with Palestinians. Similarly, my own intention is to analyze this movement of American Jews in order to shed light on and expand the study of religion and sociopolitical change, interrogating how religion participates in transformative social movement and also the inverse: how social movement reflects back on processes of religious change and innovation.

Days of Awe is, accordingly, divided into three parts. Part I, consisting of chapters 1 and 2, orients the reader to the discursive terrain that American Jewish Palestine solidarity activists navigate. It also sketches the book's central theoretical argument, that Jewish Palestine solidarity activists and other critics of the occupation and Zionism constitute a social movement operating to transform the meanings of Jewishness. Chapter 1, "Questioning the Narrative," offers an orienting map of the American Jewish landscape of Israel advocacy, the infrastructure of socialization of American Jews' narratives about Israel, and how Israel relates to their Jewish identification. The chapter traces efforts to rebrand Israel in ways that attempt to diminish the experience of cognitive dissonance. Here is where narrativity emerges as a key battlefield. Hence, the chapter examines the instruments of silencing employed by the American Jewish establishment to control the scope of debate and constrain questioning. This chapter highlights the background from which the social movement of Jews emerged and which it seeks to transform by rescripting the narrative of Jewishness. Chapter 2, "Forming a Social Movement," examines why groups of Jewish critics, conveying a deepening crisis of authority and increased questioning of the Jewish establishment's position on the occupation and Israeli policies, constitute a shift from advocacy to social movement. This chapter highlights four groups in particular: Open Hillel (OH), IfNotNow (INN), CJNV, and JVP. Drawing on sociological literature focusing on meaning-making through a movement's contentions and a dialogic turn to semiotics, this chapter anticipates the later discussion in the book of how activists participate in religious innovation and resignification of Jewishness. The dialogic perspective in the study of social movements focuses on discursive processes within movements and recognizes meaning production as the interaction between social action and systems of signs. It also foregrounds the need to unpack the hermeneutical dimensions of Jewish Palestine activists' efforts to reimagine post- and non-Zionist Jewish theology and alternative sociopolitical and cultural Jewish identity (Jewishness).

Part II, comprising chapters 3–6, engages with activists' processes of self-interrogation and transformation as well as the mechanisms and orienting values informing the reimagining of Jewishness. These processes, in both their personal and communal forms, unfold relationally through embracing the charge of a relentless Days of Awe's atonement for communal sinfulness and complicity with the occupation and through the praxis of social protest, marching, and putting one's body on the line. Chapter 3, "Unlearn-

ing," primarily addresses two intertwined processes related to the emergence
and consolidation of the Jewish diasporist social movement in the US: ethical outrage and unlearning. As the chapter's title suggests, it focuses on the
stories activists tell about their own self-transformation, or how they came
to reorient their solidarities through emphatic indignation, which was reinforced by their unlearning of ideology. Their ethical outrage is directed both
at what Israel claims to do in their name and at the failures of their own communities to take a stance consistent with what they interpret as Jewish values.
The chapter methodically analyzes the stories captured in semi-structured
interviews with activists, as well as the testimonies shared on social media.
The interviews capture how the activists portray their processes of renarration, which inform the shift of their solidarity from Israelis to Palestinians.
The chapter also investigates the relationships between prior politicization on
LGBTQI+ issues, antimilitarism, humanitarianism, and neoliberalism, and
assuming the cause of Palestinians.

Chapter 4, "Remapping the Destination," and chapter 5, "Employing
Communal Protest," together examine how Jewishness is reimagined through
the method of critical caretaking. Critical caretaking involves various mechanisms, including midrashic work by emerging religious authorities (especially identified with JVP's rabbinic council), to engage the vast resources
of Jewish traditions and to rewrite rituals with explicit calls for action. The
chapters describe critical caretaking as a relational process, continually challenged by Palestinian experiences and the narratives of other marginalized
groups and leading to intersectional rather than ethnoreligious conceptions
of liberation. Jewish Palestine solidarity activists undertake discursive processes that connect with the broader Palestine solidarity activist network, but
that also pertain specifically to the Jewish community and an effort to rescript
its narrative. This effort is grounded in reframing the meanings of Jewishness;
for this step, the rabbinic council and activist blogs play a crucial role in enabling relational critical caretaking and articulating collective action frames.
The analysis of religious innovation in the context of social activism with a
peace and justice agenda shows not only how religion works to articulate
collective action frames, but also how social activists interrogate and construct new religious and sociocultural meanings in and through the dynamic
processes of protest. Indeed, the dialogic perspective's emphasis on meaning-
making—and on activists as agents of meaning production—presents the
collective action frame of Jewish critics as a grassroots, participatory, and
democratic process of prophetic critical caretaking, dedicated to subverting
existing ideological formations and cultivating new foci of solidarity and renarrated scripts.

Chapter 6, "Reimagining Tradition," focuses on the "product" of the relational and intersectional meaning-making examined in the earlier chapters. If the preceding chapters mainly answered the *how* questions, highlighting social movement mechanisms and the hermeneutical work of critical caretaking, this chapter addresses the *what* question: What kind of Jewishness or Judaism is articulated by the Jewish Palestine solidarity movement in relation to broader trends in American Judaism? The *how* and *what* questions are deeply interrelated because in this case, process and outcome are mutually reinforcing. Pivotal to this discussion is an analysis of Tzedek Chicago, a prefigurative, Jewish, non-Zionist community that consciously attempts to reread the tradition by innovating its liturgy through a relational engagement with Palestinians and other victims of injustice. The chapter examines the production of Judaism as antimilitarist, spiritual, ethical, un-chosen, diasporist, multiracial, and postnationalist within the historical context of American Judaism, arguing that the emergence of such a community of resistance is highly consistent with the social movement of critics but not reducible to the movement's objectives. Hence, examining Tzedek Chicago's reimagining of Jewishness reveals a response to a question not often asked, one that moves beyond functionalist approach to religion and protest: How does social movement participate in rearticulating religiosity?

Part III, consisting of chapters 7, 8, and 9, captures the discomfort and enhanced critique resulting from a relentless inhabitation of the Days of Awe, the twilight where transformation occurs. These chapters, as a unit, connect the process of refiguring Jewishness to an intersectional scrutiny of American race history and the participation of (some) Jews in white privilege and the apparatuses of white supremacy, on the one hand, and with a collaborative, comprehensive, and multidimensional examination of antisemitism, on the other. Chapter 7, "Making Multidirectional Memory," discusses the deep roots of black-Palestinian solidarity in the anticolonial critique from the Global South or Third Worldism as a layered subtext for examining explicit solidarity of the Movement for Black Lives (MBL) with Palestinians. It also examines, however, histories of black-Jewish affinities in the US and the changing dynamics of such affinities precipitated by Jews' "moral choice" to become white[13] as well as the tension between the devaluation of African American and African lives and the recognition of the Holocaust as tragedy and its victims as grievable. An engagement with Michael Rothberg's notion of "multidirectional memory" reopens the possibility of connecting the narrative of the Holocaust to the colonial experiences of genocide and, with it, delinking Jews from orientalist civilizational narratives while (re)linking them to antiracist, postcolonial critique and solidarity struggles.[14]

The foundation of black-Palestinian solidarity is critical to examining the ways in which Jewish Palestine solidarity activists also articulate their solidarity with African American struggles against institutional racism and police brutality in the US and thus augment their engagement with the construction of Jews as white and the internal dynamics of Ashkenazi supremacy within the movement. Grappling with whiteness, in other words, is critical to retrieving prophetic interpretations of the Jewish tradition while refashioning the normative boundaries of Jewish identity. It illumines the embodiment of religion as a "discursive matrix." Likewise, endorsing the platform of MBL, as did JVP and a few other Jewish Palestine solidarity and anti-occupation groups, meant not only endorsing the term "genocide" to describe Palestine's predicament, but also embracing a liberatory vision that is radically anti-racist, feminist, and queer, relentlessly embodying an epistemology from the margins. The platform of MBL, examined in this chapter, illustrates the need to protect multiple marginal communities, such as gender-nonconforming persons and African American women, and to interpret the systems of oppression from their marginalized and vulnerable location. This epistemology from the margins, consistent with standpoint feminism, enhances the clarity of broad systemic sociopolitical and economic analyses. The conceptual interconnections among efforts to destabilize gendered binarism, Palestine solidarity, and criticism of the Israeli occupation by underscoring its logic of whiteness and settler colonialism resonate with Bratt's call to "break binaries, to break the power inequality inherent within them."

Chapter 8, "Decolonizing Antisemitism," continues the previous chapter's stress on marginality as a resource for refashioning Jewishness. Both chapters focus on the complex hybridities that JOCSM embody in their lived experiences, and thus challenge, through their very bodies, pervasive binaries that inform the hegemonic discourse. Jews can be black and Arab. The chapter scrutinizes efforts to decolonize and deorientalize the meanings of antisemitism, denoting a shift in the movement from simply negating the rhetorical equation of anti-Israeli occupation with antisemitism by showing up as Jews to anti-occupation protests. The shift was effected by the broader Palestine solidarity movement's increased need to name actual antisemitism. This requirement became increasingly acute in the Trump era which, as these chapters discuss, offers a moment of moral clarity on the questions of Jews' whiteness, commitment to antiracism, and the failures of Israel to condemn real manifestations of antisemitism. Chapter 8, therefore, traces JVP's effort to grapple with antisemitism in an intersectional and relational manner, while also examining patterns of inter-traditional discursive work on Christian antisemitism and the legacy of the Holocaust vis-à-vis Palestinians with

Christian churches who underwent deliberations over divestment from the occupation. The chapter also engages with efforts to deorientalize antisemitism by looking outside its exclusively European history and examining the interrelations between orientalism, Islamophobia, and antisemitism. Relatedly, the relevance of antisemitism to the underpinning of anti-black racism and white supremacy in the US exposes the fragility of Jewish whiteness but also—through challenges from JOCSM—the moral demand that white Jews relentlessly inhabit the existential discomfort of the Days of Awe, confronting their privilege and owning their sinfulness. These are the conclusions of activists in the movement whom the Trump era and the emergence of explicit antisemitism did not drive back to ethnocentric conceptions of solidarity, but rather reinforced their intersectional lens.

The final chapter, "Decolonizing Peacebuilding," asks how the examination of American Jewish Palestine solidarity activists' processes of reimaging Jewishness contributes to the broader study of religion, violence, and peacebuilding. Here, I argue that the case study pushes the boundaries of the field by foregrounding processes of unlearning as sites of research and praxis. It requires disabusing the field of its tendency to abstract "religion" from race, gender, ethnicity, nationality, and other realities, an abstraction that is itself a product of coloniality. Butler's view of religion as a "discursive matrix" with no predetermined destination resonates with my discussion of the resignification of Jewishness through social movement contentions and solidarity work. *Days of Awe*, therefore, exemplifies the peacebuilding and transformative potential of attention to discursive and epistemological violence, social movements' framing process and elastic meaning-making from the grassroots, as well as the interconnections between destabilizing binaries and certainties in one social field such as "gender identity" and the denaturalization of other fields. This chapter also places American non- or post-Zionism in tension with settlers' post-Zionism as well as Mizrahi intersectional reimagining through its own discursive critical caretaking of the relation of Jews to the Middle East and Palestine/Israel specifically. The Mizrahi-Palestinian intersectional lens, in particular, offers a challenge to American post- and non-Zionist diasporism's devaluing of Zion. I articulate the challenge only to stress that American post- or non-Zionism, as developed in continuity with the social movement of critical Jews, offers a discursive contribution to peacebuilding not limited to lines imposed by geopolitics, but rather present globally through multiple fields of meanings. Yet, the on-the-ground transformative work still needs to take place through the agentic meaning-making of marginalized sectors across the terrains that are once again particularly well situated to offer an epistemology from the margins and resources for positively resignifying normative collective boundaries and possibilities of cohabitation. I conclude by examining the limits of diasporism because my sense of extreme dislocation as an Israeli Jew living in America within this movement of Jewish critics of the occupation compels me to move beyond the one binary left undone by the movement. This is the binary that invests Jewish values in either Zion or New York City and consequently devalues the Jewish meanings of the other location. These are meanings understood in terms of space and time as well as the ethical, historical, and futurist or eschatological maps they chart. I now turn to examine the transformation of American Jewishness through ethical indignation, empathy, and prophetic and discursive critical caretaking. American Jews active in anti-occupation and Palestine solidarity work inhabit relentlessly the Days of Awe. In this book, I capture what this means and why it matters.

PART ONE

Questioning the Narrative

Which Side Are You On?

The stories by which we make sense of ourselves account for the formation of our ethical commitments on behalf or under the directives of others—whether near or distant. Such ethical commitments—and solidarity in particular—manifest in and through narratives. In my journey with American Jewish Palestine solidarity activists, I trace how they question the narratives they once embodied—narratives that taught them to stand in solidarity with Israelis and positioned Israel as a pivot (and telos) of Jewish identity and history. I also trace how and why the activists are shifting sides and decentering Israel as a touchstone for articulating their Jewishness. But before unpacking the formation of Jewish Palestine solidarity and how it relates to reimagining Jewishness, it is crucial to examine what solidarity actually means.

Solidarity, according to Richard B. Miller, "is a shared, socialized emotion, not one that can be held by individuals alone, like fear or envy. To exist, it must be intersubjective."[1] This means that, even when expressed through individual actions and commitments, standing in solidarity requires a social narrative about who we are and what ethical values guide our lives. Miller also challenges "depoliticized and depolemicized" analyses of solidarity that describe it as "a nonpartisan, cosmopolitan ideal, conceived either on the basis of an objectivist vision of common human nature or on a rejection of precisely that way of thinking."[2] Such accounts, he argues, founder on their inability to respond to the crucial question that Michael Walzer poses in his *Politics and Passion*: "Which side are you on?"[3] In contrast, Miller advances a conception of solidarity much more in line with the strong normative commitments I witnessed in Jewish Palestine solidarity work. The activists are clear about which side they are on. Genuine solidarity, as Miller contends, is not "universalist and utopian," but "a social relation that is partisan, primed for struggle, mindful of itself as organized (or close to it), and energized by feelings of resentment and indignation (among other emotions). Solidarity . . . is preferential, and it draws lines."[4] As a political form of moral agency, solidarity is always "collectively expressed in terms of organized political affiliation, a culture of shared expectations, mutual understanding, and resolve."[5] But while Miller's definition captures the collective expression and preferential commitment characteristic of solidarity, it does not convey how such moral commitments are in fact reshaped in and through the social movement within which solidarity takes actual shape. This complex process of reshaping commitments will be crucial to this book's analysis.

Nor is solidarity itself an unqualified good. Solidarity and the new communal meanings it generates do not necessarily lead to the formation of a virtuous community or, as Miller puts it, one determined by "a commitment shaped by shared norms and ideals" that are egalitarian rather than partisan.[6] The kind of solidarity formed among white supremacists, for instance, is clearly ethically undesirable, even if white supremacists themselves intensely desire and authorize it through narratives of grievances as just and normative. A desirable form of political solidarity must involve a spectrum of what Miller calls "moral reactive attitudes," which may include resentment, indignation, and guilt. It must also be subject to egalitarian claims to justice.[7] All these features, I will argue, are operative in the formation of Jewish Palestine solidarity. But how have American Jews come to develop such attitudes? This chapter focuses on one basic factor that has made solidarity possible, namely an erosion in the hold of a narrative that, through claims to necessity undergirded by basic discursive formations, had come to determine what things were capable of generating outrage, indignation, and guilt on the part of American Jews. In so doing, that narrative had diminished the humanness of Palestinians and denied the validity of their ethical claims.

In what follows, I first discuss the changing terrain of the American Jewish landscape in recent decades, before mapping the landscape of the "pro-Israel" American Jewish lobby, which Jewish Palestine solidarity activists disrupt. I then analyze the global efforts of the Boycott, Divestment, and Sanctions (BDS) movement both to subvert the logic of discourse on Israel/Palestine and to generate moral reaction and solidarity with the Palestinian struggle against Israeli occupation, thus opposing the silencing tactics typically employed to control the narrative. The chapter concludes by examining the ultimately dissatisfying attempt at a new mode of Jewish advocacy work on Israel by the group J Street.

The "Establishment"

THE CHANGING LANDSCAPE OF AMERICAN JUDAISM

The Pew Research Center's 2013 survey of US Jews maps the changing topography of American Judaism.[8] Pew's analysis suggests significant intergenerational shifts. For instance, while 93% of aging Jews (Greatest Generation) describe themselves as "Jews by religion," only 68% of younger adults
(Millennials) describe themselves this way.[9] The survey also indicates that
over a third (35%) of US Jews identify with the Reform movement, which retains its status as the largest denominational movement within Judaism. Only
18% associate with Conservative Judaism, 10% with Orthodox currents, and
6% with smaller movements such as Reconstructionist and Jewish Renewal.
However, about three in ten American Jews (including 19% of Jews by religion and two-thirds of cultural Jews) do not affiliate with any specific movement or denomination.[10] The majority of my seventy Jewish interviewees had
a strong background in the Reform movement, but had grown increasingly
critical of the Jewish establishment's position on Israel.[11] Other respondents
came from various backgrounds in religious Zionism, Orthodoxy, Reconstructionist, and Conservative currents. While critics of Israel do emerge
from across the Jewish spectrum, there are clear correlations between "denominational" affiliation and emotional attachment to Israel, an attachment
often framed in Zionist terms.[12]

Overall, the Pew survey might suggest a positive correlation between level
of religiosity and unconditional support of Israel.[13] This apparent correlation is a testament to the Zionization of the American Jewish landscape. But
the survey suggests that Zionism may be losing its traction: American Jews
over the age of 50 tend to express a deeper attachment to Israel than do their
younger counterparts: 53% of Jews 65 years and older and 47% of Jews ages
50–64 said that Israel is essential to their understanding of Jewishness. But
only 38% of Jews in their thirties and forties, and only 32% of Jews under 30,
attribute such centrality to Israel. Indeed, other aspects of Pew's findings illuminate the complex dynamics of the American Jewish landscape and point
to the multiple meanings of Jewishness that lie outside Zionist scripts. One
key question animating the survey was "What does it mean to be Jewish?"
Significantly, 62% of respondents understand their Jewishness in terms of
ancestry and culture.[14] Hence, the particular features that American Jews
identify as essential to their culture are notable: 73% identified remembering the Holocaust as an essential part of being Jewish. A close second, and
potentially related to the first, was leading an ethical/moral life, which 69%

reported as constituting an essential aspect of being Jewish. Third, 56% high-lighted work for justice/equality as the key meaning of being Jewish. "Caring about Israel" came in fifth place (43%), after the 49% who indicated that "be-ing intellectually curious" was essential to being Jewish. While "remember-ing the Holocaust" sometimes correlated positively with a sense that support of Israel—including support of its policies—is essential to Jewishness, for many of the American Jews I interviewed, it was precisely the first three of these features—remembering the Holocaust, a commitment to ethical and moral life, as well as actual social work for justice and equality—that in-formed their critique of Israel and their solidarity work on behalf of Palestin-ians. This amounts to nothing less than a self-transformative process that led them to reconnect to the legacy of the Jewish Left in Europe and North America, especially its antiracist, Marxist, and socialist legacies.[15]

When I asked Rebecca how she understood her Jewishness,[16] she told me: "I have always maintained that the basis for my activism was my Jewish ideals, the radical equality I had absorbed at home. Communism is a part of my Jewish heritage." About the cultural memory of the Holocaust, she stressed, "Growing up in Hebrew Schools, you grow up with the nightmarish Holocaust films. The conclusion of this education should have been clear: 'You can't do it to another group of people!'"[17] Another interviewee likewise asserted that her solidarity with Palestinians is grounded in the legacy of the Holocaust: "I consider myself to be in solidarity with the Palestinian people. For me, under-standing the Holocaust was hard because of the enormity of it—it happened because masses of people made a conscious decision to do nothing. I didn't want to do nothing."[18] Thus, Pew's findings on the changing attitudes and resignification of the Holocaust as a universal lesson and experience appear to be more in line with narratives of Jewish humanism than with the Zionist narrative, which appeals to the Holocaust to posit Israel as the pivot and telos of Jewish history and solidarity.[19] Nevertheless, as the Pew study suggests, as the American Jewish landscape is changing, so are its undergirding narra-tives. Even if attachments and commitments to Israel still appear to domi-nate the narration of Jewish identity, the significance Jews attribute to the memory of the Holocaust and to living an ethical life—aspects of Jewishness that do not require the state of Israel—hints at the undercurrents informing the grassroots transformation that is actively reframing Jewish narratives.

AIPAC: THE "DEFENDER" OF ISRAEL

Despite its apparently axiomatic hold, the traction of Zionism as a narra-tive frame among American Jews is quite recent.[20] Its dominance is highly contingent on events of the past century—the intensification of antisemitism and eventually the Holocaust in Europe—as well as on local concerns with integration and assimilation into American sociocultural and economic mainstreams. Thus, only since World War I has (statist) Zionism become an acceptable, even if deeply ambivalent, currency in Jewish exchanges.[21] Furthermore, in the two decades immediately following the Holocaust,[22] Judaism was increasingly construed as a religion rather than an ethnonational identity, and thus as highly consistent with both American civil religion and the Enlightenment project of universalizing the "Jewish message."[23] This universalizing spin was further compounded with an idealized projection of Israel as an extension of American ideals and values, a projection that excused the need for factual grasp of the situation in Israel.[24] Concurrently, the early decades of the Israeli state were peak years for the ethos of "the negation of exile," including provocative calls by David Ben-Gurion and other Israeli leaders for American Jews to make *aliyah* (immigrate to Israel) or, in other words, to actualize their Zionism.[25] In 1959, the Conference of Presidents of Major American Jewish Organizations was convoked in an effort to consolidate a representative body that would convey American Jewish positions on Israel to American decision-makers as well as ensure that philanthropic commitments to Israel were institutionalized. The Conference, Ofira Seliktar explains, "tried to present a unified front by denying that significant differences over Israel existed."[26] Along with the American Zionist Council on Public Affairs—established in 1954 and later renamed the American Israel Public Affairs Committee (AIPAC)—it became the center of the Jewish establishment in Washington, DC.

Furthermore, no sooner had Israel gained a central place in the American Jewish imagination than it began, especially with the watershed of the Lebanon War of 1982 and the Sabra and Shatila massacre, slowly to lose "its aura of innocence and heroism" and to face critical engagement by American Jews who disapprove of such Israeli belligerence.[27] One commentator, Dov Waxman, sees such criticism as emerging not from alienation, but from love, with all the disillusionments—but also the enduring commitment—that mature love entails.[28] But this is not what I heard from the Jewish Palestine solidarity activists I encountered. Their motivation in expressing outrage with their communal leaders and affirming ethical commitments to Palestinians was not love of Israel (in fact, many reject Zionism altogether) but indignation against injustice done in their name. What I saw was a clear politics of passion, which made it increasingly clear that the question "Whose side are you on?" could not be answered with "both," apart from a significant dismantling of Zionism's hold on Jewishness.

This brief historical overview highlights the way that crises and subsequent developments are capable of generating a paradigm shift. The twentieth century witnessed precisely such a shift among American Jews, who went from rejecting Zionism as a threat to the minority-rights discourse central to Jewish flourishing in the diasporas, to embracing it as a paradigm for Jewish identity. AIPAC and other engines of the American and Israeli Jewish establishments have sought to dominate the production of an exclusionary form of solidarity and Holocaust memory. Yet the current Zionist orthodoxy, while deeply entrenched, is itself subject to such subversion by historical contingencies and the production and retrieval of alternative meanings. Here, it may be helpful to appeal to the concept of *doxa*, as cultural sociologist Pierre Bourdieu employs it.

"Every established order," Bourdieu explains, "tends to [naturalize] its own arbitrariness."[29] *Doxa* describes a condition where "there is a quasi-perfect correspondence between the objective order and the subjective principles of organization" such that "the natural and social world appears as self-evident." Or, to use anthropologist Clifford Geertz's analogous terms, ethos and worldview are here thoroughly consistent.[30] Bourdieu distinguishes the experience of *doxa* from "an orthodox or heterodox belief," for these imply an "awareness and recognition of the possibility of different or antagonistic beliefs" in a way that *doxa* itself does not.[31] Indeed, both orthodoxy and heterodoxy are reinforced by an underpinning *doxa*. While orthodoxies need to be defended, *doxa* imprints itself in us as "self-evident and natural," an objective standard that determines how things are and ought to be.[32] Nonetheless, Bourdieu stresses, *doxas* are themselves socially constructed, historically embedded, and reflect the dominating classes' objective to retain their privilege. They are produced through "political instruments which contribute to the reproduction of the social world by producing immediate adherence to the world, seen as self-evident and undisputed, of which they are the product."[33] As an ideology, Zionism employs precisely such instruments to reproduce itself, thus (even when internally contested) preserving its hegemony by cultivating *habitus* or certain embodied dispositions that predispose Jews to authorize its legitimacy and accept without indignation its implications for Palestinians as well as non-Ashkenazi Jews (those who cannot pass as white). At the same time, the reproduction of orthodoxy relies also on orientalism, Islamophobia, and the presumption that normative Jewishness is Ashkenazi and consistent with the political and cultural project of European modernity.

The reproduction of pro-Israeli advocacy is currently threatened by a crisis in narrativity (and authority) that constitutes, in Bourdieu's words, "a necessary condition for a questioning of doxa."[34] Questioning, however, is not a sufficient condition for overcoming *doxa*. Only when "the dominated have the material and symbolic means of rejecting the definition of the real that is imposed on them through logical structures reproducing the social structures . . . and to lift the (institutionalized or internalized) censorships which it implies," can the work of denaturalizing unfold, exposing *doxa* as orthodoxy or mere "opinion."[35] Thus, to retain its hegemony, Jewish Israel advocacy in the US exhibits a concentrated effort to delimit questioning, all the while deploying a variety of mechanisms to reproduce authorizing narratives that serve to maintain the *doxa* that renders Zionism as orthodoxy. Such an effort is especially obvious in AIPAC's recent history.

Since its initial emergence as an engine of Jewish-Zionist socialization and Israel advocacy, AIPAC has continued to focus on reinforcing the alliances between Israel and the US by lobbying Congress and relentlessly engaging in advocacy that is highly consistent with an Israeli right-wing agenda that has pushed for expansion of illegal settlements and progressive annexation of territories occupied in 1967. Increasingly, AIPAC has aligned itself with the Republican Party.[36] One recent emphasis of its advocacy has been the strategic conflation of Israel's narrative of "fighting terrorism" with the US post-9/11 discourse about the "war on terrorism." This conflation is enabled by an enduring orientalism and a civilizational discourse marked by a diffuse sense of cultural affinities with Israel. These "affinities" are traced historically to the roots of Christian Zionism and the American Puritan ethos of a "City upon a Hill" or the "New Jerusalem."[37] They are further reinforced through the construction and reproduction of American identity as Judeo-Christian,[38] a construct that bears an intricate relation with the discourse of orientalism.[39]

For decades, AIPAC's lobbying mechanism has represented its work as one of "education" through bipartisan lobbying and by empowering "pro-Israel activists," ensuring that all members of Congress identify Israel's security as an "American priority."[40] AIPAC's Annual Policy Conference has become a stage for American politicians to affirm their commitment to the security of Israel and thus supposedly to secure the "Jewish vote" they need for their various campaigns. Even Samantha Power, in her capacity as the US ambassador to the United Nations, declared to an AIPAC audience in 2015 that an American commitment to Israeli security "transcends politics."[41] Hers is but one name in a long, highly bipartisan list of presidents, former presidents, and other dignitaries who frequent AIPAC's dinners, singing a refrain of "shared values" and the "special bond" between the US and Israel.[42]

Throughout its promotional materials, AIPAC declares Israel a bipartisan issue that can never be employed as a political wedge. Yet their rhetoric belies their actions and broader American Jewish attitudes.[43] The advent of the

Trump era, marked by populist rhetoric and obvious efforts to accommodate
hardline pro-Israeli arguments, has only confirmed the deepening partisan
nature of AIPAC and the framing of support of Israeli policies as a Republican
principle.[44] Despite AIPAC's repeated insistence that its work is bipartisan,
Israel has become increasingly a polarizing issue, with a July 2014 Pew poll indicating that 73% of Republicans support Israel while only 44% of Democrats
do.[45] "This difference," Connie Bruck explains, "represents . . . a significant
narrowing of AIPAC's vital core." Put within the broader American context,
a July 2014 Gallup poll of Americans under the age of 30 indicated that only
25% supported Israeli military incursions into Gaza.[46] These data illuminate
the changed landscape of American public opinion and its intergenerational
divides. It is within this context that American Jews increasingly distance
themselves from AIPAC's narrative and challenge the institutions that reproduce it.[47]

However, AIPAC remains highly influential in US policy. It is effective not
only in acquiring bundled funds to support representatives who vote in favor
of AIPAC's view of what is good for Israel, but also in promoting a network
of activists across the US who defend the occupation, disregard Palestinian
experiences, reinforce a ghetto mentality (which portrays Israel as constantly
fighting an existential threat in the Middle East), and refract any critique of
Israeli policies through the prism of the Holocaust and antisemitism.[48]

REBRANDING

But the tide is changing. The dominant narrative is eroding, as was strikingly evident in the disruptive and highly publicized protest of the youth-led
American Jewish anti-occupation group IfNotNow during AIPAC's annual
conference of March 2017. INN mustered a thousand Jews who marched,
blocking the entrance to AIPAC's conference by creating a human chain while
singing and chanting prayers highlighting their own interpretation of Jewish
values.[49] The protesters carried a banner that read "Jews Won't be free until
Palestinians are: Reject AIPAC. Reject Occupation" (see figure 1.1).

Such resistance increasingly forces AIPAC to bolster the diminishing
traction of its narrative about Israel. One example of AIPAC's own effort
to rebrand Israel is its adoption of Ari Shavit's *My Promised Land: The Triumph and Tragedy of Israel*, which offers a more candid account of the ethnic
cleansing and massacres associated with the Nakba (though without ever using this Palestinian designation for the 1948 catastrophe) than had typically
been accepted by the earlier Zionist establishment.[50] Shavit, like AIPAC and
the Israel lobby, recognizes the Palestinian experience, but only alongside an

FIGURE 1.1. Activists from IfNotNow march outside the Washington Convention Center to protest the annual AIPAC Policy Conference, Washington, DC, March 26, 2017 [Photo credit: Gili Getz]

insistence that their loss was necessary for the Zionist project to succeed. He describes with chilling detail the massacre in the Palestinian village of Lydda and the subsequent expulsion of Palestinians. "If Zionism was to be," he writes, "Lydda could not be. If Lydda was to be, Zionism could not be."[51] This attitude represents a shift away from early denial of the atrocities of 1948 to their reframing as necessary, partly through the paradigm of political realism, partly through a narrative about near annihilation. The logic of this narrative is extended to authorize continuous military operations and to underwrite the infrastructures of the occupation and the so-called policy of "conflict management." These are the hard realities of a people in a constant, existential struggle.[52] AIPAC, like many American liberal Zionists, has embraced and deployed Shavit's seemingly more sober and complicated account of Zionism, the early decades of Israel, the Israeli peace camp, and the imperfections of Israeli society. This account seeks to resolve questions by Jews and non-Jews about the ethos of security underpinning Israeli militarism and oppression of Palestinians. Shavit's narrative interprets this reality as inevitable and as a zero-sum game. Hence, Israel's bad behavior is branded as a necessity, albeit a painful one. Regardless, its army is still portrayed as "moral," and any suggestion otherwise is met with indignation. Such suggestions come from Israeli army veterans themselves—as in the case of Breaking the Silence, the organization of Israeli veterans that seeks to document the violent routines engrained in the reality of the occupation.[53] In short, Shavit's narrative constitutes a rebranding inasmuch as it supposedly acknowledges the "bad," but it does so only instrumentally in order to legitimize, by reinstating a narrative of necessity, Israeli policies and the displacement of Palestinians.

Another attempt at rebranding that likewise illuminates the enmeshment between Israeli *hasbarah* (public messaging or, literally, "explanation") and the lobby are various forms of white-, pink-, or greenwashing the occupation, that is, projecting an image of Israel as friendly to progressive interests such as LGBTQI rights and environmental sustainability. This rebranding, critics argue, serves to manipulate orientalist attitudes and sexual politics by contrasting Israel's "gay friendly" image with other areas of the Middle East, the neighborhood in which Israel is so estranged, culturally and otherwise.[54] These rebranding campaigns intend to update Israel's image, and to make its realities cohere, by projecting the image of a "villa in the jungle," thereby foregrounding its supposed progressiveness on gender issues and environmental sustainability, with the accompanying implication of cultural affinities with the West rather than with MENA's (Middle East and North Africa) authoritarianism, homophobia, and gender-based discrimination.[55] Nonetheless, my interviewees, together with other Palestine solidarity activists, contend that this is still a marketing agenda (articulated with the close advice of marketing experts) that seeks to obscure the occupation. Like the elaborate bypass roads the Israeli government constructed enabling Israelis to avoid any contact with Palestinians, so does its concentrated effort since 2005 to rebrand the occupation aim to render its oppression invisible.[56] This focus on rebranding intentionally operates, therefore, to promote exclusive (and, on Miller's account, ethically undesirable) solidarity with Israelis qua Jews in ways that draw upon inclusive and egalitarian sensibilities while nevertheless answering the question "Whose side are you on?" in an exclusive fashion, in line with non-egalitarian practices and ideological frames that appeal to political realist apparent common sense.[57]

However, rebranding Israel in this way is not sufficient for the purposes of the pro-Israel lobby. Peter Beinart, an American Jewish public intellectual, has written extensively on the change in American Jewish attitudes concerning Israel.[58] Beinart observes that the pro-Israel lobby has been increasingly distracted from its focus on a nuclear Iran by its need to oppose the BDS campaigns. The BDS campaigns, he notes, seek to collapse the narrative that enables AIPAC's effectiveness and the continued authorization of the occupation, and have gained traction with each new wave of Israeli assaults on Gaza and the West Bank.[59]

The youth-led group If Not Now (INN)—formed, like many other protest groups, around the time of the assault on Gaza in 2014—explicitly distances itself from the hostile rhetoric about Iran and its nuclear potential, which has been a focus of AIPAC and the "pro-Israel" lobby since the 1990s. For many, the Iran deal finally exposed the emptiness of the fearmongering by Israeli politicians and their backers in Washington.[60] "The greatest threat to our community isn't Iran or BDS. It's the occupation," INN wrote on its Facebook page. Two of its hashtags, #IfNotNow and #NotinMyName, capture the moral reactive sentiments of indignation and guilt, key ingredients to a form of political solidarity marked by empathy and driven by a moral imperative—embedded in a human rights discourse—to oppose injustice. Indeed, both hashtags lie at the heart of Jewish Palestine solidarity and convey the overwhelming sense of urgency to act against the occupation and the complicity of the Jewish community in this enduring oppression of Palestinians. Such urgency is motivated, in large part, by the climate of silencing, which the following section explores.

Silencing

BDS: CHALLENGING THE NARRATIVE

BDS emerged from a call articulated and endorsed by 108 representatives of Palestinian groups in July 2005.[61] Inspired "by the struggle of South Africans against apartheid and in the spirit of international solidarity, moral consistency and resistance to injustice and oppression,"[62] the BDS Call appeals for concerted action on behalf of Palestine. Yet, endorsement of BDS does not itself entail "solidarity." One prominent Jewish activist with whom I spoke critically nuanced the notion of "solidarity." She explained, "Spending three summers accompanying Palestinian villagers and utilizing my white privilege as a shield against arbitrary violence was indeed a form of witnessing and solidarity. This was actual, not theoretical, solidarity."[63] For (American and other) Jews to reach the point where their solidarity with Palestinians is not only a theoretical exercise but an embodied experience—and one driven by Palestinian directives—a serious process of renarration must have enabled the moral reactive attitudes key to the "shared, socialized emotion" that Miller describes as central to political solidarity. These contentious processes inform the response not only to the question "What side are we on?" but the more basic question "Who are we?" Any response to the latter will, of course, be fluid. As later chapters will make evident, a stable sense of self-identity is not a prerequisite for partaking in political solidarity nor for experiencing the range of moral reactive attitudes that undergird such solidarity.

Much of this resistance takes place at the discursive level.[64] This is symbolic warfare, intended to erode the discourses promoting support of Israeli policies. It aims precisely at shifting public opinion through raising awareness and challenging the production of knowledge about the conflict and occupation. In the same way that the supporters of BDS aim at crumbling not only the economic but also (and primarily) the symbolic and cultural capital authorizing Israeli policies, opponents of the BDS movement are concerned with bolstering their narrative. The critique articulated by BDS activists challenges Israel's moral standing and is accordingly interpreted by the political echelon as a symbolic threat to its identity.[65] This is abundantly clear in how Israel's official strategy has now turned toward "branding" as a way of fighting a public relations battle. Silencing and delegitimizing Israel's critics have likewise become the modus operandi in both the US and Israel.

In effect, the forces that seek explicitly to silence debate in the US by criminalizing critique, placing constraints on funding, and establishing clear parameters concerning who is allowed to speak about Israel are intricately connected to comparable forces in Israel also moving in the direction of censorship.[66] Millions of dollars are spent on *hasbarah*,[67] including a smear campaign led by right-wing Jewish activists against the appointment of David Myers, a critically acclaimed historian of modern Judaism, to head the Center for Jewish History in Manhattan. Myers's support of organizations such as the New Israel Fund and INN rendered him a target of McCarthyism for failing to pass an ideological litmus test despite his indisputable academic qualification for the prestigious position.[68] Nevertheless, efforts to rebrand Israel, cultivate its "moral" rightness, and institute litmus tests and censorship are not supplemented by any tangible changes to the policies and infrastructure of oppression. This is precisely what INN, JVP, and other critical groups repeatedly point out, but their arguments are often dismissed as self-hating and traitorous.

To preempt the argument that BDS campaigns operate within a context of a "free market" of ideas, it is important to stress why Students for Justice in Palestine (SJP), JVP, and other likeminded organizations are best understood not as just another voice in a cacophonous public discourse, but as operating against a silencing framework. The public space, as anthropologist Talal Asad observed, is inextricably articulated by power.[69] As my interviews made clear, many Palestine solidarity activists are acutely aware of the intentional and coordinated silencing of Palestinian narratives and criticisms of Zionist logic. Examples of such silencing are abundant and, in effect, are documented in venues such as the *Electronic Intifada* and *Mondoweiss*, which have become pivotal spaces for subverting hegemonic discursive framing of the Israeli-

Palestinian conflict through the production of counterknowledge through alternative media. Indeed, the very intentionality of such documentation constitutes a discursive challenge to the Zionist orthodoxy and its silencing practices. Likewise, JVP lists as one of its primary objectives the need to resist and subvert the logic underpinning efforts to silence debate about US policy about Israel and Palestine.[70]

INSTRUMENTS OF SILENCING:

ISLAMOPHOBIA AND ANTISEMITISM

Some of the most prominent means of silencing the voices of Palestinians and their allies are those that instrumentalize both Islamophobia and Holocaust piety.[71] The primary arms of this silencing agenda are organizations such as the Simon Wiesenthal Center, the Anti-Defamation League (ADL), the AMCHA Initiative, and the American Jewish Committee (AJC), which seek to criminalize critiques of Israel and render them antisemitic by definition.[72] The implication is clear: the argument and historical memory of Nazi antisemitism authorizes labeling any departure from a full support of AIPAC's type of Zionism as antisemitic or self-hating. The criminalization campaign even led to deliberations in the US Congress.[73] That organizations such as ADL participate in such systemic silencing attests to the intricate ways in which the memory of racism against Jews serves to constrain the scope of acceptable debate. In addition to the instrumentality of the Holocaust and the legacy of antisemitism, the struggle against the "delegitimizers" of Israel involves manipulating Islamophobic and orientalist undercurrents in American society (amplified after the events of September 11, 2001).[74]

Because they fear delegitimizers who would puncture the intelligibility of the Zionist narrative, the Jewish Federation conditions its financial support for Jewish activism in the US upon a litmus test of a support of official Israeli scripts. Likewise, many influential American funders and promoters of the Israeli settlement project are also implicated in intentionally exacerbating Islamophobia.[75] Indeed, the Trump moment presents a critical point where the partisan game of Israel advocacy and its instrumentalization of the Holocaust is tested, where real antisemitism is clearly on the rise and has taken hold in the administration itself—an administration that otherwise projects a "pro" Israel stance, reinforcing the rationale of Israeli policies and attitudes (as manifested in the Trump Administration's decision to decertify the Iran nuclear deal and to recognize Jerusalem as the capital of Israel in 2017). American Jews find themselves at an intersection where blatant antisemitism and even Holocaust denial from the White House coincide with a support of Zionist orthodoxy while the accusation of antisemitism is weaponized in the service of silencing critics of the occupation through legal mechanisms.[76]

Palestine solidarity activism on university campuses (especially in California) has become a key target of the Israel lobby. A central strategy is litigation based on accusations of antisemitism or of creating "a hostile environment" for Jewish students.[77] This amounts to a systematic approach—sometimes called "lawfare"—targeting universities, faculty critical of Israeli policies, and specific students active in Palestine solidarity. Often coordinated by the Global Frontier Justice Center—the US front of the Israeli Shurat HaDin, which defines itself as a legal organization focused on representing terror victims—this strategy trades on conflating opposition to antisemitism with criticism of Israel using the currency of Islamophobia.[78] The "lawfare" tactics invoke Title VI of the 1964 Civil Rights Act, which is designed to shield "against discrimination based on race or national origin in institutions that receive federal funding."[79] Indeed, Title VI lawsuits quickly proliferated, and were compounded by other initiatives, such as AMCHA, that seek to identify faculty critical of Israel.[80] Ultimately, however, such lawsuits did not go very far, and the ACLU in 2012 expressed concerns that such an employment of the 1964 Civil Rights Act "raises constitutional red flags that are significant and alarming."[81] Likewise, the ACLU was explicit in its opposition to proposed bills in Congress that sought to criminalize BDS in 2017.[82]

Even when efforts to criminalize or otherwise punish critique through appeals to "civility" or antisemitism are unsuccessful, they nonetheless create a charged atmosphere that serves to constrain debates about Palestine/Israel and characterize campuses as a threatening and intolerant environment for Jewish students.[83] But as Tom Pessah—at the time a UC Berkeley graduate student and a Jewish Israeli active with SJP—observed, many who claimed that the campus environment was hostile to Jewish students in fact conflated being Jewish with attachment to Israel. Supposedly, "most [Jewish] students feel that their identity is related to Israel and . . . that any criticism of Israel is an attack on Israel and an attack on their identity. . . . And suddenly . . . now there's just one correct opinion, which happens to be the ADL . . . line. . . . They're using their image as a protector against anti-Jewish racism, which is a great cause, to bring forward this Zionist agenda, which is not consensual, and which amplifies voices of certain students above others."[84] While many students and their parents fear the repercussions of Palestine solidarity activism, there is also a wide recognition by students and other activists of the various silencing tactics used against them. Thus, they recognize that a major component of the struggle for Palestine must be ensuring the audibility of Palestinian narratives as well as unsettling the rhetorical conflation of critiques of Israel with antisemitism.

Meanwhile, pro-Israel advocates such as those associated with Stand-WithUs have focused on cultivating youth "ambassadors" on campuses, while implementing both overt and covert censorship, occasionally under the pretense of broadening the scope of students' learning about Israel.[85] At the same time, the claim that university campuses are threatening places for Jewish students[86] was contradicted in 2017 by a qualitative study of Jewish students on five campuses across California.[87] According to this study, American Jewish students "reported feeling comfortable on their campuses, and, more specifically, comfortable as Jews on their campuses. . . . [They] parsed differences between being Jewish and supporting Israeli policy, and they objected to the expectation that their identity as Jews meant they held one kind of politics when they, in fact, hold a range of political opinions."[88] Yet the tense atmosphere, many students reported, led them to feel marginalized in both Jewish and non-Jewish activist communities on campus.

ARCHITECTURE OF SOCIALIZATION

American Jews who are critical of the occupation have come to contest the very architecture of Jewish socialization in the US. This architecture consists of Jewish day schools, summer camps, and free Birthright trips for youth and young adults. It is closely policed and underwritten by AIPAC and related groups, which employ an "Israel litmus test" to determine funding for grant seekers and the possibility of public-speaking privileges.

Taglit (or Birthright), founded in 1999, is an especially noteworthy instrument of American Jewish socialization and ideological reproduction. By 2017, at least 600,000 people had participated in this program.[89] The idea behind Birthright was to sponsor free trips to Israel for youth and young adults ages 18 to 26, especially from the US and Canada. Its objective is "to address the growing divide between Diaspora Jewish youth and the land and people of Israel."[90] Each trip costs around $120,000, with a quarter of the cost covered by the Israeli government. The remaining money is supplied by key donors such as the casino mogul Sheldon Adelson, who has deep links to right-wing Israeli and American politicians.[91]

"Trying to understand Israel by going on Birthright is sort of like trying to understand the United States by riding a fleet in the Macy's Thanksgiving Day Parade."[92] Here, Ellie Shechet describes her Birthright experience. She quotes another former Birthright participant who wrote, "Birthright's overstimulation brings about a deadening of feeling. It's hard to imagine the suffering of others when you're having the time of your life."[93] While Shechet reports that the trip she took was led by a guide who offered some nuance on the complexity of the landscape and did not totally ignore the presence of Palestinians, "there were moments when ideological suppression reared its head clearly and unpleasantly."[94] She describes an event on top of Mount Herzl, a military cemetery, when questions about Palestinian perspectives were dismissed as "political" and thus beyond the scope of Birthright conversations.[95]

As I show in chapter 3, some of the Jewish critics and Palestine solidarity activists also began their questioning while on Birthright trips or equivalent programs of immersion. While this is clearly an unintended consequence of Birthright, which aims at affirming a Zionist teleology and a "Macy's Parade" view of Israeli society, it does expose the diminishing hold of a certain narrative on a young demographic that is not only the product of American Jewish Zionist education and socialization, but is also thoroughly immersed in other social and cultural fields. The mechanisms of Birthright and the infrastructure of Jewish education eventually became key targets of protest for critical and anti-occupation Jews experiencing ethical outrage and a crisis of authority. In 2017, two new campaigns signaled these reactive ethical sentiments. JVP's #ReturnTheBirthright focuses on how the concept of a Jewish "right of return" has erased Palestinian indigeneity and their own right of return, and thus calls on young Jews to reject the offer of a free trip that "is 'free' because it has been paid for by the dispossession of Palestinians."[96] INN's #YouNeverToldMe conveys the testimonies of Millennial Jews and their explicit resentment at their elders and educators' complicity and intentional myopic production of knowledge about Israel, in simultaneously downplaying and authorizing the occupation.[97] These two campaigns mark a crucial shift from an initial experience of unease with the communal leadership and its reproductive mechanisms to the emergence of an active social movement that targets the very mechanisms underpinning the formation of American Jews. In the summer of 2018, the erosion of Birthright's narrative likewise manifested in INN's related coordinated breakaway moments, broadcasted on social media, where formal Birthright participants disrupted the trip by forcing participants and viewers to acknowledge the occupation through their choices to partake in Breaking the Silence's tour of Hebron or listen to the stories of displacement and harassment of families in East Jerusalem.[98] While disruptors of Birthright trips and summer camps' Israel education were subject to criticism from multiple sources,[99] their disruption received wide coverage and increased recognition on the part of mainstream Jewish

currents for the need to review their Israel curriculum.[100] This, combined
with the inability of American Jews to defend Israeli ethnoreligious centric
shifts manifested for example in the Jewish nation-state Basic Law passed in
2018 and ideologically driven travel bans that would deport Jewish and non-
Jewish known BDS activists,[101] marks the anti-occupation critics and activists
along a spectrum with, rather than necessarily oppositional to, the establishment. Before examining the shift to the active disruption of the mechanisms
for the reproduction of occupation-enabling narratives in more detail, let us
consider why it took place. Some who began to feel uncomfortable identifying with Israel found refuge (though perhaps temporary) in J Street or other
similarly oriented "pro-Israel, pro-peace" organizations. It is important to
attend to this phenomenon before turning, in the remainder of the book, to
deeper modes of questioning that challenge the very foundation of the Zionist paradigm, rather than embracing seemingly more appeasing versions of it.

LIMITED DIVERSIFICATION

J Street's arrival on the scene in 2008 offered, for many, a sense of diversification in American Jewish political life. This Washington-based advocacy and
lobbying group represents itself as "pro-Israel and pro-peace," thus seem-
ing to offer a platform for Jews who are dissatisfied with AIPAC's apparent
kowtowing to certain segments within Israeli politics. J Street oversees the
flow of Jewish money to political representatives whose positions on Israel
are less hawkish than those supported by AIPAC and the like.[102] J Street also
represents its work as focused on "re-shap[ing] political perceptions of what
it means to be pro-Israel."[103] "Within the American Jewish community," its
website reads, "we advocate that our institutions and leaders ground our relationships with Israel in the same values they apply to other issues, including
freedom, justice and peace—the very principles set forth in Israel's Declaration of Independence."[104] Here, J Street clearly presents itself as a counter-
voice to AIPAC, one that demands reconfiguring advocacy for Israel by calling for new diplomatic approaches, affirming a peace agenda, and insisting
on consistency of values. The latter point is an especially acute motivation for
the Jewish Palestine solidarity activists featured in the remaining chapters, for
whom consistency of values meant the shifting of the focus of Jewish solidarity and ethical commitments.

J Street's self-description shows that its inception as a counter to AIPAC
constitutes a response to a growing number of American Jews, including
those who maintain fidelity to the logic of the "two-state solution," who
feel their values to be compromised by the demand to support a militaristic

state, no matter what. J Street's objective to reshape perceptions about what
it means to support Israel suggests that, even beyond its advocacy in Congress and national politics, it aims at broadening the internal debate within
the Jewish community and "urg[ing] Jewish communal officials and institutions to demonstrate leadership by speaking out in support of policies that
align with our interests and values and against those that don't."[105] However,
despite a meteoric emergence into the political and sociocultural arena,[106]
J Street has maintained rather conventional views about American Jewish
support of Israel. If AIPAC identifies more with the Israeli Right, J Street—
like Americans for Peace Now—remains largely in continuity with historical
Labor Zionism in its various contemporary manifestations (most recently,
for instance, the Zionist Camp in the elections of 2015). J Street's language
about "our values," even with respect to Israel, operates with a Zionist ethos
that recalls Zionism's initial and foundational commitment to democratic
values and practices (hence the reference in J Street's framing to the Israeli
Declaration of Independence). Indeed, many initial supporters of J Street
eventually grew disillusioned by the way the organization was co-opted by
conventional parameters of debate, a point that became especially acute
when J Street was reluctant to criticize the Israeli assault on Gaza in 2014. But,
the organization's support in the following year of the nuclear deal with Iran,
despite the coordinated effort by Netanyahu and his allies in AIPAC to defeat
it through lobbying Congress, reinforces its location as the American voice
of a centrist Zionist position that is not beholden to right-wing Israeli interests.[107] J Street is even actively examining and displaying alternative Israeli
voices, operative in the struggling "peace camp" and various human rights–
oriented organizations.[108]

Hence, the divides between AIPAC and J Street typically fall along the
domestic American split between the Republican and Democratic parties.[109]
The intricate connections of Zionist orthodoxy and heterodoxy to the contours of the American political landscape were evident in the Bernie Sanders campaign in 2016.[110] Sanders's hiring of Simone Zimmerman as the Jewish Outreach Director of his campaign demonstrated the Vermont senator's
awareness of the changing Jewish terrains. While in college, Zimmerman was
the president of J Street U, J Street's campus arm. Later a cofounder of INN,
she repeatedly affirms the right of Palestinians to dignity and opposes the
occupation, as does Sanders (figure 1.2). The 2016 campaign exposed internal frictions within the Democratic Party, given Hillary Clinton's support of
Israeli aggressions in Gaza (specifically in 2014) as self-defense.[111] Sanders,
however, caved to immense pressures and suspended Zimmerman only two
days after announcing her hiring. Reacting to Zimmerman's suspension,

FIGURE 1.2. Simone Zimmerman protesting in front of the Jewish Federation, New York City [Photo credit: Gili Getz]

another cofounder of INN remarked that the opposition to Zimmerman reflects "how out-of-touch the American Jewish establishment is with the Jewish community."[112] Indeed, Zimmerman's suspension was met with an extensive hashtag campaign and outcry, signaling that while the establishment still holds economic and political capital, the undercurrents continue to gain cultural and social capital. The establishment's narrative is losing traction, which, as the activists I spoke to underscored, explains why they are forced to direct so much economic and political capital toward silencing alternative narratives.

That the revolutionary promise of J Street was overstated became especially evident during Operation Protective Edge in Gaza (summer 2014). J Street had emerged as a strong critic of the earlier Operation Cast Lead (2008), classifying it as a form of "collective punishment."[113] The Jewish "establishment" characterized J Street's response to Cast Lead as both "appallingly naïve" and "morally deficient."[114] By 2014, the lobbying group had "moderated" its positions, exposing its stance as nothing but conventionally Zionist. J Street's effort to articulate a more acceptable position, it hoped, would lead to membership in the Conference of Presidents of Major American Jewish Organizations.[115] The Conference of Presidents is one of the major three Jewish organizations in the US—together with AJC and the ADL—which, despite a rich history of supporting minorities, resisting and monitoring racism, and promoting religious freedom among other social justice issues, underwrite the conventional Jewish Zionist narrative. The Conference of Presidents aims at communicating on behalf of the Jewish community to the executive branch and hence has worked closely with AIPAC, which has concentrated on lobbying to legislators. With J Street's resolute efforts to find acceptance by this establishment, it became clear that this organization likewise operates within, rather than as an alternative to, the Zionist orthodoxy. "The more moderate approach," writes Josh Nathan-Kazis, "won the group praise from some former critics, while threatening to alienate core activists. It has left American Zionists critical of the war without any established Jewish organizations on their side."[116] Consequently, J Street's role in diversifying the American Jewish landscape proved to some American Jews to be merely cosmetic. They began to search, instead, for a shift from lobbying, to a movement for radical refiguring of American Jewish attitudes and attachments to Israel and Zionism. Some former J Street activists and staffers, like Simone Zimmerman, even began to protest the Israeli assault on Gaza, giving birth to the hashtag #IfNotNow.

It is not the case that J Street fails to offer a space for Jews to be critical of the occupation and perform acts of solidarity with Palestinians. It does. For instance, a young activist from the Stanford Chapter of J Street U powerfully opened a plenary session of J Street's Annual Conference in 2017, stressing that "one can fight for Israeli democracy like one fights for American democracy. We can stand for the rights of Palestinians in the same way we stand for the rights of Muslim-Americans and in the same way that they stand for us."[117] She was referring to recent acts of solidarity that American Jewish and Muslim communities exemplified in the face of rising tides of bigotry and Islamophobic policies in the Trump era such as travel bans targeting Muslims and desecration of Jewish cemeteries. She also spoke about observing the requirement of Sukkot to dwell in a sukkah and that she performed it for the first time in the middle of the Stanford campus, together with other J Street U activists, in order to protest the threat of demolition of the Palestinian village of Susiya in the West Bank. She appealed to the Jewish history of marginality, refugee-hood, and displacement as her moral compass informing action, stressing with pride how members of her St. Louis–based synagogue carried photos capturing their families' memories of being uprooted, displaced, and made refugees to protests against policies that threaten to lock the gates and turn away others seeking refuge. She also understands why the signs "Free Palestine" resonated meaningfully in Ferguson, Missouri, during the protests against police brutality of African Americans, which erupted after the fatal shooting of Michael Brown on August 9, 2014. She was there protesting in solidarity. All of this positions her and other activists in J Street U, and J Street more broadly, as already engaging potentially with an intersectional and relational reimagining of their Jewishness and interrogation of Israeli occupation policies. Yet, J Street constrains its analysis of peace and justice to a two-state paradigm, and with it a commitment to a Jewish democracy or ethnocracy as a core principle of its moral imagination.[118] J Street's official policy page cites a former Israeli prime minister, Ehud Olmert, who admits that a shift in the political paradigm from two state to one state and an anti-apartheid-style struggle for equal rights (rather than Palestinian self-determination) would spell the end of Israel as we know it.[119]

So it is not that J Street does not give space for acts of solidarity and critique. It does. The issue, for many of the activists I accompanied, is that J Street's moral imagination is so deeply entrenched in a logic of ethnoreligious nationalism that confines its acts of solidarity to dwelling in a sukkah for a night or two on the Stanford campus. Such normative confinement explains its refusal to heed the Call for BDS and thus take directives from Palestinians themselves. J Street, by its own admission, focuses on changing American policy on Israel and Palestine in ways filtered through its commitment to a "pro-Israel, pro-peace" outlook. This is no longer enough for Jews awakened by a sense of moral urgency to respond to the Call of Palestinians, which is articulated through the idiom of human rights. Their passionate solidarity with Palestinians constitutes a form of moral agency and a source for rescripting communal meanings.

The brief history of J Street suggests that—though it has presented itself as an alternative to AIPAC—its hope of being accepted by the established power structures within the American Jewish community and its reliance on an unreconstructed approach to the "two-state solution" have diminished its capacity to effectively reshape what it means to be "pro-Israel." By "unreconstructed," I refer to the uncritical presumption that the moral problems of Israel began in 1967 and that the Green Line (within which is located Israel's pre-1967 territorial scope) represents a spatial and normative boundary between the "good old Israel" and its perversion. This conceptual bifurcation is enduringly repeated even by critics deeply committed to the Jewish establishment. Their outrage with Israel focuses primarily on the extremism and racism associated with successive right-wing governments under Netanyahu and the consolidation of the political power of religious Zionism. This is not the Israel they fought for, they say.[120]

By contrast, activists associated with JVP and smaller organizations such as INN have become increasingly aware of the need to think beyond the artificiality of the Green Line. This is even if INN, unlike JVP, remains inten-

tionally committed neither to BDS tactics nor to interrogating the premises
of Zionism in order to facilitate its intentionally "Big Tent" approach, encompassing Jews critical of the occupation without an embrace of BDS or an
articulated vision concerning post-occupation reconfiguration.[121] The hope
that J Street represented a genuine alternative soon dissipated, and those who
wanted the group to become "less radical" were gratified as J Street reinforced Zionist orthodoxy (by reclaiming the internal diversity within Zionism) rather than subverting it. The upshot is that the Jewish "establishment"
in the US fluctuates along a narrow spectrum of approaches to Israel, one that
increasingly perceives its eroding narratives as the greatest security risk to
Israel and thus underwrites various silencing tactics without rectifying actual
practices. The young J Street U activist I introduced above, however, in articulating solidarity across multiple sites demonstrates how, even within the
confines of the "pro-Israel, pro-peace" paradigm of J Street, the injustices she
is able to name and catalogue push her toward moral clarity about which side
she should be on. She is not giving up on potential Israeli democratic alternatives to occupation policies (and thus her commitment to reinvigorate the
good old Israel), and she nonetheless stands for the people of Susiya in the
territories occupied in 1967. She sees the humanity of the people of Susiya,
and she is enraged by their predicament. For some other Jews who interrogate the occupation, the Green Line and a narrative about Jewish security
and democracy cease to demarcate the discourse of justice and they increasingly find it difficult to be on "both sides." The clarity of their response to
the question "Which side are you on?" becomes ever more pronounced and
transformational of the related question "Who are we?"

The work of radical questioning, necessary to the process of denaturalizing *doxa*, entails a crucial shift from advocacy to social movement activism. The task of chapter 2 is to examine how social movement spaces and
dynamics offer mechanisms for contesting religiosity and communal identity
and reimagining them nondeterministically. It does so by profiling five Jewish Palestine solidarity groups that move beyond the kind of advocacy represented by J Street toward genuinely transformative social movement work.

Forming a Social Movement

Crisis of Authority

I decided to get involved with IfNotNow when Donald Trump was elected president. The fact that he was perceived as the "pro-Israel" candidate by many within the American Jewish community due to his pro-settlement stance horrified me. Not only did I feel alienated within an America that elected a bigot and isolated in a Texas that actively discriminates against my LGBT, Latinx, and Black community members, I also felt betrayed by the Jewish community. While Donald Trump has since retracted his pro-settlement stance, I do not believe him. Now more than ever, this is the time for young Jews to get involved in anti-occupation work, and more broadly, anti-fascist work.[1]

The woman who penned this epigraph is indignant about multiple cases of injustice, including her sense that the Jewish establishment has betrayed her with its ethical misdirection. As chapter 1 suggested, a crisis of authority and narrativity in American Judaism is integral to the emergence of Jewish Palestine solidarity and activism that fundamentally challenges the prevailing discourse of Jewish Israel advocacy by reframing Israel advocacy and, more broadly, what it means to be Jewish.

As the previous chapter demonstrated, the architecture of American Jewish socialization is elaborate, and the reach of "pro-Israel" advocacy extensive. However, university campuses have become a key site of resistance to this socialization. Here, many Jewish students have become politicized and made aware of a variety of social justice issues. In college, they read, interrogate what they read, and begin to question their own locations of privilege and complicity with injustice, both locally and globally. Many of the young activists I interviewed attributed their transformation on the Israel issue to their time in college. For many Jewish young adults, the demands for self-censorship and for toeing a party line are no longer tolerable. The contradictions that produce cognitive dissonance can no longer be reconciled. This dissonance provokes a crisis of authority with respect to the institutionalized Jewish community, but sometimes even with respect to parents and other family members.

For American Jewish critics and Palestine solidarity activists, Zionism is no longer intelligible as an orienting narrative. The central theoretical question motivating this chapter is this: How does Jewish Palestine solidarity illuminate conditions that interrupt the mechanisms of social reproduction, especially in pluralistic contexts where multiple fields intersect elastically, at times with competing underpinning sensibilities and norms? This examination will shed light on broader theoretical questions about struggles over collective identities and ways of thinking about human agency, narrative change, and the relation between religion and social movement activism. This chapter maps and analyzes the American Jewish challengers of the Israeli occupation and Zionism more broadly through the lens of social movement theories that have grappled with religion, culture, and identity and meaning construction through contentious social semiotic spaces. I argue that religious discourses are not just employed instrumentally by movements, as if their boundaries and content were fixed and predetermined, but are dialogically (and creatively) reinterpreted through their emergent, relational, and dialogic dynamics.

SARURA

In May 2017, I participated in a Palestine solidarity delegation—a broad, historic coalition organized by the Center for Jewish Nonviolence (CJNV) to reclaim and rebuild the demolished village of Sarura in the Southern Hills of Hebron.[2] We were about 140 in number, mostly Jews from the US, but also from other countries, including Belgium, Switzerland, Britain, Australia, and Canada.[3] There were about one hundred more diaspora activists than the previous year. We designated three days for working with Palestinian partners in different locations, such as two villages in the Southern Hebron Hills, Susiya (see figure 2.1) and Umm al-Khair, which are under constant threat of total demolition. But we also worked in the city of Hebron itself, the Isawiya neighborhood in Jerusalem—where Palestinians face constant land seizures—and the Batan al-Hawa neighborhood in East Jerusalem.

I had left Sarura a few days before the Israeli Defense Forces (IDF) raided the camp, violently confiscating the power generator, tents, and other equipment (see figure 2.2). The raid came just moments after Jewish activists concluded the Havdalah service marking the end of Shabbat and the return of ordinary time (figure 2.3). As I anxiously watched the livestream, I noted that

FIGURE 2.1. A Jewish participant in CJNV's delegation in May 2017, in Susiya, working with the local children to plant flowers in tires, which will create a path to a structure that the Rural Women Association of South Hebron hopes to turn into a restaurant

the activists (many of whom I had come to know quite well during the previous week) were nonetheless singing, hugging one another, and strengthening their common commitment to end the occupation. We were Palestinians, Israelis, non-Israeli Jews, and other allies—all sweating together as we worked to clear caves and access paths to the village to make it inhabitable again (figure 2.4). Despite the harshness of the occupation, the images that emerged from the encampment in Sarura were of joyful co-resistance and friendship, shared *iftar* meals, singing, relaxing over sweet tea with mint, and resting together in the large tent that had to be replaced multiple times after repeated IDF raids. Despite such setbacks, the Jewish activists who went to Sarura with me were determined to actively resist the occupation and its ramifications.

This determination did not come easily, nor can its significance be overstated. It involves no less than the very transformation of the American Jewish landscape, for those on the frontlines in Sarura represent one dimension of a broader movement for reimagining Jewishness, a work that takes place through relational engagement with Palestinian narratives and lived realities. But what led American Jews, well socialized into Zionist orthodoxy, from the comfort and safety of New York City or Boston into Sarura and active civil disobedience led by Palestinian partners? This chapter explores this question

FIGURE 2.2. IDF's raid on Sarura [Photo credit: Ethan Miller]

FIGURE 2.3. Reflecting on the departure of Shabbat before the first IDF raid in the Sumud Camp in Sarura [Photo credit: Gili Getz]

FIGURE 2.4. Jewish activists working to clear a Palestinian cave to make it habitable again

by examining a shift from the kind of advocacy represented by J Street to the radical social movement activism of Open Hillel (OH), IfNotNow (INN), the Center for Jewish Nonviolence (CJNV), All That's Left (ATL), and Jewish Voice for Peace (JVP). It examines the cognitive and emotional work (and their non-binary relation with one another) that activists underwent in order to articulate their commitments to civil disobedience, to speak out against the occupation and the American Jewish establishment. Along the way, I illuminate the limits of attempts by various mechanisms of the establishment to manage cognitive dissonance and control the focus of Jewish solidarity.[4]

EMOTIONAL LIBERATION

While muzzling debate is an intentional and well-financed operation, the pro-Israel establishment cannot ultimately stifle the deep questioning many Jews undertake. Such questioning entails negotiating the meaning of being "pro-Israel" as well as whether Jewish belonging requires being pro-Israel. This work demands that, as Jews, they draw disruptively on Jewish resources to challenge the status quo and consolidate political solidarity and social movement mobilization. Jewish Palestine solidarity exemplifies a point made by sociologist Christian Smith: religion is capable not only of sanctifying the status quo, but of disrupting it too.[5] Jewish critics confront the complicity of the American Jewish community in the violation of human rights, contest Zionist interpretations of the relations between Jews and Israel, and cumulatively contribute to reshaping the American Jewish community from the ground up. This grassroots transformation is led primarily by youth, university students, and veteran Jewish social justice activists who push the scope of debate, ask questions, and engage in collective and individual cognitive processes of unlearning received narratives about the Israeli-Palestinian conflict as well as emotional processes of liberation, denoting what sociologist James M. Jasper calls "a shift of affective loyalties."[6]

Emotional liberation is often associated with the moral emotion of indignation (as the next chapter unpacks), but also with an enthusiastic hope for the future and a disruptive and prophetic protest-oriented mood. Social movements perform prophetic functions, Alberto Melucci explains, "where conflictual forms of behavior are directed against the processes by which dominant cultural codes are formed"[7] and are likewise oriented by transcendence. The latter, in Melucci's analysis, constitutes "a purely cultural form of resistance which counters the presumptions of power by affirming the right to desire—to hope that the world is more than what actually is."[8] The action in Sarura displayed a form of emotional liberation, which is as critical and as liberating as the cognitive process of unlearning ideological constructs.[9] It also displayed a prophetic intervention that can be analyzed as a mere "cultural" resistance, but at the same time was meaningfully and gratifyingly Jewish, rooted in the retrieval and appeals to Jewish traditions and histories of resistance. The Jewish activists in the CJNV delegation were indignant at what they deemed the atrocities of the occupation as well as ashamed by their collective sinfulness and complicity, but they also felt pride for standing there and resisting it *as Jews*, together with Palestinians. The action and the electrifying emotion ("collective effervescence," in Émile Durkheim's words)[10] of self-approval that it generated among the activists, therefore, exemplified Jasper's notion of moral battery, referring to the interaction between negative and positive emotions and their generative effects in terms of collective action, just as in the operation of a battery.[11] This particular case, however, contributes to the sociological work on the emotions of protest by stressing, as we will see clearly in later chapters, the role of rescripting religiocultural meanings in producing such forceful moral batteries and shifts in affective loyalties and ethical orientations.

While this shift away from Zionism and its mythologizing support of Israel breaks conventions that seem deeply entrenched within the American Jewish community, these conventions are, in fact, rather recent. Zionism, or the nationalistic option, emerged as a viable discourse only between the two world wars and immediately provoked acute tension with more prophetic and cosmopolitan approaches to Jewish politics. As Michael Barnett suggests, this history has always been marked by a contextually conditioned tension between Jewish cosmopolitanism and Jewish tribalism.[12] Barnett interprets the emergence of Jewish humanitarianism in the final decades of the twentieth century and early decades of the twenty-first century as a product of the diminishing hold of the Holocaust and Zionism as the pillars of American Jewish identity. The foci of Jewish humanitarianism are global rather than ethnocentric, framed through the popularized Kabbalistic concept of *tikkun olam* (or repair of the cosmos through good deeds or *tzedakka*) and connected with prophetic interpretations of Jewish traditions and their elective affinities with American discourses of multiculturalism and cosmopolitanism. Young Jews engage in service work globally and locally under the auspices of Jewish organizations such as the Religious Action Center and the American Jewish World Service, performing their duties in a universe that expects privileged young people to do good in the world (what Cornel West calls "do-goodism").[13]

When the humanitarian impulse meets the Palestinian "other" as the object of solidarity and long-distance normative commitment, Jewish loyalty to a Jewish ethnocracy crumbles and the possibility of post- or non-Zionist American Jewish identification emerges through a "moral shock" that, as Jasper explains, "results when an event or information shows that the world is not what one had expected."[14] The narratives of Palestinian suffering generate such shock, which is instrumental in shifting affective attachments and "rethinking moral principles."[15] The "do-goodism" of Jewish cosmopolitanism, in other words, becomes prophetic when it involves a self-interrogation of Jewish complicity with the violence against Palestinians and, as we will see in later chapters, connects this prophetic engagement to the complicity of white Jews with the structures of American white supremacy.

Even if Jewish humanitarianism did not immediately translate into a focus on Palestinian struggles, the cosmopolitan turn does denote a crucial shift in how Jews think about solidarity. While the Jewish establishment still controls economic capital, its cultural and symbolic capital is eroding, as youth increasingly prefer to engage in do-goodism in remote villages in Africa rather than in kibbutzim. Yet the matter of economic capital is significant. Critical anti-occupation Jewish education and immersion programs, led by social justice and human rights organizations, are constantly under threat of losing their funding.[16] Indeed, the Jewish establishment's concentrated focus on university campuses in the US and intensified efforts to narrow debates by imposing financial restraints on which debates can unfold, and by whom, reveal its anxiety about losing control of the narrative. It also evokes the authority crisis facing the youth, whose elders forbid them from asking questions. However, they do persist.

For instance, the waves of divestment proposals on campuses[17] propelled by a coalition of student groups cannot—as various mechanisms of the Israel lobby attempted to do—be litigated or silenced away by arguments about civility, the manipulation of Islamophobia, or accusations of antisemitism.[18] Students for Justice in Palestine (SJP), a decentralized organization minimally supported by universities, is at the forefront of campus activism.[19] Its increased effectiveness and influence, along with the movement's internal plurality, indicate that the Israel lobby's control over the narrative (even when rebranded and slightly revised) is significantly diminishing. It is likewise eroding within the Jewish landscape itself, further demonstrating a profound intergenerational crisis of authority. In what follows, I explore four sites where deep questioning unfolds through a crisis of narrativity, a precondition for disrupting social reproduction.[20]

Deep Questioning: Four Instances

OPEN HILLEL

The intergenerational divides within American Judaism are clear and, to those interested in entrenching conventional narratives and patterns of engagement with Israel, deeply alarming. One key indicator of the transformation of the American Jewish landscape is the OH movement that sprouted up on campuses in November 2012.[21] The students who participate in OH's gatherings and programs are not necessarily anti- or even non-Zionists; rather, they simply feel frustrated with the lack of open debate dictated by the standards of the umbrella organization Hillel International, which provides spaces and resources for cultivating Judaism on campuses internationally (figure 2.5). Its guidelines—similar to those governing Jewish Federation funding—mean that a lack of immediate and complete compliance with the "pro-Israel" agenda risks exclusion from participation. Hence, the Israeli *Shministim* (seniors) who refused to serve in the Occupied Territories were denied a venue in Hillel and other settings associated with the "establishment."

Notably, of the 212 Jewish students who attended the OH Conference at Harvard University in the fall of 2014, almost an equal percentage of attendees were associated with the Reform and Conservative currents of Judaism. However, the clear plurality comprised "non-denominational" and self-described "secular" Jews (35% in total). This figure does not suggest a lack of

FIGURE 2.5. Open Hillel protest in front of the Israeli consulate in New York, 2017 [Photo credit: Gili Getz]

Jewish orientation or identity among the students at the conference. It simply highlights the limits of "denomination" as a descriptive category. These limits will be important to our later analysis of how alternative conceptions of Jewishness (including appeals to atheistic Jewish traditions) disrupt the status quo and contribute to the mobilization of collective action and the rewriting of communal boundaries.

The demographic self-reporting of those who attended the OH conference highlights the immediate contexts of Jewish critical activism and sheds light on the profiles of those who sought to reorient their solidarities. The clear majority of attendees (82%) were Ashkenazi, with only 7% identifying as Sephardi or Mizrahi, and only 2% as both Ashkenazi and Sephardi. Indeed, most of my interviewees were not only Ashkenazi, but also readily admitted their complicity with and benefit from "white privilege." American Jewish critics of Israel are mostly located on the two coasts, but they can increasingly be found in other geographical locations, like the Midwest. These diverse geographical locations reflect the broader expansion of Jewish critics of Israel.

OH's challenge to the Jewish establishment's policing of the boundaries of debate indeed attracts a diversity of Jewish supporters, located across the spectrum regarding relations to Zionism and Israel, on the one hand, and BDS campaigns, on the other. The list of academics (including myself) who

came out in support of OH in early 2016 by agreeing to serve publicly on
its Academic Council further reinforces this point: the list includes outspo-
ken anti-Zionists and committed Zionists alike.[22] At the heart of this broad
scope of voices is a Jewish argument against foreclosing debates. One young
interlocutor laments, "It is shameful—I would even say a *Chillul HaShem*
[a desecration of God's name]—that Hillel's policy undermines not only the
purpose of a university education, but also is turning away Jewish students
who wish to have the same experience of give-and-take with other Jews my
family has had over the last eighty years."[23] Another activist writes:

> I've been involved in . . . Hillel since the beginning of my freshman year. Hillel
> is a place that has fostered my spiritual growth and where I've met wonderful
> friends and mentors. I deeply care about this organization and that is why I
> want it to change. Why should non-Zionist Jewish students not feel comfort-
> able experiencing the same spiritual growth and meaningful programming
> that I have experienced? Non-Zionist Jews are not any "less Jewish" than my
> Zionist peers. Hillel is not the only part of this problem. American Jewish
> institutions as a whole perpetuate the status quo reflected in the Jewish Fed-
> erations, which exist in many American cities as a financial resource for other
> Jewish organizations. The synagogue where I was raised, the Jewish camp I
> attended, and the youth movement I was a part of all reinforced the idea that
> being a Zionist is synonymous with being "a good Jew." The exclusion of non-
> Zionist Jews and the absence of Palestinian narratives and dialogue about Is-
> rael and Palestine are present in Jewish communities across the country. I
> don't find this to reflect Jewish values. Jewish texts discuss the needs to pursue
> justice, to be for oneself, to ask questions, to wrestle with G-d.[24]

As these reflections make clear, OH's push to broaden the scope of Jewish debate involves retrieving alternative scripts that construe Judaism as a tradition
of debate, questioning, and the pursuit of justice.

While on the surface this critique of the status quo might seem to signal
a departure from American Jewish trends, a closer examination of the Pew
study discussed in the previous chapter, in conjunction with the diversity
of OH's participants, suggests instead that Jewish critics of Israel are situated along a continuum: many understand Judaism not as a connection to
Israel, but as an ethics or a tradition of social justice work. By asking tough
questions, OH begins to particularize the practical ethical demands of *tikkun
olam* in ways that unsettle Jewish privilege and myopic vision. In 2017, after a
workshop involving OH activists and some members of the Academic Council that had examined dynamics of power, inclusion, and exclusion within
the Jewish community, OH activists protested Hillel International's ties to
the Israeli Diaspora Ministry's $66 million Mosaic United Program.[25] This

program was designed by Minister of Diaspora Affairs and religious Zionist Naftali Bennett to strengthen Jewish identity and attachment to Israel by imposing, in the words of OH's #OurJudaismincludes petition, "a monolithic vision of what it means to be Jewish, contradicting Hillel International's commitment to fostering an inclusive and pluralistic Jewish community on campus."[26] Mosaic United not only displays homophobic and sexist conceptions of "Jewish family values," but explicitly intends to silence "'critical discourse' regarding Israel." Such calls on Hillel International to be consistent with its professed values of pluralism and inclusion have quickly become a familiar tactic of Jewish youth activists as they navigate this crisis of authority. Locating these Jewish youth activists within the broader currents in American Judaism suggests that what led to their reorientation may in fact point to broader trends and shifts in solidarity away from Israel/Zion. Another youth-led movement, IfNotNow, further signals the profound authority crisis facing Jewish youth.

#IFNOTNOW

In the midst of Operation Protective Edge in late July 2014, INN published an open "Letter to the Conference of Presidents,"[27] calling on the Conference to "join our call to stop the war on Gaza, end the occupation, and forge a path towards freedom and dignity for all in Israel and Palestine." "We are alarmed and horrified by the death and destruction being committed in our name," the letter continues. "This is a moment of truth for the Jewish community, a moment that demands action." It goes on to explicate the hashtag's meaning: "Hillel, the Jewish sage of the 1st century, posed three questions that ring out across millennia. We come together to answer Hillel's call." The three questions are: "If we are not for ourselves, who will be for us?"; "If we are only for ourselves, who are we?"; and "If not now, when?" In response to the first question, INN affirms the diverse Jewish backgrounds of its members and affiliates, explaining that this very plurality, along with an understanding that Jewish history is defined by oppression, "has taught us that our freedom cannot be achieved absent the freedom of our neighbors." In response to the second question, the letter underscores that oppressing another population is inconsistent with liberation and security. In effect, "so long as Jewish people are caught in an endless cycle of violence, we are not safe" (figure 2.6). They also express outrage and grief "that so many speak of Palestinians as if their lives were worth less than our own," offering justifications "for the killing of so many." The question "If we are only for ourselves, who are we?" offers a challenge to *hasbarah*'s logic of security and ethnocentric interpretation of the Holocaust and the essentialization of Jewish history as a series of oppressions and persecutions. Activists at INN articulate their outrage and moral shock at the inconsistency of J Street, the more established lobby, and various other representatives of the "Jewish community" by appealing to Jewish sensibilities, signaling a move toward narrative change and shifting solidarities. Jewish sensibilities and multivalent meanings constitute this movement's main resources, which it mobilizes through what Marshall Ganz calls "public narrative," or "a leadership practice of translating values into action."[28] Ganz's focus on narrative may be situated within a broader scholarly turn.

Since the 1980s, theorists of narrative across disciplines have begun to focus on how stories threaded together from available cultural building blocks inform identity construction.[29] Francesca Polletta and her coauthors[30] identify some limitations in this turn to narrative, especially in cases where theorists neglected to account for power dynamics and sociocultural hierarchies, focusing instead on meaning-making in abstraction. Their review of sociological and other disciplinary studies of narratives demonstrates that "storytelling in institutions counters the notion that people are free to construct their own stories of the self."[31] "People can and do contest narrative conventions," they continue, "based on conventions they have learned in other settings."[32] However, those who contest narratives from outside the normative structure are, for that reason, highly disadvantaged; hence, an analysis of power is pivotal for relating narrative change to sociopolitical and cultural change. The turn to such a power-sensitive sociology of narrative[33] intersects with the literature on collective memory, especially when attention is directed to political discourse and to the question of why and how certain narratives dominate when they do.[34] Constraints on narrative change can be challenged by social movement activists who expose dissonance and flaws in the dominant narratives and subversively reimagine old stories.[35] Cultivating a subversive storyline that functions as a socially cohering public narrative (translating values into collective action), however, calls for a temporally fluid hermeneutical facility that both retrieves from and innovates within tradition.

For Ganz, "values are experienced emotionally" and motivate people to act with urgency. It is through narratives that the functionality of values for protest action materialize, intentionally and through a careful analysis of power. The sense of urgency experienced by Jewish critics of the occupation did not just happen. Their public narrative did not just emerge *ex nihilo*. It interrogates, through the mechanisms of moral shocks and outrage, and rescripts, through critical hermeneutical work with tradition and Jewish histories, the values that define the Jewish public. Experiencing, *as Jews*, the emotions of shame and indignation depends on, and emboldens through a

FIGURE 2.6. IfNotNow protest at ADL office, including arrests (Passover 2016) [Photo credit: Gili Getz]

feedback loop, an evaluative process that draws upon recovering or rewriting alternative prophetic, rather than ethnonationalist, interpretations of Jewishness. Such an act of recovery or rescripting depends upon religiocultural and historical literacies, critique of ideology, and contextually embedded constructive (re)interpretive choices that need to be accounted for theoretically.

INN's line of questioning will prove foundational to the reimagining of Jewish identity that I trace in subsequent chapters. The invocation of Rabbi Hillel to articulate a radical critique of the occupation and empathy with the victims of Zionism suggests that a reliance on a human rights vocabulary, while necessary, is not sufficient for offering a situated and particularized challenge to Zionized American Judaism and its various modes of socialization. Instead, this task requires a hermeneutical process that reimagines and reclaims Jewish resources and alternative scripts. The retrieval of Hillel is especially powerful because his legacy has been associated with Hillel International. INN seeks to recover the very basics of Hillel's teachings in the aftermath of the destruction of the Temple, and in doing so reflects its consistency with OH's challenge to the systematic and ideological muzzling of questioning.

In particular, INN invokes Hillel's wisdom to counteract the political realist logic that "we have no choice" but to employ violence.[36] "We act," INN writes, "because too many in our community endorse this dangerous view in our name. In a moment that demands courage and foresight, too many abdicate responsibility." Strikingly, INN employs Jewish rituals to grieve the death and suffering of both Israelis and Palestinians during the deadly assault on Gaza: "We will recite the Mourner's Kaddish for those who have died over the last weeks, we will consecrate their memory by reading their names, and we will call on the representatives of our community to join us as we demand an end to the war on Gaza, an end to occupation, and freedom and dignity for all people of the region."[37] The act of mourning, for non-Jews, conveys the broadening conceptions of ethical solidarity, which remains pivotal for renarrating Jewishness in ways that facilitate an alliance with a whole spectrum of social justice struggles.

The outrage INN expresses in its "Letter to the Conference of Presidents"[38] exposes the crisis of authority. It conveys the growing sense on the part of young critics that those who are supposed to represent the Jewish community not only fail to do so, but depart fundamentally from Jewish values and the kinds of lessons that Jews should have derived from their own histories. Rituals—such as the Mourner's Kaddish and weekly *dvar Torah*, a meditation on the Torah portion or *parasha* of the week—were circulated in cyberspace, where they became not only forms of protest but also resources for rescripting Jewishness.

With its #YouNeverToldMe campaign launched in late summer 2017, INN explicitly targeted mechanisms of Jewish socialization. The campaign, as chapter 1 noted, involved testimonials by alumni from key Jewish institutions expressing their disillusionment and outrage about myopic views of Israel and the rationalization of the occupation within which they had been incubated. One testimonial reads: "Growing up the Occupation had been completely hidden from me. . . . Violence erupted while we were there . . . and I saw leaders of my community completely hide Operation Protective Edge from the teen participants on the trip."[39] Another participant in the campaign writes about a social justice Jewish camp she attended for two summers: "Despite all I learned about how we are called as Jews to repair the world and stand up for those who have no one to stand up for them, I never heard a single word about the occupation. You taught me that to be Jewish is to stand up for justice, and that to stand up for justice is to celebrate my Judaism—but never told me about the grave injustices being perpetrated in my name."[40] This pointed challenge to the establishment clearly deploys shaming, by contrasting the Jewish values that had been taught with the concrete practice of and complicity with actions that violate those values.

Since its inception in 2014, INN has deepened its critique of the occupation, partly due to activists' participation in Jewish solidarity delegations to Palestine, coordinated by CJNV. In 2017, which marked fifty years of the occupation and a century since the Balfour Declaration, INN's leaders and activists reflected explicitly on why they seek to reclaim Judaism and how the Jewish establishment has failed them. One activist writes, for instance, that joining INN enabled him, for the first time since inadvertently being exposed to the realities of the occupation during a Birthright trip, to embrace his Jewishness and reconcile it with his criticism of the occupation: "It was the first time I entered a Jewish space where I didn't feel totally uncomfortable. I was shocked to learn that there are other Jews who had stayed silent on their faith or heritage for fear of being associated with the occupation. IfNotNow offered a space where Jews spoke with as much pride about being Jewish as they did with conviction for dismantling the occupation."[41] "IfNotNow," he continues, "has opened the door for my Jewish heritage to fit within my values—as a Jewish voice for ending the occupation."[42]

Another activist similarly remarked that INN offered a space for "Jews with a wide range of political affiliations who share a commitment to resist the Israeli occupation of the West Bank and Gaza."[43] This same activist grew up in the American Midwest and in Israel. Her childhood allowed her to develop a complex outlook where each return visit to Israel induced a stronger and stronger sense "of what Israel sacrifices morally to achieve 'homeland.'" A nuanced view is decidedly *not* what she found in the American Jewish context. There, "all I found was blind, unquestioning support for the Israeli government." This predicament "troubled" and "exhausted" her. "Complexity," she concludes, "was completely missing from my American Jewish life. So instead of persisting, I avoided American Jewish institutions altogether."[44]

Another INN activist likewise avers: "I know, unequivocally, that this is not my Judaism." This activist narrates her experience with the Jewish delegation to Palestine. During a protest of the occupation, she tells her audience of fellow protesters that, while she is a product of American Jewish schools and education on Israel/Palestine, her solidarity trip to Palestine exposed the occupation in ways she had never experienced before. She describes her experiences of active civil resistance against the occupation's authorities and the right-wing marchers whom INN and other activists tried to block from entering the Muslim Quarter in the Old City of Jerusalem as has been their custom on Jerusalem Day, marking the supposed unification of the city.[45] Her discussion of nonviolent resistance coordinated with a wide coalition of Israeli, Palestinian, and Jewish diaspora activists marks the deepening commitment of mostly non-Israeli Jews to active nonviolent resistance against the military occupation and its infrastructures. Indeed, CJNV provides one space from which Jews can articulate and act upon their commitments to end the occupation. It signals a shift from self-interrogation to actually putting bodies on the ground. Hence, anti-occupation activism within and through

Jewish spaces constitutes a form of "moral battery." It cultivates—even if through apparently altruistic actions motivated by ethical indignation for the sufferings of Palestinians and by indignant anger aimed at the American Jewish establishment—self-approval but also self-reshaping. The meanings of the communal "self," however, are not predetermined and involve the selective mobilization and reinterpretations of Jewish meanings and memories in narrating a transformative public narrative. INN's choice to articulate a broad anti-occupation stance without committing to BDS tactics or explicating particular positions on Zionism and a vision for Palestinian-Israeli cohabitation in the land facilitates its growth as a social force the American Jewish establishment has to grapple with in its effort to police a narrative about Jewish identity.[46] INN conveys a position of moral clarity on the occupation and in pressing the American Jewish establishment to choose its response to the question: Which side are you on, in accordance with such clarity?

THE CENTER FOR JEWISH NONVIOLENCE

Ilana Sumka founded CJNV in 2015 "to bring Jews from around the world to join the Palestinian grassroots nonviolent movement on the ground, alongside our Israeli counterparts."[47] Deriving inspiration from the US civil rights movement, Sumka writes: "I have long suspected that significant numbers of Jews joining the Palestinian grassroots nonviolent movement could be a game-changer in ways similar to Mississippi's 1964 Freedom Summer."[48] Sumka, an American Jew residing in Belgium, describes how after living in Israel for years, she gradually (and not without internal emotional resistance) became aware of the violent realities of the occupation. This prompted her to actively work to end the occupation, acting in solidarity with Palestinians who uphold the principles of nonviolent resistance. "Like many Jews around the world," Sumka writes, "it took time for me to realize I couldn't reconcile this reality of Israel's occupation with the Israel I thought I knew."[49] "There is no moral case to be made that justifies the separate legal systems, the unequal access to basic resources, the impunity that settlers enjoy or the constant harassment, violence, and displacement that Palestinians face," she writes. Most critically, she concludes, "There is certainly no Jewish case to be made for this."[50] Pivotal is her conviction, shared by many other Jewish activists, that "occupation is not our Judaism."[51]

This slogan was printed on our purple t-shirts as we, a coalition led by Palestinian partners, began our action in May 2017 to reclaim the village of Sarura. Surveilled constantly by settlers and soldiers in the nearby illegal outpost of Havat Ma'on, we came to reclaim Sarura for Palestinian families who, by 1997, were completely displaced from their caves and village when the military declared their village a closed military zone, with settlers poisoning their wells and water sources and vandalizing their property.

Our delegation's work in Sarura, an action named "Sumud: Freedom Camp," was explicitly inspired by the encampment led by the indigenous Standing Rock Sioux in North Dakota.[52] *Sumud* is the Arabic word central to depicting Palestinian *steadfastness* ("existence is resistance"). The diverse group that led the Sumud Camp spoke often of Standing Rock, reflecting a deep recognition of the intersections and analogies of struggles for justice, including equal access to water and land. CJNV's focus on concrete solidarity work and nonviolent resistance on the ground and alongside Palestinians illuminates the transition from self-reflexivity about the inconsistency of the occupation with Jewish values to a commitment to active resistance, explicitly mobilizing Jewish and international privilege. "We came to lend our bodies and our privilege to a movement led by Palestinians, just as American whites joined the Black-led civil rights movement."[53]

Among the 140 participants in the CJNV delegation to the Sumud Camp were young Jews from INN whose commitment to the slogan "Occupation Is Not My Judaism" propelled them to participate in anti-occupation work with CJNV and later, using their bodies, to counter the violent Jerusalem Day Flags Parade through the Muslim Quarter. Active, nonviolent resistance requires a willingness to suffer consequences, such as arrests, detentions, bodily injury, and deportation. CJNV activists faced disproportional force at the Sumud Camp: images of team leaders being pushed around by IDF forces—sent to dismantle the encampment and confiscate its equipment and tents—were livestreamed on Facebook. Only two days later, during the action against the Jerusalem Day parade, Israeli police broke the arm of one INN and CJNV member, as they forcibly removed her from the human chain she was a part of. Her broken arm symbolizes the transformation of Jewish resistance to the occupation, from a self-reflexive work motivated by a sense of alienation from Jewish institutions and spaces in the US, to an active reclaiming of Jewishness that involves a commitment to actual, physical solidarity with Palestinians in nonviolent co-resistance to the occupation.[54]

CJNV is strongly linked to another group, All That's Left: Anti-Occupation Collective (ATL), a Jewish diasporic organization resisting the occupation on the ground. ATL is committed to an explicitly diasporic angle of resistance. Established in 2013, the organization encompasses a wide spectrum of Jews who unambiguously oppose the occupation and focus on "empowering the diaspora to take action"[55] on the ground in Israel/Palestine, where they culti-vate strong relations with Palestinian partners for nonviolent resistance. Ac-tivists associated with ATL were pivotal in designing and implementing the CJNV delegation's action in 2017 and prior. One contributor to ATL's blog writes that ATL "taps into the umbrella idea of social change and movement—holding within its grasp a diverse array of individuals and networks that may not agree on every point, but fundamentally understand that the status quo of military occupation cannot stand. One's motivation may stem from a sense of solidarity with the Palestinian struggle or a sense of preservation for the Israeli state, or some intersection of these and other rationales."[56] Yet this emphasis on diversity does not preclude internal negotiation, contestation, and change within the movement as it consolidates its public narrative. "The point ultimately," the blogger continued, "is that our goals have to matter more than the specific reasoning. Still, how we act and the intention of said actions is constantly evolving, further reflecting the nature of the individuals who choose to be involved in more than just rhetoric."[57]

The turn to direct action and nonviolent co-resistance with Palestinian and Israeli partners by CJNV, ATL, INN, and even some activists from more mainstream organizations like J Street points to a deepening critique of the Jewish establishment conjoined with a rearticulation of Jewishness in and through the anti-occupation movement and the moral shocks and batteries it generates. The commitment to nonviolence is articulated through appeals to Jewish traditions—including the stories of Shifrah and Puah's noncoop-eration with Pharaoh's decrees and Honi the Circle Maker—as well as the historical moments of Jewish participation in the civil rights movement in the US, South Africa, and intellectual contributions to criticisms of predatory capitalism and neoliberalism. The first session of our CJNV group, which gathered in a large conference room in the Manger Hotel in Bethlehem, in-volved a rabbi who led us in a *kavanah* (spiritual attunement) that invoked Honi the Circle Maker's steadfastness, and explicitly connected it to Jewish solidarity with Palestinian steadfastness or *sumud*.[58] An engagement with Jewish resources that undergird the commitment to nonviolent resistance to injustice allows Jews to experience their activism as an authentically Jewish phenomenon. As one participant in CJNV's 2016 delegation remarks, "Rather than a hindrance, being Jewish functioned as the inspiration and the guiding principle for our work, making this one of the most empowering and positive Jewish experiences of my life."[59] These Jewish activist circles reflect a broader grassroots movement to transform communal boundaries and meanings, and this transformation unfolds precisely through anti-occupation and Palestine solidarity work. Acts of solidarity facilitate the deepening of emotional and cognitive liberation and, in this case, demonstrate the multidirectional processes of rescripting Jewish religiocultural meanings. The practice of public narratives or of translating values into action is not merely unidirectional, but rather emergenist and dialectical as well. The strong emotion of indignation that propels anti-occupation work demands increasingly, through prophetic action, to articulate positive conceptions of Jewishness that move beyond the slogan "Occupation Is Not My Judaism" to reimagining what one's Judaism actually *is*. This reimagining builds upon the strong sense of self-approval and pride that Palestine solidarity actions galvanize. The question is not only how religion works for movement mobilization but how the movement, in turn, transforms religion. We now return to JVP, which represents a larger and multifaceted dimension of this movement.

JEWISH VOICE FOR PEACE

JVP was established in Oakland in 1996 by three UC Berkeley undergraduates. At the time of its founding, other similar small local Jewish groups had begun sprouting up across the US, propelled by similar objectives, disillusionment with the American Jewish establishment, and the realization of what was being done in their name. These groups articulated a critique of Israeli occupation, especially of Israel's claims that it acts in the name of all Jews. "Not in my name!" became a rallying cry every time Israel exhibited massive levels of violence against Palestinians. In 2002, JVP was launched nationally, subsuming the smaller groups under its central leadership. The organization has always focused on building a grassroots base. By 2017, JVP had 200,000 subscribers, 10,000 individual donors, and over 60 chapters across the US. It has focused on building transformative mechanisms (see chapters 4 and 5), such as a Rabbinic Council, an Artists' Council, an Academic Advisory Council, a Health Council, a youth wing, and an Advisory Board involving key Jewish intellectuals. These constitute mechanisms for cultivating JVP's transformative mission to "build Jewish communities that reflect the understanding that being Jewish and Judaism are not synonymous with Zionism or support for Israel." They also convey the multiple registers in which JVP carries out its agenda.

The National Members Meeting (NMM) of 2015 resulted in clear guiding principles and strategies, including the objectives to "Transform Jewish communities, Sustain and support . . . allies in the Movement, Win Campaigns to Challenge Oppression and Build Power, Shift Culture and Public Discourse, and Build Capacity and Scale."[60] These objectives, JVP affirms, involve intrapersonal, interpersonal, and intercommunal change. Such change requires multivocality, involving the vocabularies of interfaith conversation, human rights, and intra-Jewish conversations, depending on the context.

JVP sees itself as participating in "the global movement for justice in Palestine," requiring that it work with "a broad spectrum of allies" in solidarity and accountability with "those directly affected by Israel's discriminatory and violent policies and practices, while working to effectively build and accountably deploy our power as American Jews and allies."[61] The focus on solidarity and accountability stresses JVP's understanding of its work as both relational and intersectional, grounded in a recognition of American Jews' particular privilege, responsibility, and capacity to participate in a global Palestine solidarity movement. The guiding principles, however, also highlight the deeply Jewish character of JVP's participation in a global movement for Palestine. In short, it seeks to renarrate Judaism beyond Zionism while actively working to "end racism, anti-Jewish, anti-Muslim, and anti-Arab bigotry, and all forms of oppression."[62] The organization's campaigns follow these guiding principles, including its leadership in the Network Against Islamophobia (NAI), its embrace of the BDS campaigns, its interfaith work with progressive churches in deliberating about divestment from the occupation, and its alliance with a variety of interrelated social justice sites.

Rebecca Vilkomerson, the executive director of JVP, opened the NMM in the spring of 2017 by celebrating the organization's increasing ability to disrupt a Jewish narrative. Specifically, she referred to JVP's support of the controversial platform of the Movement for Black Lives (MBL) in the previous year and its demonstrated capacity to be an ally by employing an intersectional analysis of social justice work and coalition building. MBL's political platform generated controversy among Jewish groups by using strong words such as "genocide" and "apartheid" to describe the predicament of Palestinians, thus challenging the Jewish establishment's invocation of a nostalgic era of Jewish participation in the 1960s civil rights movement. The way that the establishment remembers Jewish participation in the civil rights movement is both oversimplified, overlooking complexities in Jewish-black relations in the US,[63] and instrumentalized to demonstrate a history of Jewish commitment to alliance with African Americans. In so doing, it brackets black-Palestinian solidarity and "whitewashes" Israel's racist practices and military occupation. By adopting the platform, JVP (along with INN and other critics from the Jewish Left) distinguished itself from other social justice–oriented Jewish organizations in the US by attending to intersectionality.[64]

I bracket, for the moment, questions of the efficacy and accuracy of MBL's use of "genocide" and "apartheid" (see chapter 7); the point to stress here is

JVP's (as well as INN's) explicit and public support of MBL's political platform, including its controversial sections.[65] In its initial statement, JVP expressed disappointment in Jewish organizations' rejection of the platform as well as a self-reflexive admission that the organization's leadership is dominated by Ashkenazi Jews, but is undergoing its own "project to dismantle white supremacy inside of JVP." The statement then turns to the Jews of Color Caucus (JOC), which served as an authority in determining how JVP ought to respond to MBL's platform. Also using the acronym JOCSM, the Caucus describes itself as a group of "Jews of Color, Sephardi, Mizrahi, and other Minoritized Jews organizing for justice in Palestine and the transformation of our communities." Its statement of support (which became JVP's own official position) included an affirmation of "solidarity and co-resistance with the Movement for Black Lives," which it interprets as "a feminist and intersectional struggle dedicated to fighting systematic violence against Black people in the United States." This affirmation was followed by an unequivocal endorsement by JOCSM (and JVP, in turn) of MBL's platform "in its entirety without reservation," recognizing that it was drafted to articulate "a response to the sustained and increasingly visible violence against Black communities in the U.S. and globally" and expressing anger toward the "white U.S. institutional Jewish community in detracting from such a vital platform at a time when Black lives are on the line, simply because the organizers chose to align their struggle with the plight of Palestinians." Highlighting a complex history of black-Palestinian connections, JOCSM declares that "any attempt to co-opt Black struggle while demeaning these connections [amounts to] an act of anti-Black erasure."[66]

Being called into an explicit articulation of alliance with MBL, therefore, demonstrates how participation in social justice and Palestine solidarity activism deepened Jewish activists' substantial process of rescripting Jewishness. It deepened it through their internal engagement with race and the construction of Jewish whiteness. JVP's centering of JOCSM voices illustrates the elastic shifts within the American Jewish landscape, where critics of Israeli policies, Zionism, and the American Jewish establishment operate in spaces that are both relational—confronted by Palestinian experiences—and intersectional—motivated by a broader critique of interlocking systems of power and experiences of marginalization. The shift resonates with the earlier work of leftist Jewish organizers, such as the New York City–based Jews for Racial & Economic Justice (established in 1990) and its commitment, grounded in the secular tradition of Jewish socialism, to prioritize marginalized Jewish voices in cultivating intersectional and transformative grassroots organizing and solidarity in the pursuit of racial and economic justice.[67]

However, the organizations and groups examined here are distinct in their prioritization of the anti-occupation lens as an entry point into broader social justice activism that requires meaningful rescripting of Jewish public narrative and identity.

This chapter's profile of key groups that have recently emerged in response to the crisis of authority in American Judaism and through the mechanisms of moral shocks and batteries shows that this transformation of the Jewish landscape constitutes a social movement, not mere advocacy. Indeed, Jews participating in various actions, whether through JVP or CJNV, often use the word "transformative" to describe their experiences. Many relay how they finally found in the Palestine solidarity movement a Jewish space in which they could feel comfortable, meaningfully Jewish, and ethically coherent at the same time. Hence, this movement poses an especially rich topic for theoretical analysis from both social movement theory and religious studies perspectives. For here, we find a complex case of how social movement dynamics and contestations function prophetically within processes of religious and cultural reimagining. It invites us to move beyond the important theorizing of religion's potential for disruptive collective activism[68] toward illuminating activism's transformation of religiosity and ontological certainties.[69] In this case, the topic of examination is the renarration of Jewish scripts where Jewish meanings, rituals, texts, and historical memories are not merely instrumentalized by the social movement, but involve the very transformation of a religiocultural community. They surely also serve to advance the social movement's objectives. Not merely performing a "cultural" prophetic function, the social movement itself becomes a religiocultural space, as indicated by several activists who found coherence and intelligibility of their Jewish and ethical compasses therein. The following section addresses how scholarship in social movement theory might shed further light on this grassroots social movement that is transforming American Jewish communities.

Why Do Jewish Diaspora Critics of Israel Constitute a Social Movement?

IDENTITY THROUGH MOVEMENT

The cultural study of social movements helps clarify why the alternative, refigured Jewish narrative is not preconstituted, but rather is produced through social movement processes and contentions. Sociologist Sidney Tarrow's definition of a social movement is helpful for thinking about the collective significance of Jewish critics. "Rather than seeing social movements as expressions of extremism, violence, and deprivation," he writes, "they are better defined as collective challenges, based on common purposes and social solidarities, in sustained interaction with elites, opponents, and authorities."[70] Social movements differ decidedly from advocacy groups, such as AIPAC, which employ various tactics in order to influence public opinion and decision-making processes. Charles Tilly likewise offers conceptual resources for thinking about Jewish diaspora critical work in terms of social movement theory. Especially relevant is his emphasis on contentious politics and social organizing as vehicles for ordinary persons to participate politically through sustainable campaigning, a repertoire of political actions, and demonstrations of worthiness, unity, numbers, and commitments.[71] Paul van Seeters and Paul James add that the consolidation of social movements also involves the formation of "collective identity," the cultivation of "a shared normative orientation," a common "concern for change of the status quo," and "moments of practical action that are at least subjectively connected together across time addressing this concern for change."[72] The activists associated with JVP or INN engage in something more than advocacy or counter-advocacy; theirs is, in fact, a concentrated effort to produce a public narrative and radically disrupt the status quo within their own Jewish community and, more broadly and relatedly, in terms of the Palestinian predicament. JVP, in 2017, constituted the largest contingent of the global Palestine solidarity movement, a fact that, as one JVP staffer indicated, the organization must grapple with as it analyzes its own accountability to Palestinians.

The Jewish anti-occupation movement responds to the question "Whose side are you on?" with the answer "justice," and interprets its answer specifically in terms of human rights rather than through an affective loyalty to Israel as does J Street, for instance. This emphatic, normative point of departure grounded in ethical outrage and solidarity illuminates how demystifying the specific discursive or disciplinary power authorizing the occupation of Palestinians is connected to exposing the more insidious and global techniques of "biopower" that serve to render the occupation intelligible. For Michel Foucault—who coined the concept—such techniques reside in racist-statist discourses that deploy biological concepts such as purity and degeneracy to authorize practices of colonialism, segregation, apartheid, and genocide.[73] The Jewish resistance to the establishment narrative about Jewishness is thus connected, through an engagement with broader social movement dynamics, to resisting racism and biopower in their global manifestations. Jewish anti-occupation's deflation of the logic of biopower is the upshot of the erosion of mechanisms designed to reconcile incoherence among the social fields that Jews inhabit. This point invites sociological analysis.

Indeed, sociologist David Landy effectively employs a revised interpreta-

tion of Pierre Bourdieu's theory of practice to explain why Jewish critics of
Israel in the diaspora constitute a social movement that operates simultaneously within two movements: the distant Palestine solidarity movement
and the local Jewish one. Bourdieu's theory views *habitus*—the embodied
patterns of social structures in individuals in the form of their "durable transposable dispositions"[74]—as the outcome of development in one social field,
which informs, in a structured manner, relations depending on the position
and capital (symbolic, economic, social) of individual players. While afford-
ing certain players the possibility of mastering the field by manipulating its
logic and deploying its capital, in this mode the actor inhabits rather than
subverts the *doxa* that underlies the field.[75] Bourdieu's theory of social reproduction attributes little transformative role to social movement actors.
For him, they are merely complicit in reproducing silences and the *doxa*
and *illusio* that regulate the symbolic values of the field.[76] Landy, by contrast,
views social movement actors as translators whose *habitus* is the product of
the multiple, intersecting fields they inhabit. Indeed, the very multiplicity of
these fields is what enables actors to act transformatively and to be themselves
transformed.[77] Hence, one's *habitus*, contra Bourdieu, is not stable, but elastic and constituted by complex interactions. The process of translation from
one *habitus* or social field to another begins, in many respects, before active
participation in the movement, and even before the movement's formation.
It begins with a crisis related to apparent inconsistencies between the *doxa*
of one field and that of another, which generates a process of interrogating
received narratives or the scripts that render one's identity intelligible. This
mode of cognitive questioning is no longer the purview only of intellectuals, but manifests itself broadly within a counter-hegemonic movement that
aims to expose the fallacies of the orthodoxy as well as its underlying *doxa*.[78]
An analysis of Jewish critics and Palestine solidarity activists illuminates an
elastic process that moves from challenging Zionist orthodoxy to exposing
its underlying *doxa*, with self-scrutinizing analyses of biopower articulated
through concepts such as whiteness, orientalism, and antisemitism.[79] This
analytic process, examined above, is also intricately linked to processes of
emotional liberation, including shifts in affective loyalties due to moral
shocks, the experiences of which are interlinked with evaluative cognitive
processes.[80] The emotional experiences of indignation and shame, in other
words, do not merely constitute "raw" reactions to scenes of the occupation
but rather themselves are the product of unlearning ideological constructs
and *doxa*, a process that is likewise generative of reassessing and reimagining
who we are as Jews. All facets of this complex feedback loop involve substan-

tive, not merely functional, engagement with Jewish meanings, practices, and memories.

The move toward critical resistance involves refiguring Jewishness on its own terms, and thus requires constructive interpretive processes and religious, cultural, and historical literacy. In challenging the Zionist narration of Jewish identity, American Jews work to produce a new identity and a new public narrative, recognizing that the hallmark of domination is the illusion that the script one has received is the only one available. Against this logic of interpellation[81] and foreclosure, critical resistance relies upon a view of agents who navigate multiple scripts in ways that challenge those who seek to delimit such plurality by manufacturing and imposing narrative coherence.[82] The willingness to act subversively (rather than iteratively reproducing schemas and norms) illuminates what Ann Mische and Mustafa Emirbayer identify as a "projective" agentic process, which is oriented by alternative interpretations of the past and imaginations of what the future ought to be, disaggregated from other forms of less subversive agency. "The projective imagination," accordingly, "works in a way analogous to the capacity of metaphor to create semantic innovation; it takes elements of meaning apart in order to bring them back together again in new unexpected combinations."[83] This articulation of subversive agency's relation to a projective imagination offers insights into the processes of religiocultural innovation unfolding through the movement of anti-occupation Jews and their transformative rewriting of Jewish communal meanings. Their agency is prophetic not merely as a cultural form of resistance to dominant cultural codes oriented by a secularized conception of transcendence but simply as entailing the possibility of the world to be different than it is. It is also substantively prophetic in its hermeneutical facility with the Jewish tradition operative in the projective imagination. This focus on subversive agency likewise connects with a dialogic analysis that is fluidly attentive to meaning production through movement contentions[84] and a general cultural turn in social movement theory to the study of identity construction and solidarity, critical resources for any kind of collective action.[85] One key theoretical concept here is "framing."[86] Since the 1980s, social movement literature has focused increasingly on the relation between the framing processes for social movements and the dynamic production of meanings within the context of these movements.[87] "Frames," Robert D. Benford and David A. Snow explain, "help to render events or occurrences meaningful and thereby function to organize experience and guide action."[88]

"Framing" denotes active, dynamic, and contentious processes of interpretation that challenge norms and lead to "collective action frames,"[89]

defined as "action-oriented sets of beliefs and meanings that inspire and legitimate the activities and campaigns of a social movement organization."[90]
This "cultural turn," therefore, acknowledges the importance of cultural
resources that, within the sociological literature, encompass religion, values,
beliefs, myths, and narratives as available tools for movements.[91] All these
categories, however, are not merely available in a cultural "tool kit." Instead,
their generative capacity is itself subject to a process of projective imagination and critical caretaking.[92] This is one of the vectors where the study of
religion comes in. Critical caretaking entails a hermeneutical process of rescripting that draws on religious, cultural, and historical literacy, and aims
at moving beyond merely denaturalizing *doxa* to constructively reimagining
Jewish identity and reframing the Jewish ethical compass. As chapter 4 will
show in detail, critical caretaking is bound up with desubjectification and
agentic rescripting of alternative identities. Desubjectification, or desubjugation, is what Michel Foucault identifies as critical questioning of previously
doxic (in Bourdieu's sense) "natural" affective attachments to social identities. For Judith Butler, such a mode of critique is virtuous because it amounts
to "risking one's deformation as a subject by resistance not to the constraining principles per se, but to one's *attachment* to them insofar as they constitute one's identity."[93] In the case of Jewish Palestine solidarity activists, the
erosion of Zionist interpellation invites interpreting Jewishness otherwise.
Thus, critique becomes necessarily transformational even if its endpoint is
undetermined in advance. The transformational process itself is mediated
through relational and intersectional social movement dynamics as well as
moral shocks and batteries. Critical caretaking, to reiterate, expands theoretical accounts of religion and collective social movement action that focus on
the question of what "religion" can do to sociopolitical mobilization by also
looking multidirectionally at the inverse: What does social movement activism do to religion?

The indispensability of critical caretaking as an interpretive process resonates with a dialogic approach to analysis of social movement that zooms in
on "the social semiotics of meaning production."[94] The dialogic approach
underscores "the *multivocality* of collective action discourse, the multiple
meanings that can be conveyed and interpreted through any particular discourse," and that "meaning is. produced in the *interaction* between social
action and systems of signs."[95] This approach critiques the "cultural turn"
in social movement theory for potentially reifying and instrumentalizing
culture. By multivocality, the social semiotic perspective stresses multiple
meanings and the contextuality of meaning production through movement
dynamics and interactions.[96] Multivocality also contributes, under certain

circumstances, to cognitive dissonance where "the production of a coherent and compelling common sense"[97] erodes, as it did for the anti-occupation Jewish activists, whose reimagining of their Jewishness is embedded within broader social semiotic and cultural fields and thus is necessarily relational and interactive.[98]

This dialogical production of meanings contributes to transforming the worldview of the community by renarrating the meanings of American Jewish identity. Such transformation is a stated goal of JVP and other Jewish organizations operating within the space of Jewish protest to challenge and reimagine American Jewish conventions through their participation in a broader struggle for Palestinians. The social semiotic perspective, therefore, captures an intersection between social movement theory and religious studies. The former focuses on framing strategies, meaning production, and movement dynamics, while the latter illuminates the resources (both content- and function-specific) available for religiocultural and social hermeneutical processes, central to meaning-making and -remaking. Fruitfully intersecting with the dialogic lens of social movement theory, the religious studies perspective, moreover, pushes the discussion beyond movement strategy and its potential for prophetic "cultural" functionality. It allows a broader analysis of cognitive, emotional, and discursive processes and fields of meanings that influence religiocultural change and innovation.

RELIGIOUS INNOVATION

A frame analysis that theorizes the cultural dimensions of framing and reframing already acknowledges the importance of cultural resources that, within the sociological literature, encompass religion, values, beliefs, myths, and narratives. Consistent with the dialogic lens and critical caretaking, Sidney Tarrow underscores that movements are "both consumers of existing cultural meanings and producers of new meanings."[99] This insight resonates with the discussion of Jewish Palestine solidarity work and its innovative employment of religiocultural meanings. The very mobilization and the dynamics of protest and moral batteries constitute significant factors in generating religiocultural disruptive alternatives and, at the same time, capitalizing on religious resources as tools of protest and critique.[100] Frame analysis, as sociologists Snow and Byrd argue, likewise challenges the "portray[al of] individuals as passive, mimetic recipients" of values and norms. It also opens up pathways for conceptualizing processes of "innovative amplifications and extensions of existing ideologies [and discourses] or as antidotes to them."[101] This opening up facilitates a move away from attributing simplistic causality to "ideology," without, however, dismissing the complex role of religio-cultural building blocks in these processes. Since the framing perspective analyzes actors as "signifying agents,"[102] engagement with the grassroots hermeneutical process and content grants further analytic purchase to the role of religion and culture as meaning-makers in a power-sensitive sociology of narratives that likewise employs the tools of critique.[103] The dialogic perspective further embeds the meaning-making aspects of framing within a broader social semiotic of meaning production that allows us to reflect in the coming chapters on how gender, race, and sexuality—as well as Islamophobia, antisemitism, and capitalism—also interact and intersect with the relational meaning-making of critical Jews, their moral shocks and batteries, their disruptive or prophetic agency, and their projective imagination.

Indeed, social movement theorists recognize that collective action framing is instrumental to generating transformative individual and collective identity construction because, as noted, identity construction constitutes a central dimension of the framing process.[104] Hence, framing tasks' relation to cultural resources is elastic, allowing and encouraging innovation. Through the processes of frame articulation and elaboration, cultural resources are threaded and spliced in particular ways (underscoring some issues, downplaying others) to make sense of events and to cultivate collective action frames. Hence, "identity" is not a reified destination, but a process of "semantic innovation"[105] that is both dialogic and emergenist.[106] The assumption that (especially young) American Jews retrieve a readily available prophetic or atheist socialist Judaism overlooks the complex ways in which framing tasks and processes and dialogic meaning-making, as well as contextual variations, produce—in a nondeterministic fashion—novel sociocultural and religious outcomes. This brings to the fore the need to account for which conceptions of "tradition" one operates with.

Indeed, the literature on religion and violence highlights how the manipulation of religious sources and narratives can enable the mobilization, radicalism, and emergence of alternate religious and political communities.[107] Such an analysis interprets these developments as the perverse narrowing of humanistic interpretations of tradition because of the typical association of such violent mobilizations with ethnoreligious and other chauvinistic agendas. In the same way that ethnocentric and literal readings of religious resources constitute a form of contextually explained innovation within tradition (even when they portray themselves as returning to a purist or original message), so too does the reinterpretation of religious traditions cohere with inclusivist, humanistic, and pluralistic values. The theoretical puzzle resides in the scholarly affirmation of one form of innovation as "literal" and thus presumably more loyal to the tradition, and the other as a departure from, or only thinly related to, the tradition.[108] This amounts to an epistemological bias in favor of "literal" readings of tradition and the presumed "original" cultural practices associated with them as more authentic than sociocultural and political practices associated with rereadings of the tradition through contemporary sensibilities, especially those motivated by social justice concerns, relationality, and intersectional activism.

Hence, my analysis not only examines the function of religion in articulating collective action frames, but also reveals how social activists construct dialogically new religious and sociocultural meanings in and through dynamic processes of protest—but without reducing them to these. The dialogic expansion of the framing perspective, therefore, effectively foregrounds the need to unpack the hermeneutical dimensions of Jewish Palestine activists' efforts to reimagine post-Zionist Jewish theology and alternative sociopolitical and cultural Jewish identity (Jewishness). The framing perspective's emphasis on meaning and meaning-making—and thus on social movement activists as "signifying agents actively engaged in the production and maintenance of meaning"[109]—illuminates the collective action frame of Jewish critics as a grassroots, participatory, and democratic process of critical caretaking, focused on destabilizing and subverting existing ideological formations and on cultivating new foci of solidarity. Both INN's #YouNeverToldMe campaign—which challenges the mechanisms of Jewish socialization—and JVP's complementary campaign #ReturnTheBirthright—which confronts the Zionist narrative of return relationally, by exposing a narrative of Palestinian displacement and destruction in the name of Jewish "return"—signal a mode of transformational public narrative arrived at through critical caretaking, moral shocks, and indignation. Both campaigns ask the Jewish establishment how it could have failed Jewish tradition so profoundly, and in so doing, demystify interpellation and engage in an agentic process of resignification as Jews. This is because interrupting one script with presumptions of foreclosure opens up paths for multiple resources for rescripting one's identity collectively through a dialogic social movement space. The dialogic perspective's focus on the social semiotics of meaning production broadens the projective agentic process of identity in which literacy in Jewish traditions, diverse historical memories, and multivocality becomes a key mechanism in shifting affective loyalties and resignifying Jewishness from the margins and the grassroots.

My study in the following chapters, accordingly, focuses on the social semiotics of meaning production that are pivotal for the dialogic analysis of collective action. I underscore that changing the narrative about who

American Jews are as a group is integral to the active participation of Jews in the broader Palestine solidarity movement. However, this focus on narrative is itself an objective of the grassroots movement that seeks, through its emotional and cognitive liberatory processes, to transformatively reimagine American Jewish identity outside the Zionist paradigm. Valorizing the diasporic, therefore, is not only a tactic. It also becomes—instead of Zion—a goal and destination. Chapter 3, next, captures the transformative storylines that activists themselves narrate in articulating their shifts in affective loyalties and their meaning-making participation in rescripting a public narrative.

PART TWO

3

Unlearning

The Winds Are Changing

On July 8, 2014, when Israel launched Operation Protective Edge . . . I spent [work] shifts glued to my computer, distracted . . . by the most recent news, opinions, and heartbreaking stories about the assault on Gaza. My uncertainty abated, my well-cultivated connection to Israel faded into a sense of emptiness, and I woke up as I watched the mounting numbers of Palestinians being murdered in my name. In the face of isolating, useless despair, the cry of "Not in My Name" and the JVP community gave me words and action to shatter my lifelong silence and complicity. That summer I, like so many others, felt whatever was left of my carefully constructed illusions crumble and fall away.[1]

This quotation, from a young member of JVP-NYC, conveys the characteristic pain and process of unlearning that Jews who have been incubated in narratives controlled by the Jewish establishment undergo after cognitive dissonance[2] and ethical outrage provoke a crisis of authority for them. The psychological stress caused by such dissonance often drives them to a transformative process that ultimately disrupts ontological and epistemological certainties as well as the narratives that undergird them. The events in Gaza of 2014, for this Jewish Palestine solidarity activist, solidified a gradual process of unlearning, which involved observing an older sister breaking away from their parents' ideological hold, experiencing self-doubt over the course of "Israel advocacy" training, and visiting the West Bank during the early years of college—a first for someone who had spent her childhood traveling frequently to Israel. Another JVP member, a former Israeli settler, wrote about his gradual shift from "blind[ness] to the crimes and violence perpetrated in my name."[3] He said that his awakening to the humanity of Palestinians forced him to engage with "the tantalizing racism that binds the political imagination and the hearts of the young and the old."[4] "I wish I could point to a moment of clarity, to an abrupt apotheosis that liberated my tainted young morality," he writes.[5] However, his process of "transition[ing] from Zionism to (radical?) humanism was a gradual one."[6] His path of unlearning ultimately led to clarity on "the racism that surrounded me, the hatred and the settlements and the checkpoints, and the very violent stories told by soldiers who returned from the 'field,' through a new prism—one that is not solely dedicated to maintaining and justifying my own privilege."[7]

These two voices capture the mechanisms, events, and sensibilities that are crucial to the process of transitioning from Zionism to criticizing, and even subverting, its pillars and logic. They clarify the processes of emotional and cognitive liberation discussed in chapter 2, whereby moral shocks and indignation confront emotions of pride and self-approval as in moments of Jewish participation in Palestine solidarity activism. This interactive process, where a moral clarity about what Judaism is *not* is experienced collectively through solidarity action—or what James Jasper calls "moral battery"— enhances, through a feedback loop, the depth of a transformative public narrative and shifts in affective loyalties.[8] The above testimonies convey the pain, disillusionment, and ethical outrage that come from grappling with privilege and complicity, cultivating empathy for Palestinians, and acknowledging their humanity—a reality the Zionist discourse, perhaps inherently, misrecognizes, ignores, and assaults. This chapter features substantive narratives of those involved in transforming and relationally refiguring Jewishness through an engagement with Palestinian realities and narratives. Those attentive to the changing attitudes of American Jews may be unsurprised to learn that J Street's Facebook "likes" during Operation Protective Edge in the summer of 2014 flatlined at 24,000, while JVP's skyrocketed from 57,000 to 190,000.[9] This contrast indicates that Jews are increasingly recognizing that J Street does not provide a significant alternative to AIPAC, its related groups, or their instruments of Israel-branding and advocacy.[10] The images that emerged from Gaza were difficult to justify, and the surge of Facebook "likes" indicated an ethical outrage, a deepening questioning, and often an aspiration to redefine American Jewish attitudes toward Israel. The relation between emotional moral shocks and cognitive unlearning of myopic ideological constructs is not sequential. In other words, it is not that activists and critics first experienced a "raw" emotion of shock and then began to unlearn. Nor is the inverse the case. The deeply emotional experience of indignation is not self-evident, but rather requires a cognitive process that evaluates the non-binary and undetermined transformative potentialities of grassroots agentic meaning-making. Thus, the relationship between emotion and cognition is not one of simple causality, but of a feedback loop articulating new public narratives and translating values—which activists experience emotionally through the multiplicity of their social fields—into actions that then enhance and deepen the evaluative processes of unlearning and rewriting Jewish communal values.[11]

The largest counter-establishment organization, JVP, offers resources for reconceptualizing Jewish attitudes through action. Following each shocking moment, such as Operation Protective Edge, JVP's membership grows exponentially. I highlight JVP here because most of the Jewish Palestine solidarity activists I interviewed intersect in one way or another with this group. JVP's members are, together with INN, OH, and similar groups, foot soldiers in a grassroots battle that challenges the Jewish establishment through outrage, unlearning, refiguring, and (often intersectional) analysis and activism. This chapter primarily addresses the first two components—outrage and unlearning—by inviting the voices of the activists to articulate their own processes of change. However, even at this point, the intersectional character of their analyses will be evident. It is difficult, as will become clear, to discuss unlearning and ethical outrage without also examining the processes of politicization that Jews undergo on other fronts, or how those fronts inform their intra-Jewish critical work and vice versa.

In approaching my interviewees and participant observations, I wanted to learn how Jewish critics of Israeli policies and Zionism came to their critical views through a process of embodied ethical reassessment. By becoming attuned to the self-transformative process, I mean to highlight how the emotional, moral experience of indignation at the occupation participates in the ethical reframing of Jewishness and vice versa through a complex feedback loop. I asked the activists to tell their stories of transformation from conventional Jewish perceptions of Israel and Palestine to more critical outlooks on Israeli society, policies, and—crucially—their own complicity with these policies. By "transformation," I mean a disengagement from narratives of victimization, Zionist uses of the Holocaust, and inevitable militarism, on the one hand, and a reorientation of one's relation to Israel as a central component of one's American Jewish identity, on the other. Some of the interviewees experienced a sudden transformation. Others experienced a gradual process. The interviews captured the activists' own portrayals of the transformative renarration underlying the shift of their solidarity from Israel to Palestine and their revaluation of the "diasporic" as the locus of Jewish meaning and identity.

Stories of Outrage and Dissonance

Michal, a woman in her middle twenties, shared her process of awakening:

> I grew up in a Zionist family in Raleigh, North Carolina, and I attended a Jew-
> ish day camp, Jewish summer camps on a yearly basis. . . . When I visited [Is-
> rael], I experienced a sense of dissonance. I started asking questions. I went by
> myself to the West Bank and East Jerusalem. I was shocked by the [Separation]
> Wall. It provoked in me a real sense of dissonance. This set me on the path of
> learning more, so it was not exactly a sudden conversion,[12] but I started edu-
> cating myself and began a study abroad program in Tel Aviv. During this pe-
> riod, I went to Bethlehem for spring break and got a crash course on the Pal-
> estinian perspective. I experienced a major transformation of views. I found
> no common ground with the other Jews on the study abroad program. . . . I
> saw the play *My Name is Rachel Corrie* and I was profoundly moved by it. I
> identified with *her* rather than with the Israelis and I realized that I was on the
> side of "Western activists" and so I gave up my Zionist identity.[13]

Identifying with Corrie's courage to stand in solidarity with Palestinians
in front of an Israeli bulldozer to prevent the demolition of their homes—
losing her own life in the process—was more consistent with Michal's values
than was supporting the bulldozing of Palestinian homes because of the Holocaust and what might happen to Jews apart from such actions. Variations
of this story recurred throughout my interviews. I was moved to tears and
experienced a profound sense of shame as an Israeli when I listened to Corrie's parents (Craig and Cindy) talk to Tzedek Chicago's community on Yom
Kippur in 5778/2017. On that Day of Atonement, they spoke about their pain,
but also about their daughter's legacy and their resolve to dedicate the rest of
their lives to the Rachel Corrie Foundation for Peace and Justice. "Yom Kippur calls on us to let go of our fears," Cindy said, adding, "In 2012, a reporter
asked me how I felt about an Israeli judge's statement that Rachel should
have moved out of the bulldozer's way in delivering his not-guilty verdict.
I responded, 'I don't think that Rachel should have moved—I think we all
should have been standing there with her.'"[14] Not Jewish herself, Cindy encapsulated the meanings of the Days of Awe and Yom Kippur for this emerging, values-oriented Jewish community of Tzedek Chicago: "Let go of one's
fears." As a self-selected audience, members of Tzedek already exhibited a
commitment to ethical scrutiny and moral indignation, but the Corries' lessons further reinforced not only what Judaism is *not*, but also what it is—
a message preached by those most affected by Jewish communal sins. On
Yom Kippur, we atone for those sins collectively and resolve to fight against
such evils in the new year. Cindy's extension of Rachel's solidarity with the

oppressed is what feeds into and augments the moral shocks that Jewish critics experience in their concentrated efforts to reimagine their narrative outside ethnocentric and fearful paradigms. The latter, they contend, privileges
Jewish suffering and an ethos of national security. Listening to Cindy and
Craig talk about Rachel's courage reminded me of the courage I witnessed in
the young Jewish Palestine solidarity activists I worked with in the West Bank
in May 2017. Many of them were no longer beholden to the fears that keep
us stuck in our ontological and epistemological certainties. They too inhabit
the Days of Awe continuously through an active, on-the-ground resistance to
the occupation. The physical space of Palestine is not the only ground where
such resistance unfolds, but being on the ground generates moral clarity and
batteries pivotal for the process of reimagining Jewishness as a positive, ethical, political subjectivity, not merely defined by what it is not.

However, the path to such clarity and the possibility of reimagining Jewishness is neither self-evident nor straightforward, for it works against the
normative boundaries of the community, its underpinning narratives, and
its historiographies. Another young organizer with JVP told me about her
upbringing in a "casually Reform and Zionist home" and how, at one point
during high school, she became aware of the occupation, the demolition of
houses, and all that was related to it. "But it didn't sink in entirely," she said.
The turning point for her was in 2008. "I went on a Birthright tour . . . during the time of bombing in Gaza." "On that trip," she said, "the contrast
between the images of Israel I grew up with and the image that Birthright
projected [and] the war I knew was going on, and yet was entirely silenced,
was very upsetting to me."[15] She grew frustrated and increasingly inquisitive
when her questions were silenced over the course of the trip. Upon returning to college, she joined SJP, reflecting a pattern highlighted in the previous
chapter concerning Jewish representation in SJP and other similar forms of
Palestine solidarity activism, especially in colleges. From this point on, the
Birthrighter-turned-SJP-activist's politicization deepened, and she later returned to Israel and Palestine to volunteer with the Israeli Committee Against
House Demolition. It was then that she finally received a full, on-the-ground
education about the complexities of the issue. Her awakening was the result
of an increasing conflict between the multiple, intersecting fields she inhabited: Jewish, progressive, young, American, college student. The *habitus* of the
college student immersed in and sensitized to progressive politics ultimately
generated a sense of dissonance and outrage, which resulted in unlearning
and denaturalizing Zionist orthodoxy as well as the *doxa* that underpins the
established Jewish framework.

The young activists I interviewed frequently mentioned Birthright trips

in their narratives. Although they did not always feel the dissonance immediately, it typically contributed to their transformative process and eventual
unlearning of the Zionist narrative and the mechanisms (such as rebranding
Israel as gay friendly) that the established Jewish community employed to
overcome apparent incoherence and contradictions among social fields. This
widely shared experience eventually led to JVP's #ReturnTheBirthright campaign, which was launched in late summer 2017—involving the testimonies
of alumni of the program and urging potential recruits to forfeit their "right"
for a free trip and to recognize that "Israel is not our birthright"[16]—as well as
INN's #YouNeverToldMe campaign, which shames Jewish educational institutions for failing to teach young Jews about the occupation.[17] The Birthright
program's misfire was not the only path leading to transformative questioning, however.

Hila, a young organizer with JVP, told me her story of gradual transformation: "I grew up as a liberal Zionist within the Reform context. In our congregation, we had a female rabbi and many gay couples."[18] Her positive experience with her congregation's inclusiveness anticipated a growing sense of
dissonance between so-called "Jewish values" and Zionism. Such dissonance
related not only to the Israeli occupation of Palestinians, but also to domestic
Israeli discriminatory practices that eventually became impossible to identify
with. However, Hila first experienced a thorough immersion in the conventional narrative: "I was indoctrinated in Zionist summer camps. . . . I had to
unlearn all of that. I also went to scouts glorifying Israel. I grew up with all
that. I also went to Israel on a nine-month Birthright-type gap year and went
through training on how to defend Israel on campuses." For Hila, everything
changed when she went to college at one of the University of California campuses, which was a target of AMCHA's efforts to repress any manifestation
of Palestine solidarity work.[19] "I traveled to the West Bank and joined the
famous weekly nonviolent demonstrations in Bil'in."[20]

Hila's unlearning deepened after college. She continued, "I went to South
Tel Aviv and witnessed racism toward African asylum seekers. . . . This on-
the-ground experience . . . informed my shift."[21] What Hila encountered were
inconsistencies between racism and what she had been told about the Jewish
meanings of Israel and its *raison d'être*: the history of the Holocaust and the
treatment of asylum seekers. Of course, what Hila's narrative does not mention is that South Tel Aviv is a poor, mostly Mizrahi area where the majority
of the asylum seekers were channeled before being subjected to deportation
threats by the Israeli government in 2017. The cultivation of anti-Arab racism among the Arab Jews has its own historicity that is very much related to
Palestinian experiences within Euro-Zionist discourse. For Hila, the racism

she encountered in South Tel Aviv vindicated her estrangement from Israeli society. Gone are the days, for activists like Hila, of the romantic depictions of the Sabra[22] and their transformation of the desert into a flourishing oasis. This romantic depiction—as many Jews have come to recognize—needed to be decolonized and likewise interrogated for its Eurocentricity, orientalism, and heteronormativity.

The stories of transformation highlight experiences of estrangement and occasionally revulsion toward Israeli-Jewish society. One key activist in JVP told me about her first journey to Israel: "I come from a family of Zionist refugees from Europe, and so I grew up of course thinking of Israel as a mythical place," she began. "I ended up sitting at the back of the airplane in New York City, chatting with a young Israeli couple, immediately making connections that their family came from the same village in Poland as my grandparents. But then very quickly they made racist remarks about 'Arabs' and I felt . . . transported to 1950s Mississippi." "What was so shocking," she continued, "was that there was no social restraint on the level of racism. We are talking about two white, Ashkenazi professionals, born in Israel. This experience frames my memories of that trip. When visiting Israel, I saw everything colored by this brutal racism, with no shame."[23] This reflection is worth close attention. Note that she first conveys the fantastic image of Israel she received at home, which was then shattered by the unfiltered racism she so casually encountered on her trip. Second, it is significant that the Ashkenazi couple on the airplane traced their roots to the same Jewish Polish origins as my interviewee, because it attributes the radical distinction in sensitivities to the accidents of history: the couple is racist because their family's journey from Poland ended in Israel rather than the US. This logic enables an understanding of Zionism as profoundly derailed and antithetical to progressive American Jewish sensitivities. Indeed, American Jewish critics and anti-occupation activists exercise relentless criticism of American racism, which they interpret as a site of injustice and see as interrelated with their Palestine solidarity work (along with fighting other bigotries and exploitative patterns). However, the overtly racist Ashkenazi couple embodies, for this critic, the corruption of Judaism by Zionism.

A critical distance from Israel also manifested in a growing estrangement from the mainstream American Jewish community for my interviewees. Hila recounted this estrangement shortly after participating in a counterprotest surrounding pro-Israel mobilization during Operation Protective Edge: "Yesterday I had a very intense day in San Francisco during the Palestine solidarity protest. I actually went to the counter-demonstration 'Stop the Sirens,' standing there with a sign protesting the protestors. I was attacked verbally and I had to disengage. There was a moment of realization that this political moment has been about . . . reclaiming Jewish humanity, and I wanted to say, 'You are not my people anymore.'"[24] However, Hila acknowledged that her activism did make her feel at home, for the movement served to create or prefigure a new model of an American Jewish community that is ethically relational and grounded in a non-Zionist outlook. Hila's experiences confirm that Jewish Palestine activist circles constitute moral batteries where the intense emotions of shame and indignation interact with the collective effervescence of self-approval for standing on the right side of history and, in the process, rescripting Jewishness from the margins.

Hila's sentiments are echoed by Yael who, together with a non-Jewish, Arab American friend, established an SJP chapter on her college campus. After being raised in a Zionist and Reform-turned-Reconstructionist home, she experienced cognitive dissonance for the first time as an adolescent, when she came across a photograph on the internet showing a Palestinian boy who was beaten by Israeli settlers for waving a Palestinian flag. She became further confused when she saw an article covering Israeli Jews who chanted anti-Arab slogans. "I felt angry and betrayed," Yael exclaimed. "My rabbi and parents shut me down, but I began to research independently and I couldn't believe how they were telling me that the State of Israel is good!" Like Hila, Yael felt estranged from her previous identification with and love for Israel. She spoke of racist and militant remarks that her Israeli cousins wrote on Facebook. Like Hila, she also described her resentment toward the Jewish establishment and her elders' uncritical support of Israel and suggested that the community of activists itself prefigures a post-Zionist Jewish identity: "The young generation of Jews is not interested in free [Birthright] trips. My generation is reclaiming Judaism. . . . I love finding a community of activists with whom I can express my doubts and commitments to social justice."[25]

Such ethical outrage and revulsion, as I show below, is typically more gradual. Often, the activists had already been politicized on other issues and were thoroughly embedded within particular sociocultural contexts that had formed their ethical sensibilities. Even while subjected to the Zionist orthodoxy, their inhabiting of multiple social fields and subsequent cross-fertilization provided a key for understanding their stories. Their ethical indignation in the face of what appears to constitute grave violations of human rights produced new forms of political solidarity with Palestinians and provoked a critical interrogation of the ethical limitations of Jewish solidarity and any commitments to Israel. This process, as noted, unfolds nonsequentially and through a complex nexus of dialogic interactions, moral batteries, and semiotic navigations and innovations.

American Jews undergoing ethical transformation are confronted by the realities of the occupation—and thus Palestinian suffering—with which they do not want to be complicit. Their encounters with internal Israeli racism against Mizrahi, Ethiopian, and other minority groups lead to, on both an individual and a collective level, not only estrangement, but a self-interrogation informed by a refigured Jewish community—one that such critical interrogation serves, in turn, to cultivate. This reimagining takes place also through an intersectional lens that calls into question Ashkenazi hegemony in Israel and also unsettles Ashkenazi normativity in the US through the work of the JOCSM Caucus, which operates in partnership with JVP.

I will address the intersectional dynamics operative in refiguring Jewishness in later chapters, but for now I wish to stress its relevance to the way estrangement and ethical outrage are enhanced through the cross-fertilization of the social movement, thus facilitating the very processes of resignifying communal meanings through grassroots agency. The increased audibility of JOCSM in the movement—along with its visibly intersectional reality—helps draw Israel into a broader analysis of white settler colonialism from which American Jews can more easily be estranged and disentangled. Cataloguing the atrocities that Ashkenazi hegemony has inflicted on Mizrahi, Ethiopian, and other marginalized Jews—from sterilizing Ethiopian women to kidnapping Yemeni children—can be interpreted through the explanatory frame of whiteness, orientalism, and colonialism, which activists want to distance themselves from while interrogating their own complicity with them.[26]

Exposing the interconnections between Israeli Ashkenazi hegemony and enduring patterns of white supremacy in the US, indeed, requires deeper levels of unlearning and a dismantling of the ideological constructs of Zionism and the *doxa* enabling them. Such a transformative effort requires more than just waking up to the suffering of Palestinians; it also requires a decolonization of the scaffolding that underpins the multiplicity of oppressive narratives. Indeed, the routes to Jewish Palestine solidarity activism often traverse politicization on many other issues. Such critical work reinforces and deepens the experience of ethical outrage as well as its generative capacity as a mechanism for reimagining Jewishness.

Prior Politicization

The role of politicization on other issues—whether prior or concurrent—is indeed pivotal, but assumes different trajectories depending on different generational patterns. Elders in Jewish protest activist circles usually cite their involvement in the anti-war and civil rights movements of 1960s America, but not without self-interrogation of their blind spots.[27] Intersecting with an antimilitarist critique is a deep and complex history of American Jewish feminist work against the occupation, dating back to the 1982 Lebanon War and images from the massacre in the Sabra and Shatila Palestinian refugee camp, enabled by the IDF and executed by the Lebanese Phalange forces.[28] Jewish feminist (mostly Ashkenazi) organizing has relied heavily on universal discourses of human rights and transnational feminist solidarity frames to assert its critique of chauvinistic Israeli practices and to cultivate dialogue across national lines.

Ashkenazi-dominated feminist organizing, however, has typically failed to connect Mizrahi struggles for social justice with the peace agenda, thereby foreclosing the possibility of substantive Mizrahi-Palestinian alliances and alienating Mizrahi feminists.[29] In the American context, the feminist response was nonetheless one of the earliest instances of collective Jewish organizing for dialogue between Israeli and non-Israeli Jews and Palestinians and for the promotion of Palestinian self-determination. Predating feminist organizing was the short-lived Breira ("Alternative") organization (1973–1977), which recognized (in conceptual continuity with the older generation of left-wing American Zionists) the legitimacy of Palestinian claims and thus departed from the hard line increasingly pursued by the American Jewish establishment in the aftermath of the Yom Kippur War of 1973.[30] Jewish feminist anti-occupation stances also developed within antimilitarism feminist organizations such as Code Pink (founded in 2002). While not explicitly Jewish, Code Pink's opposition to US wars, invasions in the Middle East, and torture practices in Guantanamo is highly consistent with opposition to the Israeli occupation.[31]

The politicization of the older generation of American Jewish critics during the 1960s was not typically motivated by the Palestinian-Israeli conflict even if a deeper examination, as I conduct in chapter 7, shows that attitudes toward Israel and Palestine have been constitutive of, not auxiliary to, black-Jewish relations in the US. Sharon, an activist in an Arab-Jewish Partnership based in Chicago, told me that while she attended Hebrew school as an adolescent in the 1960s (where she received some "Zionist propaganda"), the broad intoxication with the 1967 War seemed odd to her. "At the time, I began attending anti-war demonstrations against Vietnam," she told me. "So I was clearly against the one war and thus I was puzzled by how people embraced and celebrated the '67 War."[32] Despite this sense of inconsistency, her consolidation of a position on Israel as it related to her Jewish identity was gradual. While she grew up in a "secular" home that put minimal emphasis on Jewish education, she married a man whose family "did embrace the Zionist outlook. Our kids went to Hebrew School and received a heavy dose of the conventional narrative." "But," she continued, "my husband grew uncomfortable with Israel's actions and we started talking at home about Israel a lot in the 1990s and 2000s, and so, by the eruption of the Second Intifada, I was already aware of what was going on there."[33] Sharon and her spouse became further politicized in 2001 "because we were appalled by the war on Afghanistan." Anti-war activism on one front eventually became explicitly connected to anti-war activism on another. The analogies between US militarism and orientalism and the Israeli occupation increasingly drove them to protest. "By the Second Intifada," she told me, "our family wanted to be active with respect to how Palestinians were being portrayed as terrorists, not humans." Indeed, it was a family process. "My daughter discovered the organization 'Not in My Name!' [a local group later assimilated into the national JVP] and so, when she came back from college, we went to demonstrations."[34] Sharon's gradual transformation into active participation in the movement of Jewish critics shows how this process necessitated her drawing connections among the war on terrorism, American militarism, and the legacy of orientalism that enabled new forms of colonialism and imperial involvement in the Middle East. As her experience suggests, various entry points are often necessary to erode the hold of the narrative that renders the Israeli occupation intelligible.

For Avram, a young activist, Palestine solidarity and BDS work intersected with work on women's and feminist issues: "I got involved," he told me, "with a women's shelter feminist collective and this experience began to shape my political maturation. I realized I didn't have to engage with Israel to find a focus for my desire to be active for social justice, but I realized that I needed to take a position. I saw that I was directly connected to Israel and Zionism because the state claims to represent me. I started to inform myself. During the invasion of Iraq, I went to demonstrations. Within this context, there was a memorial for Rachel Corrie who died for her Palestine solidarity activism; this is where I heard of the International Solidarity Movement."[35] Like Michal, whose reflections we encountered earlier in the chapter, this young man identified far more with Corrie's principled defense of the helpless than with the occupation, which is purportedly necessary for the security of Jews all over the world. "That Rachel made the ultimate sacrifice," he continued, "moved me and I got involved with the local chapter of the International Solidarity Movement. . . . I spent seven weeks in the West Bank and Israel. . . . I moved to Chicago . . . where I met likeminded Jews. I became a part of the IJAN [International Jewish Anti-Zionist Network]."[36] Avram's narrative also highlights the construction of pre-movement communities of Jewish activists who feel either estranged from or overly "civil" with their families. They are able to find "likeminded Jews" with whom to engage in refiguring their self-understanding as American Jews. The movement itself provides a field of contentions and moral batteries that generate prefigured, collective modes of Jewish identity.

Rebecca, another Chicago-based activist of the older generation, described the humanistic and social justice values she acquired at home during the civil rights era. Her grandparents and parents were affiliated with the Orthodox and then Conservative movements. And, while she had received a traditional Zionist education in Hebrew school, she absorbed a commitment to fighting against discrimination at home. When she went to high school, the family reaffiliated once more, this time with Reform Judaism. "I did not feel very much at home in this synagogue," she recalled. Her discomfort was mainly the result of the rabbi, with whom youth her age were required to meet weekly prior to a trip to Israel, conveying an uncritical celebration of Israeli militarism. "I asked, 'Why are you celebrating the killing of other human beings?,' [but] the rabbi dismissed me." Unsurprisingly, Rebecca chose not to join her peers on the trip. Her outrage, untypical of her generation, focused on the apparent inconsistencies between Jewish values and unconditional support of Israeli policies. This type of outrage would become more ubiquitous beginning with the Second Intifada and continuing with the repeated assaults on Gaza. Like many of my interviewees, Rebecca had a long history as an activist, specifically with anti-apartheid campaigns. Her activism for Palestinian rights emerged organically from her focus on South Africa. Rebecca's story, in many respects unusual because of its foresight, is nonetheless characteristic of others' gradual realization of the need to interrogate their positions in relation to the mainstream Zionist narrative.

While most of the Jewish activists in Palestine solidarity work come from Reform or Conservative backgrounds, some have arrived via other routes. Daniel, a cantor in a Reconstructionist synagogue in the Midwest, began his journey within a religious Zionist framework, first in the UK and then in Israel, before he moved to the US. For him, the turning point was the assassination of Israeli prime minister Yitzhak Rabin by a Zionist zealot. Even then, though, Daniel's process was gradual. First, he removed his kippah and became "secular." Then, while he was in the US, the 2008 assault on Gaza motivated him to take a more active, public stance. So, he immersed himself in rereading the tradition relationally from the perspective of the Palestinians in order to connect to it "more authentically," as he put it. "In previous generations," he told me, "when our ancestors said, 'Because you were slaves in Egypt . . . ,' they were able to connect to this experience because they spoke of themselves. Today, the only way to connect to this foundation is by connecting to the Palestinians. Their experiences connect us to the Jewish experience of powerlessness."[37]

Rebecca's and Daniel's stories demonstrate two different trajectories leading to solidarity with Palestinians. Both stories illuminate the increasing diversification of meanings of Israel for American Jews.

Like Daniel's unusual path from religious Zionism to non- or anti-Zionism of an American variety, Yehezkel, an emerging scholar from New York City, came from a Lubavitch Hasidic background. He told me about his gradual exposure to Marxist ideas in college and graduate school and the consolidation of his own lens through socialism. "This[exposure] relates to my religious transformation as well as my politics around Israel and Palestine."[38] Describing his exit from Hasidic Judaism, Yehezkel told a story of self-creation:

> I learned how to read English on my own because I grew up in Brooklyn, speaking only Yiddish. I had a burning desire to read everything. This resulted in challenging my understanding of *Halakha* as immutable. . . . I also had philosophical disagreement with my community's treatment of women and gay people. . . . Upon deeper reflection, it is clear to me that the death of the *Rebbe* whom I thought was the messiah also shook the foundations of my spiritual universe.

Unlike other interviewees, who were incubated within Zionist orthodoxy, Yehezkel arrived at his Zionism through what he viewed as Lubavitch's tacit acceptance of Zionism even while dismissing it as heretical. "Lubavitch are Zionists in a functional sense," he told me. "They support Israel and tend to be right-wing in their support."[39] He recalled, for instance, joyful reactions to Rabin's assassination. When Yehezkel joined a Birthright trip during the Second Intifada, he remembers staying on the bus, refusing to go to Mount Herzl where Theodor Herzl's grave[40] is located because it appeared to him to constitute idol worship. He also recalled his effort, on a later trip during 2006, to go to Hebron and visit the Cave of the Patriarchs. He remembered realizing the absurdity of spotting an American Jewish soldier fully weaponized, walking down the segregated streets of Hebron. "I wanted to shout, 'What the hell are you doing here, pointing a gun at a Palestinian?'" This was the moment when Yehezkel began to understand the occupation. The trip precipitated his involvement in antimilitarism on his campus and in SJP. While Yehezkel's trajectory is unique, his participation in Palestine solidarity is the outcome—as it was for other Reform, Reconstructionist, Conservative, and nondenominational Jews—of an ethical outrage based in conceptions of justice outside exclusively Jewish discourses. As in the other stories, prior politicization, questioning, critical theory reading, and trips to Israel and Palestine all contributed to Yehezkel's position and emotional experience of moral shocks. In each case, the transformation required generating substantive meanings and alternative scripts through resistance and protest.

As is clear by now, disillusionment and anger with the American Jewish establishment characterize the sentiments of the Jewish activists to whom I spoke. They felt betrayed and censored; hence, they profoundly exemplified the crisis of authority and narrativity discussed in the previous chapter. The young JVP organizer whom we encountered earlier, whose sense of dissonance was heightened during a Birthright trip in 2008, expressed this anger explicitly: "From a specifically Jewish perspective, when I realized the degree of censorship within the Jewish community—that we were not able to hold events that could have facilitated honest engagement—I grew very frustrated and involved. Hillel rejected us. We fought for inclusion, we petitioned with many signatures, but they wouldn't budge. I felt ashamed of the lack of acknowledgement of the humanity of Palestinians."[41] OH has sought to address this very frustration.[42] The sense of betrayal by the Jewish establishment and its various institutions and scripts is a major factor in the activists' political maturation as well as their refiguring of their identities as Jews.

Yuli, who grew up in a practicing Reform household and went through the usual socialization path of day school and a Birthright trip, became involved in anti-war activism following the attacks of 9/11. She was in college then, and this attack, she told me, "was very foundational for [her] activism." She protested the invasion of Iraq—a protest that, on her campus, was largely led by Muslim and South Asian students. While also active on immigration issues, she encountered Jews Against the Occupation, because of this group's intersectional justice work around Islamophobia. She subsequently became "aware and involved."[43] She traveled to Palestine for solidarity work with Jews Against the Occupation, where she met her Muslim-Palestinian spouse and had a child with him.

Like Yuli's, Batya's path to Palestine solidarity began with anti-war politicization on a college campus in New York City. "I was a very committed Jew . . . and I certainly believed Israel was a good thing. In 2003, I was against the Iraq War and that was *my* conversion moment."[44] Like other Jewish critics, she began reading more, always a subversive act in a landscape so constrained ideologically: "I started reading Edward Said's work and, at the time, I also befriended a Palestinian play writer who wrote a play about the *Nakba*—this blew my mind!" Batya's transformation was not immediate, however. "I went on a personal journey: reading on the internet and exploring books." This journey offered her entry into the necessary process that other activists refer to as "unlearning." She continued: "Then I was one day in my apartment in Brooklyn, when I saw in a newspaper a picture of an anti-war demonstration. To the side of the photo, I saw a group of people carrying a sign: 'Jews Against the Occupation.' This is how I met Yuli. I went to their [Jews Against the Occupation] Passover Seder and I worked for their agenda 40 hours per week. Unexpectedly so—since I am from NYC, Jewish bourgeois, and privileged— the issue has taken over my life!"[45]

Beyond antimilitarism, politicization on the Palestine issue has taken various other paths. LGBTQI+ consciousness and activism has proved to be another conducive channel. A young rabbinical student named Sarit underscored how embracing her lesbian sexual orientation related to her process of unlearning Zionism:

> I went to college and became involved with "Third Path," which was an organization of religious Jews trying to change the dialogue on campus. . . . I became at the time radicalized on other issues: race, radical theoretical approaches, including queerness. I came out. . . . After college, I lived in Chicago and did some organizing within the Jewish community and became involved with Jewish anti-Zionist organizing where I saw the intersection of various struggles, but also a commitment to build alternative Jewish communities. So we were committed to Jewish education and we devoted ten weeks to a reading group and as soon as I did that everything fit together and was in line with other kinds of unlearning I was doing.[46]

"Now that I am in rabbinic school," she continued, "I am blessed to be in a cohort with feminist and queer people who are marginalized from the tradition and who are trying to figure out how to live within the tradition in integrity as feminists. Zionism, in some respects, is easier to deal with because it is so modern as opposed to the inherent patriarchy inscribed into Judaism." Sarit's experience embracing her sexual orientation, in conjunction with her Jewish activism and unlearning, predisposed her to interrogate the Jewish tradition while still inhabiting it. The stress she places on Zionism's modernity resonates with the general tendency of other activists and critics to portray this turn to Zionism as an accidental perversion or derailment of Judaism, which could be overcome by reclaiming a more authentic interpretation of the tradition. Disentangling the tradition from its patriarchal and heteronormative underpinnings, however, proves infinitely more complex.

JVP's intersectional approach echoes Sarit's personal journey. Wendy Elisheva Somerson, a self-identified "queer Jew," writes about celebrating a Passover Seder with over one hundred other queer Jews in the anti-occupation Passover Seder sponsored by JVP in Seattle in 2010. "After leading the concluding prayer," she writes, "I told everybody that only six years ago I didn't know any other radical Jews with whom to celebrate *Pesach*. This year, I felt like I was taking a deep nourishing breath after years of shallow breathing. As a queer Jew who is deeply critical of the Israeli government and deeply inspired by Jewish ritual, my desire for both political and spiritual fulfillment was finally being met."[47] Somerson's exhilaration about finding a new community is evident: "The experience highlighted for me how important it is for radical Jews to create alternative spiritual and political spaces, instead of begging to be let into Jewish institutional spaces that offer us inclusion only when we leave our anti-Occupation politics behind." Somerson's search for radical alternative spaces coincides with a critique of mainstream LGBTQI organizations that "represent us only if we validate heteronormative institutions such as marriage, militarism, and the prison industrial complex." She suggests that both queer and anti-occupation Jews need to actively construct "spaces outside of institutions that help us envision a world in which we want to live." Somerson's reaffirmation of the connections between queer and radical Jewish politics illumines the simultaneity and interweaving of various forms of politicization for Jews.

Somerson's story also raises a critical question: What does it mean to engage in Jewish queer activism? As she iterates, it means a commitment to resisting the Jewish establishment's and Israeli efforts to "pinkwash" the occupation by constructing an image of Israel as a "gay-friendly oasis," and to resisting the reframing of LGBTQI struggles according to heteronormativity.[48] LGBTQI issues have thus become a fertile ground for exposing the tactics of the Jewish establishment, including its reliance on Islamophobic tropes. Employing a queer lens demands highlighting the need to be "woke" (an African American slang word popularized by MBL, implying social awareness) on a wide array of social justice issues, not bracketing one at the expense of others. Hence, LGBTQI can function neither as a fig leaf nor as a discrete issue compartmentalized from other issues of marginality, vulnerability, and discrimination. Challenging such an instrumental use of LGBTQI issues has become an important focus for collective action frames.

One example of this challenge is a letter signed by over one hundred rabbis and rabbinical students denouncing Hillel International's financial connections with Mosaic United, a right-wing Israeli initiative dedicated to promoting a conservative agenda among American Jews. Mosaic United frames its agenda in terms of Jewish ethnocentricity, but also in terms of heteronormative, homophobic, and patriarchal "family values."[49] The letter was sponsored by OH and included a demand for the readmission, without preconditions, of B'nai Keshet, an LGBTQI group at Ohio State University, to campus Hillel, despite its violation of Hillel's guidelines by cosponsoring a fund-raiser

Purim event with JVP for LGBTQI refugees. As the letter explains, this spon-
sorship violated the "'Standards of Partnership' for campus Israel Activities,
which bar speakers and groups deemed too critical of Israel." The letter first
praises Hillel International's increased "commitment to fully supporting
LGBTQ students," as was evident in, for example, the 2007 publication of a
LGBTQ Resource Guide. But its authors also insist that the expulsion of B'nai
Keshet works against the inclusivity guidelines, "isolat[ing] LGBTQ Jewish
students from the broader Jewish community . . . [and] signal[ing] to LGBTQ
Jewish college students around the world that Hillel International views them
as disposable, rather than as an integral part of the Jewish campus community." This letter challenges an apparent internal incoherence between inclusivist rhetoric, on the one hand, and exclusionary practices, on the other. In
this case, the ideological commitment to Zionist orthodoxy blatantly hurt
a marginalized Jewish community that Hillel International otherwise claims
to embrace.[50] The case of B'nai Keshet demonstrates that sensitization on
LGBTQI issues does not necessarily result in becoming "woke" about the
struggle for Palestinian rights. But it also shows that, for Jewish critics whose
narrative frames have shifted, LGBTQI and Palestinian issues intersect, and
any compartmentalization must be resisted.[51]

Nonetheless, anti-occupation Jews also find themselves on the defensive in their fight against pinkwashing. The complicated relation of gender
and anti-occupation activism was especially evident following JVP's action
against the Celebrate Israel parade in Manhattan on June 4, 2017, which
marked fifty years of the occupation (figure 3.1). The action, intended to disrupt the LGBTQI contingent of the parade, was just one of six disruptions,
but it gained the most controversial press for its apparent targeting of marginalized groups, resulting in the arrests of JVP disruptors and calls for labeling JVP as a "hate group."[52] Ironically, the disruption itself was enacted by
queer Jewish activists protesting pinkwashing. Yet it resulted in broad backlash from the Jewish community, which portrayed JVP activists as threatening LGBTQI youth and as disrespectful of free speech and the diversity of
opinions within the Jewish community.[53] Jewish Queer Youth (JQY), one of
the LGBTQI groups in the parade, described the marchers as highly vulnerable teens from Orthodox and Hasidic backgrounds "who were kicked out
of their homes, schools, and synagogues" because of their gender identities.[54]
Thus, JQY complained, to "target" them was highly unethical. Other groups
under the LGBTQI frame, however, were known promoters of pinkwashing,
especially A Wider Bridge, an explicitly pro-Israel, North American–based
advocacy organization known for pinkwashing and for promoting stereo-
types of Muslim and Arab queers.[55] Nevertheless, JVP's targeting of the queer

FIGURE 3.1. Protesters from JVP disrupt the LGBTQ marchers in the Celebrate Israel Parade, June 4, 2017 [Photo credit: Jewish Voice for Peace]

contingent was framed as a violent and cowardly form of censorship, even as antisemitic and homophobic. The act was allegedly "antisemitic" because it violated the religious freedom of Jews to celebrate Israel, and "homophobic" because JVP, not officially a queer organization, chose to specifically target this part of the parade.

But others—including many self-identified queer Jews within Jewish Palestine solidarity circles—contested JQY's complaints. One commentator, referring to the case of B'nai Keshet and other failures of the establishment to respond to concerns raised by INN and OH about the institutional and financial links with Mosaic United, concludes that the institutional concern for vulnerable LGBTQI youth is opportunistic and conditional on an "adherence to the party line on Israel-Palestine."[56] "As a queer Jewish college student," she continues, "I am troubled by these dynamics. Though the stated support of LGBT Jews is better than rejection, acceptance is only meaningful when it is consistent, not when it's there to underline or undermine political agendas." "When I want to act on my values as a Jew as much as I want to act on my values as a queer woman," she continues, "will my community stand up for me?" The queer activists with JVP saw themselves as being consistent in resisting the employment of Pride to authorize the occupation, while standing in solidarity with Palestinians among whom gender nonconformity or homosexuality is often a target for blackmailing by the Israeli intelligence infrastructure.[57] These protesters "stood in formation, holding signs that read 'No Pride in Apartheid' and 'queer Jews for a Free Palestine.'" In one participant's words, "as queer and trans people, we needed to interrupt this moment of pinkwashing to claim queer space from those who would align it with forces of racism."[58] "Our action," the same activist continues, "emerged from JVP leadership's recognition and validation of our queer political analysis" and an effort to realign LGBTQI with antiracism and Palestine solidarity, as well as with the Palestinian LGBTQI community. Labeling the disruption as a homophobic hate crime is "a patently absurd claim that is meant to discredit us," especially given that some of the LGBTQI youth parading came from Orthodox families and suffered from intense levels of homophobia. The aim of the action was to "[interrupt] a story that to be Jewish is to align yourself with the state of Israel, to accept and support the ethnic cleansing of Palestinians. And [for] everyone in the LGBT contingent to . . . remember that just because we experience oppression as LGBT people does not abdicate us of responsibility for injustices done to other communities, especially when it is done in our names. In fact, when we recognize the links between our various oppressions—between homophobia and racism, for example—we can forge life-saving connections to other communities." Here is a Jewish queer activism articulated through Palestine solidarity in ways that enhance the renarration of Jewishness and its ethical commitments.

Another transgender lesbian activist with JVP likewise wrote to defend the disruption of queer Jews by JVP's queer activists: "It is not homophobic to object, as queer and trans Jews, to the use of our identities to justify horrific violence against Palestinians. These are the contradictions that anti-pinkwashing demonstrations . . . seek to expose, and precisely why critics woefully miss the point when they brand JVP and our members as violent homophobes: we are the ones using non-violence to protest violence, homophobia, and the deployment of queer and trans Jewish lives to erase Palestinian ones."[59] In response to the controversy,[60] the queer-identified rabbi and deputy director at JVP Alissa Wise articulated this very point, describing direct actions, such as disrupting the parade, as coming "from a place of love. . . . You do it because violence has been normalized, and you know the status quo will not change unless you bring that violence to the public square." For Wise, her queer and non-Zionist identities are closely interlinked. "In fact," she continues, "I first 'came out' to my family as both queer and non-zionist when I protested in this very parade in 2002 with my comrades at Jews Against the Occupation."[61] She further explains that the disruptive action "did not target vulnerable youth," as reactions had suggested. Instead, according to Wise, "they targeted a jingoistic, nationalistic parade to celebrate a state that . . . brutally controls Palestinian life and land."[62] Many of my interviewees echoed Wise in connecting processes of politicization on gender and Zionism—a connection that intensifies the struggle at the level of narrativity. Indeed, the establishment's narrative draws heavily on homophobia, Islamophobia, and orientalism to undergird its concentrated efforts at pinkwashing the occupation.

The examples of B'nai Keshet and the Celebrate Israel parade signal the charged terrains of meaning within which Jewish activists operate as signifying agents. Activists navigate relationally—offering an analysis of pinkwashing as it affects the Palestinian struggle—an intersectional, critical turn that connects sites of injustice. They do so in order to imagine coalitional work and ethical consistency across social fields. In one case, the offense was the failure of LGBTQI youth to recognize that their focus of solidarity as marchers in the Israel parade was misguided; it was complicit in a storyline that ethically enraged the disruptors and that the disruptors were eager to dispel. In the other case, LGBTQI vulnerability was leveraged to challenge the exclusionary logic of Hillel International's ideological litmus test. LGBTQI spaces have become intricately related to politicization on Israel and Palestine, with an increased pressure on queer Jews to articulate their ethical location vis-à-vis the Palestinian struggle against Israeli occupation. The centralization of queer identities and the engagement with gender fluidity and sexuality also refines, for some activists, their sense of estrangement from Zionist and Israeli conceptions of masculinity and heroism in ways that contribute to revalorizing diasporic depth beyond facile militarist physicality.[63]

A third example that foregrounds LGBTQI spaces as critical terrain for contesting narratives emerged during the Chicago Dyke March on June 24, 2017. Marchers carrying rainbow flags featuring the Star of David were asked to leave the march or use other rainbow flags. The forbidden flags were precisely those used by A Wider Bridge and thus produced strong associations with Zionist pinkwashing. However, the exclusion of the marchers generated a wide discussion on social media and in Jewish publications about who "owns" the Star of David and whether Israel has a monopoly over it, challenging a presumption that the marchers carrying the flags innocently wanted to articulate pride as Jews. This assumption once again brought accusations of antisemitism against the parade's organizers and the broader Palestine solidarity movement.[64] This critical response met by LGBTQI Jews for their advertent or inadvertent participation in pinkwashing, therefore, illuminates how refiguring Jewishness unfolds in a symbolically contested terrain of sexual politics where censoring a form of pinkwashing that also thrives on Islamophobic tropes can be framed as an antisemitic act. At the same time, many queer and trans activists are involved in active solidarity with Palestinian liberation and BDS.[65] These controversies, therefore, elucidate how Jewish Palestine solidarity often leads to a deepening of queer politicization, and vice versa.

As this section has shown, queer rights, antimilitarism, women's rights, and a broad spectrum of politicization on other social justice issues either predisposed or enhanced some activists' critical reorientation toward Israel. These other sites of politicization—whether concurrent or prior—underscore the multiple forms of socialization that compete with the Jewish establishment to exert influence and to cultivate sensibilities in American Jews who seek thereby to reclaim a Jewish historiography of relentless commitment to social justice. Now, it is important to underscore, as does intellectual historian Michael E. Staub,[66] discrepancies between popular American Jewish romanticizing of Jewish participation in antiracist protests of the civil rights movement and the intra-Jewish tensions and contentions revolving around Jewish consistency with American progressive and liberal politics. Indeed, the post-WWII era was defined by such tensions. Some Jewish sectors were uncomfortable with Jewish involvement with the radical Left and the threats it ostensibly posed to Jewish interests. A few even actively supported militarism and racist policies. The late 1960s, for instance, witnessed the emergence of the extremist Jewish Defense League led by Meir Kahane (1968) as well as endorsements by some American rabbis of US policies in Vietnam.[67] The apparent synonymy between Jews and liberalism ignores internal pluralities and currents that pulled in conservative and neoconservative directions and contributed to Jews' participation in whiteness and white privilege. This trend, together with the emergence in the mid-1960s of a separationist Black Power movement that rejected Martin Luther King Jr.'s consensual and interracial approach to social movement work, attenuated Jewish-black alliances and their capacity to fight effectively against racism.[68] As historian Marc Dollinger puts it: "What started as nonviolent civil rights protests in the 1950s developed by the mid-1960s into the apparent balkanization of American life."[69] Identity politics and Jewish socioeconomic mobility were key forces fracturing the memory and vision of the civil rights movement, likewise signaling a shift in American Jewish priorities, away from the struggles of African Americans to self-centered foci of activism or self-advocacy.[70]

In many respects, the contemporary movement of critical Jews seeks to subvert this balkanization (or fragmentation according to identity-perceived boundaries), and their processes of becoming "woke" testify to the challenge of non-intersectional identity politics, that is, a politics that fails to make central an analysis of the interlocking patterns of structures and ideologies of privilege, oppression, and domination. Dollinger attributes the consolidation of Zionism as the hinge of American Jewish identity to the emergence of Black Power and its affirmation of African American identity and black nationalism. This development, he argues, emboldened muscular interpretations of Jewish nationalism participating in a broader landscape of identity politics as the Jewish versions of Black Power.[71] Jews no longer were apologetic about

publicly asking, in a self-centered manner, whether certain policies were
"good for the Jews."[72] The movement of Jewish Palestine solidarity that began
to consolidate in the early decades of the twenty-first century, however, conveys that this is decidedly the *wrong* question to ask. It revisits, as we saw in
the case of JVP's support of MBL's platform, the potentiality of Jewish-black
alliance.[73] Alliances, rather than parallel self-affirmation and promotion of
an ethnoreligious national agenda, are now interpreted through a scrutiny of
Jews' complicity with whiteness rather than their positionality as a supposedly comparable minority group. In the process of reshaping the meanings of
alliance, the movement of critical Jews centralizes its own JOCSM's narratives
of marginality as a mechanism of self-transformation.

Indeed, activists in the movement are able to connect *unambiguously* to
left and progressive politics because they tackle the questions of Zionism and
whiteness as constituting key dimensions of American Jewishness, with an
understanding that participation in progressive politics requires shifts on
both these fronts. Their novelty, however, should not be exaggerated. They
stand within a longer tradition of American Jewish interlocutors, some of
whom challenged the Jewish establishment and sought to redefine Jewishness
over and against its synagogue-centric approaches to tradition and some for
whom their alliance with radical black politics ultimately did not sustain Black
Power's turn to an anti-Zionism that also trafficked in antisemitic tropes.[74]
Others grappled with how an apparent denial of Jewish liberation in the form
of Israel (political self-determination) delimits Jews' capacity to partake fully
in progressive social justice politics. The tension revolves around whether
participating in progressive politics, especially when its operative critique of
militarism and imperialism is turned on Israel, threatens the security and
continuity of Jews and thus amounts to the dreaded label of "self-hate."[75]
Breira, in particular, was briefly successful in creating a broad coalition of
Jews supportive of meaningful peace between Israelis and Palestinians, but it
did so by insisting that the motivation for holding such a position revolved
around "our love and respect for the people and the land of Israel as well as
our understanding that the continuity of Jewish life in the Diaspora is inextricably linked to the existence of Israel."[76] The obligation that "we shall not
be silent," the same statement reads, constitutes an imperative "for the sake
of Zion." This articulation, therefore, shows that, in the mid-1970s, efforts to
connect the American Jewish Left with constructive approaches to supporting coexistence in Israel/Palestine were still refracted through a Zionist lens
that understood Jewish continuity in terms of Israel and, relatedly, American
Jewish commitments to the "people of the land" in terms of self-love. Breira's
initiative collapsed from the pressure of an intense attack from hardliners

and a general decrease in Jewish involvement in social justice struggles in the 1970s. However, the left-leaning liberal impulses that generated an initial endorsement for Breira among Jews sympathetic to its message were later channeled into organizations such as the New Jewish Agenda (established in 1980) and *Tikkun* magazine (in 1986),[77] constituting the so-called camp of "liberal Zionism." Yet the social movement of Jewish critics of the occupation subverts the presumption that these terms could be held comfortably and unambiguously together.

Contemporary activists challenge all axiomatic claims about a Jewish "self" and the discourses that construct it. They also interrogate the "self" through solidarity with Palestinians and through their own normative commitments to the "other" of Jewish violence—a normativity that is both an outcome and an instrument of self-transformation undergone through social movement's spaces and contentions as well as the various mechanisms of (pre-)politicization. They do so not for the sake of Zion, but for the sake of Palestinians and, importantly, *also* for the sake of Jews. As noted, Jewish solidarity actions with Palestinians provoke an enhanced experience of self-approval or love of self that is also captured in one of INN's trending hashtags, #WeWillBeThe-Generation to fix what, according to INN, amounts to the moral disaster of the occupation. This relational reimagining of "self-love" is also intersectional. Connecting unambiguously to American progressive social justice work and fighting against racism (being "woke") means turning the tools of critique internally to challenge romanticized or filiopietistic accounts of Jews during the civil rights movement[78] in order to offer a self-critique of the construction of Jews as white and the broader colonization of the Jewish imagination. This includes accounting for the failure of segments of Jewish communities, even in the 1950s, to act according to their sense of ethical exceptionalism.[79] The resources of this critique are emerging from the margins of Jewish communities and prove foundational for the grassroots transformation of Jewish communal meanings. For the Jewish Palestine solidarity activists, Judaism should not be equated with Zionism. But it should also not be equated with whiteness or Ashkenaziness. In other words, Mizrahi, Sephardi, and Jews of color participate centrally in rewriting Jewishness, its normative boundaries, and thus also the meanings of self-love and liberation. Similarly, participation in alliances with African American and other marginalized communities consolidated a cognitive recognition that one's liberation is linked to all other struggles for liberation, including along gender and sexual lines. Israel or Zion as the destination of Jewish liberation and the touchstone for Jewish continuity through the struggle for self-determination, from the perspective of Jewish Palestine solidarity activists and anti-occupation critics, constitutes a misdirection of self-love that is ultimately detrimental to Jewish continuity.[80] Hence, the accusation of self-hate, they argue, betrays a derailed sense of self and itself operates against the projective imagination of one group's liberation as interlinked with all others—an imagination that works against communal balkanization and the logic of non-intersectional identity politics. The interrogation of whiteness comes into focus in later chapters (especially 7 and 8), but it nonetheless participates in much of the analysis preceding these chapters. In the following section, I turn to the concept of unlearning as a pivotal mechanism in the activists' stories of transitioning from Zionism and the meaningfully Jewish arguments they articulate along the way.

Unlearning

Simply being confronted by facts that contradict a narrative frame or storyline does not in itself change anyone's perception, necessarily. However, when a narrative loses its intelligibility, change and innovation often ensue, even within well-entrenched social fields.[81] The erosion of intelligibility precipitates unlearning, and vice versa. Shaming campaigns such as #ReturnTheBirthright and #YouNeverToldMe constitute an outcome of unlearning and a concentrated effort to effect grassroots transformation through public narrative (translating values, which are themselves fluid and open for reimagining, into action).

One young Jewish artist and solidarity activist who identifies as anti-Zionist, whom I will call Aaron, told me about his trajectory from a Conservative home to a Birthright trip and volunteer work on a kibbutz to anti-Zionism. His story is worth quoting at some length:

> I grew up in a suburb of Chicago in a Jewish area and my family is a part of the Conservative movement. I went to Jewish school and received a biased education when it came to the Israeli-Palestinian situation. My family was Zionist. My grandparents met in a Zionist youth movement before '48 [in the US]. On my mom's side, my grandma was a refugee from Europe during WWII. I grew up in a very Zionist environment, but from a young age I identified strongly as a Jew and thus, without reflection, also with Zionism; my strong identification as a Jew led me to an interest in Zionist ideology. I remember the signing of the Oslo Accords. I was 11. . . . This was the first time I became aware that there is such thing as a Palestinian people; that was the first time I paid attention and started forming my own opinions. Throughout high school, I started identifying more with cultural Zionism and socialist threads. I still identified as a Zionist at this point. The first time I started questioning my position was in college as an undergrad. There were two Palestinian students there and we

became good friends. This was the first time I became aware that pro-Israel people weren't aware of the history and purposely obscured what was actually going on. I became very political in college (on other issues as well). I became aware that I could be Jewish and take their side. I took a Birthright trip and in the following summer I worked in a kibbutz for five months. I was critical, but still identified as a Zionist. I identified with the socialist and cultural Zionist and Hebrew Revival. I went to a kibbutz. After the kibbutz program, I became disillusioned in general. I got to experience a bit more of Israeli society outside the Birthright trip and at this point I stopped identifying as a Zionist. I was well aware the kibbutz movement wasn't what it used to be. I didn't expect it to be an experience of what the kibbutz used to be. But I thought I would witness innovative approaches there, but I didn't and instead I had encountered a lot of racism. It was a culture shock! I didn't feel comfortable interacting with people there and there was a general level of bruteness. When the Jewish community in the U.S. talks about Israel, it idealizes it. What kind of racism did I encounter? Against Arabs, Druze, Ethiopians—"don't leave things outside because the Ethiopians will get them"—remarks along these lines.[82]

Aaron's story reveals a gradual process of interrogating received narratives about Israel. Like many of the other activists I interviewed, Aaron was encouraged to exercise his critical thinking on all topics except Israel, but, like many of his peers, he eventually overcame the Zionist taboo and began to see for himself its underpinning illusions. Once again, as with the JVP activist who felt transported to Mississippi in the 1950s, it was not only the realities of the occupation and the predicament of the Palestinians that opened his eyes, but the everyday racism that he witnessed during his visits. He felt estranged from the place that was supposed to be "home."[83] The transformation unfolded through the intersecting emotive (revulsion at casual racism, which itself evokes ethical and evaluative frames) and cognitive (analysis of the occupation and Israeli society) experiences of moral shocks.

Another important motif in Aaron's unlearning is that the process involved rereading Jewishness relationally through telling Palestinian stories for the first time. The concept of unlearning was also key for the activist whose reflections formed the epigraph to this chapter. "On my journey of unlearning the Zionism I was raised with," she wrote, "I discovered new histories, ideologies, and political views. I have learned to love and celebrate the diaspora and all that it means for me and my family. I have met the very same civil rights veterans I learned about in school, heard their unapologetic and undiluted views, and seen them turned away by the Jewish establishment that taught me to be proud of their legacy."[84] Here, she challenges what she deems the hypocritical employment of the Jewish legacy during the civil rights era

in the US. Indeed, for many Jewish Palestine solidarity activists and critics
of Zionism, the failure of progressive Jews to endorse the platform of MBL
exemplifies an ethical incoherence.[85]

Batya, who became active in resisting the occupation of Palestine through
her embeddedness in the anti-war climate surrounding the American invasion of Iraq, described her personal journey. Characteristically, her unlearning was enabled by the pluralistic nature of her college. "I met Palestinian
people when I went to college and I met a woman who told me about how
her grandmother was kicked out of Palestine. She was just like me, but one
cannot even compare the amazing rights of *olim hadashim* [new Jewish im-
migrants to Israel] to her condition of absolutely no rights. I connected to her
story. I could trace my ancestors to Lodz [a major Jewish urban center in pre-
WWII Poland], and she traces her roots to specific locations in Palestine."[86]
As Batya's story illustrates, the process of unlearning involves cultivating
personal relations with other Americans, just like them, who happen to be
Palestinian, or who are active in various Palestine solidarity initiatives. Campus organizing, as we saw in the previous chapters, offers opportunities for
co-resistance, meaningful exchanges, and friendships across communities.

Another Jewish activist, Caleb, in the broader (though not explicitly
Jewish) Palestine solidarity movement told me that his process of self-
interrogation and unlearning came about organically during college, where
he encountered Said's *Orientalism*. "This was the first time I came across
a critique of Zionism. It was emotionally provocative, but I couldn't really
challenge him intellectually. I did not have the resources. So I began to study
Arabic and then studied abroad in Jordan and, through my interactions and
reading, I became more aware of the Nakba and of Palestinian perspectives.
Everybody I met in Amman was a Palestinian. So I became aware of the refugee situation and that it was an outcome of a massive event. This bothered
me."[87] Caleb's odyssey continued with a Birthright trip in 2008: "I was so
acutely aware that the trip went on while people were massacred in Gaza.
This made me realize I needed to learn more Arabic, and I went back to
Jordan and lived there for a while in order to learn more Arabic. I then went
to East Jerusalem and learned more about the Palestine solidarity movement." Caleb and Aaron's stories represent, in many respects, idiosyncratic
journeys of reorientation vis-à-vis Zionist axiomatic claims. However, their
processes of unlearning through reading and challenging immersion experiences are typical and mutually reinforcing with the emotion of moral shocks
they inhabit—as well as their journeys through radicalization on the axes
of gender, sexuality, and feminism—of the trajectories of Jewish critics and
Palestine solidarity activities.[88]

It is no wonder that season 4 (released in 2017) of the popular and award-winning dramedy *Transparent*[89]—which focuses on the self-actualization of Maura Pfefferman, a Jewish trans woman coming out later in life, and her family members, in an exploration of American Jewishness—included a trip to Israel and Palestine and a side plot that examined the ethical wrongs of occupying and interloping on someone else's property. The questioning of sexuality and gender, for the Pfeffermans, exposed deep family secrets and led to self-discoveries for all of the main characters in ways that connected self-actualization with a retrieval of family history back in Europe before, during, and in the aftermath of WWII. The interrogation of sexuality and gender associated with Maura's coming out as a trans woman collapsed the layers of secrecy and sublimation that had been central to appearances. These events resonate with my earlier point that the drive to destabilize ontological and epistemological certainties inevitably shapes the meanings and scope of selfhood, in which one experiences (self-)hate (as alienation) or love (at-homeness). *Transparent* is enormously popular among young Jews active in Palestine solidarity and in broader Jewish circles. INN's chapters in New York City, the Bay Area, Boston, and Los Angeles even hosted viewing parties in September 2017, celebrating the show's examination of how American Jews relate to Israel and the occupation.[90]

One episode of *Transparent* shows Ali (played by Gaby Hoffmann), Maura's youngest daughter, journeying with a celebrated social media activist by the name of Lyfe from a posh area of Tel Aviv to Ramallah, through obvious landmarks of the occupation. Her journey, even if not conveyed explicitly as such, likely unfolds in Ali's fantasy because, when she returns to the supposed location of her encounter with Palestinians a few days later, the place looks desolate and the man who drove her to the checkpoint simply disappears on the other side as if he had never existed.[91] Nevertheless, the fantastic journey is significant for how it consolidates the connections between destabilizing gender binaries and a Jewish narrative about self-determination. In Ramallah, Ali meets with LGBTQI youth, who educate her rapidly on the specific meanings of the occupation to their communities, which serve as targets for surveillance and blackmailing. This episode's connection between Ali's exposure to the occupation and her pre-sensitization to LGBTQI issues resonates strongly with the stories that I heard from activists in the movement and their resistance to the complex semiotics of pinkwashing. Traveling with her family through the traditional landmarks of Jewish tourism—threaded with layers of orientalism, such as riding camels in circles in a parking lot and eating in a Bedouin tent—became intolerable for Ali, who felt compelled to go back to the West Bank and her friends there. Her jour-

ney with Lyfe and Janan (a Palestinian woman), to Janan's idyllic family farm
that Palestinian activists reclaimed from Israeli authorities, may have been
imaginative—as opposed to Ali's examination of the ugliness of checkpoints
and barbed wire—but no more imaginative than the narrative that American
Jews normally receive through Birthright trips. On the trip, Ali, an American Jewish gender-questioning person, ignorant on Israel/Palestine, under-
goes a mirror experience of the utopic *hasbarah* trips that paves the road for
her own self-transformation into gender nonconformity.[92] Ultimately, her
encounter with Palestinians appears to connect narcissistically to her own
process of self-discovery and actualization, not unlike the aim of Birthright
trips, which seek to solidify a naïve sense of American Jewishness qua Zionism. Nor is it unlike the emotion of self-approval and self-creation American
Jews experience through the moral batteries that their apparent altruistic acts
of solidarity with Palestinians generate. When the Pfeffermans stop in an illegal settlement to deliver a gift for a friend's mom, Ali reaches her breaking
point and confides in Maura that she may be gender nonconformist, that
she is unsure she is comfortable in a woman's body, and that she is searching
for spaces outside gender binaries. With Maura's blessing, Ali embarks on a
journey of self-exploration, returning to the West Bank and their (note my
intentional change in pronoun) Palestinian and activist friends. Once again,
we follow them through ugly checkpoints. *Transparent*'s linking of Ali's political and sexual self-interrogation and the undoing of prior axiomatic certainties about who they are exemplifies the mutually reinforcing operation of
multiple social fields in undoing the naturalness of a variety of binaries or the
presumed ontological certainty about one's identity. The lens of emancipatory narratives about gender and sexuality provides substantial resources for
challenging claims of "self-hate" as foundationally misconstruing the very

FIGURE 3.2. Multidirectional mechanisms for unlearning and disrupting conceptions of communal
"self"

meanings of the self. Likewise, politicization and sensitization on gender and sexual identities (which remain fluid and open to transformation along the journey) become transformative mechanisms in the processes of reimagining Jewishness relationally and intersectionally in ways that enable Jewish Palestine solidarity activists to cohere comfortably with American progressive outlooks and to disrupt the logic of ethnoreligious balkanization and non-intersectional identity politics.

I now turn to examine, in further detail, the construction of Jewishly informed alternative scripts motivated by ethical indignation.

Remapping the Destination

Reclaiming Judaism as Social Justice Activism

I was never connected closely with Zionism or Judaism as a cultural and religious identity. I grew up in an assimilated environment. . . . As a child, I personally enjoyed discussions after Torah reading. I didn't think of Israel until they passed around the JNF
[Jewish National Fund] box in synagogue. Israel was distant from my world. . . . Many
of my friends went to Israel during high school for various camps and so forth. I didn't
feel any interest in going to Israel at the time. I started to look at it as a way to think more
deeply about my identity. I didn't know much at all about my ancestors in Belarus. I
never felt that Jewish. . . . Eventually, I identified with Jewish culture and especially the
tradition of social justice. My grandparents were very involved during the New Deal era
politics. My grandfather fought in the army and as a scholar went to Berlin in the 1930s
and witnessed a Nazi protest. Reportedly (the story was in the paper), he refused to give
the Nazi salute and was horrified by the experience but stood his ground. It was exciting
for me to discover this story of a principled struggle for justice and especially compar-
ing this with friends involved with Jewish day camps and their preoccupations. I had a
cousin who even made *aliyah*. There is one narrative of Israel that connects to leftist sorts
of struggles—this is at least what I had in my head. But the rabbi in my dad's synagogue
was and still is hyper-Zionist and the language he used was striking because it sounded
chauvinistic like Nazism or fascist type movement. I am not sure why as a young person
I was so quick to make this shift. I was around 16 or 17 years old and by then I had friends
who came back from summers in Israel. It sounded like a lot of fun (lots of making out),
but it didn't at all sound to me like principled social engagement I was hoping for.[1]

Above are the words of Yuda, a young Jewish critic of Zionism. Much like the
activists we encountered in the previous chapter, he underscores the legacy of
secular prophetic social justice orientation as central to his own Jewish identity and commitment to activism. Accordingly, his narrative of transformation depicts not a sudden ethical revulsion, but a gradual process of political
maturation through which he strove to connect a legacy of left-leaning Jewish

prophetic history with the realities of Israel. Evident in Yuda's account is the profound influence on him of leftist Jewish idealism and his grandfather's principled resistance to Nazism. This legacy stood in sharp contrast both to what the rabbi at his synagogue taught and to the mundane adolescent fun his friends had on Birthright trips. Yuda now aspires in his own activism to reclaim a sense of Judaism as a tradition of standing with the marginalized, however filiopietistic this conception of tradition may be.[2]

Yuli, whom we encountered in chapter 3, attributed her commitment to Palestine solidarity to "the influence of the Jewish community [she] grew up in." "I went to Israel and I saw a society speaking highly of itself and seemed tough. So I asked myself, what kind of a Jew am I."[3] Yuli's and Yuda's words point to what by now has emerged as a common thread among American Jewish advocates of Palestine. They seek, on the one hand, to reclaim Judaism as a humanistic tradition by appealing to its prophetic and leftist strands, and on the other, to relinquish forms of nationalism or tribalism that they associate with Israel.

This chapter examines the grassroots emergence—at a moment of crisis in authority—of prophetic moral leadership and alternative conceptions of Jewish tradition. In particular, it explores attempts at reimagining Jewishness by means of "critical caretaking." Several key trends are the focus here: the retrieval of Jewish tradition as social justice oriented and joyful, rather than beholden to narratives of death and destruction and exclusionary forms of tribal solidarity; the work of rabbinic activists in refiguring Jewish traditions along lines dictated by grassroots communal authority; and various tactics for creative hermeneutical engagement with text, history, and memory. In bringing resources from their tradition to the Palestine solidarity movement, these activists have critically refigured that tradition. The upshot is a conception of Jewish liberation as interlinked with that of others—and thus freed from the constraints of a Zionist teleology and the balkanization of non-intersectional identity politics. The process of critical caretaking sheds light on the transformative capacities of moral shocks[4] to generate new communal meanings or public narratives, not only in terms of identifying sociological mechanisms operative in moments conducive for subversive agency, but also in terms of accounting for multifaceted layers of tradition-specific historical, symbolic, and textual interpretations and memories.

Critical Caretaking

As the previous chapters have shown, Jewish activists often undergo a journey where they need to "unlearn" certain received axioms about Israel, a process with profound significance for their own understanding of what it means to be Jewish. Unlearning or denaturalizing what appears self-evident is crucial to critique, but is only one dimension of it. In exposing the relations between power and knowledge, critique challenges previously axiomatic certainties. The loss of such certainty is necessary but ultimately insufficient for developing a constructively critical and transformative intervention. Yet, beyond and through the dissonance that critique generates is a concurrent process of refiguring Jewish identity outside the hegemonic logic that has just been deconstructed. In many respects, Jewish critics are critics precisely because they are caretakers of their tradition, opting not to reject that tradition, but to reassess it by probing its meanings in the wake of the loss of prior certainty. A helpful category for understanding this complex endeavor is "critical caretaking." The activists I interviewed not only claim Jewish traditions for themselves, but draw on resources from those traditions in order to reinterpret and critically inhabit them. Though most of them have not been trained at rabbinic schools or in midrashic literatures and methods, they are, in effect, critical caretakers of Jewish traditions, histories, and narratives. They thus challenge the presumption that, to be a critic of religion, one cannot operate from within the tradition. Their critical caretaking enables them to move beyond merely demystifying Zionism and challenging the American Jewish establishment, toward the more profound work of refiguring Jewish traditions and constructing alternative scripts.

The practice of critique, as Michel Foucault understood it, is itself self-transformational and virtuous because it requires challenging norms rather than obeying or reiterating them. Chapter 2's discussion of identity in social movement explored this process as unfolding through grassroots meaning-making and dialogic tensions among multiple social fields.[5] In her reflection on Foucault's "What Is Critique?," Judith Butler explains that "to be critical of an authority that poses as absolute requires a critical practice that has self-transformation at its core."[6] Here, Butler emphasizes the intimate relationship between critique and active stylization of the self, by which she draws on Foucault's view of critique as "the art of voluntary insubordination, that of reflected intractability."[7] By resisting governance, and the illegitimate ethical demands governance entails, one exposes the illegitimacy of the norms underlying those demands. But such resistance also constitutes "a practice of freedom" by subverting certainties that foreclose acts of moral and political imagination.[8] "Critique," in Foucault's words, "essentially insure[s] the desubjugation of the subject in the context of what we could call . . . the politics of truth."[9] But critique is not an exclusively negative task. Of course, it tears down; but it also builds up. Its deconstructive work is transformative, for the "certain exercise of disobedience" it demands ultimately allows "for the inventive elaboration of the self."[10] Critique, in other words, enables the cultivation of transformed selves, whose endpoint is not predetermined. Indeed, for Jewish critics of Zionism, who think "beyond the domain of the thinkable,"[11] desubjectivization not only demands the hermeneutical work of probing their Jewishness, but represents a form of critical virtue ethics pivotal in cultivating their projective imagination and transformative agency.[12] The projective imagination refers to "the specific culturally embedded ways in which people imagine, talk about, negotiate, and make commitments to their futures"[13] and illuminates the degrees to which human social action is minimally agentic (reinforcing existing norms and practices through iteration) or maximally transformative (subverting norms and practices).

The hinge that leads Jewish critics of Zionism to active prophetic intervention in Palestine solidarity activism, I argue, is the work of self-refashioning according to alternative norms they themselves rescript. In their work as critical caretakers, these activists employ ethical resources—both Jewish and otherwise—thereby demystifying and refashioning Jewishness and foci of solidarity. They do so not "from nowhere," but through deep engagement with Jewish resources, on which they draw to reinterpret apparent axioms. This often unfolds through the social mechanisms of moral shocks and battery they experience through acts of Palestine solidarity and the moral emotional experiences of indignation and shame, which generate both a profound sense of self-critique and an intensified sense of self-approval and pride. The "self," as noted, is not predetermined but rather conveys semiotic and dialogic fluidity and the capacity to innovate from the margins through retrieving alternative conceptions of the past and new imaginations of the future. Such retrieval typically involves recovering competing motifs from the vast tradition, and so the relevance of religiocultural and historical literacy cannot be overstated. In so doing, these activists demonstrate that critique is not necessarily secular. Indeed, to conflate the critical with the secular betrays an uncritical acceptance of the modernist dichotomy of reason and faith.[14]

Yet that these developments happen specifically in the context of Palestinian solidarity illuminates the degree to which the broader tradition of human rights, as well as activist agendas, can influence and substantially modify religious practice, texts, and norms of engagement. In reflecting on his participation in CJNV's 2016 solidarity trip to Hebron, Rabbi Brant Rosen insists that Jewish solidarity with Palestinians is not merely "a benevolent human rights campaign," but a response to a call from Palestinians. "We were not there to assuage our guilt," he adds. Instead, "we were there because our privilege was a source of power that could [be] leveraged to help [Palestinians] stand down their oppression."[15] Rosen's focus on solidarity points to the dynamic connection between practices of Jewish solidarity with Palestinians and the critical refiguring of Jewish norms.[16] Hence, the transformative act of self-critique through solidarity is morally gratifying and generates, as earlier chapters have noted, self-approval and new belonging. Naomi Klein describes the Jewish space JVP has constructed as a way of recovering Jewish imperatives to uphold "values of human rights and solidarity with Palestinian people. It's an alternative Jewish community that allows me to have a home."[17] By fostering solidarity, indignation, and ethical, humanistic conceptions of tradition, this space becomes a "home" for refigured Jewishness.[18]

Notably, however, this process does not amount to a simple subordination or dilution of tradition to a set of norms that stand over and against it; rather, it constitutes an effort to reclaim, through refashioning, alternative ways of being American Jewish. Critical caretaking, therefore, is highly relational: Jewish meanings, texts, and practices are interrogated and reframed by directly examining their implications for Palestinians and, to a lesser extent, other victims of Zionism, such as the Mizrahim/yot and Ethiopian Jews. Such attention to marginalized others makes critical caretaking also deeply intersectional.

Critical caretaking involves various mechanisms, one of which is midrashic work that engages Jewish traditions. Two key sites of such work are JVP's Artistic Council and its Rabbinical Council. The Artistic Council, which includes Jews and allies, aims at retrieving radical Jewish histories to help decolonize Jewish aesthetics and challenge the use of trauma in service of state violence. At the same time, it seeks to mount support for a cultural boycott of Israel, while cultivating connections with Palestinian artists.[19] The emphasis on artistic production reflects the importance of Jewish literacy in the work of desubjectivization and constructive projective imagining. Such work also involves rewriting rituals with explicit calls for action. This is the focus of the Rabbinic Council, whose aim is to support and promote the objectives of JVP, including communal transformation, by providing Jewish resources, cultivating literacy in Jewish traditions, and offering a public rabbinic presence for the movement and a rabbinic community rooted in solidarity and guided by values of *Tzelem Elohim* (the divine image), *Tzedek* and *Rachamim* (justice and compassion), the prophetic call, and *kehila* (community).[20] Hence, this network of rabbis exemplifies critical caretaking through developing liturgy and resources to embolden Jewish framing of protest repertoire, but also to construct new, transformative Jewish meanings.[21]

In the following section, we continue our examination of grassroots retrievals of alternative Jewish traditions by turning to "voices in the wilderness" who point to the moral erosion of religious and communal authority. This provides necessary background to examining the emergence through movement of new religious authorities and mechanisms for reframing Jewishness.

Rabbinic Responses: Outrage and Reclaiming an "Authentic" Judaism

The CJNV embodies an active reclamation of alternative Jewishness that is itself rewritten through the very act and experience of solidarity. The t-shirts we wore in the Sumud Freedom Camp in the space of the demolished Palestinian town of Sarura in May 2017 read "Occupation is not my Judaism." While the slogan emphasizes what Judaism is *not*, the path to this slogan required the hard work of self-reflexive reimagining of what Jewishness *is*, not only what it is not. Responding to this question demands hermeneutical and historical fluency, revisiting and scrutinizing the resources of the past in constructing new meanings.

In identifying the relatively recent centrality of Jewish devotion to the State of Israel, Jewish critics aspire to reorient Judaism to its ethical kernel or historical legacy, itself a presumption subject to historicist scrutiny.[22] Brian Walt, a South African–born rabbi who is now active in BDS campaigns and sits on JVP's rabbinic council, seeks to reorient Judaism by reclaiming the diasporic dimensions of Judaism. For Walt, such a reversal requires interrogating and historicizing the Zionization of Jewish resources.[23] Noting the Reform current's roots in non-Zionism,[24] he objects to a Zionized Jewish liturgy as a perversion of Judaism.[25] Walt's historicizing of the Reform prayerbook indicates the profound link between his moral outrage—about Israeli oppression in his name and the sanction of Israeli policies by the American Jewish establishment—and the impulse to recover "authentic" Judaism, untainted by state power, essentially diasporic, and "non-Constantinian."

Many of the interviewees cited their desire to retrieve an "anti-Constantinian" construal of Judaism as motivating their break with the American Zionist orthodoxy. One activist explained: "Strong Jewish roots is something I cherish. I am more attuned to cultural [than to statist] Zionism. Valuing collective culture and wanting to thrive culturally isn't the same as engaging in state power, so when you associate Jewishness with state power it is destructive." "Jewish culture," she continued, "can be stronger by disassociating it from political hegemony. Look at New York City, Jewish cultures and Jewish plurality flourishes there."[26] Variations of this connection between estrangement from Israel and critique of Zionism as a perversion of Judaism emerged repeatedly in my interviews.

While the designation "Constantinian Judaism," a curious appropriation of a concept in Christian history, has deeper roots in Jewish and Christian theological reflections,[27] activists in the movement often trace the designation to a scholar of American and Jewish studies, Marc Ellis.[28] The term resonated with many of my interviewees, who saw their own diasporic location as more authentically Jewish than homeownership in Zion, thus challenging the Zionist valorization of autochthony and indigeneity.[29] This emphasis on diaspora coheres with their desire to unsettle chauvinistic interpretations of Jewish liberation as well as Zionist readings of Jewish history and narratives of the land of Zion. It also resonates with counter-hegemonic scholarly discourse that aspires similarly to dismantle the Zionist discourse[30] and to de-link a narrative of trauma from the diasporic condition.

As Daniel Boyarin emphasizes, such scholarly work unfolds by actively reappropriating conceptions of diaspora as a homeland that had been dynamically contained in and produced by particularistic textual and interpretive practices, trans-locally and trans-historically.[31] Diasporism, for Boyarin, is embodied in the Talmud, "a book [that] has been the portable homeland of the Jewish people."[32] Diasporism takes many forms. Some diasporists seek to retrieve modernist articulations of Jewish diasporism, whether that of Simon Dubnow or resources within modernist currents of Judaism (Reform, Conservative, and Reconstructionist). Others emphasize culturally fluid and open conceptions of Jewishness that amount to seeking justice through leftist politics and destabilizing Ashkenazi hegemony. Diaspora is a creative and dynamic religious, intellectual, ethical, and cultural destination. Crucially, however, it does not necessarily negate the "profundity of our attachment to the Land."[33] This profundity does not depend on a myth of autochthony (which presupposes a natural and continuous right to the land of Zion), but rather recognizes that at the heart of the Jewish narrative is the condition of "always already coming from somewhere else."[34] This conception of the land leads Boyarin and his brother Jonathan Boyarin to articulate the diasporic "as a theoretical and historical model to replace national self-determination."[35] This is to reject Zionist indigeneity-based claims of territoriality and their reliance on modernist conceptions of self-determination, which in themselves constitute "a Western, imperialist imposition on the rest of the world."[36] Such imperialism represents a departure from a more authentically diasporist approach to land and communal preservation.

Ellis likewise identifies Zionist attitudes toward the state of Israel as a derailment of the Jewish tradition. He argues that the post-Holocaust tendency to attend exclusively to Jewish suffering constitutes a betrayal of the prophetic dimensions of Judaism and produces tone-deafness to the sufferings of others.[37] "When we assimilate to the state and power, whether in Israel or

America," he writes, "we move toward a Judaism that is passive in the face of injustice with the sophistication of real politik." This transformation constitutes a radical departure from Ellis's historical and theological reading of Judaism as a counterargument to Constantinian Christianity. "Judaism, as it developed within the shadow of an empowered Constantinian Christianity," he underscores, "is a sustained engagement with state-oriented religiosity." The emergence of what he identifies as a post-Holocaust Constantinian Judaism "is ironic for a variety of reasons, not least of which is our recent survival of Constantinian Christianity in the death camps of Nazi Europe."[38]

Motivated by similar insights, the rabbis I highlight here also challenge this Constantinian frame. Brant Rosen acknowledges the influence of Ellis's *Toward a Jewish Theology of Liberation* on his own cultivation of multiple foci of solidarity: "Here was a Jewish thinker thoughtfully and compellingly advocating a new kind of post-Holocaust theology: one that didn't view Jewish suffering as 'unique' and 'untouchable,' but as an experience that should sensitize us to the suffering and persecution of all people everywhere."[39] In his own theology, Ellis opposes Jewish thinkers who interpret Israel and Zionism as a liberationist path for Jews after the Holocaust. This view remains blind to the suffering of others and problematically valorizes militarism. To describe Judaism as "Constantinian" suggests, therefore, that Judaism's marriage to power in Zionism entails a transformation analogous to Christianity's shift in the fourth century from a persecuted minority that stood against the corrupting aspects of power, to the official religion of empire.

As noted, while Ellis's Jewish Palestinian liberation theology became a central reference point for some in the contemporary movement of Jewish critics, the labeling of Zionism as "Constantinian Judaism" is not originally his. It goes back to Mennonite theologian John Howard Yoder (1927–1997),[40] who understood Zionism as undermining the true message and mission of Judaism, namely "*galut* [exile] as vocation."[41] He was criticized for his construal of Zionism by American Jewish theologian Peter Ochs, who claimed that Yoder's anti-Zionism betrays his unwillingness to relinquish Christian supersessionism (or his "non-non supersessionism," as Ochs puts it) and, with it, his failure to engage in what Ochs views as the potential of post-liberal theology to participate in and model the repair and alleviation of human suffering. Relinquishing supersessionist claims is, Ochs contends, the *sine qua non* for constructive and reparative interreligious engagement. For Ochs, Zionism constitutes "a reparation for the suffering of the Jews,"[42] and thus Yoder's failure to acknowledge this and his willingness to instead analyze Judaism only to the extent that it promotes his understanding of Christian ends excludes him from the task of postliberal theology to which

Ochs is committed. For Ochs, "Yoder's anti-Zionism is dyadic and thus not reparative."[43]

Magid rereads Yoder against Ochs's critique. This does not amount to an endorsement of Yoder's theological ends. Instead, Magid views Yoder's labeling of Zionism as "Jewish Constantinianism" as generating "a kind of inner-Jewish reparation, whereby dormant dimensions of the tradition that do not fit into the Zionist narrative can once again be given a voice."[44] The intention is to illuminate the potential of this internal critique to more deeply engage in the promise of postliberal theology to be reparative in ways that acknowledge not only Jewish suffering but also Palestinian suffering produced by Zionism and its historical realities. This approach resonates with Ellis's critique of Jewish monopoly over the economy of suffering. But the reparative potential does not entail, in Magid's reading, inversing a dyadic outlook that reinstates supersessionism, whether intentionally or not. Instead, it entails employing "particular lenses" with which to navigate "the multivocality of tradition"[45] in a particular historical moment that concurrently demands accounting for the suffering of others caused by Jewish actions and ideologies. Ellis's theology, in distinction, coalesces with Christian supersessionism in its dyadic impulse to revalorize the diasporic and "prophetic" as the most authentically Jewish set of values and ideas and in its foreclosing the potential for an intra-Jewish reparative process. Ellis's call to listen to and atone for the suffering of Palestinians is a key motif and mechanism in the process of reimagining Jewishness relationally in ways that demand reinvigorating and retrieving prophetic memories, impulses, stories, and scriptural threads. However, such resources, as noted earlier, are not simply available untouched for retrieval. Rather, retrieving them demands a process of critical caretaking, a projective and transformative agency oriented by alternative interpretations of the past and imaginations of the future, and complex dialogic interactions that facilitate the innovative capacity of these semiotic interactive exchanges.[46] Magid's rereading of Yoder's anti-Zionism as an intra-Jewish reparative opportunity, historically located in the realities of Israel, moves the conversation beyond dyadic claims. Such claims oscillate between the labels of authenticity and non-authenticity (Zionism as the perversion of Judaism) and thus obscure generative capacities to imagine new meanings dialogically through critique (desubjectivization) but also hermeneutically through constructive meaning-making work from the margins that enhances the causal impacts of moral shocks. Of course, critique is already and necessarily hermeneutical because it disrupts, on Butler's reading, "certainties that foreclose acts of moral and political imagination," while refashioning the self through positive ethical engagement. Thus, the relation between critique and reimagining is not sequential but concurrent and mutually reinforcing. The aforementioned Jewish-specific critical and constructive resources do not emerge *ex nihilo*. Thus, they point to the multivocality of tradition as well as the relevance of fluency in such multivocality to broadening and reshaping the scope of moral and political imagination. The focus on critical caretaking and reparative possibilities does not necessarily reject or supersede the enduring "profundity" of the land, even while involving a critique of political theology that valorizes peoplehood while relying on modernist autochthonous logic of self-determination.

Ellis's more dyadic interpretation of "Constantinian Judaism," however, played a central role in Rosen's inaugural Rosh Hashanah sermon to the newly formed community of Tzedek Chicago. Rosen called on his audience to resist Constantinianism: "We now embrace a new narrative—one that responds to trauma not with a message of healing and hope, but by placing our faith in humanly wielded power. Our new narrative teaches that the pain of our Jewish past will inevitably become our future unless we embrace the ways of power and privilege; nationalism and militarism."[47] Emphatically, occupation is not *his* Judaism. The use of the label "Constantinianism" here highlights Zionism as an erroneous turn, a poisonous political theology that needs to be subverted and *aufgehoben* through re-accessing an ostensibly more authentic Jewish experience of powerlessness.

Indeed, one common tactic of Jewish Palestine solidarity activists is to reinterpret Jewish meanings in distinctly non-Constantinian ways, thereby reclaiming the Jewish prophetic tradition. Rabbi Michael Lerner, a leading voice of American Jewish dissent, points to the tragic connotations of marking the Ninth of Av in the midst of the destruction of Gaza during Operation Protective Edge (July–August 2014). In an article titled "Mourning for a Judaism Being Murdered by Israel," he stresses that the Ninth of Av ought to be marked as an occasion to commemorate "disasters that happened to us throughout Jewish history."[48] Thus, he continues, "I'm going to be fasting and mourning also for a Judaism being murdered by Israel."[49] The traumatic events of the Holocaust, Lerner suggests, informed this turn from Judaism as a "religion of compassion and identification with the most oppressed that was championed by our Biblical prophets" to "worship[ing] power and . . . rejoic[ing] in Israel's ability to become the most military powerful state in the Middle East." This led to a grave distortion where Israel, rather than its victims, is prayed for in synagogues across the world.

The distortion Lerner underscores is profound: "The worship of power is precisely what Judaism came into being to challenge. We were slaves, the powerless, and though the Torah talks of God using a strong arm to redeem the Israelites from Egyptian slavery, it simultaneously insists, over and over again, that when Jews go into their promised land in Canaan (now Palestine) they must 'love the stranger/the other,' have only one law for the stranger *and* for the native born, and warns 'do not oppress the stranger/the other.'" The subversion and loss of these motifs is what Lerner mourned on the Ninth of Av.[50] He mourned the "murdering" of an authentic Judaism that is, by definition, diasporic, displaced, and resides optimally in the metaphorical land of Egypt.

Walt's testimony likewise illustrates the role that ethical outrage, unlearning, and a turn to Palestine solidarity play in creatively reinterpreting Jewish traditions.[51] His own relation to Zionism changed radically in 2008 after he visited the sites of demolished Palestinian homes as part of his work with Rabbis for Human Rights and the Israel Committee against House Demolition. These visits "shook [him] to [his] core." "I remember standing on the site of a recently demolished Palestinian home seeing the children's toys lying in the rubble." This sight prompted him to question: "What does it mean for me to believe in a Jewish state that demolishes Palestinian homes using bulldozers to destroy everything including the toys of children, while it builds and subsidizes thousands of homes for Jews, homes that house among others, friends of mine who make *Aliyah* from America? How can I understand this reality as a Jew? Is this the Jewish state I believe in and support? As a supporter of Israel, a Zionist, am I implicated in this evil act?" Even while seeing the realities of the occupation firsthand, Walt struggled with his love of Zionism: "It was hard for me to even think of relinquishing my Zionism. It was so much part of me." The final turning point happened during a solidarity visit in 2008 that included a tour of Hebron. There, the rabbi realized that his group was walking on a "Jews-only street." "In the past I believed that the discrimination I saw—the demolished homes, the uprooted trees, the stolen land—were an aberration of the Zionist vision. I came to understand that all of these were not mistakes, not blemishes on a dream; they were all the logical outcome of Zionism."[52] His outrage concerns both the violation of the humanity of Palestinians and the distortion of the Jewish tradition as he understands it. The analogy with apartheid became very real for this South African rabbi. For him, not only the occupation but also Zionism itself were not *his* Judaism.

The outrage of rabbis like Lerner, Rosen, and Walt is critical for the process of refiguring Jewish meanings and identity. This task requires not merely exposing inconsistencies, but the intentional hermeneutical work of examining meanings within the Jewish tradition. But the impulse to identify some "authentic" kernel of Judaism has itself a modernist genealogy, and thus its own dangers. We must tackle these before further scrutinizing appeals to the prophetic Jewish tradition that account for dialogical and historically located dynamics operative in processes of religiocultural innovation through *other-oriented* solidarity.

Situating the Diasporist Moment

Reform Judaism was born together with Jewish emancipation and assimilation into European societies, a process that gained momentum especially in the aftermath of Napoleon's defeat in 1815, which led many Jews to convert to Christianity in order to retain their rights and status. Leaders of this movement explicitly downplayed the messianic and ethnocentric particularistic motifs of the Jewish tradition and accordingly sought to render the liturgy more colloquial, accessible, and aesthetically appealing, thus minimizing conflicts between Jewish practice and secular European civic life. The German roots of Reform are important not just historically, but also conceptually and theologically. Abraham Geiger (1810–1874) was instrumental in construing Judaism as a modern religion that needed only to relinquish obedience to Mosaic law as "external shackles of historical accident" and celebrate its historical role in anticipating Protestantism.[53]

Geiger's insistence on the Jewish spiritual genius and the originality of the Jewish monotheistic impulse challenged normative assumptions of Enlightenment intellectuals such as Immanuel Kant, who had dismissed Judaism as a relic of the past that accordingly bore no relation to Christianity. Likewise a child of his era, Geiger's refiguring of Judaism is consistent with Moses Mendelssohn's bifurcation of the religious from the political in accordance with the new possibility of Jewish emancipation through acquiring full citizenship in Germany. For Jews to become German citizens necessitated inventing Judaism as a religion that could be privatized, a process that demanded identifying—through the *Wissenschaft des Judentums*—a Jewish essence, a kernel that had survived only by hiding under the tombs of halakhic laws. This essence, for Geiger, was the "universal, ethical contribution that Judaism makes to culture at large."[54]

The narratives in this chapter and chapter 3 confirm what the Pew survey of 2013 had suggested: the influence of Reform on contemporary expressions of ethical outrage that are pivotal in generating social activism. Rather than rejecting the Reform current, Jewish critics of Israel—as we saw with Reform liturgy—seek to recover the original impulse of Reform as a refiguring of Jewishness that eschews messianic and communal expectations of Zion as the locus of redemption. Although the circumstances motivating the contemporary retrieval of a non-messianic Jewish diasporist orientation differ from those that initially underpinned the Reform movement, the similarities between how Jewishness is reconfigured are significant. The institution of the modern nation-state and the relevance of religiocultural and social meanings authorizing this institution are apparent both in nineteenth-century Germany and in contemporary twenty-first-century Jewish critics of Israel whose ability to trade Zion for New York City depends, in part, on their ability to read Zion metaphorically and associated valorization of the diasporic condition. Yet these processes rely, to a certain degree, on Protestant modes of turning religion into a "confessional" affair, with attendant assumptions about the correct boundaries of "political" and "social" spaces.[55] In particular, contemporary critiques of Constantinianism presume the capacity of the "state" as an infrastructure of power to be legitimated independently of conceptions of "nation," which always draw upon, however selectively, narratives about who we are, narratives that always intersect in complex ways with cultural and religious meanings. Jewish modernity constantly navigated these twin developments of confessionalization and the emergence of citizenship as a political category.

Indeed, while the ascendancy of Zionism within the Reform current in American Judaism denotes a sharp departure from Reform's foundational commitments, the Reform current itself radicalized the Jewish tradition. American Reform Judaism emerged with the arrival of German Jews in the mid-1880s. Its institutionalization and "confessionalization" were shaped particularly by Rabbi Isaac Mayer Wise (who arrived in the US from Bohemia in 1846). This legacy typically manifested in an opposition to Zionism or Jewish nationalism as the framework for resolving the "Jewish problem" in Europe.[56] The "confessionalization" of Judaism and associated rejection of Judaism as a nation also made way for the "enthusiastic endorsement of America as the new Zion."[57] This embrace of the new Zion was popularized by the German-born American Reform rabbi Max Lilienthal (1815–1882), who wrote that his contemporary Jews ought to relinquish restorationist ambitions: "America is our Palestine; here is our Zion and Jerusalem: Washington and the signers of the glorious Declaration of Independence—of universal human right, liberty, and happiness—are our deliverers."[58] This celebration of diaspora as home is a function of the Jew's "admission in many lands to full citizenship," exclaimed another German-born American Reform rabbi. The ability to integrate into one's culture rendered obsolete "the hope voiced in Synagogal liturgy for a return to Palestine, the formation of a Jewish State under a king of the house of David, and the restoration of the sacrificial cult."[59]

Initially, Reform in the US was decidedly opposed to Zionism. But some advocated for a Reform Zionism. These included Gustav and Richard Gottheil, Rabbi Stephen S. Wise, and Justice Louis Brandeis. By the time the Balfour Declaration was issued in 1917, American Jews associated with the Reform movement sent funds to sponsor Zionist settlement in Palestine, the Hadassah Hospital, and the Hebrew University. The Columbus Platform of 1937 denoted this decisive shift from Reform's initial anti-Zionist stance. This platform also signaled the coalescing of a current within Reform that sought to reembrace traditional ritual.[60] Later statements of Reform principles (the Centenary Perspective of 1975 and the Statement of Principles of 1999) both affirm prophetic social action as in the Pittsburgh Platform of 1885 (the most radical articulation of Judaism as a modern religion—that is, as an ethical or spiritual orientation rather than an orthopraxy, or uniform set of ritual practices) and retain ritual observance as articulated in the Columbus Platform. They also express strong commitments both to the Israeli nation-state and to a robust pluralism that includes women and LGBTQI constituencies meaningfully within the community.[61] This tension between a Jewish ethnocultural-centric narrative about Israel and an otherwise progressive outlook is at the heart of many Jewish critics' experiences of dissonance and ethical outrage. This outrage leads them to recognize the impossibility of occupying a progressive position that excludes Palestine. Thus they relinquish Zionism in favor of progressivism and, in turn, develop their own interpretation of the prophetic threads of the Jewish tradition.

But beyond the tensions between statist Zionism and prophetic Judaism's intersections with humanism and progressivism in the US, the history of Reform is marked by contestations between a classical emphasis on spirit over form—which underpins its humanistic and rationalist currents—and a more traditionalist thread that emerged in the 1960s.[62] The reaffirmation of the Pittsburgh Platform's commitments, however, does not encompass Pittsburgh's categorical rejection of Zionism. The latter legacy, indeed, continued to be contested because Reform's suspicion and rejection of Zionism was not a settled tenet nor a homogeneous position. From the late nineteenth century until World War II, some thinkers rejected Zionism as having secularist and atheistic tendencies.[63] Others struggled to reconcile Zionism with liberalism.[64] Yet still others, like Abba Hillel Silver, a Lithuanian-born leader of American Reform, strongly supported statist Zionism while vehemently criticizing radical Reform as "Paulist." He spoke of Jewish anti-Zionism as "'a candle which lights others and consumes itself.' They [like Paul] tried to erect Jewish life upon the slender, sagging stilts of a few theologic abstractions. They, too, felt the Law to be a burden."[65]

This brief detour into the contested history of Zionism within the current of American Reform Judaism and its supersessionist motifs provides illuminating background context to the contemporary language about reclaiming an authentic ethical kernel of Judaism that is so central to Jewish Palestine solidarity activists and other critics of the Israeli occupation and Zionism. The Jewish activists and critics I interviewed, as well as others who share their views on social media and in other public venues, describe their processes of disengaging from Israel in terms of recovering their identity as Jews, which they often painted as identical to "humanism" and "social justice." This portrayal of "Jewish values" is consistent with the modernist search for an ethical humanist kernel and thus resists ethnocentric conceptions of solidarity. However, even while often portraying solidarity as the retrieval of a readily available if marginalized "kernel" of authentic Judaism, the *other*-centric mode of solidarity exposes the historically specific reparative and innovative grassroots meaning-making journey enacted through a social movement's navigation of a complex semiotic topography, necessarily pushed beyond intra-Jewish resources and interrogative tools.

Jewish Palestine solidarity activists overcome the conflation of Zionism and Judaism by interpreting, in a manner consistent with the Reconstructionist movement,[66] the Jewish tradition or "civilization" as coinciding with humanistic values and concerns. This does not involve a simple choice between liberalism and Zionism,[67] but rather constitutes a reworking of Jewish meanings and motifs through the prism of contemporary sensibilities about justice and human rights. Mordechai Kaplan's notion of Judaism as a "civilization"[68] that is elastic and always subject to reinterpretation animates many of the religious "technologies" deployed by organizations such as JVP. By framing Judaism as a civilization encompassing "secular" aspects such as cuisine, history, and literature, Kaplan broadened the scope of Jewish participation to those who were not necessarily beholden to theological and ritualistic prescriptions. However, the Reconstructionist current, like the Reform and Conservative ones, remains entangled, like Orthodoxy,[69] with the other modernist Jewish movement, statist Zionism. Thus, critique of the one entails critiques and innovations in the other. Kaplan's own Zionism, Rebecca Alpert asserts, was ethical—not statist—and sought to cultivate cross-fertilization among Jewish centers in Israel and the diasporas.[70] Alpert applies Reconstructionist principles to Zionism, thus subjecting its practices and ideas to values in an effort to transvalue such practices or theorize them out of existence. "The tension between the reality of Israel and the Zion of our dream is too great," she writes, "to allow for me to claim that these words [*Israel* and *Zion*] are equivalent." Thus, she concludes, "to uphold Reconstructionist values, I must stand, as a Jew, in solidarity with Palestinians."[71] This is not to attribute causality to the Reconstructionist outlook but to highlight the mainstreaming of this current's interpretive tools and approach to tradition as an effective resource for *other*-centric processes of critical caretaking.

The Reconstructionist movement has struggled, from the time of its inception, with the motifs of chosenness and election, regarding them as inconsistent with the values of human rights, humanism, and pluralism. Instead, the Reconstructionist movement reinterpreted and reshaped liturgical texts and rituals to render these consistent with universal and humanistic values. The strategy of reading allegorically rather than literally is apparent in JVP's efforts in liturgical innovations and transvaluation of practices. This process, however, does not suggest a movement toward overcoming Judaism, but rather celebrating Jewish particularity and distinctness in a post-Zionist mode.

This celebration reflects sociocultural developments in the American Jewish landscape. Shaul Magid traces patterns suggestive of the cultivation of postethnic conceptions of Jewishness in the US.[72] He analyzes this process partly as the upshot of an increased rate of intermarriages and Jews of choice and partly as rooted in intellectual developments specific to American Judaism. He highlights two developments in particular: the cross-fertilizing of American Judaism with the philosophical tradition of pragmatism, which contributed to the emergence of the countercultural Jewish Renewal movement in the 1970s; and the thought of Zalman Schachter-Shalomi, one of the founders of the Jewish Renewal movement. Schachter-Shalomi, in promoting postethnic Judaism, reflects elective affinities with the Reconstructionist movement, specifically the legacies of Kabbalistic traditions, Mordechai Kaplan's writings, and Felix Adler's Ethical Culture Society, as well as their combined intellectual efforts that allowed relinquishing Jewish "ownership" of God. Magid illumines the unique challenge to which Jewish Renewal offers a "metaphysical, (post) halakhic, societal, and pragmatic template."[73] "While secular Zionism offered Jews Jewishness *without* Judaism, post-ethnic America has challenged Jews to consider whether Jewishness can exist *beyond* Judaism," he stresses.[74] Overcoming the links of Jewishness to blood- and land-based conceptions of peoplehood whether as imprinted in fears of assimilation into the diasporic contexts or as celebrated in the ethnocentric nationalist project, in other words, demands imagining Jewishness otherwise, not as occupation with an intricate infrastructure of segregated spaces nor as bounded by the control of marriages. What remains of Jewishness once ethnic boundaries (however contested) are subverted?

In David Landy's analysis, the social movement of critical diaspora Juda-

ism seeks, through a particular praxis, to "*re-cognise* or theoretically reconstitute what it means to be a diaspora Jew," and does so "in direct contestation with dominant Zionist praxis."[75] At the heart of this resignification is
the reversal of the "negation of diaspora" integral to the Zionist ethos.[76] The
movement's resignification and the progressivism it espouses have deep historical roots in earlier developments such as the American Council for Judaism (ACJ), established in 1942 as an internal challenge to the shift of Reform
toward an embrace of Zionism.[77] Significantly diminished in traction and
membership in the post-1967 era, the ACJ promoted an anti-nationalist approach to Judaism and actively supported, in the aftermath of WWII, a joint
Jewish-Arab (Palestinian) state rather than an exclusionary ethnonational
frame.[78] Additionally, the movement's intellectual scaffoldings evince a robust legacy of critical interlocutors including, in the 1950s, Kaplan's critique
of exclusively statist Zionism[79] and Simon Rawidowicz's concern with the
unfolding of "cruel Zionism," the subsequent immorality of this project of
political self-determination, and a relinquishing of "the Jewish author and his
pen as the embodiment of the Jewish spirit."[80] Earlier, during the period between the world wars, theorist of nationalism Hans Kohn similarly lamented
the Zionists' reliance on force: "The means will have determined the goal.
Jewish Palestine will no longer have anything of that Zion for which I once
put myself on the line," he wrote in 1929.[81] Other marginalized internal critics whose voices reverberate loudly in the movement of contemporary Jewish critics of the occupation, amplifying the movement's ethical outrage and
reparative potentiality, include Hannah Arendt, Ella Habiba Shohat, Daniel Boyarin, Noam Chomsky, Sara Roy, Judith Butler, and Jacqueline Rose,
among many others.[82] Butler, in particular, is often heralded in the contemporary movement as one of its key public intellectuals. In her background,
however, stands, among other intellectual influences, Arendt.[83]

Arendt is often cited for lamenting that "the solution of the Jewish question merely produced a new category of refugees, the Arabs," and that this
predicament is linked to the logic of colonialism because "what happened
in Palestine within the smallest territory and in terms of hundreds of thousands was then repeated in India on a large scale involving many millions
of people."[84] Arendt's comparison among instances of colonialism and displacement would go on to resonate deeply in the later movement of critical
Jews. Their intersectional approach to the struggle for Palestinian rights and
their concomitant retrieval of Shohat's and other Mizrahi critical theorists'
rereading and expanding of Edward Said's critique of Zionism elucidates the
multiperspectival implications of the liberatory narrative of European Zionism not only from the perspective of its Palestinian victims but also from

that of its Arab-Jewish *other*.[85] It also clarifies why an engagement with co-lonialism and Eurocentricity is a transformative site pivotal for reimagining Jewishness through Palestine solidarity.

In earlier chapters, I showed that when American Jews work on the ground, in solidarity with Palestinian partners, they display a form of what James Jasper calls moral battery, reinforcing the negative emotion of indignation but also augmenting the positive emotion of self-approval. The sentiment of belonging in the movement, expressed by my interviewees, stresses how critique tends to generate communal self-transformation while also cultivating positive conceptions of a refashioned communal self. In this transformative semiotic process of critical caretaking, a group constructively and innovatively navigates and reconfigures religiocultural and other resources in rewriting or prefiguring the response to the question of "who we are." To effect sociocultural change on a broader level than the intellectual endeavor requires rewriting collective passions—in an embodied and embedded manner—and refiguring what and who is included in conceptions of one's community. For Arendt, belonging to the Jewish people was simply a matter of fact, not passion. This distinguishes her intellectual prophetic contribution and the contemporary movement's transformative public narrative that seeks to translate the rewritten values and moral and political imagination into action.

Arendt, in particular, was subject to the label of self-hatred. After the publication of her *Eichmann in Jerusalem: A Report on the Banality of Evil* (1963), Gershom Scholem famously accused her of failing to demonstrate the obligation of *ahavat yisrael*, or the love of Israel. Her reply to this accusation quickly became a classic refutation of its logic. She wrote: "You are quite right—I am not moved by any 'love' of this sort, and for two reasons: I have never in my life 'loved' any people or collective. . . . I indeed love 'only' my friends and the only kind of love I know of and believe in is the love of persons. Secondly, this 'love of the Jews' would appear to me, since I am myself Jewish, as something rather suspect." It is "suspect," in her observation, because it leads to an idolatrous worship of the community: "Now this people believes only in itself? What good can come out of that? Well, in this sense I do not 'love' the Jews, nor do I 'believe' in them; I merely belong to them as a matter of course, beyond dispute or argument."[86] Arendt's profound challenge to Scholem's homogenization of the Jewish people in light of a Zionist teleology resonates in the Jewish critics' refusal of this homogenizing narrative and the worship of Israel and its ethos of security. Indeed, they refuse the kind of *ahavat yisrael* Scholem espouses. However, this refusal persists in a feedback loop with their otherwise shift in affective loyalties and their reparative response to the call of Palestinians to stand in solidarity with them. Unlike Arendt, they do not simply belong as a matter of course, beyond dispute or argument. Their very belonging entails a critical transformative process through *other*-centric solidarity, grappling with Jewish sinfulness, social movement dynamics, and dialogic resignification of the very meanings of Jewishness. But even Arendt— despite her distancing from any *ahavat yisrael*—underscored, in the same response to Scholem, her sense of particularistic *shame*: "Wrong done by my own people naturally grieves me more than wrong done by other peoples."[87] Indeed, the contemporary critics of the occupation stand within a robust and legitimate historical trajectory. Like Arendt's friend Walter Benjamin, they focus on the debris of a history of progress and liberation for some, or the "anonymous vanquished," in Benjamin's words, in order to "read history against the grain,"[88] a critical mechanism for renarrating one's script.

The movement's challenge and resignification of Judaism qua diasporism, therefore, is a novel development not because it invented an ethical Jewish critique of Zionism, but rather because its critique unfolds at the broad grassroots level of a social movement and because it centralizes the perspectives and experiences of Palestinians and JOCSM and other marginalized Jews. It scripts an alternative narrative. Among the Jewish activists I encountered, post-Zionism was most evident in interpreting their own dissimilation in terms of a discourse of American multiculturalism. That they function according to a countercultural calendar, for instance, or living according to a different cyclical time than the majority culture, was repeatedly mentioned as something they cherish and cultivate.[89] Their religious tradition, hence, does not only carry a sentimental value; it offers a space they embrace, but they embrace it as critical caretakers.

One such critical caretaker is Ben Lorber, a writer and a former campus organizer for JVP. He challenges the reliance of American liberal Judaism on ethnic continuity and security, and claims that their mutually reinforcing logics impoverish Jewishness: "A Jewishness reduced to the simple imperatives to preserve a blood line that is increasingly intermingled, and to defend a nation-state whose policies are increasingly indefensible, cannot last. . . . What is exciting, energizing, enlivening about a Jewishness framed solely as a defensive struggle against extinction, a Jewishness lived in the shadow of death?"[90] He laments that "the ready-made containers of nation-state and blood-tribe" have obscured "the ritual and song that made our ancestors tremble; the texts they pored over by candlelight; the values that girded their footsteps; the secular Jewish theatre, dance, and poetry that enflamed their hearts; the pious traditions of radicalism that gave direction to their days."[91] For Lorber, critique entails self-stylizing in a way that reclaims the complexity of diasporism by challenging both endogamy and Zionism. American post-Zionist or postethnic Jewishness, therefore, is not merely an outcome of increasing assimilation into Americanness, intermarriage, and the construal of Jewishness as choice; it is also, crucially, the result of grappling with Jewish violence.

Ethical outrage at such violence motivates Jewish critics to interrogate, unlearn, and reimagine their identity and tradition because—although they resist the Jewish establishment—they do not want to stop being Jewish, which requires them to reimagine Jewish ethics and rewrite Jewishness through the mechanisms of moral batteries and shocks as joyful and enchanting rather than tragic and defensive. Their outrage is chiefly directed at the perceived failures and silencing patterns of Jewish leadership outside Israel. But some moral leadership has emerged. The first is the kind that emerged from the grassroots in the form of a movement of Jewish critics. The second is the prophetic outcry from established religious authorities such as Lerner, Rosen, and Walt. The following section examines these prophetic voices.

The Prophetic Mode

"To actually stand in solidarity with Palestinians would amount to communal heresy." Here, Brant Rosen—who eventually resigned from his leadership of a congregation in Evanston, IL, before becoming the rabbi of the innovative, non-Zionist Tzedek Chicago—describes his experience in a collection of blog posts, *Wrestling in the Daylight*.[92] But he eventually felt obliged to challenge Zionist interpretations of Jewish identity and history by retrieving and articulating a different understanding. Consistent with my findings that major Israeli military operations propelled many to join JVP, INN, or equivalent organizations, Rosen's outrage was finally provoked by the images emerging from Gaza and the West Bank.

After years of questioning the Zionist assumptions that inform the American Jewish establishment's positions on Israel and Israeli policies and its mechanisms for managing dissonance, Rosen finally went public with a post on his blog, *Shalom Rav*, during the early stages of Operation Cast Lead in Gaza (2008–2009). Titled "Outrage in Gaza: No More Apologies," the post opens with outrage: "The news today out of Israel and Gaza makes me just sick to my stomach. . . . I don't buy the rationalizations any more. I'm so tired of the apologetics. How on earth will squeezing the life out of Gaza, not to mention bombing the living hell out of it, ensure the safety of Israeli citizens?"[93] Rosen ends this initial post with a pointed question: "There, I've said it. Now what do I do?"[94] Part of the reason action has been difficult to contemplate is that Rosen realizes that he speaks against the Jewish mainstream's convention. Yet he recognizes that he must speak up because he holds a leadership position within the community.

Rosen's blog post generated heated discussion. One commenter cited Zechariah 4:6, "Not by might and not by power, but by my spirit, said the Lord of Hosts," to affirm Rosen's outrage and the need to articulate a specifically Jewish response to the Israeli attacks on Gaza.[95] Another commenter wrote: "I'm so happy that the synagogue I grew up in now has a rabbi willing to openly support the Jewish values I thought I'd learned."[96] Critics also responded. Arlene, writing from Israel, asked: "Have you ever decried the killing by the Palestinian Authority of so-called collaborators? Have you ever expressed concern about the fact that the PA does not allow freedom of the press?"[97] Here, she appeals to a familiar mode of justification embedded in orientalist tropes. Similarly, another critic wrote: "The people of Gaza sowed the seeds of terror when they elected Hamas, and now they are reaping the whirlwind. I feel no sympathy for them." The violent implications of Israeli policies are deemed justifiable because of supposed Palestinian violence. Yet Rosen could no longer employ such technologies to reduce his own cognitive dissonance and sense of ethical outrage. He continued to struggle with the morality of Israeli actions.

"Thank you for sharing your very honest outrage and grief," a commenter named Elaine wrote to Rosen. Responding in a "Jewish" fashion, she continued: "If it is the traditional Jewish custom to tear one's garments upon hearing of a death, then perhaps this can also be understood as a call to tear down the pretenses by which we rationalize the violence that leads to those deaths."[98] Lynn, another commenter, agreed with Elaine: "We should sit *shiva* . . . mourning the death of innocent Palestinians; the deaths of innocent Israelis; the death (for some) of a dream of an Israel that is a 'light unto the nations.'"[99] Lisa K. wrote: "I just wanted to thank you, from the bottom of my heart, for truly being a Jewish leader and speaking out when the establishment has such strong forces to silence us. You provide me with the invaluable spiritual reassurance that my moral compass is on track."[100]

Rosen's *Shalom Rav* blog became a space where debates both clarified and deepened the ethical outrage concerning Israeli practices, the Zionist paradigm itself, and the intensifying cognitive dissonance between American sensibilities and Jewish-Zionist *habitus*. Ethical outrage is not mere raw emotion but rather amounts to intentional "cognitive activities." The ethical outrage of Jews illumines how emotions themselves are, as Richard B. Miller writes, "rule-governed and depend on a wider system of shared meanings"[101] that can be disrupted and reconfigured by moral shocks.

The exchanges in *Wrestling in Daylight* indicate that some Jewish activists and critics were simply waiting for someone like Rosen to articulate for them—employing his religious and communal authority as well as his literacy in Jewish textual resources—inconsistencies between the conventional narrative and the realities on the ground. It was not the case, however, that Rosen's leadership (or that of other rabbinic "voices in the wilderness") was the impetus for the social movement, though leaders (religious or otherwise) are often highlighted as exemplars who lead their communities through processes of change. In this case, the leaders came much later than the movement. But now, in effect, the movement is educating a new generation of rabbis who have been transformed by the movement, as well as by other social justice issues such as LGBTQI, anti-Black and anti-Latinx racism, xenophobia, and antimilitarism.

Affirming the need for rabbinic responsibility in the midst of Operation Protective Edge, Magid, who is a rabbi as well as a Jewish studies scholar, lauds the initiation of an intra-Jewish conversation involving rabbinic dissent and outrage about the deaths in Gaza. However, he raises a critical question: Where were these rabbis during the decades of occupation, humiliation, house demolitions, land confiscation, and "administrative detention," which requires no habeas corpus, all of this in the name of the Jewish people?[102] This line of questioning illuminates the convenience of suddenly speaking out against obviously unnecessary violence, all the while sidestepping a substantive discussion of the root causes of the escalation in Gaza: decades of Israeli occupation. "Standing in righteous indignation only when one sees corpses of women and children lying in the streets of Gaza is troubling. This terrible mess, the fault of both sides, did not happen in a vacuum. It is the cumulative effect of decades of terrible policies and bad behavior."[103] It also illuminates the subordination of Jewishness to the apparent demands of realpolitik.

Magid's ethical outrage targets the failures of Jewish leadership. "Rabbis are not lawyers," he continues. "Their job is not to justify their 'clients'' behavior by showing us how badly the other side is behaving. . . . The prophets were not obsessed with the evil of the other side."[104] Like Arendt, Magid is particularly upset about the wrongs committed by his own community. Like Yuli and Yuda, he appeals to the tradition of Jewish social justice activism epitomized by Abraham Joshua Heschel. "He would be at the weekly protests against house demolitions in the Sheikh Jarrah neighborhood [of East Jerusalem] just as he marched on Selma." Here, Magid echoes the activists' own refiguring of their Jewishness through the retrieval of a historicity that conveys Judaism as a tradition of social justice activism. This retrieval further furnishes the ethical outrage and propels American Jews to shift their orientation from Zionism to diasporism and challenge the complicity of the Jewish establishment with the radical religious and nationalist Israeli agenda.[105]

The Knesset's March 2017 legislation denying entry to foreigners who support BDS and subsequent barring of Rabbi Alissa Wise of JVP from a flight to Tel Aviv, however, did mobilize over 200 rabbis, cantors, and rabbinic students to sign a protest letter.[106] Not all the signatories are supporters of BDS, but they came together in their reaction to the prevention of a rabbi from entering Israel. Of course, this "travel ban" is highly consistent with the patterns of silencing discussed in earlier chapters, but in 2017, it finally reached the point of absurdity. Rabbi Laurie Zimmerman, one of the letter's authors, writes that the debate over BDS is "controversy for the sake of heaven," quoting, as does the letter, from Pirkei Avot (a compilation of rabbinic ethical teachings) 5:17. "It is a controversy that could lead to vigorous discussion and deep self-reflection about the obligation of American Jews to speak out against Israel's policy toward the Palestinian people."[107] She also remarks that moral leadership and impetus now derives from the grassroots and the younger generation's disappointment with its elders: "As I watch a generational shift occurring in our communities, with increasing numbers of young Jews appalled by Israel's harsh policies toward the Palestinian people, I have noted how many of them are baffled by the larger community's unwillingness even to discuss nonviolent approaches to create social change. . . . But they won't be silenced. They are speaking up, and older Jews are beginning to listen."[108] This is an outcome of critical caretaking driven by and embedded within conceptions of tradition rooted in Reconstructionist and Reform currents. However, at the same time, the work of refiguring Jewishness unfolds through solidarity with Palestinians and indignation against injustice and Jewish complicity in such injustice.

My interviewees struggled to interpret this unprecedented moment in Jewish history when Jews must stand in solidarity with the victims of Jewish power. This is what is meant by post-Zionist theology, which is the upshot of relational critical caretaking. Simply put, activists do not care solely about Jews as the destination of their moral commitments or, conversely, the rest of humanity and social justice in general; instead, they focus specifically on the victims of Zionism. What does it mean, however, to channel Heschel's legacy? Here, we shift from what Judaism is *not* to what Judaism *is*, reimagined through solidarity. In doing so, we revisit the earlier discussion of how the critique of Jewish Constantinianism through the selective retrieval of tradition carries a reparative but also supersessionist potential.

In her "Introduction" to her father's *The Prophets*, Susannah Heschel writes about his experience of accepting Martin Luther King Jr.'s invitation to join the 1965 voting rights march from Selma to Montgomery. "The greatness of that Selma march continues to reverberate because it was not simply a political event, but an extraordinary moral and religious one too. For my father, the march was a deeply spiritual occasion. When he came home, he said, 'I felt my legs were praying.'"[109] Abraham Joshua Heschel's participation in the march reflected his understanding of the prophets as "not simply biblical figures . . . but models for his life." For him, the significance of the prophets "was not the content of their message, but the kind of religious experience they exemplified."[110] Articulating the prophetic in terms of a disembodied message functioned in supersessionist ways to order the Hebrew Bible hierarchically, connecting the prophets' message to Jesus's, while discounting their personalities and embodiment[111] and perhaps even their connection to Zion. Heschel's conception of the prophetic as a bodily mode that involves emotional engagement animates his notion of "divine pathos," relaying his view of God, contra the Aristotelian tradition, as "'the most moved mover.'"[112] This view of "divine pathos" informed his solidarity with African Americans, his friendship with King, and his opposition to the Vietnam War.[113] "Prophecy," he wrote, "is the voice that God has sent to the silent agony, a voice to the plundered poor, to the profane riches of the world."[114] His only regret, Heschel later wrote, was that "Jewish religious institutions have again missed a great opportunity, namely, to interpret a Civil Rights movement in terms of Judaism."[115] Palestine solidarity, however, offers the space for precisely such an opportunity. Praying with one's legs constitutes, therefore, a distinct form of spiritual practice when marching with another also entails interrogating and relentlessly atoning for one's own responsibility. In the midst of such relationality, Jewishness itself is refigured. Clearing paths and cleaning caves in Sarura at the Sumud Freedom Camp felt, for many of my fellow participants, like a concrete actualization of relational critical caretaking.

Reimagining Jewishness, as this chapter has suggested, involves a complex retrieval of the prophetic tradition, demanding transformation through reckoning with one's complicity and with the violent meanings of tradition. This reckoning, however, can occasionally tend toward supersessionist readings of tradition, shaped by Christian histories of interpretation. This happens, for instance, when attempts at rescripting Jewishness appeal to disembodied conceptions of the prophetic to counter the physicality and ethnocentricity of the Zionist project. Ellis's use of the Christian label of Constantinianism, for instance, shifts the discussion of the prophetic from divine pathos to cognitive propositions.[116] He highlights that a post-Holocaust theology of libera-

tion needs to confront Jewish power and relinquish conceptions of Jewish innocence. Such confrontation requires drawing non-chauvinistic conclusions
from the history of Jewish suffering and foregrounding the ethical threads
of the Jewish tradition. Only through such cognitive retrieval and attendant
solidarity work, he stresses, can Jews themselves be liberated from their en-
slavement to a narrative of power and oppression. A Heschelian prophetic
impulse, in distinction, returns to (rather than overcomes) the Hebrew Bible
in a non-sanitized manner through critique and embodied actions. Ayelet
Wachs Cashman, for instance, wrote:

> One of the many ways that I brought Judaism to that space [the march from
> Charlottesville to Washington, DC, to protest white supremacy in 2017]
> is with Jewish texts and songs. Whether praying *Tfilat Haderech* (Traveler's
> Prayer) in Emancipation Park, teaching *Olam Chesed Yibaneh* off the side of
> some highway, or singing Kiddush in a Mexican restaurant in central Virginia,
> my traditional Jewish prayers were present on this march. Yet these texts took
> on new meanings than they had before this march. These Jewish prayers and
> songs had been rewritten, recontextualized, revolutionized. They will always
> have a piece of this march with them.[117]

This sense of critique as the audacity to confront white supremacy, both
within and without the Jewish community, led Cashman to self-consciously
reimagine the Torah portion called *parashat Ki Tavo*, which conveys the
Tochachot, or the curses of divine wrath, to which Israelites will be subjected
in response to unethical behavior (Deut. 27:15–26). INN invited her to write
a *dvar Torah* on this *parasha*, in the midst of her aforementioned march.
Here, for instance, she reimagined "Cursed be anyone who makes a sculp-
ture or molten image" (Deut. 27:15) as "confronting white supremacy [and]
taking down all Confederate statues, as well as all . . . monuments dedicated
to white supremacists." This connection might be dismissed as an inappro-
priate instrumentalizing of tradition in service of protest. However, such an
analysis fails to grapple with the deeper reasons why she, INN, and other
groups engage in hermeneutical critical caretaking, or why the deployment
of Jewish resources exerts such power on their prophetic activism. Grounding themselves in Jewish resources, histories, memories, symbols, and songs,
they embody a form of prophetic intervention and reimagining of alternative scripts of Jewishness—one that concurrently depends upon and per-
forms critique. The prophetic comes not in the form of a few exemplars,
but in and through social movement contentions, dialogic interactions, and
identity rescripting. The social movement, grassroots, critical caretaking of
Jewish Palestine solidarity and anti-occupation activists, unlike the dominant

mode of post-Holocaust theology of liberation, does not pivot exclusively on the Jewish experience of suffering as the ground for emancipation through solidarity.

The activist space constitutes a multidirectional prophetic sphere where one stands with the other, praying with one's legs, as the other's "other." It is also, of course, a space for speaking truth to the Jewish community with the intention to transform it. Jewish Palestine solidarity activism produces, through the social movement's dynamics, a grassroots retrieval of the Jewish prophetic tradition. It embodies a prophetic pastiche. The many Jews who partook in the civil rights movement may not have understood their movement in terms of Jewish prophetic traditions. Contemporary Jewish critics of Zionism, however, cannot afford to think of their movement in generic human rights terms. Thus, they find themselves grappling with tensions that have long ungirded the landscape of modern American Judaism, between ethnonationalist and communal conceptions of Jewishness, on the one hand, and postnational and inter-communal conceptions, on the other.[118]

To be prophetic, as Heschel understood, is to challenge complacency and indifference toward the suffering of others. He famously wrote: "Few are guilty but all are responsible."[119] The prophetic task, therefore, is to challenge indifference and to generate ethical and emotional indignation, and in so doing, to atone relentlessly for the sins of one's community. Socialization into modernist conceptions of religion risks framing contemporary manifestations of the prophetic in terms of reconnecting to a history of prophetic Jewish actions and "Jewish values" rather than—like Heschel—connecting these more carefully to the biblical narratives of the prophets. Nevertheless, Jewish Palestine solidarity has become a true site of prophetic interruption of complicity and indifference, through its action on the streets, where activists put their very bodies on the line. Like Heschel, the contemporary prophetic social movement challenges chauvinistic conceptions of solidarity. Susannah Heschel describes how, in the aftermath of her father's own losses of many family members, he reflected on the communal experience of European Jews in WWII, and committed himself to ensuring that "never again" would this happen to other human beings. He explained: "What is the task? Not to forget, never to be indifferent to other people's suffering."[120]

As Magid insisted, Heschel—though not an opponent of Zionist developments or of the centrality of Zion to the Jewish tradition—would have certainly shown up for the nonviolent resistance actions in Sheikh Jarrah as he did in Selma. Heschel's words and actions exemplify Miller's "empathic indignation," a key element in the formation of political solidarity across identity boundaries. "Religions," Miller writes, "have bases for cultivating feelings of political solidarity with those who are justifiably aggrieved, and they serve the wider public by drawing on those resources to cultivate dispositions and fellow-feeling among their adherents to build ties with strange bedfellows."[121] Prophetic resources, furthermore, provide "strong bases to fuel social criticism within and among groups bound together in political solidarity."[122] INN's conception of ethical solidarity is rooted in grassroots critical caretaking. It thus requires seizing upon what Heschel lamented as a missed opportunity during the civil rights era: a broad realization of the significance of this moment of protest in terms of connecting to the Jewish prophetic tradition.

INN retrieves Rabbi Hillel's three questions—If I am not for myself, who will be for me? If I am only for myself, what am I? If not now, when?—amid a crisis of authority, to call for transformative critical caretaking in an effort to save the Jewish soul from a misguided history of pain and tragedy, and to articulate a vision of solidarity with others. This is, indeed, the obligation of INN's generation. INN sees itself as rooted in the Jewish tradition. The group, as chapter 2 described, was born from indignation at the silence and complicity of the American Jewish community in the face of the assault on Gaza in 2014. INN's frustration with institutional Judaism in the US has only deepened since 2014, propelling the group's commitment to build an anti-occupation movement rooted in Jewish conceptions of tradition. Indeed, the INN logo itself represents the burning bush, "symboliz[ing] our generation's call to leadership in the Jewish community. Just as Moses was commanded to return to Egypt to fight for the liberation of his people, we too feel called to take responsibility for the future of our community."[123]

The transformative work is rooted in an understanding of the resilience of the Jewish tradition, as the commitment of the ancestors to preserve light, songs, and joy in the face of darkness, despair, and brokenness. It is also rooted in the diverse ways in which Jewishness is lived and in recognizing that multiple lived experiences invite, in a highly Reconstructionist mode, reimagining what Jewishness means contextually. "The Jewish tradition has flourished across continents and centuries because each generation of Jews has kept its flame alive by adapting and renewing it for their time and place," INN's website asserts.[124] This understanding of tradition is empowering because it invites a grassroots refiguring amid a crisis of authority. The task of grassroots prophetic transformation, therefore, is to end the occupation also because the Palestinians' lack of freedom cages Jews in their communal trauma and exclusionary interpretation of their liberation. The activists seek to unsettle the tragic through reclaiming traditions of Jewish diasporic joy with singing traditional and rewritten Jewish or Jewishly inflected melodies and songs in protest transforming into a praxis and mechanism of subversion. They reconnect to their Jewishness through joyful singing, rather than only through remembering Jewish tragedies and narratives of marginality. Indeed, songs and singing constitute key dimensions of Jewish protest actions and repertoire. This grassroots prophetic transformation with its challenge to trauma as definitional to the Jewish experience likewise reflects the location of American Jewish Palestine solidarity activists in changing universalizing conceptions of the Holocaust as an event in Jewish history. INN's meaning-making agents from the grassroots see themselves as constituting a generation "born wandering in the desert" and thus are particularly situated to emerge joyfully and with an enhanced sense of self-love out of "our people's trauma in order to move us toward the ongoing promise of liberation." Liberation is the destination, *not* Zion.

Conclusion

Certainly, the grassroots social movement of the younger generation of American Jews accounts for the vibrancy of contemporary hermeneutical critical caretaking. Alternative leaders such as Rosen became influential within the movement because they challenged the complicity of rabbis and scholars with the logic of Constantinian Judaism. However, the process of religious innovation is participatory and broad based, not the result of a single, exemplary, prophetic leader. The religious authority of the rabbis does not stand outside the social movement of non-Zionist Jews; instead, it is intricately related to dynamic contention and identity (re)construction.

   This is not to suggest a reductive or instrumental understanding of the role of religious hermeneutics. It is to underscore that the religious meanings participating in critical caretaking are not simply available for retrieval outside the relational ethical discourse of the movement. Hence, critical caretaking is thoroughly relational, a point that suggests religious innovation is a multiperspectival process spanning contested social fields. The movement of Jewish Palestine solidarity activists channels Heschel's prophetic mode and capacity to reject exclusionary narratives of solidarity. For Heschel, the prophetic is intimately connected to his mysticism and the Kabbalistic Hasidic view of good deeds as mechanisms for the release of divine sparks from the evil of racism.[125] Like Heschel, Jewish Palestine solidarity activists recognize that Jewish liberation is bound up with others. "The tragedy of Pharaoh," Heschel told white Americans in 1964, "was the failure to realize that the exodus from slavery could have spelled redemption for both Israel and Egypt. Would that Pharaoh and the Egyptians had joined the Israelites in the desert and together stood at the foot of Sinai."[126] In an effort to more fully address the question of how critical caretaking serves to refigure Jewishness, I now turn to address the common tactics, innovative spaces, and activist patterns that enable and promote the reframing of Jewish meanings and the emergence of religious leadership within protest and social movement activism.

Employing Communal Protest

Shabbat of Resistance

A central claim of this book so far has been that solidarity movements contend fundamentally at the level of narratives in order to transform them. As one organizer with JVP told me, "The motivation for my activism derives partly from solidarity, but also from an aspiration to see a more just Jewish community."[1] Hila, whom we encountered in chapter 3, likewise explained that her activism derives from her self-understanding as a Jewish person: "I consider myself a spiritual Jew. I am able to separate Zionism from Judaism and I believe in equality. Because I am Jewish, I protest—I am informed by values of humanism, which is the main framework for organizing. The experience of doing solidarity work actually strengthened my Jewish identity. Things are starting to crumble for Israel *Casbarah* and I want to be the voice of morality. I'm hoping that my activism helps in shifting Jewish political thought; I want to shift Jewry around the world as well as end the occupation. My Judaism translates into my commitment to uphold universal humanist values." Hila exemplifies how the relation between indignation and *other*-centric solidarity work constitutes a moral battery, enhancing her sense of self-approval through critical caretaking, reimagining "self" hermeneutically and dialogically and within the activist context of a social movement. Another activist from the Bay Area ended up in social activist circles because of the understanding of Jewish identity she gained from her upbringing in a progressive Jewish community in Santa Fe. Despite a rather conventional Zionist education in the US, her exposure to Israel showed her where her solidarities should lie: "Once I went to Israel/Palestine with a perspective about who is really the underdog here and with a sense that the commitment to the underdogs is so engrained in my understanding of Judaism [I saw that] you have to be on the side of the underdog, the minority, the oppressed."[2] "The

Jews weren't powerless . . . the Jews were not the victims here." This recognition constituted nothing less than a paradigm shift for her.

This process of retrieval, as the previous chapter showed, is often accompanied by careful hermeneutical work. For Aaron, criticizing the idolatry of the state is intricately related to the gradual deepening of his religious commitments:

> Over time I became more observant. I don't identify with the Conservative movement anymore. I consider myself cross-denominational. The more religious I become, the more comfortable I am with being less Zionist. I see my religious identity as a huge motivation. I never had a religious community I strongly identified with until I started engaging with pro-Palestine Jews. We had a positive Jewish identity. From a religious perspective, conflating Judaism with Israel is very dangerous; it is idol worship. You don't have to believe in the state to be Jewish, but worshipping a state isn't a replacement for morality. I read lots of pro-Israel arguments that [Israel] is instrumental for Jewish survival. It is important to care about Jewish continuity. I am afraid that the more blood Jews will have on their hands, this continuity is under threat— this is a huge motivation for me as well. Similarly, I am motivated by the tradition of Jewish social activism, but more deeply by a morality embedded within Jewish culture.[3]

Aaron's reflection expresses resentment toward Israel's militarism and hegemony and a sense that this "Constantinian" chapter in Jewish history has, ironically, come to threaten the survival of Jews and the Jewish tradition. Aaron's remarks also illuminate how, in a context where conventional denominational spaces are constraining or silencing, social activism has transformed the way he relates to Jewish communal space. Like other activists, he cites his understanding of Judaism as an ethical tradition as motivating his activism.[4] He therefore suggests a need to retrieve what seems to have been forgotten or derailed in modern Jewish history. This process of retrieval—as we saw especially in chapter 4—is typical of the religious innovation provoked by ethical outrage, critical caretaking, and the social movement's focus on public narrative, translating values (rewritten from the grassroots and through the mechanisms of moral shocks and batteries) into protest action.[5] Another common feature is a resistance to ideological control over religious practice, including mourning practices surrounding the Holocaust.

The appeal to ostensibly authentic "Jewish values," however, often assumes that such values exist in a codified form.[6] Some Jewish activists who otherwise understand tradition as hermeneutical engagement with texts in context nevertheless dispute this modernist assumption. One shomeret Shabbat (observant of the commandments associated with Shabbat) activist told me she reads Torah as a way of stopping violence, of challenging the Jewish people as the prophets had done, and making the ancient texts speak to the present moment.[7] She does so *not* by searching for some ethical "kernel" consistent with a reified conception of the "prophetic" and translatable into secular humanism, but rather through immersion in deep layers of learning and interpretation that span millennia. Resisting their reduction to discrete values, she strives to cultivate deeper literacy in the tradition. She expressed some frustration with the fact that so many Jewish activists lack a knowledge of Hebrew, relying instead on English translations and thus remaining at an introductory level of engagement with the rich layers and methods of Jewish tradition. Though her approach is deeply traditionalist, it nonetheless coheres with the more Reconstructionist norm of Jewish Palestine solidarity in its ethical indignation at the unjust predicament of Palestinians and construal of Israeli violation of their humanity as an idolatrous perversion of the Jewish tradition. The "Reconstructionist norm" alludes to a strong opposition to the language of chosenness and its reinterpretation in the service of ethnonationalism. These activists' sense of indignation is rooted in a conception of justice that is not necessarily or entirely intra-traditional. Indeed, their experiences of moral shocks demonstrate their embeddedness in multiple social fields and the increased incompatibility of these fields with one another. At a time when the American landscape is associated with balkanized identity politics within which Israel advocacy once thrived, this incompatibility exacerbates activists' diminished capacity to rationalize and manage dissonance.[8] Hence, the objection to pillaging and occupying the lands of other people reflects a normative assessment that is not simply taken, ready-made, from the textual and other resources of tradition. Rather, because these diverse resources also contain grounds for affirming such practices, constructive engagement with them requires a historically grounded interpretive process that concurrently constructs new norms.

While more traditionalist approaches surfaced less frequently in my interviews, the language of reclaiming authentic diasporist Jewishness is ubiquitous among these activists. Hila's aspiration to reclaim an ethical, humanistic Judaism that underscores principles of equality and non-Zionism aligns with the broader trend evident in previous chapters. Another interviewee underscored her religious commitments and upbringing within the Reconstructionist current, which relinquished ideas of chosenness and election, yet maintained a commitment to reconstructed Jewish liturgy and texts. "I believe in the importance of seeing the world through a particular lens and I derive lots of meanings from living in a Jewish time, a Jewish calendar," she told me.[9] Her solidarity work was explicitly shaped by her passion for Jewish liturgy, her commitment to a particular ethical message she attributed to Judaism and, like many of the activists, a broader enculturation into queer-trans activism during college. Another Jewish Palestine solidarity activist I met at a JVP-Chicago event told her story of transitioning from a religious Zionism that even resulted in *aliyah* to her exposure to feminist blogs that drew explicit connections between Palestinian and feminist struggles. She abruptly decided to return to the US, where she found other likeminded Jewish and non-Jewish activists who furthered her understanding of the Israeli occupation of Palestinians.[10]

As chapter 3 observed, sensitization to gender critique and feminism constitutes a significant form of prior politicization that has led many Jewish critics to unlearning Zionist orthodoxy. This is not only because of the type of systemic critique feminism offers, but also because, as one participant in JVP-Chicago observed, engagement with feminist critique has led many to see themselves as, in one way or another, "misfit Jews." This suggests, in turn, a broader need to scrutinize various types of marginality within Judaism, including those rooted in heteronormativity and patriarchy, but also those of JOCSM. Indeed, as the next chapter will explore, reimagining Jewishness from the margins and through broad-based solidarity work has emerged as a normative orientation for Tzedek Chicago (henceforth Tzedek) and other intentional activist communities.

Gender plays a profound role in the movement's critical caretaking processes. This role is of course evident in public ritualistic parades, such as Celebrate Israel, where semiotic tensions came to the fore through the dynamics of pinkwashing and misappropriation of symbols.[11] But it is equally evident in other contexts. A reception by A Wider Bridge (an organization dedicated to creating opportunities for LGBTQI people) at the Creating Change conference in 2016, which aimed at cultivating relations between Israeli and North American LGBTQI communities, provoked predictably charged reactions. While the conference led to an explosive protest by the queer left at attempts to pinkwash the occupation, in turn provoking counteraccusations of antisemitism,[12] it also offered the space for an innovative deployment of liturgy. The conference featured a Kabbalat Shabbat service framed as an alternative, non-Zionist, queer Shabbat. Those who undertook this innovative hermeneutical work wanted, as they explained a few weeks later, to think of Shabbat in terms of resistance, not rest. Notably, the service included a feminine version of the *Sh'ma* ("Sh'ma Yisrael, ha-Shekhinah b'Kirbainu ha-Shekhinah Ahat"), employing the feminine name of God and a reading that called for outrage: "Shock us, Adonai, deny to us the false Shabbat which gives us the delusions of satisfaction amid a world of war and hatred; Wake us, O God, and shake us. . . . Let your Shabbat not be a day of torpor and slumber; let it be a time to be stirred and spurred to action."[13] The service continued with a reading of a poem by Samah Sabawi, a Palestinian Canadian writer. The poem describes a profound liberation: "The day I rise / From the ashes of your oppression / I promise you I will not rise alone / You too will rise with me / You will be liberated / From your own tyranny / And my freedom / Will bring your salvation."[14]

The Kiddush at the end of the service likewise affirmed solidarity and a commitment to social justice work, and acknowledged the interconnections among various sites of injustice. "We dedicate this cup of wine to the struggles for justice, dignity and freedom that people all over the world are part of every day," it commences. Next, the Kiddush clarifies the meaning of intersectional solidarity: "Each of our struggles is specific and important both for their own sake and for the strength that each struggle for justice brings to every other struggle. The humanity and dignity of each of us is necessary for the humanity and dignity of all of us." It concludes, "Raise a glass to affirm and celebrate joint struggle toward collective liberation and remind ourselves of our commitment: 'never again for anyone,'" and with "N'varech et eyn hachayim matzmichat p'ri hagafen" (a feminized version of the liturgical verse that reads "Let us bless the source of life that ripens fruit on the vine").

In its emphasis on both gender and non-Zionist interpretive lenses, this innovative Kabbalat Shabbat echoes the work of Fringes: A Feminist, Non-Zionist Havurah, founded in 2007 in Philadelphia to cultivate a specifically feminist spirituality from the "fringes" that is ethically connected to non-Zionism. Before turning to Fringes' innovation, it is important to stress that in the same way in which the contemporary movement of Jewish critics participates in a longer trajectory of American Jewish critique of Zionism,[15] so too is the feminist critique of Jewish ritual and communal meanings rooted in a deep historical context and built upon broad intellectual shoulders. Pivotal for the trajectory of feminist critique and constructive reparative engagement is the scholarship of Judith Plaskow. Plaskow's centrality in cultivating a Jewish feminist ethics and theology emerged from her view of Jewish theology as androcentric and in need of reimagining its very foundations. In a notable response to Cynthia Ozick's "Notes Toward Finding the Right Question," Plaskow's "The Right Question Is Theological" challenges Ozick's focus on halakha or legal reasoning as a mechanism for enhancing the position of women within Judaism.[16] For Plaskow, who rejects Ozick's interpretation of women's marginality within Judaism as only a sociological question, halakhic marginalization is merely symptomatic of a masculinist theology. Thus, this theology needs to be confronted. She subsequently theorized pathways for change that emphasized a rereading of the Torah, employing a feminist lens that destabilizes men's position as normative Jews and renders the invisible visible and the inaudible audible through a critical hermeneutical engagement. This feminist insight for rereading tradition in order to reimagine it and its normative boundaries as one's own resonates with the movement of critical Jews' grassroots critical caretaking and their intersectional focus on the margins and its silences. This process is itself intricately related to activists' pre-politicization on gender, feminism, race, and other sites of critique.

These two threads—Jewish non-Zionism and feminist reimagining of Jewish ethics, theology, and praxis—have not been co-extensive, but their critical force and insights coalesce in the contemporary movement of critics of Jewishness as prescribed and reproduced within Zionist orthodoxy. If Plaskow imagines herself as *Standing Again at Sinai* (1990)[17] in order to generate a "new understanding of God that reflects and supports the redefinition of Jewish humanity [and] a new understanding of the community of Israel,"[18] the young activists of INN imagine themselves as Moses standing again in front of the burning bush, *their* logo.[19] It entails, like Plaskow's, a "redefinition" of Jewish humanity and community but not its theorizing out of existence. "The Bush burns bright but is not consumed," INN's statement conveys, "the fire is not a mechanism of destruction, but rather a force of inspiration and transformation."[20] In its intersectional understanding of liberation, INN returns to the place where the template of Jewish liberation narrative commences as a way of rewriting its meaning, decentering its apparent ethnocentric foundations, and reconfiguring Jewishness through an active reparative grappling with the silences and suffering produced by Jewish sinfulness and violence. Plaskow returns to Sinai, the site of the Covenant, in order to similarly decenter and deconstruct the patriarchal underpinnings of tradition by asking, "What would have been different had the great silence been filled?"[21] This is the silence of women who lived but were made inaudible and invisible. Reimagining Jewishness through listening to silences amounts to denaturalizing common sense and apparent ontologies because "a silence so vast tends to fade into the natural order," Plaskow explains.[22] Yet "silence," she continues, can become "an invitation to experiment and explore."[23] The contemporary movement of critics engages in such innovative exploration in articulating a non-Zionist Jewishness that is also necessarily feminist and non-binary and also deeply relational and thus *other*-centric, as exemplified by the alternative queer Kabbalat Shabbat at the Creating Change conference.

Fringes, likewise, sees itself as a liturgical laboratory, whose databases of liturgy and poetry it makes widely available, especially to Jews whose activism on Israel/Palestine has estranged them from other communities, so they can launch their own intentional communities and havurot.[24] The name itself refers to the tzitzit of the tallit, or prayer shawl. "Far more than just trim," Fringes' founding statement reads, "it is the fringes that define the tallit, that make fabric into a sacred garment. Fringes dangle on the edges, are sometimes stepped on, yet are necessary to define the boundaries of community, and are brought together at the Sh'ma as an act of love and courage."[25] Beyond Fringes' explicit non-Zionism, it represents a quest for spiritual and religious alternative scripts that go beyond members' otherwise activist location as feminist non-Zionists.

Fringes' innovative Shabbat of Solidarity service exemplifies the explicit aspiration—widely articulated by the activists I interviewed and observed—not only to connect their spirituality or religiosity to social justice actions and agendas, but to actively rescript an alternative community within the context of critical, counter-hegemonic social movement work. The Shabbat of Solidarity embodies queer, feminist, and non- or post-Zionist aspirations to imagine a different kind of a Jewish community.[26] It suggests that reimagining Jewishness can be analyzed not only as a tool of social movement, but non-reductively on its own terms.[27] It thus invites attention to actual knowledge about Judaism and Jewishness produced through and within the complex terrains of the social movement. The Jewishness that emerges from the matrix of Palestine solidarity not only deconstructs Zionism's hold on the Jewish imagination but also and concurrently challenges patriarchal and heteronormative frames. Moreover, it invites a deeper investigation of how Jews have been constructed as white, and of the relevance of this history to the movement's commitment to various struggles against racism. In each of these cases, the hermeneutical mechanisms for de-Zionizing Jewishness are rooted in a grassroots practice of critical caretaking that destabilizes exclusionary conceptions of Jewish liberation while also constructing new normative boundaries for what Plaskow calls "Jewish humanity."

De-Zionizing, certainly, is a key area for hermeneutical work as Jewish activists seek to constructively refigure their Jewishness outside the reigning paradigm. One activist who described her upbringing as "Jewish-Buddhist" formed a small community of other Jewish college students who studied Jewish liturgy and worked to denationalize it.[28] Although political positions concerning Israel-Palestine were not explicitly discussed in this forum, they were assumed. The Jewish members of the community were all active in other campus-wide Palestine solidarity activism, but felt they needed to supplement this activism with Jewish learning. This is because they recognized that Jewish Palestine activism entails a complex reworking of the meanings of Jewish identity, with implications for de-Zionizing ritual practice and liturgy. Liturgy, as the previous chapter emphasized, is reimagined through grassroots critical caretaking, carried out by meaning-making agents. The following section turns explicitly to how liturgical and ritualistic innovation not only serves as protest repertoire but also functions to rescript Jewishness beyond the movement's immediate objectives.

Ritual, Protest Liturgy: Religious Innovation through Protest

"Symbols of revolt," Sidney Tarrow wrote of the civil rights movement, "are not drawn like musty costumes from a cultural closet and arrayed before the public. Nor are new meanings unrolled out of whole cloth." Instead, "the costumes of revolt are woven from a blend of inherited and invented fibers into collective action frames in confrontation with opponents and elites."[29] This fluid conception of the movement's activists as producers of meanings (though never *ex nihilo*) allows for a non-reductive analysis of the causal forces of identity and ideology in articulating the movement's public narrative. Alternative counter-hegemonic ideas are not simply available for retrieval from a "cultural closet." For many Jewish activists, reclaiming their Judaism involves reinterpreting Jewish history and culture as an uncompromising commitment to the oppressed and to challenging oppressive structures. This prophetic critical caretaking is rooted in traditional histories, and cross-fertilized with resources from multiple social fields. Many of the Jewish activists I interviewed engaged in hermeneutical work grounded in their own facility with Jewish traditions and histories. This chapter elaborates on the previous chapter by attending to intentional efforts at transforming the American Jewish landscape and communal meanings from the grassroots. The grassroots process generates new forms of religiocultural and historical literacy as well as new sites of authority. This amounts to an intentional effort to prefigure novel meanings of Jewishness whose newness is often framed in terms of reclaiming a kernel that had been obscured by the ascendance of Zionism(s) as a hegemonic script.

One mechanism for reimagining or reclaiming alternative Jewishness is the work of groups like the JVP Rabbinical Council, which, as its self-description reads, "has come together to speak out on behalf of justice for *all* peoples in the Middle East."[30] The Rabbinical Council consists of a network of rabbis, cantors, and rabbinical students who employ their fluency in the tradition in order to innovate and de-Zionize liturgies, textual interpretations, communal praxis, and normative commitments. Their aim is to transform the Jewish community through de-Zionization, and their methods are hermeneutical. These involve both intra- and inter-communal outreach, including interfaith intersectional work[31] and efforts to inform mainstream rabbis about injustices related specifically to the Israeli occupation of Palestinians. The Rabbinical Council engages in mobilizing grassroots activism as well as lobbying Congress.[32] The Council produces alternative Jewish liturgies for holidays, which also include calls for action. Indeed, many of these liturgies are enacted as explicitly Jewish protest. This hermeneutical work serves not only to inform the call for action and solidarity, but also to fundamentally reshape American Judaism from the grassroots and the margins.

But before turning to the liturgical aspect of protest, which can be understood bi-directionally as either a protest that refigures liturgy, or a liturgical reframing that deepens ethical outrage and commitment to social justice work, it is important to highlight other spaces where the hermeneutical mechanism informs discursive relational critical caretaking. Rabbinic blogs, such as *Shalom Rav*, where Brant Rosen interrogated his own complicity and rethinking in expressing publicly his break with the Jewish establishment's narrative, constitute spaces for both established and emerging Jewish authorities to engage dialogically in the work of reframing.

Another earlier venue for producing alternative scripts was the now-defunct *Palestinian Talmud* blog of JVP's Rabbinical Council. Here, explicit allusions to talmudic passages offered a pivot around which the grassroots rabbinic voices that emerged on the *Palestinian Talmud* blog expressed the imperative to stand in solidarity with the Palestinians. This blog was motivated by a conscious effort to rewrite tradition relationally in ways that read history against the grain and highlighted the voices and experiences of Palestinians. This constitutes a central mechanism for the reparative process of reimagining Jewishness. It amounts to standing again in front of the burning bush and revisiting the meaning of "wandering in the wilderness," but with the historically specific sense of communal sinfulness and the resolve to be accountable to the suffering and liberation of others. The destination of the Exodus is not, as noted in chapter 4, Zion, but liberation, the meanings of which are now being interrogated multiperspectively. For example, one rabbi activist with INN reflects on *parashat Va'era*—the reading portion from Exodus 6:5–7 where God promises that God will rid Israel from their slavery and, subsequently, "bring [Israel] in to the land concerning which I swore to Abraham, Isaac, and Jacob" (Exodus 6:8)—about the significance of God's preventing Moses from entering the land. The promise to enter the land, for this rabbi, requires a spiritual commitment to struggle against "modern-day slavery and oppression throughout the world." It should not translate into "keeping control of land where only a very specific group of people can find safety and liberation."[33] "I believe," she continues, "we can be the generation that is finally ready to enter the Promised Land, spiritually speaking. I believe we can all get free, but first we've got to join hands together and march forward to justice for everyone."[34] In this rereading of *parashat Va'era*, the rabbi returns to the definitional and foundational biblical narratives in order to reread them in ways that decenter the monopoly and dispel the myopias of Jewish suffering, and conveys what I highlighted in earlier chapters as a sense of enhanced self-approval experienced by the contemporary movement of Jewish critics and anti-occupation activists. They see themselves as the generation that stands again in front of the burning bush, responds to its call to lead, and uses its flames to illuminate an intersectional approach to liberation from slavery. And so they bring to their experience with the "burning bush" the tools of critique, instrumental in making silences audible and alternative scripts imaginable, but also an intra-Jewish supersessionist spiritualizing of the meaning of Zion.

The *Palestinian Talmud* blog's very name foregrounds an aspiration to revisit the rabbinic turn, in which the early rabbis invented Judaism as a text-based tradition, thus shifting the focus of Jewish religion from the cult of the Temple to the Torah and the connected body of synchronic translocal, transhistorical, and intertextual interpretations.[35] Indeed, Daniel Boyarin echoes this aspiration in his probing into the Babylonian (Bavli) Talmud as a key source of lived Jewish meanings before the onset of European modernity. His focus on the diasporic significance of the Babylonian Talmud, most critically, refutes the centrality of trauma in constituting a diaspora and, relatedly, diminishes the significance of organic metaphors about a common origin story traced back to Palestine or Zion. This point resonates with Daniel and Jonathan Boyarin's rejection of nativist Zionist narratives that seeks to authorize a "return" that involves ethnic cleansing and domination of the indigenous population.[36] The Bavli, in other words, provides Jews a shared intercultural identity that avoids relying on an ethnonational story of common origin. The upshot is a move from negative Zionist framing of diaspora (or exile) to a positive valorization of the diasporic as comprising "bonds of language, religion, culture and a sense of a common fate."[37]

There are two versions of the Talmud, and one of them—the Yerushalmi (or the Palestinian version)—is traditionally deemed less authentic than the Bavli, which represents the synchronic, intercultural, translocal, multidirectional, and transhistorical interpretive discursivity that Boyarin valorizes as constitutive of the Jewish diaspora. Despite the yearning to return to Zion captured famously in Psalm 137 and often cited in Zionist interpretations of Jewish history and memory, Boyarin foregrounds the talmudic affirmation and prioritization of Mesopotamia over Zion as a place of abode. Indeed, while the Palestinian Talmud was composed in Palestine or *Eretz Yisrael*, the Babylonian Talmud was composed in what is today Iraq. That the hermeneutical team of JVP and related groups named their online space the *Palestinian Talmud* also stresses the hermeneutical principle of reading the resources of tradition through a Palestinian perspective. The name *Palestinian Talmud*, in other words, trades on the ironic double significance of the name, for here "Palestinian" refers to present-day Palestinians, foregrounding their concrete and embodied suffering in their own diaspora and dislocation.

Exemplifying the *Palestinian Talmud*'s function as a midrashic space, Alana Alpert—at the time a rabbinic student and thus an emerging authority from the grassroots—criticizes the Jewish National Fund's tactic of planting trees to displace Palestinian and Bedouin communities. In her 2012 midrash on Genesis 2:9, Alpert imagines a Tree of Violence in the garden: "The Tree of Violence is placed just behind the Tree of Knowledge, for it only takes effect after you become aware of right and wrong," she writes. "When you eat of its fruit," she continues, "what you have learned to be true will become false and what you have learned to love will turn against you." The focus on the symbolism of the tree, "the most basic human symbol," enables Alpert to shift the discussion to the actual uprooting of trees "as tools of displacement, as facts on the ground, as soldiers in the quiet war against the Bedouin in the Negev."[38] Rabbi Rachel Barenblat similarly engages in a midrash in order to stress violations of the basic human right to water. Referring to Genesis 26:19–21, Barenblat recalls Isaac's restoring his father's wells as well as his quarrelling with herdsmen over the wells. She draws parallels to the current day, asking: "Who may drill, and who only gets the infrequent rains?"[39] This question is followed by a link to a report by the Israeli human rights organization B'Tselem on Palestinian and Israeli water consumption.

While each of these midrashic engagements is motivated by an ethical outrage grounded in human rights norms (not merely a humanitarianism that allows for making moral obligations global), they also offer substantively Jewish responses to Zionism's assault on Palestinian lives and hegemonic hold over American Judaism. If each activist is to remain a Jewish person, then a constructive hermeneutical response is necessary to de-Zionize Jewishness. Thus, JVP's concentrated efforts through blogs and other interpretive mechanisms are not mere instruments of anti-occupation protest but also, galvanized by the force of moral batteries, constitute sites of religious innovation. The constructive effort to articulate alternative meanings is especially evident, for example, in Rosen's *Yedid Nefesh* blog. In this second blog, he moves beyond *Shalom Rav*'s primary focus on social justice issues to an emphasis on poetry, liturgy, Jewish life, and spirituality, more broadly. Yet even here, each of these meditations fundamentally confronts Zionism for its violations of Jewish values, which are themselves construed through the modernist impulse to recover an authentic kernel and an alternative conception of tradition. Indeed, the midrashic hermeneutical turn draws self-consciously on extra-traditional as well as intra-traditional resources. Hence, articulating the process of critical caretaking as deeply relational is not simply about choosing the "prophetic" option from the "cultural closet" for enacting one's Jewishness. It involves a fundamental reattunement to the prophetic through extra-traditional and human rights–oriented ethical indignation, interrogation of their own complicity (and responsibility) as Jews, and processes of alternative meaning-making. The latter often requires returning to the definitional memories and narratives of Jewishness in order to rescript them relationally and intersectionally.

As is now clear, a key site of Jewish Palestine solidarity activism is its reimagining of Jewish liturgy and the meanings of holidays. For example, Rosen's prayer for Tu B'Shvat in 2016 (used also in Tzedek's Tu B'Shvat Seder[40]) employs the metaphor of sprouting plants to illumine the "inevitability of liberation." It reads: "New life is returning / Sprouting through cracks in the concrete / blooming out of villages long buried / and homes demolished." The reference to budding life evokes the resilience or steadfastness of the oppressed: "Like the almond blossoms spreading across the hills / like the olive trees standing steadfast in rocky soil, new life is rising / And soon, so very soon / the land will open its arms / to welcome you home." The destructive images of demolitions and buried homes serve to de-Zionize Tu B'Shvat by recontextualizing its images of "resurrection," foregrounding those who have steadfastly endured the abuse of their land and destruction of their homes: "New life is stirring / Can't you feel the blood coursing once more / through awakened hearts?" The final lines resolve the tension and anticipate a liberatory moment: "And soon, so very soon / the land will open its arms / to welcome you home." Here, Rosen subverts (or transvalues) the meaning of Tu B'Shvat within Zionist praxis by highlighting its colonial dimensions through a relational justice lens, and retrieving its ethical impulse about rebirth. Crucially, he directs this liberationist emphasis toward the victims of Zionism, "the olive trees standing steadfast in rocky soil."[41]

In another blog post, titled "Reclaiming a Tu B'shvat of Liberation," Rosen reflects on historical variations of marking this "New Year for the Trees," which also denotes a general celebration of nature. In the contemporary context, however, the challenge is to "decouple Tu B'shvat from [the] destructive legacy of colonialism and disenfranchisement." Since the emergence of political Zionism, Tu B'Shvat has been increasingly associated with the effort of the Jewish National Fund (JNF) to cover the land of Israel/Palestine with pine trees, creating "facts on the ground." Cantor Michael Davis similarly remarks that "it is deeply symbolic . . . that the early-20th-century Eastern European settlers chose a non-native, barren tree. Symbolically and in a real sense, this foreign tree displaced the olive trees of the indigenous population."[42] This Zionization of the holiday, Rosen underscores, "led to tragedy for the Palestinian people." Rosen's effort to decouple this "harbinger of spring" from its Zionist appropriation illustrates a broader inclination to revalorize the diasporic and to challenge Zionist teleology. For him, therefore, celebrating the holiday of spring during the coldest season in Chicago, when the ground is covered with snow, serves to rekindle its authentic meaning: "While some might think this would be an unlikely setting to celebrate Tu B'shvat, I actually find it quite profound to contemplate the coming of spring in the midst of a Chicago winter. It comes to remind us that even during this dark, often bitterly cold season, there are unseen forces at work preparing our world for renewal and rebirth."[43] The first time I participated in a Tu B'Shvat Seder was at Tzedek on an icy evening. The text, "New Life Is Rising: A Tu B'shvat Haggadah," intended to de-Zionize and decolonize the meaning of the holiday. It drew on Kabbalist interpretations of the Seder, in which eating symbolic foods becomes a redemptive act that invokes "a cosmic Tree of Life." Thus, the ritual itself was conceived as producing an alternative Jewish script with redemptive qualities.[44]

Among the Jewish holidays, Hanukkah presents perhaps the greatest challenge to rabbinic reinterpretation. Lynn Gottlieb finds it ironic that the traditional focus on active nonviolence and the spiritual meanings associated with Hanukkah emerged in the midst of the Roman occupation of Palestine. "The rabbinic sages," she writes in the *Palestinian Talmud*, "framed the holy day as a reminder that our spiritual power comes from remaining steadfast to compassion and good deeds." Once again we see here a (re)interpretation of Judaism in opposition to Constantinianism. Hanukkah, Gottlieb underscores, is about "refusing to cooperate with Roman militarism." Appealing to its central motif of light, she adds: "Yes, BDS has Jewish roots in rabbinic tradition. So, how do we increase light today? By supporting resistance to Israeli state militarism through peace education as well as noncooperation with militarism through BDS."[45] This passage exemplifies the fluid move from textual retrieval to a call for social action. While critics may argue that such retrieval renders the text merely instrumental to the cause of a social movement, many activists in the movement aspire to articulate alternative forms of post- or non-Zionist Jewish imagination that will offer greater congruence among the various social fields American Jews inhabit. "The true miracle of Hanuka," Gottlieb concludes, "is giving public witness to the absolute necessity of putting militarism aside and rededicating our commitment to human dignity as a force more powerful for achieving security and peace."[46]

Gottlieb's midrash reflects broader reinterpretive patterns that thread through various efforts to present deeply Jewish humanistic responses and alternatives to the Zionist readings of Jewish sources and calendrical events. The first motif includes a reclaiming of rabbinical tradition eclipsed by the Zionization of Judaism. The second motif includes the refashioning of Jewish classical interpretations to fit with human rights norms, principles of nonviolent activism, and contemporary challenges such as militarism and struggles against ethnic cleansing, capitalist exploitation, and racism. The midrashim also include a call and prescription for action, be it the act of marking Tu B'Shvat by buying olive oil[47] from Palestinians or by supporting BDS campaigns. To this extent, ritual and liturgical de-Zionizing becomes instrumental to distinctly Jewish mobilization and protest. A hermeneutical mechanism is integral to generating protest repertoire, but liturgical and Jewish refiguring cannot be reduced to the objectives of the broader Palestine solidarity movement. Participation in the broader movement necessitates refiguring Jewish meanings and conceptions of identity, an elastic process enriched relationally through the social movement's activism itself.

For instance, the global call for action framed as a #ShabbatAgainst Demolition offered a Jewish frame for Jewish resistance to imminent demolitions planned for a variety of Palestinian villages in August 2016. However, Kabbalat Shabbat can serve as a protest repertoire only because of underlying processes of hermeneutical reclaiming that then led the CJNV (one sponsor of this globally coordinated event) to frame its solidarity trip with the now familiar slogan "Occupation Is Not My Judaism." The call for #ShabbatAgainstDemolition explained, "As Jews, we say emphatically that forced displacement, dislocation, and demolition do not represent our values . . . As members of a people who have experienced expulsion, persecution, and dispossession, we stand with all Palestinian communities facing eviction."[48] The organizers also underscored that this action is in response to a call for help from Palestinians themselves and thus constitutes an authentic act of Jewish solidarity. Significantly, this global action took place on the eve of Tisha B'Av (the Ninth of Av) and involved a reading of a reinterpreted version of Lamentations written by Rosen, foregrounding the tragic ironies of Jews' role as oppressors and demolishers.[49] The prayer highlights Zionism as a source of illusion and self-deception:

> For now we know
> we've been in exile all along,
> comfortable in our illusions
> of homeland security
> even as we wandered mindlessly
> into dark and narrow places.

All "we once valued," Rosen continues, "were mere delusions" about safety and refuge. But on the contrary:

> Our strength was nothing but dread,
> our might, our weakness,
> our victories, celebrations of vanity.

Exposing the Zionist project as a delusional narrative about "home" and "safety" leads Rosen to address explicitly Jewish "culpability / in this destruction, / this ruin that has now / blown upon us." The "us" here appears to refer specifically to a Jewish experience of shame upon realizing the truth about Israel and Jewishly authorized oppression.

> How deep the shame
> that comes with this terrible knowledge.
> How can we not have known
> what others must have known . . . ?
> For we assumed a future of plenty,
> presuming our prosperity
> was somehow our entitlement.

Reading this prayer of lamentation atoning "for our complacency and complicity, / our willful blindness" as a part of a protest action constitutes more than an act of protest, or even of broader Palestine solidarity. It is also an act of reclaiming and refiguring Jewishness, not by reaching out to preconfigured "values" but through a grassroots, active projectionist, agentic process of resignification through a relentless atonement and an imaginative process of standing again in the wilderness and in front of the burning bush.[50]

The prayer concludes with a plea for reclaiming that also constitutes a reimagining of Jewish commitments:

> We are ready to shoulder the blame,
> to accept our responsibility.
> We just don't know
> how to unburden ourselves
> from this awful shame and loathing
> that blocks the way forward.

> For now it is all we can do
> to send forth our pain
> that it might somehow renew our days,
> not as they were before,
> but rather as they somehow
> might be.

Rosen's *Lamentations* signifies something beyond its functional purpose in Jewishly framed solidarity action. It evokes a broader process of challenging, subverting, and atoning for Jewish complicity and culpability. In fact, the process of lament undergirds the mechanisms of unlearning and ethical outrage that are antecedent to protest, even while reinforced by it.

The Mourner's Kaddish and other grieving and atonement rituals have become integral to Jewish Palestine solidarity's protest repertoire, where the subjects of grieving expand beyond ethnoreligious centric boundaries to emphasize the grief of Palestinians, Israelis, and loss of illusions. Consider once more, for instance, the Jews who acted in solidarity with Palestinians during CJNV's 2016 action in the West Bank. They marked Shabbat while in the Palestinian village of Susiya not because it functioned as a protest mechanism, but for their own spiritual strengthening as they worked to reclaim Judaism through solidarity with Palestinians. In an interview for the *Jerusalem Post*, Rosen discussed his experience of marking Shabbat in this Palestinian village under a constant threat of demolition and where Jewish prayers and melodies are typically associated with the violence constantly inflicted by the occupation and its settlers: "It's powerful and redemptive to say these prayers in the heart of territory occupied in our name and say: 'No, that's not the Judaism we stand for.'"[51] Another activist told me about the profundity of reading *parashat Behar* about the rules of jubilee (*sh'mita*) in Sumud Freedom Camp, on the fiftieth year of the occupation of 1967, in the presence of the Palestinian farmer who was reclaiming his land. She will forever read this text through this relational lens, which makes evident just how contradictory the realities of the occupation are to the ethical principles animating the Jewish concept of jubilee, in particular the notion of sojourning in, not owning, the land, and the sabbatical obligation to the poor, dispossessed, and marginalized. Here, once more, we see Jewish praxis functioning in multiple ways, as protest mechanism against the occupation and its infrastructure, but also as a relational "redemptive" refiguring. Liturgical innovation and ritual praxis constitute tools of protest that are already also tools for reimagining Jewishness through the movement's ethical commitments to Palestinians.

Consistent with Gottlieb's tenor, Rosen wrote a new blessing on the occasion of Tzedek's first Hanukkah in December 2015, amid national solidarity actions and protests in response to intensified Islamophobia in the US. The reinterpreted *Hanerot Hallelu* includes a stanza alluding to the intersectionality among sites of injustice, from Palestine and the logic of the occupation to the streets of Chicago where black men and boys are especially prone to brutality: "We light these lights," the prayer reads, "for the spirit of resilience that remains after our strength has ebbed away, for the steadfast knowledge even as the bullets echo repeatedly off bodies lying in the streets that the impunity of the powerful cannot last forever." It concludes by affirming a non-Zionist embrace of Hanukkah's other meanings: "It is not by might nor by cruelty but by a love that burns relentlessly that this broken world will be redeemed." The image of brokenness plays upon the mystical underpinning of *tikkun olam* as a modality of enacting Jewishness in the world. It is effective in reframing Hanukkah's message as a relentless struggle for social justice, rather than a Jewish-centric celebration. The Hanukkah demonstrations orchestrated by JVP's Network Against Islamophobia, Jews Against Islamophobia, and Jews Say No! involved signs in the shape of eight candles and a *shamash* in the center that read "Jews against Islamophobia and racism—rekindling our commitment to Justice." The other candles express protests against racism, anti-immigration policies and xenophobia, and militarism and state surveillance, and call for opening the gates to refugees (see figure 5.1).[52] This protest, which employs Hanukkah's key ritualistic symbol, illustrates how the refiguring of Jewishness relates to the broader terrains of socioeconomic and cultural justice issues in the US as it rearticulates Jewishness as a mode of ethically motivated (not ethnocentric) solidarity.

In her Hanukkah midrash, "Light a Candle for Gaza," Rabbi Alissa Wise,

FIGURE 5.1. JVP's Hanukkah protest (Chicago, 2015) [Photo credit: Jewish Voice for Peace]

like Gottlieb, confronts the sufferings of Gazans. She opens with a description of the launching of Operation Cast Lead on the morning of December 27, 2008, the sixth day of Hanukkah. The words "Cast Lead," Wise tells her readers, refer "to a popular Hanukkah song written by the venerable Zionist poet Chaim Nachman Bialik: 'My teacher gave a dreidel to me / A dreidel of cast lead.'"[53] The Operation ended on January 18, 2008, but only after approximately 1,400 Palestinians had been killed, including 300 children. It was launched during Hanukkah, and its name resonated deeply with Israeli lore. Three years later on the sixth day of Hanukkah, Wise urges her readers to remember the victims of Operation Cast Lead and to reflect on the continuous blockade on Gaza. "This Hanukah," she writes, "we invite you to light a candle for Gaza."[54] Wise follows this invitation to solidarity action with a request that the sufferings of Gazans become integral for the commemoration of the holiday. "As you gather to light the Hanukkah candles with your community and/or family," she writes, "consider adding some moment of reflection on Gaza." This might include a discussion of how Hanukkah, which she understands as commemorating "the ongoing human struggle for freedom" and "shed[ding] light on the dark places of our world," entails a requirement to stand in solidarity with the oppressed. The discussion about Gaza, therefore, must include attention to how Israeli restrictions "continue to rob the people of Gaza of a life of normalcy and dignity," and reflection on the testimonies of Gazans who describe their sufferings under occupation and arbitrary violence. Wise's reflection exemplifies a common strategy: she draws on ethical outrage and empathy with an "other," precisely the *other* whom Jews have wronged, to orient a reinterpretation of traditional texts that emphasizes relation with that *other*. This strategy recognizes that reclaiming Jewishness necessitates a more complex engagement with Jewish resources and histories than simply retrieving the "prophetic" by means of global service works or do-goodism through a secularized currency of *tikkun olam*, as though Zionism and Israel had never happened. It requires a Jewishly embedded process of atonement and cultivation of empathy, pivotal ingredients for ethical solidarity.

Sukkot in 2013 also offered an occasion for protest and a constructive reimagining of Jewish identity. Activists associated with JVP marked the holiday publicly by constructing ritual *sukkot* (temporary huts) outside Israeli consulates in key American cities, such as Boston and Chicago. The public Sukkot was meant to protest the Prawer Plan (to ethnically cleanse Bedouins) by emphasizing what the holiday was meant to commemorate. As they later did with the symbolic menorah in 2015 to protest Jewish complicity with Islamophobia, and again in the days leading to Rosh Hashanah in 2017 with images of honey and shofars to protest Jewish organizations funding the Islamo-phobia industry as a part of the #DeFundIslamophobia campaign of JVP-Chicago, the activists protested Israeli policies by constructing a Jewish space (the sukkah), which is a ritualistic act, and by reclaiming the Jewish meanings of the holiday. The "Stop Prawer Plan Sukkot Toolkit 2013," developed by JVP's Rabbinic Council, explains the significance of the protest: "The holiday of sukkot is marked by constructing and then living in a sukkah—a tempo-rary dwelling, like the ones the Israelites lived in when wandering through the desert. Sukkot remind us of the importance of stability and home. They are open, designed to encourage welcoming in guests, both strangers and familiars. As we gather in Sukkot aware of the reality of vulnerability and the possibility of openness we will strategize how to stop the mass displace-ment and forced transfer of Palestinian Bedouin in the Negev."[55] The toolkit explains that the sukkot "represent Jews' liberation from slavery" as well as "the precariousness of our freedom. The ancient Israelites were freed from slavery, but they didn't move into palaces. Instead, they lived in collapsible homes that were portable, vulnerable and temporary."[56] After establishing the symbolic meanings of the sukkah, the toolkit draws a connection to the predicament of the Bedouins. "Today, in a desert not far from Sinai, another group of people is standing up for their liberation."[57] Once again, the effort to reach congruence among social fields within which American Jews are em-bedded means downplaying the uniqueness of Jewish suffering. Instead of a restricted story of liberation, the narrative functions allegorically.

Pesach (Passover) also offers, through intentional practice, the possibility of universal and humanistic interpretations of the Jewish tradition through a relational justice lens. In 2012, or the Jewish year 5772, following the dramatic flotilla that sailed to Gaza to protest and break up the Israeli blockade, JVP devised its own Haggadah for the ritual Seder. Echoing the ethical impulses behind INN's hashtag #WeWillBeTheGeneration and resting on a deeper tra-dition of social justice–oriented rewriting of the definitional Jewish narra-tive,[58] the Haggadah repeatedly emphasizes that Jews are obligated to side with the underdog, remember their bondage while dispelling the illusion of security associated with Zion, and embrace the aspiration to reach the Prom-ised Land as a form of spiritual practice and destination. A quotation from Grace Paley, an American Jewish writer, sums it up: "I began to understand in my own time and place, that we had been slaves in Egypt and brought out of bondage for some reason. One of the reasons, clearly, was to tell the story again and again—that we had been strangers and slaves in Egypt and there-fore knew what we were talking about when we cried out against pain and op-pression. In fact, we were obligated by knowledge to do so."[59] The Haggadah prepared for Passover of 2015 (5775), in the aftermath of Operation Protective Edge, included a *Nizkor* (a prayer of remembrance): "Even as we give thanks for the gift of being together at this time, we take a moment of silence, in memoriam of all those who we have lost in the past year. . . . We remember those killed this past summer during the 50 days of death and destruction in Gaza." The *Nizkor* then moves to remember victims of police brutality in the US. "We remember the Black people killed in this country by police and vigilantes. Michael Brown, Eric Garner, Yuvette Henderson, Tamir Rice, and too many others."[60] Next, it commemorates trans people who have been killed by targeted violence. The move from Palestine to racism and queer struggles reinforces the metaphorical reading of the Haggadah while also reflecting the intersectional turn of Palestine solidarity.[61] Like those who marked Shabbat in Susiya and who read *parashat Behar* in Sumud Freedom Camp, JVP's Rabbinical Council innovatively reclaims the prophetic, metaphorical, and humanistic meanings of Jewishness by rewriting rituals. Like other forms of grassroots critical caretaking, this offers audacious critique of Jewish complicity with power and oppression.

The Seder plate, consistent with other versions of the Haggadah that emphasize gender justice, is expanded to include an orange, "symbolizing building Jewish community where women, queer, and transgender people are welcomed and recognized as full, valued participants." The plate also contains an olive, "symbolizing the self-determination of the Palestinian people and an invitation to Jewish communities to become allies to Palestinian liberation struggle."[62] In the *Maggid*, or storytelling portion, the response to the question "This olive: why do we eat it?" highlights the olive as a symbol of peace, but also an awareness that "olive trees, the source of livelihood for Palestinian farmers, are regularly chopped down, burned and uprooted by Israeli settlers and the Israeli authorities. . . . As we eat now, we ask one another: How will we, as Jews, bear witness to the unjust actions committed in our name? Will these olives inspire us to be bearers of peace and hope for Palestinians— and for all who are oppressed?"[63] The *Maggid* concludes with the traditional "blessed are you, *Shekhinah*, who is within us, spirit of the world, who brings forth fruit from the trees." The inclusion of both the orange and olive on the Seder plate exemplifies how discursive grassroots innovation within the tradition can be informed by ethical and historical challenges that are thoroughly relational and intersectional. Similarly, the performance of the reinterpreted Passover Seder itself generates new communal meanings and boundaries. Participants in both public and private rituals report relief at finally feeling ethically coherent and truly belonging to a Jewish community. The symbolic acts produce new meanings and, in their capacity as moral batteries, also augment activists' sense of self-approval, not mere representations of alternative scripts.[64] They are joyous in their resistance through rituals that, in turn, causally function as mechanism in the process of reimagining Jewishness.

Clearly, the Seder becomes an occasion to retell the story of liberation metaphorically in order both to regenerate energy for social justice work as a form of spiritual practice and to illuminate the interconnections among struggles against marginality and oppression. The *Yachatz*, the point of the Seder in which the middle of the three matzahs is broken in half, is likewise infused with universal symbolism. JVP's Seder discusses the *Nakba* (or the Palestinian Catastrophe of 1948, also known as the Israeli War of Independence) and the hurried departure of people who would become the first wave of Palestinian refugees. This portion begins with a poem by Taha Muhammad Ali:

> We did not weep
> when we were leaving—
> for we had neither
> time nor tears,
> and there was no farewell.[65]

Once the poem has ended, the *matzah* is broken, with one half hidden as the *afikoman*, which stands as a substitute for the Korban or sacrifice and is hidden for the children of the house to find. "Once the *matzah* is broken," the instruction reads (again echoing *tikkun olam*), "it cannot be repaired completely. Irreparable damage has been done—but the pieces can be reunited."[66] As with the reading of Bedouin testimonies from the Naqab during the Sukkot protest, the breaking of the *matzah* is followed by a recitation of the names of the villages destroyed in 1948. These practices of remembrance and atonement are central to the process of rereading Jewishness relationally, as in feminist methodologies, by foregrounding positionality, invisibility, and silence. The Seder concludes by reciting the plagues of the occupation: poverty, restrictions on movement, water shortage, destruction of olive trees, home demolitions, settlements, political prisoners, profiteering, denial of the right of return, and erasing histories.[67] With this recitation, contemporary Israel becomes the metaphorical Egypt and thus the very source of Palestinian suffering and oppression rather than an embodiment of Jewish liberation. This is, of course, meant to counter the traditional recitation of plagues inflicted (by God) on the Egyptians in liberating the Israelites from slavery. The message aims to generate awareness of how one's liberation story may be intertwined with another's story of oppression—"our freedom was bought with the suffering of the others."[68]

Grassroots Religiocultural Hermeneutics and Remaking Meanings

This chapter has demonstrated how a social movement that offers a Jewish critique of Israeli policies and the American Jewish establishment can, at the same time, substantively expand and alter the meaning of Jewish traditions. It is now pertinent to ask what broader implications this movement has for the study of the connection between religion and socio-political change. In the case of Jewish Palestine solidarity actors in the US, religious innovation is typically motivated by ethical outrage and solidarity with Palestinians. Such innovation amounts to a highly relational and self-reflexive process of reinterpretation and refiguring of the meanings and implications of Jewish identity for their activism. Jews who are outraged by what is being done to Palestinians in their name do not simply stop being Jewish. Neither can they simply declare, as Hannah Arendt did in her response to Gershom Scholem's accusation that she did not love Israel, that they are Jewish as "a matter of course beyond dispute and argument."[69] Instead, their critical caretaking takes root in a focused reconsideration of what it means to be Jewish, a contestation that foregrounds Rabbi Hillel's three questions: If I am not for myself, who will be for me? If I am only for myself, what am I? If not now, when? This process also entails challenging the established communal leadership structures from the ground up. Jewish critical caretakers draw on their historical and religious inheritance and their sociocultural location as Americans to reframe their relations to Zionism, the Israeli state, and Israeli policies, in particular. In some cases, this hermeneutical effort also entails a process of becoming "Jewish" for the first time. Here, the activist context motivates Jews who had professed ignorance about the tradition to become literate (or deepen their literacy) through their activism, even as this very activism constitutes a form of grassroots innovation within the tradition.

A *Tashlich* liturgical ceremony on the first day of Rosh Hashanah 2014, in the aftermath of Operation Protective Edge, illuminates the complex interconnections between protest and religious innovation. *Tashlich* (literally: "you shall cast away") is a symbolic shedding of sins and wounds into a body of water while participants recite biblical passages. JVP explains, "The idea is not that we suddenly get rid of our sins, but that we set our intention to transform them."[70] As in the *Nizkor*, the point is to rekindle participants' commitments to working toward justice: "We are not throwing 'away' our sins. We are transforming their energy in order to renew our commitment to the struggle for justice."[71] This point underscores the activists' confrontation of their own complicity with injustice. It also emphasizes their commitment to transforming such injustice by reclaiming and reimagining the meanings of the Jewish tradition, while recognizing that these meanings are not mere old "costumes" in the closet of tradition, passively and statically waiting to be retrieved. On the contrary, the retrieval of the prophetic, and with it a fundamental commitment to *tikkun olam* understood as social justice, is not merely a choice from a menu of Jewish options. Instead, it conveys a relational process of rescripting. Making Palestine central to the process of refashioning Jewishness is essential for confronting and owning up to Jewish complicity with injustice.

The Jewish Palestine solidarity movement demonstrates the need for scholarly analysis that moves beyond construing innovation within tradition as merely instrumental to the broader Palestine solidarity movement, just another tool among others on which Jewish activists may draw at will. In such a reductive account, Jewishly articulated critique and protest might be interpreted as simply a means of inuring Palestine solidarity to accusations of antisemitism, given the discursive context that often equates criticism of Israel with antisemitism. While arguing Jewishly against Jewish praxis and discourse does carry instrumental value to the broader intersectional effort to advance Palestinian causes, it cannot be analyzed only through the prism of movement strategy or reduced to its objectives.[72] American Jews who are Palestine solidarity activists, for instance, assume an interpretive frame that subverts Zionist ideology and offers an alternative lens through which events are refracted. Hence, refiguring Jewish identity through the mechanisms of critical caretaking is both a condition for and a dynamic outcome of the cultivation of new collective identity. Such relational critical caretaking already informs the process of renarrating Jewishness—both before and through the movement's systematic subversion of dominant ideological formations, in which diagnostic frames identify Jews as victims rather than perpetrators of violence.

Jewish Palestine solidarity activists engage in discursive processes that connect both with the broader, intersectional Palestine solidarity activist network and with the Jewish community and an effort to argue against a prevailing Jewish narrative. Such counterargument is grounded in a reframing of the meaning of Jewishness, a process for which the rabbinic council and the activist blogs are instrumental by fostering relational critical caretaking and articulating collective action frames and public narrative. Critical caretaking and the renarration of identity are pivotal for developing public narrative, or the mechanism of "translating values into action," as Marshall Ganz explains.[73] The activist orientation became clear in our examination of the "calls for action" embedded in performances of liturgy qua protest (as in the above examples of Sukkot, Pesach, and Hanukkah) and in the meditations on

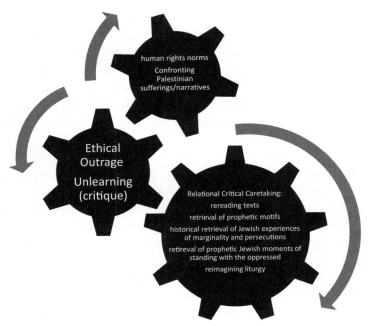

FIGURE 5.2. Reinforcing processes and mechanisms generative of new public narrative and religious innovation

alternative de-Zionized meanings of holidays such as Tu B'Shvat or Shabbat. Thus, cultivating public narrative also involves hermeneutical work that leads to reinterpreting tradition dialogically through interaction with multiple semiotic landscapes. Religious studies offers a crucial contribution to the study of social movements grounded in identity claims: fluency and literacy in religiocultural resources, and an emphasis on interpretive approaches, thick description, and redescription. The production of collective identities through the social movement requires religious literacy and relational hermeneutical skills and fluency. Figure 5.2 illustrates through a set of metaphorical gears the mutual relationships among these processes. The following chapter explores the "outcome" of these mutually reinforcing processes in terms of religious innovation by examining the Jewish script articulated and enacted by Tzedek. The question is not only what religion can do for the movement. I also ask: What does the movement do for religion?

Reimagining Tradition

all we valued were delusions
our strength nothing but dread
our might our weakness
our victories celebrations of vanity
that shielded us from the awful truth
of our powerlessness[1]

Tzedek Chicago

On Friday night, August 7, 2015, I sat in the basement of a Lutheran church in Chicago's Lincoln Park that served as a gathering space for a new, explicitly non-Zionist, Jewish synagogue. Here, a "congregation" without a space of its own has found an occasional resting place in a Christian church, a handful of whose welcoming members were there that Friday, celebrating the emergence of Tzedek Chicago as a "prefigurative" Jewish community oriented by a social justice compass. Since then, Tzedek has met not only in the Lutheran church but in several locations around town, including the Irish American Heritage Center in Irving Park, which would hold major services for Rosh Hashanah, Yom Kippur, and Passover, accommodating about 500 people on location as well as hundreds of others virtually, via livestream. That night, I was in the church's basement to participate in Tzedek's first public Kabbalat Shabbat. Rabbi Brant Rosen, the liberal Zionist turned radical non-Zionist Palestine solidarity activist, led the service. However, the work of meaning-making, reclaiming, and innovating within the Jewish tradition has been a collaborative, communal project from the very beginning, from that exhilarating Friday through the community's continued democratic effort to envision itself beyond mere resistance.

As I stared at the metallic folding chairs, struggling to keep cool in the hot church basement, I knew this was an important moment. It represented the culmination of years of ethical outrage and unlearning of the Zionist axioms of Jewish discourse in America. I immediately noticed the familiar faces of some of my interviewees from the Chicago area amid an otherwise mixed group that included JOCSM. The group included the very young and the old, with some kids running around. My own children were impatient, but I had felt compelled, despite the late hour, to drag them along from South

Bend, Indiana (a two-hour drive). One day, so I told my partner Jason, they
will appreciate having been part of this moment marking the birth of a new
synagogue that explicitly sees itself as not only challenging the Jewish establishment through unlearning and demystifying received narratives, but prefiguring an alternative American Jewish community.

Social movements often prefigure in their practices the society they aspire
to create. At stake here are not only shifting political structures, but the very
meaning of American Jewish identity.[2] This refiguring of religiosity bears a
complex relation to the reframing of Jewish politics and identity: it is both
an outcome and a necessary condition for such reframing. The new Jewish critique cannot be reduced to the movement's efforts at constructing a
counter-hegemony, because the refiguring of Jewish identity is not only an
instrument for advancing the movement's objectives of undoing Zionist teleology and challenging orientalism.[3] It is also about reimagining American
Jewishness along non-Zionist, antimilitarist, universalist, and prophetic lines
in ways that reflect a reparative intra-Jewish contestation of Jewish Constantinianism through *other*-centric solidarity.[4] The creation of a refigured communal religiocultural space indicates a crucial move beyond the movement's
immediate objective of opposing the occupation and promoting Palestinian
rights. While JVP and other similar organizations do focus primarily on how
Jews can contribute—as Jews—to broader Palestine solidarity, Tzedek's prefigurative intention (which it shares with other similar emerging intentional
communities) is to articulate a substantive alternative for American Jews that
goes beyond these activist objectives and beyond the modes of outrage and
unlearning summed up by the slogan "not in my name."

This constructive turn is necessarily hermeneutical, involving innovative retrieval from tradition that is informed by the contemporary context.
Tzedek exemplifies the process of imagining a new collective identity and
an intelligible alternative public narrative. This process involves contentions,
solidarity, and intra- and inter-tradition hermeneutical work, as well as grassroots intersectional analysis and activism. In short, the refigured Jewishness
Tzedek embodies is not a pre-constituted identity. Rather, it is generated
through action and is the product of complex relational and dialogic challenges as well as the contentious forces generated by broader social justice
movements that intersect with and influence Jewish critics of Zionism. The
previous chapter highlighted the mechanisms grassroots prophetic critical
caretakers employ in articulating their self-transformative critique of Jewishness through ethical solidarity with Palestinians. It also illuminated the
agentic force of symbols and sacred texts themselves as they concurrently
represent and construct Jewish protest. This chapter engages specifically with

Tzedek's work of reimagining Jewishness. Tzedek, while a unique development, is nonetheless highly consistent with this broader grassroots refiguring of Jewish identity via ethical outrage and unlearning. Here, I focus specifically on Tzedek because it offers a systematic and exceedingly self-reflexive account of its values, boundaries, and commitments.[5]

Prefigurative Core Values

Tzedek emerged in Chicago in late 2014 as the organic upshot of a growing frustration by American Jewish critics of Israeli policies with the existing Jewish leadership and infrastructure, especially for their complicity in injustice.[6] This intentional American Jewish community is not an outlier, but the most explicit consolidation of the prefigurative community many Jews had already identified in explicitly Jewish spaces of organizing, such as JVP, INN, OH, and CJNV.[7] Tzedek—motivated by an intentional effort to imagine a non-Zionist Judaism that is nonviolent, prophetic, humanistic, universalist, and focused on local and global struggles for equity—is consistent with the broader movement of refiguring Jewish identity through activism and interactions with other social influences. Notably, Tzedek is not a one-issue community, but recognizes the integral connection of its non-Zionism to broader social justice and progressive commitments. It defines these commitments in terms of six "core values," each of which is a positive statement about the Judaism that Tzedek seeks to embody.

Tzedek's first core value is "a Judaism beyond borders," which informs its activism and advocacy "for a world beyond borders," "reject[s] the view that any one people, ethnic group or nation is entitled to any part of our world more than any other," and "bids us to care for the earth that we share with all peoples and all life."[8] This emphasis on a Judaism beyond borders explicitly leads to the synagogue's call for "personal behaviors and public policies that will ensure preservation of our planet's natural resources and its survival for future generations." This chapter's epigraph, a brief excerpt from Rosen's poetic reworking of the traditional liturgy for the Ninth of Av (*Eicha* or Lamentations), conveys Tzedek's view of Jewish un-chosenness by deflating the conception of Jewish suffering as unique, a conception often connected to this liturgy marking the successive destructions inflicted on Jews throughout history. In a way reminiscent of Allen Ginsberg's "Howl," Rosen depicts in his "Lamentation for a New Diaspora" a dystopian vision of the growing environmental catastrophe caused by human actions, failure of political will, and complicity in systems of predatory capitalism, militarism, and racism. Explaining his creative hermeneutical process, Rosen asks, "What if we experienced [Lamentations] not as a dirge of grief for the past, but of anticipatory grief for a cataclysm that has yet to come? And given the current globalized reality in which we currently live, what if Lamentations was a song of loss in response to a cataclysm experienced not just by Jews, but by the entire world?"[9] Exemplifying the view of Judaism beyond borders, he adds: "It's not that I think we should stop acknowledging our uniquely Jewish communal pain, but I do think it's time to admit that our fate as Jews is bound up with the fate of all who live on this planet." And yet, the specific rabbinic theology of "'*mipnei chataeinu*'—that it was 'because of our sins' that we were exiled" at the heart of Lamentations also underlies Rosen's vision of a generic dystopian city (not necessarily Jerusalem). "Not that I believe in a supernatural God that willfully punishes—I don't. And I also don't believe in blaming victims. But I do believe this theology compels us to think seriously about our communal complicity in the misfortunes that befall us. . . . Global climate change, permanent war, predatory capitalism—this is all our doing. We can't pin this mess on God."[10] In their emphasis on communal sins and atonement, Rosen's poetic renditions convey the perpetual and relentless Days of Awe that framed this book's introduction.

This affirmation of Judaism beyond borders connects to another of Tzedek's values, "spiritual freedom," which emphasizes non-chosenness and the internal diversity of the community, where some members "adhere to more traditional views of the divine while others view God as a human expression of our highest, most transcendent aspirations. Others do not define themselves as religious, but identify with the humanist and cultural aspects of Jewish tradition." Several members and frequent guests are Christians whose own pursuit of justice for Palestinians led them to Tzedek. The laxity of expectations about fidelity to Jewish praxis, such as fasting on Yom Kippur or refraining from the use of iPhones and other technologies, is apparent. Often, members will read their portions from their devices and will live-tweet their experiences during services. Such broad flexibility concerning traditional praxis within a Jewish space points to Tzedek's continuity with Reform and Reconstructionist currents, which focus on identifying some ethical kernel, rather than any ritual laws, as the truly normative aspect of the tradition. Accordingly, Tzedek's liturgy typically revises the chauvinistic language of prayers to reflect a more pluralistic and universalist outlook, though the male-pronoun reference to God is harder to theorize out of existence. The community's critical struggle with the ways that heteronormativity and patriarchy are hardwired within prayers and texts is rooted in its recognition that challenging racism by deconstructing Zionism invites critique of interrelated wrongs. Thus, the Tzedek community traverses many of the same paths toward de-Zionization that we have seen in earlier chapters, including politicization on matters of gender, race, and militarism.

Jay Stanton, at the time a member of Tzedek (later also a rabbinic intern), delivered a sermon at the first Kol Nidrei service on the eve of Yom Kippur. In it, he explicated Tzedek's resolve to unlearn "Islamophobia, sexism, transphobia, classism, ableism, heterosexism, Ashkenormativity, militarism, capitalism, and nationalist exceptionalism."[11] He described his choice to focus on Jacob's reconciliation with Esau, rather than the traditional Yom Kippur reading from Leviticus, as signaling *teshuvah*—or atonement—as a process of personal transformation and forgiveness rather than transference of guilt to a scapegoat. In an explicit call to action, in line with the activist approach central to the previous chapter's discussion of liturgical innovations, Stanton urges members to interpret the moment of *Ne'ilah* (when sunset denotes the end of Yom Kippur and the conclusion of the Days of Awe) as an invitation to a renewed commitment: "When Jacob wrestled with the man the night before reconciliation with Esau, he did not let the man go until the man gave him a blessing. Similarly, we can't let God go until She accepts everyone's *teshuvah*, which might be until some people are ready to change. So tomorrow night, let's occupy Heaven. . . . Let all who are hungry for justice enter the gates!"[12] Stanton's remarks display the connections among sites of critique, from gender and Ashkenazi normativity to feminism and Zionism.

Consistent with its goal of reclaiming "anti-Constantinian Judaism," another of Tzedek's explicit values affirms "a Judaism of solidarity," which entails the "tradition's sacred imperative to take a stand against the corrupt use of power. We also understand that the Jewish historical legacy as a persecuted people bequeaths to us a responsibility to reject the ways of oppression and stand with the most vulnerable members of our society." This value informs various activities, including participation in broad-based coalitions combating institutional racism, Islamophobia, and xenophobia. "We promote a Judaism rooted in anti-racist values and understand that antisemitism is not separate from the systems that perpetuate prejudice and discrimination." Two of Tzedek's very first actions were to participate in the movement to save Dyett High School in the South Side Chicago neighborhood of Bronzeville, threatened to be closed like other public schools that cater to brown and black communities, and to support the campaign to establish a long-needed trauma center to serve South Side residents.[13]

The value of solidarity also manifests in Tzedek's commitment to refugees, undocumented people, and MBL. This commitment translates to specific forms of activism. For instance, in 2013, Rosen identified the Ninth of Av as "an opportunity to examine our responsibility in the contemporary tragedies that occur in our world." He later called for "a real communal reckoning over structural racism" following the murder of Trayvon Martin.[14] In 2017, Tzedek observed Tisha B'Av with other Jewish congregations and organizations on the South Side, focusing on the brokenness and desolation of Chicago by reading Lamentations and contemporary reflections on racial violence, police brutality, and gentrification.

Likewise, as a part of Tzedek's tradition of action on the second day of Rosh Hashanah, a group gathered at Chicago City Hall to support the #NoCopAcademy campaign demanding that (Jewish) Mayor Rahm Emanuel redirect $95 million from building a police and fire training center in West Garfield Park to investing in kids' education. Here, Stanton reinterpreted a traditional Sephardi *piyyut* (liturgical poem) for Rosh Hashanah, drawing connections between the binding of Isaac and police violence in Chicago:

> In the season of open gates
> When you blow the shofar
> Bear in mind how we got here
> The binder, the bound, and the altar
> . . .
> Abraham! Abraham! Put down your gun!
> Will this be the year the mayor listens to the shofar's call?
> When will Rahm repent?
> When will he say "Hineni—Here I am"
> In the season of open gates
> when you blow the shofar
> Bear in mind how we got here
> The binder, the bound, and the altar.[15]

This piyyut, recited as a part of an action-service involving blowing the shofar in City Hall, exhibits a Judaism of solidarity that channels its focus to the suffering inflicted on black and brown people by structural racism in Chicago. "At our action," Stanton writes, "the shofar was blown to wake the city and its mayor up to social justice."[16] As Tzedek's active opposition to intersectional oppression shows, solidarity rooted in a conception of un-chosenness is necessarily also antiracist.

The urgency generated by class and race dynamics in Chicago features centrally in Tzedek's services. This is often displayed in original prophetic poetry like that of poet and musician Adam Gottlieb, who in Rosh Hashanah 5778/2017 offered a powerful prophetic supplement (*haftarah*) on "O Sing unto the Lord a new song; Sing unto the Lord, all the earth! Let the skies be glad, let earth rejoice, Let the sea and all within it thunder praise" (Psalm 96). Gottlieb pleaded:

Let the prisoners be freed
Let the refugees return
Let the Water Protectors rest
Let the organizers sleep
Let the truth-speakers read novels
Let the poets write about rivers
Let the rivers fill with fish![17]

The biblical narratives and motifs, even with their legacies of violence, still inform the grammar and symbols of prophetic outcry. They inform calls for social justice, including those that reinterpret the concept of "Zion" as *tikkun olam* or a repair of specific injustices. In the case of homelessness and gentrification in Chicago, this means addressing the displacement of people by greed and racism, whose victims are the "ungrievable," the black and brown bodies on whose backs coloniality was enacted.[18] The prophetic fight back exemplified in liturgical innovation and social justice action resonates with Heschel's notion of divine pathos and his emphasis on the need to pray with one's legs. This legacy animates the activists' decision to fight the occupation with their bodies. Tzedek thus stands in continuity with the prophetic grassroots transformative social movement, demonstrating the relevance of Jewish traditions to the very process of critique and rescripting alternative Jewishness outside Zionist and Israeli emphases on militarism and hypermasculinity, settler colonial and orientalist frameworks, and exclusionary deployment of the Holocaust's memory.[19] Critically, this process does not merely involve accessing the memory of Jewish powerlessness and identifying an ahistorical kernel of Jewish ethics as a basis of activist stances. Rather, it pivotally entails grappling with histories of Jewish sinfulness and complicity with power.

In his sermon on Yom Kippur 2015, Rosen laments the diminishing traction of "our sacred tradition [that] demands that we show solidarity with those who wander in search of a home,"[20] and connects this erosion of value to unprecedented Jewish privilege. His analysis of privilege draws on the African American essayist James Baldwin's discussion of the assimilation of Jews into "whiteness," which the next chapter addresses in detail. Rosen affirms Baldwin's assessment, stressing that "the price for Jewish acceptance into white America was the betrayal of the most sacred aspects of our spiritual and historical legacy. We, who were once oppressed wanderers ourselves, have now found a home in America. But in so doing we have been directly or indirectly complicit in the systematic oppression and dislocation of others."[21] The amnesia that underlies the construction of Jews as white though marginalizing and silencing the experiences of JOCSM is deeply connected, for Rosen, with the perversion of Judaism by Zionism and by Israel's displacement of Palestinians in order to actualize a narrative of Jewish liberation and "homecoming." The sermon's recognition of the enormity of the complicity in multiple crises of refugees and indigenous populations and the interlacing of Zionism with the legacies of settler colonialism once again leads to a call for action. As Rosen explains, the shift from merely acknowledging wrongs to *teshuvah* or transformation (personal and communal) begins "by joining together, by building coalitions, by creating movements. . . . And that is why we've prominently identified 'solidarity' as one of our congregation's six core values."[22]

Tzedek's commitment to solidarity amounts to a retrieval or augmentation of leftist Jewish politics and socioeconomic critique represented, for instance, by Jews for Racial & Economic Justice (JFREJ), founded in New York City in 1990.[23] JFREJ also identified the need to forge broad coalitions in social justice struggles through transformative grassroots organizing informed by the secular Jewish socialist Bundist tradition of *doikayt*, or "hereness," which emphasized that "Jews should root [their] struggles in the places where they live, working for liberation and justice alongside [their] neighbors. It stands in opposition to assimilation, and to both the idea that Jewish liberation is not worthy of struggle, and that Jews can find a separate justice for [themselves]."[24] JFREJ likewise recognizes "the webs of power and resistance that weave together the local and global." Thus, while focused on New York, it "oppose[s] oppression, colonialism, occupation, and displacement everywhere" through strategic solidarity that will enable resistance to "white supremacy, capitalism, and other forms of structural oppression."[25]

Tzedek's participation in the #NoCopAcademy campaign and actions against such wrongs as Islamophobia and white supremacy all constitute *doikayt*. But in Tzedek's work of prefiguring a new form of Jewish community, it cannot simply add the occupation as one more example of how local issues connect to global concerns, as JFREJ tends to do. Grappling with Israel and Zionism, though not Tzedek's only focus, is central to its work of reimagining Jewishness through atonement or *teshuvah* that comes from grappling with personal and communal complicity with the wrongs it has come to recognize. Jewish Palestine solidarity relies on interrogating and atoning for communal complicity not only with the occupation of Palestinians, but also with white supremacy, orientalism, and coloniality more broadly.

Such solidarity relates closely to another of Tzedek's values, "a Judaism of equity," which sees in the Torah an "imperative that there should be no needy among us." This requires "solidarity with those who assert that poverty has no place in a civilized and moral society—and that all people have the right to safe food and water, safe living spaces, health care and education." Solidarity also connects to yet another core value, "a Judaism beyond nationalism." "We are non-Zionist, openly acknowledging that the creation of an ethnic Jewish nation state in historic Palestine resulted in an injustice against its indigenous people. . . . We reject any ideology that insists upon exclusive Jewish entitlement to the land, recognizing that it has historically been considered sacred by many faiths and home to a variety of peoples, ethnicities and cultures." The relation of non-Zionism to the values of solidarity, equity, and *doikayt* was central to Rosen's inaugural sermon on Rosh Hashanah 2015, in which he drew on Marc Ellis's claim that "Constantinian Judaism,"[26] the marriage of Judaism and empire, derailed Judaism from its prophetic profession. Tzedek, therefore, is "intentionally standing down" the Zionist narrative of Jewish meanings by "reclaim[ing] a sacred legacy—a liberatory narrative that has long been indigenous to Jewish life" by assuming clear political stances and engaging in action. Tzedek's non-Zionist stance manifests in its activist mode against racism of all forms. However, to reiterate a key point, Tzedek's aim is not strictly identical with Bundist secular *doikayt*, because Tzedek also seeks to cultivate an intentional spirituality through *teshuvah* and the grassroots work of critical resignification of Jewishness.

Rosen's second Rosh Hashanah sermon at Tzedek likewise focused on the topic of non-Zionism and the celebration of Jewish diasporism. Deliberately claiming the value of non-Zionism "out loud" is important, he explained, because "we *need* congregations that openly state they don't celebrate a Jewish nation built on the backs of another people. That call out—as Jews—a state system that privileges Jews over non-Jews."[27] Subsequently, he reframes the concept of "non-Zionism"—formulated negatively—in positive terms as "diasporism." He argues, echoing the Boyarins, that "Jewish tradition was actually born and bred in the Diaspora . . . as a kind of 'spiritual road map'—a spiritual response to the trauma of dispersion and exile" or a "spiritual prism through which we viewed the world and our place in it." The definitional experience of dispersal of both people and God and the reshaping of that experience into a "spiritual statement about the human condition," Rosen argues, is "the intrinsic beauty and genius of the Jewish conception of peoplehood." Because "we all know the experience of being strangers in a strange land," this experience becomes the ethical foundation for a Judaism of solidarity.

The pivotal experience of exile and dispersion also generated an alternative conception to military and political power evident in the reworking of the Hanukkah script: "Lo b'chayil v'lo b'koach"—"Not by might and not by power but by My spirit says the Lord of Hosts" (Zechariah 4:6). The rabbis' genius, Rosen explains, was their "idea that there is a Power even greater than the mightiest empire," which is why they selected Zechariah 4:6 as the *haftarah* portion for Hanukkah's commemoration of the eventually disastrous Hasmonean dynasty. For Rosen, Zionism amounts to a false messianism: "The messianic ideal is not the notion of Jewish sovereign independence in their ancient homeland. It is the vision of universal redemption: of justice and peace for all." This vision is captured in a song repeatedly sung during Jewish acts of civil disobedience and resistance, "Olam Chesed Yibaneh" ("I will build this world from love/compassion"), which is based on Psalm 89:3 and mishnaic interpretations of *gmilut hasadim* (good deeds) and lovingkindness in the stories of Ruth and the prophet Hosea[28] as crucial exemplars of *tikkun olam*.[29] By contrast, chauvinistic redemptive impulses are highly misguided and inconsistent with an understanding of Jewish liberation as necessarily interlinked with that of others. The "Faustian bargain with Empire" Zionism made in its Constantinian turn betrayed the truth of "not by might and not by power." In doing so, Rosen underscores, it departed from the rabbinic understanding that survival depends not on militarism, "but rather upon 'Torah, Avodah and Gemilut Hasadim'— Learning, Worship and Acts of Righteousness."

The interpretation of Zionism as Constantinian Judaism reaches back, as chapter 4 discussed, to the Mennonite theologian John Howard Yoder's anti-Zionism, rooted in a complex supersessionism. Yoder links apostolic Christianity and early Judaism in ways that render exile, based on his reading of Jeremiah 29:4–7, as divinely willed and as mission. His concentrated effort to recover Christianity from its Constantinian turn led him into a recovery project, interpreting "Judaism *as* Christianity, or Christianity *as* authentic Judaism."[30] For him, the diasporic moment allowed for power to shift "from the political to the pietistic," which is, accordingly, Judaism's (and Christianity's) authentic non-Constantinian message and contribution. Hence, his anti-Zionism is grounded not in a denial of Jews' right to exist and survive, but rather in his view of this modern movement as a violation of the principle of "the separation between church and political and military power,"[31] a subversion of Judaism's diasporic destiny, and its transformation of ethnic identity into a locus of worship and fulfillment.[32] This brief detour to a Christian pacifist critique of Zionism as Constantinian Judaism carries, as Magid argues, reparative potential when put in conversation with intra-Jewish critics of Zionism. It thus constitutes an engagement with the multivocality of tradition that can constructively respond to the Palestinian suffering caused by Zionism's narrative of Jewish liberation. The deployment of the label "Constantinian" within the contemporary movement of Jewish critics often valorizes diasporism in ways that interpret Zion metaphorically and spiritually, recover an authentic essence that can be articulated in terms of "values," and risk a dyadic supersessionist approach that, in turn, coalesces with Yoder's ahistorical interpretation of "Judaism *as* Christianity." To reiterate, however, reimagining Jewishness as non- and post-Zionist entails, for the contemporary moment of intra-Jewish contestation, not only accessing a story about powerlessness and landlessness as a virtue and a source of ethics but also grappling with Jewish sinfulness and violence as experienced by internal and external others. The process of rescripting through the critique of Jewish power and *teshuvah*, therefore, is *other*-centric, deeply historical and multiperspectival, and open to the margins and the silences of Jewish traditions, histories, and memories. The sources of ethical reflection, therefore, are diverse and not contained only within the textual and other resources of tradition. Nor does the process of reimagining give epistemological primacy to earlier interpretations of religious traditions at the time of their emergence, even when trying to reimagine such moments anew, like the INN members who stand again in front of the burning bush and seek to recover the wilderness experience as one about relocating a moral compass and direction.[33]

Accordingly, Rosen's post-Zionist diasporism is influenced by a non-Zionist Jewish feminist outlook, which emphasizes an epistemology from the margins. It radically unsettles conceptions of Jewishness as Ashkenazi and white European by highlighting lived multicolor and multiracial Jewish experiences and imagining, on this basis, various paths for cross-group solidarity in struggles against racism.[34] As the feminist lens makes clear, creating "space for multiple expressions of gender is not separable from space for multiple expressions of understanding of Jewish peoplehood."[35] Tzedek's values thus cohere with feminist and queer critique and other forms of power analysis that seek to interrogate critically Jewish tradition and the historical complicity of Jews with power. Yet once more, Tzedek's aim cannot be reduced to such power analysis, even as it innovates in specifically feminist ways within the tradition.

Tzedek's non-Zionism, in other words, is driven primarily (even if not exclusively) by the Jewish concept of *mipnei chataeinu,* which is awakened through empathic and ethical indignation, responsibility to Palestinians (on whose backs Zionism was actualized), and other foci of alliance and solidarity. Tzedek's work of demystifying Zionism is not the upshot of an abstract analysis of capitalism, colonialism, militarism, gender, and nationalism. Rather, it arrives at such abstractions and broad systemic analyses from the ground up, beginning with the personal, yet intersubjective, and thus communal experience of outrage, mourning, and *teshuvah.* The result is a prophetic commitment to praying with one's legs, spending sacred times such as Rosh Hashanah or Hanukkah on the streets or at City Hall. Tzedek's intentional spiritual community is both constructed through and embodied in these actions. The relationship between religious texts, liturgies, and rituals, on the one hand, and political actions of protest, on the other, is not simply causal. The discussion of the contemporary movement of critical Jews, including the Tzedek community, has shown that tradition is rescripted in and through the movement and its mechanisms of moral batteries and public narrative and that these complex processes, generative of meaning-making from the grassroots, are also interpretive and hermeneutically innovative.

Clearly, the emotional experience of ethical outrage is itself rooted in rearticulated shared norms of egalitarianism that also animate feminist and Bundist critiques of Zionism. However, to be propelled by *mipnei chataeinu*—or to inhabit relentlessly the liminality of the Days of Awe, as Scout Bratt's Kol Nidrei sermon on Yom Kippur of 5778/2017[36] urged—places the emphasis on religious practices of atonement and mourning rather than on subjecting the tradition to impersonal abstract principles and commitments. Indeed, for the Tzedek community, the process of liturgical innovation requires clarity about the basic ethical question: Whose side are you on? One's response, as chapter 1 showed, demands engaging with the interrelated question: Who am I? To effect liturgical innovation through solidarity and emphatic indignation means that renarrating the meanings of communal boundaries is a personal, intersubjective, and relational undertaking. Hence, Tzedek emphasizes moral reasoning as an outcome of intersubjective and relational process. Put simply, the relationship of solidarity with various others, but primarily Palestinians, functions as a moral source for critical caretaking, while this very relationality depends on relentless atonement—itself a form of critical caretaking. Tzedek's Jewish Palestine solidarity exemplifies religion's capacity for disruption, which makes religion an important ingredient in social movement mobilization, public narrative, and identity construction.[37] It also demonstrates that the disruption of *doxa* is itself a site of religious, as well as political, innovation.

Reimagining Jewishness, therefore, is a fundamentally relational process. This relationality plays a crucial role in intentional spaces, whether the prefigurative community of Tzedek itself or online interpretive communities such as the *Palestinian Talmud* and other activist blogs that are reinforced by progressive Jewish venues such as *Tikkun* and *Jewschool,* as well as a handful of radical podcasts.[38] These are key locations for the hermeneutical reframing that grounds discursive critical caretaking. If critical caretaking constitutes a mechanism of social change, it unfolds not only within individuals' own self-scrutinizing outrage and unlearning, but also more methodically through the Rabbinical Council of JVP and similar mechanisms, which innovate and reframe liturgies and de-Zionize (and in some instances also feminize) Jewish meanings.

Crucially, this process of resignification is never simply instrumentalized in the service of protest. Such instrumentalization would in fact undermine the very vitality of this critical caretaking. This became evident in Tzedek's membership meeting at the end of March 2016, which marked the community's first full year. One of the insights emerging from this interactive meeting was that members—many of whom are also active in JVP-Chicago, SJP, and other activist communities focused on Palestine, Islamophobia, racism in America, and other causes they recognize as interrelated—desire spiritual and religious nourishment beyond their social activism and non-Zionist protest, outlets that they can and do seek elsewhere. In Tzedek, some participants underscored, they wanted a community where they could meaningfully fulfill life cycle needs, children's programing, and adult education in Jewish traditions and Hebrew. In a related fashion, others stressed a need for a creative tension between spiritual and ritual activities and activist agendas, highlighting the importance of building a community not only around the principles of social justice.

Others, however, embrace the near synonymy between Jewishness and social justice activism that they hope Tzedek will continue to embody. For instance, one person told me after the first members' meeting that he was terribly puzzled by the discussion of Judaism as "faith" and the "congregation" (another term he used with great caution) as a space for spiritual nourishment. Given his strong connection to his family's legacy of communism and the Bund, reclaiming Judaism means, for him, recovering an atheistic form of social and economic justice activism (*doikayt*). The complex aspirations for Tzedek foreground the point that refiguring Jewishness requires vigorously negotiating the very contours of the prefigurative community. The renarrated community in turn constitutes a source of spiritual nourishment—whether configured religiously or non-religiously—to animate and embolden a Judaism of ethical solidarity.

A veteran exemplar of a non-Zionist Judaism that—like Tzedek—emphasizes solidarity and equity is Rabbi Lynn Gottlieb. She calls, for example, for a high holiday fast for Palestinian human rights through a midrash on the tradition that, based on Psalm 91:15, entails that "the pious . . . fast from dawn to dusk during the Ten Days of Teshuvah" as a means of solidarity with those who suffer. Gottlieb points out the ubiquity of immense suffering: "We mourn the unnecessary loss of life that stems from preventable harm: racial, gender and economic oppression, police violence, military occupation, forced dispossession and deadly conflict." "These harmful conditions," she continues, "deny millions of people the opportunity to fulfil their dreams." To offer spiritual resources to those struggling against systems of oppression, Gottlieb's reflection on her reframed traditional fast is followed by hyperlinks to various actions one can take to stop this acute violation of human rights. Gottlieb's call for *ta'anit* (fasting) is highly intersectional in its solidarity. She declares that her public fast is also meant to "give public witness to the persecution of Native Americans, African Americans and Latinos by the United States in the form of police brutality, the war on drugs and gangs, closing of schools, mass incarceration, the militarization of the border, deportation and economic exploitation." Engaging in such solidarity, she underscores, is what Jews have always done. She explains: "I was 12 during the time of the civil rights movement and the first liturgy I ever wrote was 'what can we do for the movement?'"[39] Regardless of how problematic this narrative of black-Jewish alliance is,[40] she experienced it as authentic, exclaiming: "My reform Judaism education was all about what can we do. We stood in solidarity with African Americans."

Tzedek's Yom Kippur liturgy likewise emphasizes the inconsistency of genuine, justice-oriented solidarity with Zionism. For instance, it adapts the communal *vidui* or confession—the traditional moment in the liturgy of *mipnei chataeinu* where Jews publicly articulate their communal sins—to the contemporary moment. Once the community has recited its complicity in the general American sins of racism, capitalism, and militarism, the liturgy moves to the specific plight of the Palestinians: "*Ve'al kulam eloha selichot selach lanu, mechal lanu, kaper lanu* (For all these, source of forgiveness, forgive us, pardon us, receive our atonement) . . . for the destruction of homes, expropriation of land and warehousing of humanity . . . for a brutal and crushing military occupation . . . for blockading 1.8 million Gazans inside an open air prison . . . for repeatedly unleashing devastating military firepower on a population trapped in a tiny strip of land . . . for wedding sacred Jewish spiritual tradition to political nationalism and militarism . . . for rationalizing away Israel's oppression of the Palestinian people."[41]

This contemporary recitation of the *vidui* conveys Tzedek's aim—consistent with the social movement's discursive critical caretaking and activism—to confront its own complicity with violence, while acknowledging that the Jewish tradition contains rich resources for such confrontation. In particular, the *mipnei chataeinu* motif of Lamentations pushes the community to examine itself and acknowledge its complicity. Atoning (relentlessly) for such complicity becomes a way of committing to actions that promote social justice. Foregrounding the intricate connection of solidarity to non-Zionism thus invites reimagining Jewishness not only through broad power analyses, like those afforded by feminist critical theory. It also centrally demands that such reimagining unfold through Palestine solidarity, a space of constant atonement and critical caretaking. The imperative to promote social justice, for Gottlieb and other grassroots interpreters, is thus definitional to Jewishness. It constitutes its supposed prophetic kernel, which they all seek to reclaim through critical caretaking.

If the Book, Then Not the Sword

The self-transformational aspect of critique also involves confronting the contemporary legacy of Jewish violence. Gottlieb's articulation of a non-Zionist Judaism of solidarity that is informed by intersectional analysis reflects the movement's commitment to nonviolence. Indeed, another of Tzedek's values, "a Judaism of nonviolence," entails "honor[ing] those aspects of our tradition that promote peace and reject the pursuit of war as a solution to our conflicts. We openly disavow those aspects of our religion—and all religions—that promote violence, intolerance and xenophobia." Tzedek thus pledges its active support for "practices of nonviolence, civil resistance, diplomacy and human engagement. Through our advocacy, we take a stand against militarism and colonialism, particularly when it is waged in our name as Jews and Americans."[42]

The hermeneutical work necessary for Jewish critical caretaking, therefore, is not restricted to engagements with texts, liturgy, and symbols, but also extends to historical cases of alternative, non-hegemonic forms of Jewishness. Communities like Tzedek push the boundaries of theory on religion and social movement, destabilizing conceptions that limit tradition to transcendence, symbols, and sacred texts.[43] Religion's disruptive force is also located in the retrieval of historical and cultural memories and embedded communal experiences in ways that motivate, as noted, relinquishing the epistemological priority assigned to the sociocultural practices of tradition's historical moments of origin. One such tradition is *doikayt*. Another is the rich history of Jewish activism. For instance, the CJNV's team leaders highlighted the work of Jewish activists in the Student Nonviolent Coordinating Committee (SNCC) during the civil rights movement in the 1960s and in the struggle against apartheid in South Africa. One of the main learning sessions leading up to the action in Sarura was devoted to retrieving biblical legacies of nonviolent resistance. Here, the two midwives Shifrah and Puah were offered as models of civil disobedience for their refusal to obey the Pharaoh's order to kill newborn boys.[44] Their likely identity as Egyptian women (though a midrash suggests they were Moses's mother and sister[45]) emerged in the discussion as crucial to the question of inter-group solidarity. The mid-wives' manipulation of the Pharaoh's own racism against himself brought to mind the righteous non-Jews, whose courageous act of hiding Jews dur-ing WWII—which involved lying and lawbreaking—saved many Jews' lives. This biblical narrative of nonviolent disobedience—like the stories of Ruth Furst in South Africa and Dorothy Zellner in SNCC, as one CJNV leader explained—foregrounded the intimate connection between feminist and nonviolent motifs in Jewish activist traditions. Here, the renarration of Jewish tradition with deliberate attention to its history of civil disobedience shows how a retrieval of "Jewish values" can amount to an act of critical caretaking that manifests in solidarity with Palestinians and others.

Tzedek's liturgy conveys the significance of nonviolence to the move-ment. For instance, instead of reciting the Ten Plagues in the Passover Seder, the community recites ten sacred acts of liberation, including "civil resis-tance"—invoking here the disobedient midwives—and "reaching out to the Other"—here referring to Exodus 2:6, which describes the compassion the daughter of Pharaoh felt for the crying boy even after determining he was a Hebrew.[46] Once again conveying complex and mutually reinforcing interpre-tive, cognitive, and emotional processes by which religion becomes causal in the world, these liturgies often lead to explicit calls for members to undertake acts of nonviolent resistance and protest in Chicago, whether through anti-Islamophobia campaigns or protests of deportation policies, police brutality, or immoral economic, educational, and housing policies.

INN's weekly *dvar Torah*, which promotes rereading biblical motifs through the contemporary experience of ethical outrage, solidarity, and al-liance with marginalized communities, reflects this animating value of non-violence. In chapter 4, we encountered this method of self-fashioning critique via the resources of Judaism in an INN member's rereading of the *Tochachot* (curses or divine rebukes) in Deuteronomy, explicating the wrath of God in response to unethical conduct and calling on contemporary Jews to be fearful and rectify the communal moral corruption. Another INN member acknowledges struggling, in his *dvar Torah*, with "the violent, racist, sexist, and otherwise terrifying things plainly written in the Torah." In particular, he speaks of Exodus 30:11–34:35, which, following the narrative of the golden calf and broken tablets, describes the terrible violence to be done to Israelites (if they become idolatrous and violate commandments) and their enemies. He resists the strategy of simply ignoring the violence in biblical texts, as his Conservative upbringing had conditioned him to do. This, he suggests, was organically linked to their community's ignoring of the violence associated with the Israeli occupation of Palestinians. "Without fully confronting the

'bad stuff,' he writes, "we'll remain spiritually static, guilty of the fundamental sin in [this text], the sin of the golden calf: idolatry."[47] This *dvar Torah*
was published in the days leading to INN's protest of the AIPAC meeting
in Washington, DC, thus expressing the movement's prophetic challenge to
the Jewish establishment's complicity with violence. Jewish critical caretakers
engage seriously with the violence threaded through the biblical tradition, for
they find this hermeneutical and dialectical exercise consistently meaningful
and conducive not just to their activism, but to their self- and communal
transformation.

One cantor on JVP's Rabbinical Council similarly reflects on the profound challenges posed by the Exodus narrative (Ex. 23:20–32) of "what
today," he writes, "we could only call 'ethnic cleansing.'" The story of expulsion, killing, and displacement, he underscores, comes at the end of the
traditional Talmud curriculum, after a focus on the laws for correct conduct
elucidated from the Torah portion of *Mishpatim*, which also contains these
verses from Exodus. "By excluding the end of *Mishpatim* [from] prayer and
liturgical readings, while keeping the beginning of *Mishpatim* within the Talmud in the curriculum," the cantor continues, "Judaism laid out for us a path
of constructing our moral universe in an often violent, unjust world." "It is
up to us to decide: war or peace and justice."[48] Like the midrashic engagements with the rabbinic legacy of "not by might" described above, this cantor
strives to reclaim the old rabbinic wisdom while intentionally suppressing
any nationalist, messianic impulses. His engagement with the tradition involves a critical examination of Zionist practices, how they have been authorized biblically, and a multiperspectival approach to questions of justice. He
is thus confronted by a sense of injustice done to the "Hivite, the Canaanite,
and the Hittite" of the biblical narrative and to the indigenous Palestinians
of today. This relational and decolonial reading exemplifies how Palestinian
narratives participate in refiguring American Jewish identity.[49] Another rabbi
likewise told me about her struggle with the violence in the textual tradition: "So much within Jewish tradition . . . is quite objectionable and outright
advocates genocide. These texts are being read by the right wing in Israel,
not just to give them inspiration but also some sort of divine permission to
oppress the Palestinian people and kick them off their land. You can avoid
or ignore these texts, try to justify them, or confront them. I usually opt to
confront them, because to do otherwise is irresponsible, but that does mean
that I have a much more oppositional relationship to Judaism than I used to,
and I struggle with that."[50]

Expressing a similar sentiment, Gottlieb begins her book *Trail Guide to
the Torah of Nonviolence* with quotes from Deuteronomy 31:1 and *Babylonian*

Talmud, Sanhedrin 21b: "each generation writes its own Torah."[51] This sentiment animates the efforts of INN and other youth activist circles to reclaim tradition in a moment of a crisis of both authority and narrativity. Gottlieb explicates nonviolence as "the primary lens through which Judaism is interpreted and practiced."[52] In short, "If the sword, then, not the book. If the book, then not the sword."[53] She realizes that, in challenging militarism, she directly confronts Zionism because "militarism is the backbone of Jewish nationalist ideology,"[54] and challenging the one entails challenging the other. Like the cantor, she insists that Jews must choose unequivocally "the sword or the book."

These reflections by critical caretakers illuminate their acknowledgment of the multivocality of tradition and its historical vastness that defies simplistic abstraction of an authentic and ahistorical ethical message. Yet, their activism demonstrates a commitment to engage tradition through a particular lens whose sources of ethical reasoning are multiperspectival and thus destabilize the epistemological and ontological certainties underpinning exclusionary accounts of Jewishness. The effort to demonstrate Judaism's consistency with antimilitarism—an endeavor that demands reading the tradition from multiple perspectives—displays the inevitable embeddedness of the tradition within multiple social semiotic terrains. Jewish activism against the occupation draws strongly on the language of universal human rights in articulating ethical indignation and recovering the prophetic tradition. "In this time of tremendous suffering and fear, from Jerusalem to Gaza, and from Hebron to Be'er Sheva, we reaffirm that all Israelis and Palestinians deserve security, justice, and equality, and we mourn all those who have died."[55] These are the opening lines of an Open Letter released by JVP concerning the events of Operation Protective Edge during the summer of 2014. In rejecting the notion of chosenness and the singularity of Jewish suffering, the letter is clear that the occupation—and not Hamas aggression—is the root cause of violence in Palestine.[56]

Rosen rejects not just the apparent valuing of Jewish lives over Palestinian lives, but also the incitement of vengeance he traces all the way to the highest political and religious echelons. Vengeance, Rosen writes, is not an authentically Jewish way of processing grief. "We stand with the great sage Rabbi Ben Azzai, who famously taught that the concept of humanity being created in the divine image is the most central value of Torah. If we ultimately view all life as sacred, then *empathy*—not isolation or vengeance—is the most healing response of all. . . . Let us affirm that the loss of Jewish children is *inseparable* from the loss of innocent children everywhere who fall victim daily to hatred and violence."[57] As Rosen recognizes, empathy (feeling *with* an *other*), which differs conceptually from compassion (or feeling *for* an *other*), is pivotal for the formation of political solidarities that seek "not to alleviate distress but to rectify an injustice."[58] Hence, like solidarity, desirable (as opposed to self-serving) empathy depends on other virtues and experiences of indignation in the face of injustice.[59] Rosen's words and actions (and those of the Tzedek community) express an emphatic indignation rooted in a prophetic pastiche. This emphatic indignation cultivates a robust capacity to partake in political solidarity through the lens of *mipnei chataeinu* in ways that require feeling *with* an *other*, as well as *teshuvah* and reimagining one's own identity through critical caretaking. Disruptive appropriation of such religious traditions provides consistently effective resources for emphatic indignation animating robust forms of solidarity.

Tzedek's commitment to a nonviolent Judaism is highly consistent with the reimagining of Jewishness undertaken by the broader movement of Jewish critical caretaking and Palestine solidarity activism. Indeed, its pilot Shabbat service directly confronted the most violent passages from Deuteronomy, which describe the conquest of the land of Canaan—*parashat Eikev* (Deut. 7:12–11:25). This biblical story echoes today in the Israeli occupation of Palestine and the ideologies sustaining it, according to Ashley Bohrer, a scholar and an activist with JVP and CJNV who gave the day's sermon. "If we cannot confront this part of our tradition, if we cannot do the hard work of undermining the conquest mentality that has made us, we are not only agents of violence, we have lost an essential component of Judaism." The passages from *Eikev*, she explained, "teach us today, as Jews engaged in building a better and more just world, that we can neither deny nor sanitize our heritage. . . . If we say we have only been victims, we affirm the narrative that Jews cannot be oppressors. *Eikev* shows us that this is not true: We cannot ignore one side of our inheritance at the expense of the other." Bohrer's constructive grappling with the dark, violent passages of the Torah embodies Tzedek's commitments to activism informed by intersectional analysis and *doikayt*: "We live, here in Chicago, on stolen land of the Potawatomi. Just as Chicagoans we must confront this history of genocide, and on the first Yahrzeit of Michael Brown's murder, we as Americans must confront the living history of structural racism, so too as Jews we must recognize in our traditions the living history of the conquest." Bohrer's invocation of Michael Brown, one of many African Americans brutalized by American policing and institutional racism, sharpens the intersectional purchase of reimagined Jewishness, a point the final two chapters will more fully explicate.

Why Engage Tradition?

This chapter has explored Tzedek's quest to form a robust Jewish community that is committed to a postnationalist form of Judaism, seeks genuine relationship with others, and remains attentive to the intersectional nature of social injustice. As I have emphasized, it does so not by jettisoning Jewish traditions, but by critically refiguring them. It draws on these diverse traditions—constructing a prophetic pastiche—to ground its activism and even its critiques of Jewish history and tradition. But my account of Tzedek may raise, for some readers, a critical question: If Tzedek's nonviolent, prophetic, humanistic, universalist commitment to both local and global struggles for equity can be grounded in principles found outside Jewish traditions, why go to such great lengths to base this commitment in tradition-specific concepts and practices? In other words, why do activists find it important to ground their solidarity in reimagined Jewishness in addition to ethical commitments expressed in terms of human rights? One answer is found at the end of the previous section, in Bohrer's call to relentlessly confront the violence in Jewish history and tradition. But this response is not entirely satisfying. Given that JFREJ grounds its similar social justice activism in the secular and atheistic Jewish tradition of *doikayt*, the question remains: How does religious innovation really contribute to the work of personal and communal transformation?

My account of Tzedek has shown that, while its concerns are consistent with the other activist circles of Jewish Palestine solidarity work, Tzedek's meaning as an intentional spiritual community cannot be reduced to its activism. Judith Butler's account of religion, cited in this book's introduction, helps in further articulating this point. For Butler, religion constitutes "a matrix for subject formation whose final form is not determined in advance, a discursive matrix for the articulation and disputation of values, and a field of contestation."[60] The social movement of Jewish critics that this book has traced—including the Tzedek community—inhabits precisely such a matrix, which it seeks to rework hermeneutically for both individual and communal reformation. The movement thus illustrates how the process of religious innovation and change is intricately interwoven with processes of sociopolitical and cultural change, including the meaning-making work that unfolds within social movement spaces. Tzedek's emergence is both consistent with and an outcome of the prophetic pastiche that characterizes the social movement. Both sites involve the practices of *vidui* and *teshuvah*. Political action by the Jewish social movement for Palestinian rights relies on ritualizing Jewish mourning and atonement for communal sins, and Tzedek's definitional values likewise pivot on these religious practices. This analysis allows us to ask not only how religion contributes to disrupting the status quo, to mobilizing, framing, and renarrating identity, but also how religiosity itself, understood in Butler's sense, is transformed through the movement.

Given that Judaism constitutes a matrix of subject formation, critically refiguring it requires literacy in Jewish traditions and historical memories, which function as one crucial source of authority in the process of disputation of norms and communal practices. It also involves appealing to other sources of moral authority, which are embedded in relationality, hereness, and the ethical work of atonement and emphatic indignation. Therefore, the scope of interpreting Jewish resources is significantly expanded within a social movement that seeks to rescript communal boundaries. Religion, as Butler understands it, plays a pivotal role in the deployment of emphatic indignation and prophetic audacity to subvert *doxas* and illusions.[61]

Hence, the question "Why not relinquish tradition altogether for the sake of promoting social justice?" relies on the absurd—and decidedly modernist—presumption that people who are Jewish might just as well cease to be Jewish. The case of Jewishness and its complex relation to "peoplehood" is particularly instructive because Jewish modes of identification could never easily be classified in modernist terms of belief in a set of propositions. Instead, they always also articulated themselves in particular historical, sociocultural, and collective ways that embodied both secular and religious frames. Hence, reclaiming atheistic Bundism is just as authentic a case of Jewish hermeneutical retrieval as reclaiming the legacy of the biblical prophets. When these strands appear together, they generate what I have called "prophetic pastiche." They also illuminate the complex causality by religions that can be transformative in the world.

This points to what sociologist Christian Smith views as religion's "unique social ontology," which "under certain conditions can endow human commitments and actions with a depth, intensity, and tenacity normally not found in non-religious contexts—even when the means and processes by which religion inspires those actions are similar to those in non-religious contexts."[62] My analysis moves away (as do many of the Jewish activists I engage) from Smith's *sui generis* view of religion's causality as grounded in help-seeking practices engaging superhuman powers. Smith classifies identity, community, meaning, social control, and other aspects of religion as secondary or emergent features, products, and powers sociologically forceful yet derivative.[63] Indeed, his insistence on the causal powers of religion amid "complex combinations of forces, usually both religious and non-religious,"[64] remains relevant to the analysis of tradition/religion and transformative social movement work. Their relevance resides not only in *how* religions exert causal forces but also in *why* they still do.[65] Smith attributes religion's uniqueness to the fact that "religion alone is about accessing the help of superhuman powers" and thus, "under certain social circumstances," it "generate[s] a level of *intensity, depth, and persistence in people's motivations, commitments, and endurance* not often seen in non-religious life."[66] However, my use of the concept of prophetic pastiche conveys that the prophetic stance and retrieval activists embodied in Tzedek and other communal and activist spaces constitute, as in art, an eclectic imitation of prophetic style for the purpose of reclaiming and transforming it.[67] It likewise denotes how their activism, influenced by multiple forces, participates in the proliferation of the meanings of the prophetic through intertextuality,[68] as the activists' social, cultural, political, and religious texts are shaped significantly through the grammars and semiotic landscapes of a broader social movement.[69] Hence, the pastiche is not mere imitation but retains a sense of parody, an eclecticism with a critical and self-transformative edge.[70] Accordingly, its intertextual meaning-making mechanisms and causal power are not necessarily derivative of nor grounded in efforts to seek superhuman assistance, even while seeking to transcend historical and ideological constraints of Jewish meanings by reconnecting with Jewish traditions that cohere with the values of antimilitarism, non-chosenness, and solidarity. This act of transcendence through prophetic pastiche tends to generate *intensity, depth, and persistence* in activists' resolve to resist the occupation, even with their own bodies and sacrificing their own safety. The case study of Jewish activists, many of whom are non-religious and explicitly reject conceptions of the superhuman, amplifies that explicating religion's causal world-transforming, -transcending, and -disruptive powers does not depend on isolating its *sui generis* definition as involving superhuman powers.

Certainly, the case of Jewish activists illustrates the limits of abstracting religiocultural and political meaning-making from the analysis of identity and social movement theory and practice, and thus ghettoizing the specifically religious work of communities like Tzedek. It requires that we explicitly broaden our analytic capacity to grasp the role of religiocultural resources in public narrative, where critical caretaking as self-fashioning entails—as chapter 4 showed—crucial hermeneutical work as agents rescript their stories within a complex semiotic terrain. It likewise stresses that the ethical outrage and indignation at the heart of refiguring Jewishness through Palestine solidarity is embedded in a context-specific personal (not abstract) engagement with ethical commitments. Jewish Palestine solidarity activism is deeply personal in reimagining what it means to be Jewish. Its forcefulness and resolve to put bodies on the ground are propelled not just by atonement and solidarity but also by a commitment to a diasporist, joyful, and humanistic Jewishness. We observed activists deriving spiritual meanings from explicitly Jewish spaces, and in the process of working for Palestine solidarity, reconfiguring these spaces. We also highlighted how promoting this struggle requires a hermeneutical discursive work that cannot simply theorize Jewishness out of existence. Indeed, it requires opening up spaces for agentic innovative work on identity and narrative because the epicenter of the oppression of Palestinians is that of narrativity formed through epistemic and discursive violence. I will return to this point explicitly in the concluding chapter.

This chapter focused specifically on the making and unmaking of meaning—a process necessary for Jewish activists who wish to operate within explicitly Jewish spaces, as they reimagine the very contours of their collective identity. This dialogic process involves not only accessing and reclaiming a more "authentic" Jewish narrative and message of powerlessness, but also, centrally, it demands grappling relationally and intersectionally with the historical ramifications of Jewish power. I pointed to a broad consistency between the use of liturgy and rituals in social movement protest and intentional liturgical spaces, but also showed that such consistency does not entail that reimagined liturgy and rituals are merely instrumental to the movement's objectives. Instead, prefigurative spaces—whether in street protests where rituals are employed as protest repertoire, or in services where reimagined liturgy cultivates new communal boundaries—signal a rescripting of Jewishness through agentic meaning-making processes of grassroots resignification. This interrogation, however, is not merely internally contained as a form of self-scrutiny. Instead, it cross-fertilizes and is challenged by movement dynamics and broader discussions of race, colonialism, and white supremacy. In the next two chapters, I turn to examine the movement's processes of decolonizing and deorientalizing Jewishness, both of which are crucial to the work of refiguring collective meanings through solidarity.

PART THREE

Making Multidirectional Memory

> There is no doubt that Gaza is not just a "kind of" concentration camp; it is the hood
> on steroids. Now in the black community, located within the American empire, you do
> have forms of domination and subordination, forms of police surveillance and so forth,
> so that we are not making claims of identity, we are making claims of forms of domi-
> nation that must be connected. And those are not the only two—we could talk about
> the Dalit people in India and the ways that their humanity is being lost and there are
> parallels there; we could talk about peasants in Mexico. So all of these are going to have
> similarities and dissimilarities. But there is no doubt that for the Ferguson moment in
> America and the anti-occupation moment in the Israel-Palestinian struggle, there is a
> very important connection to make and I think we should continue to make it.[1]

In this quotation, Cornel West draws pointed analogies between racism in
the US and Gaza's predicament under Israeli occupation. Calling Gaza "the
hood on steroids," he underscores interlocking systems of domination, local and global. The concept of "the hood" evokes the related concept of the
"ghetto," which, like "concentration camp," is laden with shifting meanings.
Each term connotes a dehumanizing form of spatial segregation that is authorized by a complex racial logic. West's observation distills the complicated
terrain of black-Palestinian solidarity as it appears within a global, intersectional social justice movement of which Jewish Palestine solidarity is just one
part. In order to further explore what it means to unlearn a narrative—a
critical mechanism in the efforts of American Jews to ethically refigure their
tradition—this chapter addresses the importance of connecting Jewish unlearning with American race history, including the construction of Jews as
white. It locates black-Palestine solidarity within the global Palestine solidarity movement, but also scrutinizes the roots of black-Jewish affinities, which
present possibilities for decolonizing the Jewish narration of the Holocaust
and for destabilizing the identity of Jews as white. Decolonizing Jewishness,
which requires grappling with the intersection of race and religion, is just
as critical a tool as a retrieval and reinterpretation of prophetic traditions of
social justice in the process of reframing ethical commitments and participating in the broader "geographies of liberation."[2] Hence, Palestine plays a
key role in American Jewish efforts to cultivate an anticolonial and antiracist
imagination.

Global Palestine Solidarity

Global Palestine solidarity is a grassroots, counter-hegemonic movement that demands justice for marginalized communities and individuals. It is no wonder that the World Social Forum (WSF) adopted the banner of Palestine solidarity in its 2012 gathering in Porto Alegre, Brazil.[3] The adoption of Palestine as a leftist revolutionary symbol has roots in a long history of interconnectivity with anticolonial and anti-imperialist agendas in the Global South.[4] Palestine began to gain the attention of the global political Left after the 1967 war. As Helga Tawil-Souri explains, the Palestinian Liberation Organization (PLO) resonated with other nationalist and anti-imperialist struggles in the Global South or the "Third World." But in the 1990s, as leftists began to emphasize a "global civil society" and to deploy the concept of the Global South instead of the Third World, they also reframed the meaning of Palestine, putting a stronger premium on the legacies of slavery, colonialism, and economic exploitation as well as the ideologies that authorize such modes of domination (e.g., racism, orientalism, capitalism).[5] Importantly, the framing of Palestine as a human rights cause (not an Islamist one) is key to understanding the broad support the cause of Palestine has garnered through the BDS campaigns and other solidarity activism.[6] Linking the Palestinian struggle to broader analyses of colonialism and racism requires an intersectional outlook, one that, in the words of Keith P. Feldman, scrutinizes "the cultural and historical ligatures linking the United States and the Middle East"[7] in order to expose the operative force of Israel for US "imperial culture." The analytic concept of "imperial culture," Feldman continues, "names the crucible within which an enduring U.S. national ideology of territorial expansion and its attendant regimes of racial domination and war-making have been codified, reified, naturalized, and contested." Accordingly, black-Palestinian solidarity challenges "a symbolic architecture to secure consent for extraterritorial violence as essential for protecting the national home."[8]

The first level at which intersectionality is operative in terms of collective actions is in exposing demonstrable connections between the security machinery of Israel and the militarization of US police.[9] Many reports point to the direct contacts and training sessions that one commentator terms the "Israelification" of the American police in its racial profiling, discrimination, and harassment of racialized minorities, especially Muslims.[10] Angela Davis, the African American feminist scholar and activist, was an early voice in exposing the interconnections between Israel and the prison-industrial complex in the US.[11] JVP made this issue a focus of activism when it launched, in 2017, a campaign outlining the "deadly exchange"[12] between Israeli and American police, military, and security apparatuses, likewise deepening connections between the plights of Latinx, African American, Palestinian, and other marginalized communities. The #DeadlyExchange campaign exemplifies an intersectional frame and aims at exposing the complicity of the Jewish establishment with both the occupation of Palestine and police brutality against marginalized communities in the US.[13] Solidarity, however, moves beyond merely adducing such "hard data," which might justify cross-movement activism against transnational militarism as well as the securitizing and racializing of minorities.[14] One important site of intersectionality, critical for decolonizing Jewish narrativity, is black-Palestinian solidarity, to which I now turn.

From Ferguson to Gaza and Back Again

Gaza, Palestine, and Ferguson, Missouri, though separated by over six thousand miles, are threaded together in the narrative of a global social justice movement. They were joined on August 9, 2014, when eighteen-year-old American Michael Brown was shot by a white police officer in what many understood as yet another instance of police brutality against and disregard for black lives. Brown's shooting sparked outrage and protest not because it was an unusual event, but rather because such killings have become routine in what Michelle Alexander calls "the New Jim Crow," a regime marked by disproportionate incarceration rates of African Americans and systemic obstacles to mobility and dignified lives.[15] Thousands flooded the streets of Ferguson in protest. The hashtag #BlackLivesMatter—which emerged in July 2013 after the acquittal of George Zimmerman, who killed an African American teenage boy named Trayvon Martin—accelerated as a movement with the killing of Brown and a host of other black men and boys that same year (e.g., Eric Garner in New York City and Tamir Rice in Baltimore). At the same time, the deaths and injuries of black women and girls and trans persons remained far more inaudible and marginalized.

"We wish to express our support and solidarity with the people of Ferguson who have taken their struggle to the street, facing a militarized police occupation,"[16] read a statement shortly after Brown's shooting, signed by Palestinians—in Palestine and in diasporas around the world—only days after the cease-fire that concluded the most recent chapter of Israel's assault on Gaza. Cyberspace was filled with images of Palestinians holding signs that expressed solidarity with the people of Ferguson and commiseration about the hyper-militarized police brutality that met their protests, as well as tweets sharing practical advice for handling tear gas attacks.[17] The striking similarities between images from the Israeli occupation and the confrontations with the Ferguson police reinforced the underpinning logic of intersectionality as operationalized by the solidarity movement. As Davis concisely explains, "the Ferguson struggle has taught us that local issues have global ramifications."[18] The connections and parallels between Ferguson and Palestine tightened with the endorsement of BDS campaigns by Dream Defenders, a movement related to #BlackLivesMatter. These connections deepened with its decision to send a delegation (the first of several) to Palestine in January 2015, organized by the Institute for Middle East Understanding. The delegates reported that the trip solidified their understanding of the connections between the American struggles for racial justice and the Palestinian struggles against the occupation. During a solidarity demonstration in Nazareth, one delegate said, "We come to a land that has been stolen by greed and destroyed by hate. We come here and we learn laws that have been co-signed in ink but written in blood of the innocent and we stand next to people who continue to courageously struggle and resist the occupation. People continue to dream and fight for freedom. . . . From Ferguson to Palestine the struggle for freedom continues."[19] This proclamation underscores how structures of greed, racism, and colonialism have operated globally in generating parallel narratives of dispossession, humiliation, and ungrievable death.

The Dream Defenders (see figure 7.1) stand in a long tradition of African American affinity with Palestine, a trend that came to fruition when Black Power emerged in the 1960s, breaking with Martin Luther King Jr.'s approach to interracial and interfaith civil rights activism, which was accused of embracing white (including Jewish) allies and their commitment to liberal gradualism.[20] Primarily comprising the Nation of Islam (NOI), the Black Panther Party, and the Student Nonviolent Coordinating Committee (SNCC),[21] Black Power, along with the broader New Left, articulated an explicitly anti-Zionist position in the aftermath of the 1967 occupation. This position was grounded in a global critique of Zionism as colonialism and identified Israel as a mechanism to promote American imperialism. "American Jews, once viewed as allies of African Americans because they understood what it meant to face persecution," writes Marc Dollinger, "emerged in the post-1967 era as partners of a white Israeli government responsible for subjugating its people of color, the Palestinian Arabs." As a result, he concludes, "the black-Jewish alliance of the 1950s became the black-Arab alliance of the 1960s."[22] The consolidation of this alliance also generated explicitly antisemitic expressions by some activists in Black Power circles, such as SNCC program director Ralph Featherstone, who spoke of the "evil of Zionism" in "those Jews in the little Jew shops in the ghettos,"[23] echoing NOI rhetoric.[24] The emergence and consolidation of black antisemitism in the US is intricately related not only to the local struggles of African Americans, but also to their increasingly global critique of colonialism, how they interpret Zion and Zionism, and how such interpretations play out within the scope of African American communal self-understandings as well as the narratives and metaphors that determine them. Palestine and Zion function as metaphors but also as subjects of solidarity in ways that illuminate how constitutive they are to interpreting Jewish-black relations.

The African American novelist and social critic James Baldwin wrote in his 1948 essay "The Harlem Ghetto" that "the Negro identifies himself almost wholly with the Jew. The more devout Negro considers that he *is* a Jew, in bondage to a hard taskmaster and waiting for a Moses to lead him out of Egypt."[25] Accordingly, Baldwin explains, the Jewish liberation narrative has been interlaced in the African American imagination with the definitional narrative of Christianity, the crucifixion. "The images of the suffering Christ and the suffering Jew," he continues, "are wedded with the image of the suffering slave, and they are one: the people that walked in darkness have seen a great light."[26] Such imagery, which motivated coalitions of American Jews and African Americans during the civil rights movement to fight side by side for redemption in the form of democratic inclusion in America, ultimately lost traction for Black Power. This shift was already articulated in Baldwin's later recognition in *The Fire Next Time* (1962) of the forcefulness (regardless of the flaws of its theology and its racist conclusions about Jews) of the NOI's critique of white Christian America. Describing his own process of spiritual crisis and disillusionment with the Church's capacity to disrupt white domination and cultivate a sense of self-worth in black Christians, Baldwin acknowledges the NOI's effort to decolonize the African American imagination. The NOI, accordingly, constructed a new vocabulary that was able to expose Christianity for its history of oppression, its sanctification not only of dominating structures but also of suffering, its manufacturing of a false sense of security, and its failure to act *in the world* on so urgent a matter as racial justice.[27] Baldwin's critique in *The Fire Next Time* of religion as containing an emancipatory mechanism anticipates the diminishing force of the "Hebrew" or the "Jew" as a metaphor for Black Power. This erosion was precipitated by the incomparability of Jewish and black predicaments and by white Jews' benefiting from whiteness in the aftermath of WWII.[28] Precisely against this narrative that attributes the divergence of Jews and blacks to the emergence of Black Power's separatism—and with it black antisemitism and anti-Zionism—Dollinger retrieves, as I discuss in chapter 3, an account of a different kind of black-Jewish alliance, in which the black separatism that emerged in the late 1960s emboldened and consolidated Jewish separatism. Instead of a story of dual retreat of Jews and blacks from their legacy of alliance during the civil rights movement,[29] Dollinger points to connections among various internal critics who historically resisted the romanticization of this "good old alliance," ostensibly spoiled by the emergence of black militarism and anti-semitism. For instance, Albert Vorspan, a former director of the Commission on Social Action of Reform Judaism of the Union of American Hebrew Congregations and Central Conference of American Rabbis, challenged in 1969 the logic of this narrative that "black-Jewish relationships used to be good and now they have turned sour." "The truth is," he continues, "that they never were really good. We Jews did a great deal *for* black people, and that is precisely the point. . . . It was kind and benevolent but it was also colonial."[30] Accordingly, moving forward with racial and social justice will involve taking on a "supporting role."[31] Anticipating the later movement of critical Jewish allies, Vorspan's remarks gesture toward the requirement for decolonizing Jewishness through self-interrogation and grappling with the sins of Jewish power, rather than merely accessing a narrative of Jewish powerlessness.

Dollinger shows that, even while expressing explicit animosity toward one another, the (white) Jewish and black communities cross-fertilized in the late 1960s and 1970s. In the early stages of Black Power and the transition to non-intersectional identity politics, leaders within the Jewish community were willing to tolerate overt expressions of black antisemitism and appreciate black militancy as a form of "Negro Zionism,"[32] to quote Rabbi Arthur Hertzberg. Or, in the words of another Jewish leader, "Africa is [the Negro Zionist's] Israel."[33] Likewise, echoing Baldwin's "The Harlem Ghetto," Rabbi Alan W. Miller described African Americans as "America's 'Jews,'"[34] interpreting their social justice struggles and plight for self-actualization through the prism of Jewish experiences, but with a lucid critique of New York's Jewish Federation of Teachers, which in 1968 instrumentalized antisemitism in a fight to segregate education according to patterns of "white flight."[35] Claims of black antisemitism, in other words, were cited "against the legitimate aspirations of black and Puerto Rican parents and children in a school system which has abysmally failed them."[36] Miller, who held a leadership position in the Reconstructionist movement in the late 1960s, wrote self-reflexively about black-Jewish confrontation and the emergence of Black Power at the time: "some blacks are as ruthlessly desperate in their search for their *Jerusalem* as some of our people were in the search for ours."[37] Jewish militancy and terrorism, Miller reminds his readers, "was born . . . in the concentration camps of Europe."[38] This suffering undergirds hatred and militancy and provides an explanatory frame for interpreting black militancy. "The possibility of a *black* holocaust in America," he writes, "seems *much* more probable than a Jewish one. After all, it is blacks, not Jews, who have been mowed down in the streets of American cities with scarcely a demur."[39] Accordingly, the predicament of blacks in America was refracted through "the lens of Jews suffering under Nazism in World War II,"[40] both in order to diminish the apparent threat of emerging black antisemitism and to affirm the impetus of black militarism and intra-communal focus on self-affirmation, which contributed to Jewish self-affirmation and advocacy. This parallelism of Black Power and militant Zionism also operated in reverse, as leaders like Malcolm X and Stokely Carmichael identified Jewish Zionism as a separationist, identity-based course of action to emulate.[41] Hence, Zion's metaphorical hold remained forceful, even if the actual objectives of Black Power contradicted the content of Zionist ideological frames and its affective affinities.

The landscape of identity politics and the consolidation of Black Power produced many ironies. One of these was the emergence of the Jewish Defense League (JDL) in 1968 under the leadership of Rabbi Meir Kahane. This development amounts to a historical irony because it shows how the African American Left enabled, through the aforementioned cross-fertilization of militant tactics and metaphors, the emboldening of the Jewish (or neoconservative) Right.[42] The motto "Never Again" was first articulated by Kahane, who—while mobilizing vigilante organizations aimed to protect Jews against African American urban violence in the US—embraced "black militancy [expressed in his admiration for the tactics of the Black Panthers] as an answer to Jewish powerlessness," which he resented.[43] Even if marginalized at the time within the American Jewish community, Kahane's legacy and the operative force of his motto not only persisted, but became mainstream in a landscape defined by identity politics and Jewish advocacy that, quite unlike that of Miller and other Jewish leaders in the late 1960s, amplifies the threat of antisemitism (read as anti-Zionism) in America.[44] The emergence of Black Power's Palestine solidarity and Jewish nationalism, therefore, is not merely the outcome of a split between these communities. Instead, Dollinger's closer scrutiny demonstrates a complex symmetry and mutual borrowing, even while African American grassroots activism relinquished its identification with the Jew as a metaphor for liberation.

According to Feldman, whose *A Shadow over Palestine* demonstrates the indebtedness of Black Power to Palestinian scholarship's critique of colonization,[45] reading US racial politics needs to be refracted transnationally through the lens of Israel/Palestine and its relevance to US imperial culture, illuminating the complex semiotic interrelation among Palestinian liberation, black freedom, and Jewish self-determination. This entails challenging the domestication and assimilation of the issue of black-Jewish relations under an "ethnic relations" paradigm. This discursive turn allows for analyzing Israel and Palestine merely as "epiphenomenal" to "ethnic relations," which otherwise can be assessed in terms of black-Jewish "cooperation and confrontation" confined within the framework of the liberal pluralistic nation-state. "This framework," Feldman writes, "reduces a heterogeneous historical field of affiliations to Israel and Palestine to expressions of Black anti-Semitism or Jewish racism, which then become the linchpin in a narrative of the tragedy of Black radicalism's dissolution of the civil rights promise."[46] Hence, Feldman, like Dollinger's rereading of the narrative about Jewish-black alliances, challenges a "declentionist" narrative of Jewish-black relations, but Feldman transcends the US logic of identity politics (for still being beholden to the delimiting ethnic relations paradigm). Instead, he underscores the declentionist narrative's failures to identify "transnational circuits of racialization, migration, and cultural exchange," thereby misreading the question of Israel and Palestine as epiphenomenal rather than "constitutive of . . . the meaning and function of race in the United States."[47]

Feldman's intervention is similar to other scholars in American studies working beyond the conceptual limits that the nation-state imposes in order to decolonize and reconceive political imaginations. Alex Lubin, in particular, illuminates the emergence, through a critical race analysis (and in a context of neoliberal governance), of Afro-Arab political imaginaries. He underscores that black criticism of Israel needs to be interpreted in terms of a broader analysis of African American internationalism and its attendant disengagement from earlier support of Zionism by African American luminaries such as King and W. E. B. Du Bois. Lubin, like Feldman, challenges US-centric, domesticating, explanatory, "inter-ethnic" paradigms, which bracket global semiotic dynamics that foreground the comparative study of racialization. He retrieves Jewish and black genealogies of critique that connect anti-semitism, orientalism, and anti-black racism in ways that resonate with the global social justice movement's effort to recraft public imagination. Lubin's excavation of subaltern genealogies throughout the late nineteenth and twentieth centuries intends to trace ways to "reconstitute . . . the geographies of modernity into . . . a geography of liberation."[48] "Geographies of liberation," Lubin continues, "are dialectical spaces produced in the collision between nationalism and colonialism, on one hand, and subaltern decolonial and liberation politics, on the other." These dialectical spaces constitute "a transgressive geography" where Afro-Arab intellectuals can cultivate "radical political understandings of liberation that emerged through a comparative and spatial politics between the United States and Palestine."[49] It is "transgressive" in that it challenges and deconstructs "coloniality" or colonial modernity.[50]

The contemporary moment—to return to the Dream Defenders—not only conveys an activist construction of a transgressive and relational geography of liberation, but it also offers another ironic turn. Now, Zionism as a metaphor is employed by ethnoreligious white nationalists, as we will see in chapter 8, who admire Jewish Zionism even while relying on antisemitic nostalgia and ideological frames. This self-described "white Zionism" gestures toward the interrelation between white supremacy and antisemitism in the US, marking the metaphorical limits of Zionism, aligning the Jewish Right with the American Right, and exposing the need to center an analysis of Europe as a cultural and political project of modernity involving race theories, colonialism, and other forms of exploitation. The project of Europe (or Euro-America), in other words, is not outside the analytic scope of the case of Israel and Palestine. Nor is it outside the formation of global solidarity (more below). White ethnonationalists' employment of Zionism as their metaphor, likewise, clarifies a path for black-Palestinian solidarity, where anti-Zionism is not also an expression of "black Zionism" and where "Africa" is not "Israel"; rather, its story of displacement, suffering, and oppression is the story of Palestine. The struggle for Palestinian liberation is but one site in a broader and intersecting struggle for justice where one group's liberation is interlinked with, not parallel to or the same as, all others.[51]

Radical black feminists such as Davis and Beverly Guy-Sheftall have worked for Palestine solidarity for decades, underscoring antiracist forms of black feminism as pivotal for imagining the intersectional social justice struggles within which Palestine liberation unfolds.[52] These antiracist movements differ from the civil rights era because they attend to issues of gender and other intersectional markers. "The assumption that Black freedom was freedom for the Black man created a certain kind of border around the Black struggle which can no longer exist."[53] Davis draws on feminist methodologies to recover the critique of capitalism at the heart of intersectionality theory and connect it to interrogation of racism, colonialism, gender nonconformity, and postcolonialities.[54] Feminism, therefore, unlocks "a range of connections among discourses, and institutions, and identities, and ideologies that we often tend to consider separately" while also cultivating epistemologies from the margins as well as recognizing "connections that are not always apparent."[55] For this reason, Davis interprets Palestine liberation as a feminist struggle, deploying feminist methodologies to facilitate solidarity and affinity among "what appear to be separate" issues, while also operating to untangle what might appear to be naturally interconnected.[56]

The platform of MBL, discussed in chapter 2, is thoroughly informed by this mode of radical antiracist feminism. This is clear from its recognition

FIGURE 7.1. A Palestine solidarity delegation of African American activists, August 2016 [Photo credit: Christopher Hazou]

of the vulnerabilities of gender-nonconforming people and black women as well as its advocacy of special protections for vulnerable people, thus relating their marginality to a broader socioeconomic and political analysis.[57] As the previous chapter noted, antiracist feminist approaches and a related transnational critical race analysis of US imperial culture are critical for the paths that led some American Jews to refigure their ethical commitments and focus of solidarity. Many, for instance, could no longer tolerate the ethical incoherence between their embrace of gender inconformity and their communities' complicity with the occupation, nor could they cohere their antimilitarism with Israelism.

Indeed, front and center among those who flooded the streets of Ferguson in solidarity protests were Jewish activists critical of Israel. Their dedication to fighting racism and police brutality was reinforced on the first Hanukkah following the clashes in Ferguson. A national Jewish Day of Action to End Police Violence was announced, and many employed the holiday's rituals to reconfirm the Jewish commitment to fight publicly for racial justice.[58] Here, Jewish activists subverted ethnocentric interpretations of Hanukkah by articulating their universal commitment to stand with the marginalized and the victims of oppression, recognizing the interconnections among all sites of injustice. For them, a commitment to the cause of Ferguson symbolized the same kind of struggle they experienced when standing in solidarity with Palestinians, when insisting within their own communities, and more broadly, that Palestinian lives matter (see figure 7.2).

Here, critical Jews' contexts and processes of pre-politicization are clearly evident in how they reimagine Jewishness also through denaturalizing the transnational circuits of racialization. Some American Jews' embeddedness in progressive politics and antiracism, in particular, reinforces their analytic grasp of the Palestinian predicament and enhances their moral shocks and indignation.[59] The latter emotion, as earlier chapters discussed, contributes to a new public narrative, demonstrating once again the view of identity as an emergent and dialogic process of semiotic innovation. Identity transformation does not merely involve a retrieval of alternative interpretations of traditions; rather, it actively demands a process of critique through increasing employment of an intersectional analytic lens. Indeed, participation in collective actions against deadly exchanges also generates activists' engagement with the discursive and semiotic layers of white supremacy.

Before turning to a more detailed engagement with black-Palestinian solidarity, let us contextualize the intersectional moment further. As we will examine below, opening up possibilities for deeper forms of black-Jewish solidarity than the ones reliant on JVP models of alliance requires destabilizing the construction of Jews as white and European as an integral dimension of the critique of Zionism qua settler colonialism. Only once Jewish "whiteness" has been challenged, but also grappled with as a social fact, can the place of

FIGURE 7.2. Pro-Palestinian march over the Brooklyn Bridge, 2014 [Photo credit: Gili Getz]

Jews in the global struggle against racism and imperialism be fully understood and inhabited. Here, the voices and experiences of JOCSM are especially crucial. Indeed, JVP's statement reinforcing its alliance with MBL in
the aftermath of MBL's controversial policy platform—including an explicit
statement of solidarity with Palestinians and a condemnation of Israeli practices as genocidal—was articulated by the Caucus of JOCSM. The lived experiences of JOCSM and their complex hybridities constitute an entry point
into the intersectional movement from a place of lived marginality rather
than "white privilege," even while being Jewish. JOCSM's critical caretaking
as well as feminist and queer lenses facilitate and deepen the refashioning of
Jewishness by interrogating Jews' participation in whiteness, a process accelerated in the ethically clarifying presidency of Trump.[60] In sharp relief against
JVP's support of MBL's use of the word "genocide" (and "apartheid") in explaining the movement's solidarity with Palestinians was the long aforementioned history of black-Palestinian solidarity and African Americans' affinity
with Third Worldism or the Global South. Such solidarity is also consistent
with African Americans' historical engagement with the commemoration
and recognition of the genocide against European Jews within the American
public discourse and its contextualization within the stories of colonialism,
imperialism, and racism.

In this context, reestablishing black-Jewish alliance can rely neither on
a perception of comparable marginality and powerlessness through an invocation of the generic experience of Jews, nor on a non-intersectional
identity politics through the employment of Zionism as an emancipatory
(militant) paradigm to ensure that Jews will never face powerlessness or extinction again. Nor can it simply rely on Jews' accessing their "prophetic"
resources. The prophetic pastiche is also an outcome of confronting Jewish
sinfulness and complicity with multiple layers of violence, including violence
against JOCSM. The centrality of JOCSM to the process of confronting Jewish "whiteness" and nationalist separatism points to the need to revisit the
operative force of European racialization and racism on the development
of Zionism and racialized modern conceptions of Jewishness. Through the
multiple hybridities they inhabit, JOCSM challenge the racialization of Jews
as a distinct group (or race), the roots of which are found in the scientific
study of race, a taxonomical tool of empire and colonialism.

Notably, the Jews of Europe were not only victims of racial scientific antisemitism, deeply rooted in, yet distinct from, classical Christian antisemitism. They also participated in producing racialized modern Jewish thought,
which was already determined by their milieu and thus reflective of internalized antisemitism and its turn toward biology and science.[61] Jewish racialized

scholarship in the nineteenth and early twentieth centuries, as Mitchell Hart explains, challenged the biological determinism that had made its way into debates about potential assimilation of emancipated Jews in Europe by underscoring the inferiority of the "Jewish race" as prohibitive for Jews' inclusion in Europe.[62] "What most Jewish social thinkers," Hart stresses, "could not accept was a causal explanation for the Jewish condition rooted in a fixed, immutable racial or biological essence or identity. They could not accept the view that the Jews were degenerate *because they were Jews*."[63] This refusal to embrace biological determinism while nonetheless internalizing negative imagery of "the Jews" informed the political drive toward either integration into European societies or Zionism.[64]

In particular, Zionism employed race to underscore its distinct claims, Volkist personality (as in Herder's formulation), and aspirations for self-actualization. This entailed cultivating a sense of self-worth that redirected the focus of Jewish longing toward national self-determination. The latter no longer needed to depend explicitly on Jewishness as tradition contained in the Torah and mitzvot, though the concept of Jewish peoplehood (or ethnicity) and tradition will always be entangled. This language of "blood" and "race" was especially associated with Revisionist Zionism and later found strong expression in the emergence of JDL and the eventual mainstreaming of its Jewish-centric advocacy and its blood- and land-centric conceptions of peoplehood.[65] The concept of "Zion" as a form of separatist racial or ethnic liberation, and the supposed alliance emerging from parallels between Jewish and Black Power, is thus still beholden to and interlaced with a racial legacy that JOCSM are especially well positioned to challenge by denaturalizing it.

The contemporary Jewish critics of Zionism attempt to subvert this legacy in their symbolic effort to stand again metaphorically in front of the "burning bush" and to recommit to an intersectional conception of liberation while being confronted by the Jewish communal sins of an occupation that, as they interpret it, itself relies on and is authorized by orientalist and racist discourses. Cultivating an antiracist outlook that also distances itself from racial conceptions of Jewishness and interrogates Europe as a political and cultural project is therefore necessary for a black-Jewish alliance that conceptually links the Jewish Holocaust of European Jews with a broader analysis of colonial legacies, including slavery and racism. Hence, a Jewish-black alliance involves decolonizing "race" as well as "religion" (as Baldwin illuminates in *The Fire Next Time*), thereby destabilizing conceptions of such an alliance as "inter-racial" while pluralizing the meanings of Jewishness through a multiperspectival rather than separatist conception of liberation and through an unlearning of Zionism's Euro- and Ashkenazi-centric monopoly over contemporary accounts of Jewishness. Unlearning Zion qua blood- and land-centric conceptions of Jewishness illuminates pathways for intersectional black-Jewish alliances that centralize Palestine, not Zion, as its metaphorical engine as well as concrete site of activism and mechanisms for cultivating intertextual prophetic pastiche, as the previous chapter explicated.

Black-Palestinian-Jewish Solidarity?

The MBL platform discusses Israel's genocidal and apartheid-like practices under a broader heading of divestment from militarism and prisons as mechanisms for black liberation.[66] "The US justifies and advances the global war on terror via its alliances with Israel and is complicit in the genocide taking place against the Palestinian people."[67] Its complicity, the platform continues, manifests in "requir[ing] Israel to use 75 percent of all the military aid it receives to buy US-made arms," thus transferring US taxpayers' wealth to arms corporations that then lobby for increased militarism. The upshot, accordingly, is not merely a diversion of funds from social policies, but the complicity of US citizens in Israel's apartheid policies of discrimination, land theft, and checkpoints that inflict humiliation (or worse) on Palestinians daily. The platform, therefore, clearly connects militarization, neoliberalism, and the Palestinian predicament with which African Americans identify as they too suffer the consequences of militarism, neoliberalism, and the legacy of uprootedness, racism, and genocidal experiences.

Although both scholarly and popular perceptions contest the portrayal of Israeli actions and policies against Palestinians as genocidal,[68] the force of this comparative category has been a source of African American affinity with Jews as well as Palestinians. As longtime civil rights and Israel/Palestine activist Dorothy Zellner underscores, African Americans have had "a long and tormented relationship with this word, 'genocide.'"[69] It started with appeals by the National Negro Congress to the United Nations already in 1946 and by the NAACP in its 1947 "Appeal to the World," written by Du Bois and other black scholars and attorneys, to apply "genocide" to the historical experiences of African Americans. Neither effort bore any results. These efforts were followed, in 1951, after the ratification of the 1948 UN Convention on the Prevention and Punishment of the Crime of Genocide, by another petition to the UN, "We Charge Genocide," presented by the Civil Rights Congress. This petition explicitly employed the convention's definition of genocide in order to seek justice for African Americans: "It is sometimes incorrectly thought that genocide means the complete and definitive destruction of a race of people. However, the Genocide Convention . . . defines genocide as any . . . intent to destroy, in whole or in part, a national, racial, ethnic or religious group." "We Charge Genocide" received little traction in US media. One exception, Zellner reveals, would be the Jewish press, specifically *Jewish Currents*, which she reprimands for later rejecting the MBL platform for its use of the word "genocide."[70] But, in a 1952 editorial, *Jewish Currents* applies the convention's definition to the Jim Crow South, where "the Negro people, as a people, are subjected to second class citizenship . . . [in order] to enforce on the whole Negro people unrelieved oppression that adds up to genocide."[71] MBL's choice of the word "genocide," therefore, to describe the predicament of Palestinians[72] reflects a history where African Americans' efforts to frame their own experiences and memories through this legal lens were not successful, with black intellectuals and others wondering what other word, despite the "compatibility of black conditions with the standards of the UN Convention on the Prevention and Elimination of Genocide,"[73] could be used to describe the narratives of African Americans.

Efforts to employ the label "genocide" comparatively, as well as Jewish participation in such efforts, are indicative of the operative force of the narrative of Jewish "powerlessness" and marginality as a source of alliance formation with African Americans in the immediate aftermath of WWII. The knee-jerk reactions of mainstream Jewish organizations to MBL's contemporary employment of the word show why the aforementioned shifts in Jewish-black relations emboldened Jewish-centric advocacy. Such advocacy nevertheless relies on a declentionist historiography of black-Jewish alliance. MBL's radicalism is assimilated into this narrative, which leaves American Jews indignant in their nostalgia for the civil rights era and their understanding that the source of the alliance resided in a comparable marginality of the two communities. Such reactions, however, also rely on a balkanized topography of identity politics, which demands communities to tell and enact their stories of liberation and oppression in isolation from one another and sometimes as a zero-sum game. Jewish allies demonstrated, echoing earlier voices such as Miller and Vorspan's, that the path to alliance must involve explicitly naming Jewish power and violence, not merely heralding a memory of Jewish "powerlessness." Even if the process of renarrating Jewishness does involve critical caretaking—by which it reconnects to the prophetic motifs and histories of marginalization—this transformative work involves relinquishing monopoly over suffering through a multiperspectival prism that grapples relentlessly with complicity and communal sins through a transnational critical race analysis too. As noted, this process also involves grappling with the logic of racism (including antisemitism), the undoing of which is critical for the possibility of forming antiracist intersectional alliances.

As Michael Rothberg shows, Du Bois was exemplary in interrogating the connections between blacks and Jews (assuming the latter do not identify as JOC) in ways that attend to the connections between their respective narratives of race, dehumanization, and Western colonialism and nationalism.[74] Writing in the aftermath of WWII, while frequenting the sites of destruction in Poland, Du Bois was able, in his "The Negro and the Warsaw Ghetto" (1952), to rethink race and violence outside the specificity of "the color line" as he experienced it. "The result of these three visits," he reports, "and particularly of my view of the Warsaw ghetto, was not so much clearer understanding of the Jewish problem in the world as it was a real and more complete understanding of the Negro problem." Visiting the site of the Jewish ghetto, accordingly, clarified for him that "the problem of slavery, emancipation, and caste in the United States was no longer . . . a separate and unique thing as I had so long conceived it. It was not even solely a matter of color and physical and racial characteristics, which was particularly a hard thing for me to learn, since for a lifetime the color line had been a real and efficient cause of misery." "The race problem," he stresses, "cut across lines of color and physique and belief and status and was a matter of cultural patterns, perverted teaching and human hate and prejudice, which reached all sorts of people."[75]

Not unlike West's emphasis on systems over specific identities, Du Bois's visit to the sites of genocide against Jews clarifies for him an intersectional approach (beyond the color line) to the "race problem" and to the real and specific suffering of African Americans. However, this clarity does not lead him, Rothberg argues, to conflate one narrative of destruction with another or to posit them as entirely distinct.[76] Witnessing the aftermath of the destruction reoriented Du Bois from the earlier connection he drew between Nazi Germany's violence and European Christian colonial violence against people of color[77] to a more focused contextualization of Jim Crow America by examining (and witnessing) how "absolute erasure [was] predicated on absolute separation." Du Bois's experience in Warsaw "reveal[ed] the more subtle and insidious operation of the color line,"[78] anticipating what Giorgio Agamben, drawing on Michel Foucault's concept of biopolitics, identified as a "biological continuum."[79] Racism, accordingly, underwrites the capacity to differentiate, separate, and dominate populations through the construction of racial geography, in which Warsaw represents an empty space along a continuum with Jim Crow.[80] To this, West would add Gaza, "the hood on steroids." Hence, "rethinking the color line from the ruins of Warsaw means grasping legalized segregation as a part of a shared logic of biopower. Not simply confined to their own 'ghettos,' blacks and Jews are linked by virtue of the very caesura that divides them along the biological continuum."[81] Just as MBL deepened its solidarity with Palestinians and its intersectional analysis through visits to the West Bank, so too did Du Bois's nuanced account of the connections between genocidal manifestations of violence develop through witnessing the aftermath of the destruction of Warsaw and European Jews. What has changed over the past seven decades is the augmented assimilation of Jews into whiteness and the civilizational (orientalist) narratives that differentiate, rather than connect, the atrocities of colonialism to European fascisms and antisemitism.[82]

The question of the comparability of such evils as the Holocaust, slavery, and the extinction of indigenous populations in the Americas has not only been the purview of African American intellectuals and activists. It has also animated much research in genocide studies, with some scholars analyzing and problematizing the centrality of the Holocaust to the study of genocide[83] and others locating the Holocaust within a broader global history of imperialism and colonialism.[84] Pluralizing the scope of genocide as a category allows for interpreting the atrocities of colonialism, and even the Holocaust itself, as chapters within a broader history of modernity, which relied on race theory and various other mechanisms of dehumanization, dispossession, and destruction.[85] A. Dirk Moses, a genocide studies scholar, for example, challenges a teleological (Hegelian) reading of history through the language of theodicy he finds in Walter Benjamin's plea to narrate history from the perspective of its victims. The Hegelian spin, Moses argues, appears in a widespread hegemonic tendency among scholars to accept the massive destruction of indigenous populations in the Americas, Australia, New Zealand, and Africa as somehow a necessary evil for the story of civilizational progress ("development"), highly dependent on economic profitability of settler colonialism, while nonetheless expressing shock at the systematic plans for destroying European groups. "The upshot," Moses writes, "is that the genocide of European peoples in the twentieth century strikes many American, Anglo-European and Israeli scholars as a more urgent research question than the genocide of non-Europeans by Europeans in the preceding centuries or by postcolonial states of their indigenous populations today."[86] Critics seek to dispel this "hegemonic Eurocentrism" by decolonizing the category of genocide, a process that first requires contextualizing Nazi Germany within a history of colonial policies of destruction, annihilation, and dispossession. Such policies themselves relied, of course, on racializing "subjects" through religious and ethnic taxonomies.[87] The work of decolonizing then requires rejecting relations of affinity or solidarity with "white" Jews, for whom *their* genocide is purportedly unique and unencumbered by imperialism and colonialism.

Hence, when MBL describes the Palestinian predicament as "genocidal," this description conveys MBL's own standing in a black intellectual tradition that has engaged in decolonizing (and therefore deorientalizing) grievability, to recall Judith Butler.[88] In examining what counts as a "grievable" life, Butler refers to those humans who, for whatever reason, are excluded from the definition of the human and stresses that what is at stake is not a simple addition to a preexisting ontological conception of the human, but "an insurrection at the level of ontology, a critical opening up of the questions, What is real? Whose lives are real? How might reality be remade?"[89] The lives of the excluded are considered unreal, an act that in itself constitutes a form of violence. Unreal lives, accordingly, "cannot be mourned because they are always already lost or, rather, never 'were,' and they must be killed, since they seem to live on, stubbornly, in this state of deadness."[90] Butler highlights the ungrievability of Palestinian deaths. And outrage over the ungrievability of black lives led, of course, to the hashtag #BlackLivesMatter, underscoring the need to oppose racist ontologies in ways that draw connections among multiple cases of ungrievability, reminiscent of Du Bois's analysis of biopolitics.

The institutional American Jewish reaction to the use of the word "genocide" to refer to Israeli practices reflects its reliance on a mono-causal analysis of the Holocaust as the sacred pivot of modern Jewish identity and the unique outcome of ahistorical, Christian Judeophobia, which developed into and was abetted by modern race theory.[91] It also reflects blood- and land-centric Zionist interpretations of Jewishness, themselves beholden to modern racial discourses. And it conveys a refusal to interpret Israel itself through the lens of settler colonialism and its reliance on orientalist frames that render indigenous populations both inaudible and disposable (and ungrievable).[92] For Moses, the question is how to overcome the zero-sum game in order to illumine "the processes that link the genocides of modernity"[93] during what he terms the "racial century" (1850–1950), which was marked by "people making" and "nation-building" through imperial competition.[94] Du Bois, likewise, provides resources to think beyond the color line in ways that can reintroduce anti-Jewish oppression into the interconnected struggles against racism. This discussion of racism and biopolitics consequently reveals the centrality of Europe as a narrative and a set of discourses that unfold on transnational and global semiotic sites of contention. It reveals why processes of communal self-transformation employ the tools of decolonizing critique.

This mode of critical investigation complements and enhances critical

Jews' return to the metaphorical "burning bush" and their resolve to interlink their own struggle with all other struggles for liberation.[95] This constitutes a concentrated effort to shift from the non-intersectional approach to the identity politics exemplified by JDL's militant Jewish-centric advocacy and diffused within the broader organizational Jewish landscape where "Never Again" *to Jews* authorizes Jewish support for the logic of the occupation. Retrieving a narrative of Jewish-black alliance, therefore, cannot simply rely on a historiography that glorifies the alliance of the civil rights era embodied in the iconic images of marches. The contemporary process of standing in alliance with African Americans cannot be, Jewish activists have come to realize, grounded in the apparent comparative marginality of Jews and blacks. This, to recall Dollinger's analysis, constitutes a false comparison that disintegrated with the emergence of a separatist Black Power in the 1960s.[96] The separatist approach, which also involved purging Jews from key positions in civil rights organizations, not only marked, as Vorspan stressed, the end of Jewish-black alliance, but also exposed a Jewish lack of engagement with power differentials and the distinctiveness of these communities' experiences within an American topography increasingly defined by non-intersectional identity politics. Standing in alliance with African Americans also, consistent with Feldman's outlook, conveys that, for critical Jews, the formation of this position is necessarily processed through their transnational analysis of American hegemony, but also through their specific complicity as Jews with Palestinian suffering, a predicament that feeds back into and cross-fertilizes with African American critical (feminist) race analysis.

A substantive alliance that moves beyond both optics and a parallelism based on separatism[97] would have to entail active grappling with Jewish participation in the forces and ideologies of oppression and racism. Hence, JVP, by way of JOCSM, stressed that articulating its alliance with MBL had to involve contending with and atoning for the Jewish community's own histories of relying upon and participating in white (and Ashkenazi) supremacy. The process of critical caretaking is hermeneutical (navigating the vastness of traditions through a particular lens), but also deeply historical, shedding light on the historical dynamics of identity transformation and religiocultural innovation. Linking the genocides of modernity constructs possibilities for Jewish-black solidarity, while delinking them precludes it. Such solidarity demands grieving the ungrievables of the colonial project. MBL's platform and intersectional analysis broadly interconnect, through an overwhelming focus on structures, the stories of slavery, indigeneity, and racism in the underbelly of the enduring dominance of colonial and Eurocentric imaginations.

Interlocking Structures of Domination

The limits of a comparative and transnational critical analysis of racism as a mechanism for imagining liberation revolve around its lack of engagement with the multiple ethical, cultural, and religious resources that diverse communities may draw upon for and reinterpret in their own rewriting of their emancipatory imaginations. The geographies of liberation cannot only involve an analysis of colonial modernity in their construction of public narratives. The MBL platform exemplifies both solidarity based on a comparative analysis of racialization and the limits of this approach as the only grammar for emancipatory struggles. Rachel Gilmer, one of the authors of the controversial section of the MBL platform, admitted during a panel at JVP's 2017 NMM that, once confronted with the backlash, some in MBL wondered whether they moved too fast to explicate the case of Palestine. The answer, she stressed, was an emphatic no. However, the reactions did help the movement elucidate its values, grounded in the later legacy of King, and interrogate whether they "cared about being popular and safe for the liberal establishment or . . . about doing the right thing."[98] JVP and JOCSM, she added, helped the movement "be courageous" in this respect as well as the ancestors of radical black activism that always identified the global dimensions of the African American struggle. In this connection, references to King's fifty-year-old speech (given as a sermon) against the Vietnam War were invoked to mark the rich legacy of black internationalism and Third Worldism. Gilmer affirmed that the problem with Israeli apartheid is deeply rooted in Zionist ideology, at the core of which resides white supremacy that needs to be debunked, highlighting that it is impossible to have a "softer Zionist movement for peace." In the same way, a nicer version of capitalism, colonialism, and militarism will not redress root causes of oppression and injustice. "I [Gilmer] am so thankful to the Palestinian people for helping us make these connections," from their Twitter solidarity about how, drawing on their experiences with the IDF, to survive tear gas (manufactured by the same corporations) in Ferguson to the aforementioned analysis of deadly exchanges between Israeli military and security infrastructures, American corporations, and the incarceration of black and brown people in the US. For Gilmer, Israel is pivotal for the counterterrorism machinery where Palestinians and blacks are always perceived as risks to the "public order" and conceptions of safety, executed only through the technologies of biopolitics: aggression, exclusion, incarceration, and borders. Israel, she said, has become a "one-stop shop for homeland security," with an economy based on selling "counterterrorism" and "repression around the world." There is "no incentive for peace," and so "this is not about some solidarity . . . but a real sense of shared fate." The word "solidarity" does seem for her to indicate that the struggles of Palestinians and MBL are actually one "global war for dignity," which would involve illuminating the alliances of white supremacy and Zionism's antisemitic roots. Hence, Gilmer seeks to make the stories of JOCSM central to decolonizing Jewish discourse and to articulating a vision of a world beyond Zionism, that is, to "recapture the public imagination," so that we will not live in somebody else's imagination. Her words reflect the push to relinquish the metaphorical hold of Zion as an emancipatory paradigm. Unblinkingly confronting the parallels and interconnections between Ferguson and Gaza, she unambiguously embraces Palestine as her metaphor.

When Gilmer underscores the "shared fate" of Palestinian and African American communities, she conveys the tendency of intersectional analyses to overemphasize structures, thus succumbing to unsituated critiques of power.[99] One limit of intersectionality as a critical feminist methodology is its silence on matters of religion (especially the question of religious women's agency) and its related presumption of baseline consensus about the significance of non-oppression, freedom, agency, and human flourishing.[100] This silence also delimits the interrelated comparative and transnational critique of colonial modernity through an analysis of racialization and biopolitics. Recapturing the imagination requires more than a structural critique of power. It necessitates hermeneutical work that is firmly grounded, as Jakeet Singh explains, in identity understood not merely "as a site of oppression but also as a source of values, normativity, ethical aspirations, and political projects."[101] Such a central focus on identity recalls intersectional theory's initial commitment to standpoint feminisms, which insisted on grounding epistemology in women's standpoints. The latter are not the same as merely perspectives born out of social locations but rather denote an epistemic reframing through a collective political struggle.[102] However, intersectional theory's later emphasis on critiquing structures of domination and oppression signaled a shift away from standpoint feminism to an unsituated focus on power.[103] This development constituted not only a departure from standpoint feminist insights about identities as sites of moral imagination, but also a departure from Du Bois, who cautioned against conflating sites of violence, while nonetheless recognizing that each site is linked on a continuum of biopolitical logic. Hence, Gilmer's attempt to reclaim the public imagination is constrained because her solidarity with Palestinians—which relies on an unsituated critique of power—results in equating black and Palestinian struggles. She assumes a commitment to "anti-oppression" in all its forms as self-evident and not as internally contested. The MBL platform clearly represents a moment in black-Palestinian solidarity that relies on a structural power critique and the discourse of human rights to posit Israel (or Zionism) as a key culprit in a global structure of interlocking oppressions refracted through the lens of white supremacy.

Black-Palestinian solidarity, however, did not begin in Ferguson. It has, as noted, roots in anticolonialism, antimilitarism, and attention to the plight of black, brown, and other marginalized communities. Even when MBL resists acknowledging its religious roots, preferring to rely exclusively on secularist human rights discourse—despite employing specifically Christian concepts like love—it sees itself as standing firmly within the African American prophetic tradition, which refuses to be domesticated.[104] Similarly refusing domestication, JVP and INN stood apart from other Jewish organizations that opposed the naming of Israeli practices as genocidal.[105] This indignant reaction points to its embeddedness in Zionist orthodoxy and indicates that only when the logic of this orthodoxy has been disrupted—by decolonizing both "Zion" and "genocide"—can a genuine black-Jewish alliance emerge. JVP's departure from this orthodoxy via its own self-scrutiny of white (Ashkenazi) supremacy signals the deepening of the movement's intersectional analysis and activist approach. However, this deepening requires also further critical engagement with American race history, black antisemitism, and the memory of the Holocaust. This deepening of critical caretaking illuminates, as Feldman does, "transnational circuits of racialization"[106] and, as Lubin stresses, the need to examine racialization comparatively in order to expose Euro-Zionism as a form of racialized Judaism beholden to colonial modernity and to reimagine Jews within a geography of liberation. This reimagining of Jewish participation in a geography of liberation not beholden to the project of nationalism as a product of coloniality cannot rely solely on retrieving the prophetic tradition through textual exegesis. It requires a comparative analysis of racialization and a careful examination of the relations between race and religion in Jewish modernity.

As this chapter has traced, the history of black-Jewish relations in the US is complex and has, particularly since WWII, been entangled with Zion and Palestine. While initially embracing Black Power as "good for the Jews," despite its apparent trafficking in antisemitism,[107] the Jewish establishment became increasingly fearful of black antisemitism, as manifest in explicit pronouncements by Leonard Jeffries, who blamed Jews for slavery, and Louis Farrakhan of the Nation of Islam.[108] Violent eruptions such as the Crown Heights riot of August 19–22, 1991, apparently vindicated this emerging narrative about black antisemitism.[109] This fear was often cited in Jewish oppositions to affirmative action, conveying European (Ashkenazi) Jews' assimilation into whiteness.[110]

Baldwin argued in his 1967 piece "Negroes Are Anti-Semitic Because They're Anti-White"[111] that black antisemitism constitutes a reaction to Jews' embrace of whiteness and, subsequently, offers resources to explain why African Americans have come to relinquish the metaphorical hold of "the Jew" as the emancipatory paradigm that Baldwin had described in his 1948 piece "The Harlem Ghetto." The later piece emphasizes African American experiences of Jews as agents of white exploitation. Anticipating the transnational, comparative, critical race theorizing of twenty-first-century thinkers, it offers, nonetheless, a nuanced treatment of Jewish suffering:

> The Jew's suffering is recognized as part of the moral history of the world and the Jew is recognized as a contributor to the world's history: this is not true for the blacks. Jewish history, whether or not one can say it is honored, is certainly known: the black history has been blasted, maligned and despised. *The Jew is a white man, and when white men rise up against oppression, they are heroes: when black men rise, they have reverted to their native savagery.* The uprising in the Warsaw ghetto was not described as a riot, nor the participants maligned as hoodlums: the boys and girls in Watts and Harlem are thoroughly aware of this, and it certainly contributes to their attitude toward the Jews.[112]

What the moral history of the world fails to recognize, Baldwin underscores, are the silenced massacres in the Congo or South Africa, which are attributed to Western Christian colonialism. Jews' whiteness, for Baldwin, is evident in the grievability of their deaths and suffering. Like white Christians, Jews are grievable. "In the American context," he writes, "the most ironical thing about Negro anti-Semitism is that the Negro is really condemning the Jew for having become an American white man—for having become, in effect, a Christian. The Jew profits from his status in America, and he must expect Negroes to distrust him for it. The Jew does not realize that the credentials he offers, the fact that he has been despised and slaughtered, does not increase the Negro's understanding. It increases the Negro's rage."[113] The Jew is despised for embracing whiteness. Hence, "the descendants of the slave" will always consider the Jew to be "part of the history of Europe. . . . Always, that is, unless he himself is willing to prove that this judgment is inadequate and unjust."[114] Baldwin thus allows space for the Jew, as he does for whites broadly, to make a different kind of moral choice, to reject participation in whiteness through his concept of "love."[115] He imagines the possibility that "relatively conscious" whites and blacks will act "like lovers" and in alliance with one another to "end the racial nightmare, and achieve our country."[116]

The condition for such alliance is consciousness of the relational operation of race and the cultivation of love as a locus for critiquing exploitative practices and ideologies but also as a locus for imagining "new modes of relationality."[117] Love, for Baldwin, constitutes an activity of self-transformation and resistance, transforming whites from their condition of lovelessness and unexamined racial innocence and furnishing blacks with technology for overcoming self-destructive tendencies and hatred.[118] The focus on love does not mean the delegitimization of indignation. For Baldwin, the transformation of society will entail validating and redirecting rage's force constructively in ways that both destabilize white comfort and false innocence and enhance accountability to the questions of history and positionality. As Butorac concludes, for Baldwin, "love creates the conditions for structural transformation by enabling white Americans to sacrifice the promise of safety that was never their rightful inheritance."[119] Acting thusly "like lovers" becomes even more urgent for American Jews' processes of relinquishing their sense of safety and certainty through grappling with their whitening and Zionization. To this extent, Baldwin affirms the earlier point that a black-Jewish alliance would require interrogating coloniality or Europe as a set of discursive formations, a process that posits JOCSM as inhabiting an epistemic privilege in the process of reimagining through decolonizing Jewishness.

Baldwin's work, therefore, clarifies why the contemporary movement of Jewish critics and allies cannot unlearn Zionism without also unlearning Jewish whiteness and their positionality within American race history and even broadly within the projects and ideologies of modernity. One of Baldwin's key points in "On Being White . . . and Other Lies" is that whiteness is a moral choice, not an ontological reality.[120] "No one was white before he/she came to America," he writes. The Jews were certainly not white in the countries they came from, and "they came here, in part, *because* they were not white." The moral choice that whiteness represents for him entails the choice to subjugate, rape, and colonize. A moral choice to decolonize Jewish whiteness in tandem with decolonizing those communities comprising the "wretched of the interior," Houria Bouteldja argues decades later but in intellectual continuity with Baldwin's intervention, would be indispensable in cultivating meaningful antiracist coalitions and solidarities that will disrupt the logic of coloniality.[121] By "wretched of the interior," Bouteldja conveys the spectrum and gradation of wretchedness (invoking Frantz Fanon's anticolonial critique) in a power analysis encompassing the excluded and marginalized within the Global North.[122] Unlike Fanon but consistent with Baldwin's white and black "lovers," however, she proposes "revolutionary love" as the pathway for decolonization and one that, for Jews, will denote a moral choice to disrupt their complicity with the legacies of racism, white supremacy, and imperialism through forming alliances with the "wretched of the interior" and becoming together with them an anticolonial "us."[123] Such intersectional alliances will necessarily involve seeing beyond "the color line" and demystifying the construction of Jews as a "buffer community" differentiating white Christian Europe and Muslims.

Baldwin and Bouteldja both illuminate alternative horizons, the paths to which would depend on decolonization but also convergences and alliances that denote a moral choice to relink the genocides of modernity (by uncovering "the colonial genes of National Socialism"[124]) in order to recover Jewish non-whiteness. Asserting that Israel turned Jews "into the most passionate defenders of Empire on Arab soil,"[125] Bouteldja reaffirms the clarity communicated in MBL's platform and increasingly in Jewish Palestine solidarity activists' own grappling with multiple layers of complicity: the moral choice to overcome Jews' entanglement with whiteness entails a disengagement from Zionism. This decolonization constitutes the *sine qua non* for Jewish-black alliance. Speaking directly to Jews qua whites, Bouteldja writes: "They managed to make you trade your religion, your history, and your memories for a colonial ideology. You abandoned your Jewish, multi-secular identities; you despise Yiddish and Arabic and have entirely given yourselves over to the Zionist identity."[126] This assertion resonates with why decolonization also requires or is concurrent with, as we saw in earlier chapters, grassroots religiocultural hermeneutics. The Jewish activists I encountered shifted their affective loyalties and rewrote their Jewishness in accordance to this moral compass. In other words, making a different kind of moral choice requires decolonizing a multipronged racial legacy that enabled white Jews to assimilate into whiteness (as they have in the US) and to articulate a national narrative (as embodied in Israel) that likewise carries with it many of the ills of Europe. These ills include orientalism, colonialism, and an internalized antisemitism that contributed to the transvaluation of Jewishness, dubbed "Constantinian" and characterized as militant, muscular, and powerful. Against such ills, Tzedek Chicago redefines Jewishness as diasporic, nonviolent, and non-Zionist and recommits itself to the diasporic acts of *doikayt*. Indeed, the self-definition as "non" or "anti" Zionist reflects a rejection of what is interpreted as yet another one of the ills of Europe, linked to internalized antisemitism and embedded in colonial and racial discourses. Decolonizing Jewishness, therefore, involves recovering it from its racist legacies.[127] The question of whether Zionism is reducible to coloniality is precisely the question that the intersectional and critical race analyses telegraphed by Gilmer cannot respond to without theorizing Zion out of the Jewish imagination.[128]

Thus, extricating Zion coheres with Tzedek Chicago's moral choice to grapple with American Jewish complicity with whiteness, a struggle constitutive of the congregation's value of non-Zionism. It similarly sheds light on how disentangling from Zion and whiteness are intertwined for Jewish activists.

Baldwin's essays thus convey the complexity of relations between African Americans and American Jews. They ask precisely what it means for blacks that Jews became assimilated into whiteness, how this development relates to African Americans' solidarity with Palestinians, and why refashioning Jewishness in the way that the Jewish grassroots transformational movement aspires to depends on decolonizing Jewishness and disabusing it, concurrently, of whiteness and Zionism. Ironically, black antisemitism relies on the construction of Jews as white. Likewise, this construction motivates MBL's interpretation of Israel and Zionism through the prism of white supremacy and critical globally oriented race theory, which exposes the interweaving and interconnections among sites of domination. Reimagining Jewishness, therefore, involves not only the retrieval of a prophetic pastiche, but also the decolonization of Jews' whiteness even while acknowledging and owning Jewish whiteness in atoning for Jewish complicity in oppression. The prophetic intervention, in other words, demands the tools of postcolonial critique, but also vice versa.

A Community of Barbarians

By underscoring solidarity with Palestinians and employing a structural intersectional lens, Jews' participation in anti-oppression struggles can assume either the form of alliance (as with JVP) or a hybrid model involving both allies and insiders (JOCSM). How might the struggle against antisemitism fit into this dynamic? What interpretive work might serve to reimagine Jewishness outside its co-optation by whiteness and colonialism? Indeed, the refusal by American Jewish institutions to acknowledge the interconnections among modern genocides, including the Holocaust, amplifies this co-optation, especially when aided by an orientalism that renders Palestinians ungrievable. To enlist Jews in the resistance against racism and oppression requires a discursive work that traces, as Santiago Slabodsky does, how the existence of the Israeli state prevented and confused Jewish anticolonial critical work and the cultivation of alliances with the Global South and other communities oppressed by enduring colonial legacies. Slabodsky examines the work of Jewish philosophers who embraced, through their colonial and postcolonial encounters, a critique of colonial discourses about "barbarism." This critique involved reinterpreting, subverting, and resignifying the binaries of civilized versus barbarians, which authorized the colonial project of domination. However, profound inconsistencies emerged in these thinkers' analyses of Israel and where it might fall along the civilized-barbarian spectrum. The inconsistencies are grounded in the discursive power of Zion as an emancipatory metaphor.

For instance, Emmanuel Levinas had a deeply influential encounter, in the 1970s, with Argentinian thinker Enrique Dussel, who represented the Global South's genre of barbaric philosophy. Consequently, Levinas "expanded his critique of the West, mobilized the positive conception of barbarism from his new conversation partners, and recognized that the future of humanity resided in the barbaric margins of the West."[129] He argued for "the need to form a large community of barbarians [that] would be instrumental in challenging criminal imperial formations represented symbolically by Rome and contextualized as Europe and the United States."[130] However, given Levinas's otherwise appreciative approach to Israel as the space where Jews could practice their social law, it was through Israel as a political entity that he sought to (re)integrate Jews into the "community of barbarians," subscribing to the liberationist/redemptive Zionist narrative of Jewish history that amplifies Jewish victimization. This decision exposes the internal contradictions and blind spots in Levinas's philosophy, especially since Israel itself reproduces the Eurocentric civilizational narrative and the broad support that Palestinian resistance has gained among intellectuals in the Global South who otherwise influenced Levinas's own anticolonial critique.[131] The resignifying and subverting of the "barbarian" as an entry point for alliances among anticolonial marginalized communities, including Jews, in other words, is confounded by the contradictions that Israel itself represents. What Slabodsky refers to as "positive counter-narratives of barbarism," articulated by post-Holocaust Jewish thinkers, failed even as they provided insights into the possibility of anticolonial struggle.[132] It follows that decolonization and the elucidation of intersectional alliances will need to address the contradictory ways in which Israel and Palestine feature in accounts of these alliances, their transnational dynamics, and their semiotic interweaving. Decolonization demands an analysis of Zionism through the lens of settler colonialism, but also an analysis that engages with the legacies of antisemitism and the interpretation of the Holocaust as a unique event rather than one deeply connected to the enduring legacies of imperialism and colonialism.

In line with Bouteldja's critique of Zionism as an obstacle for the inclusion of Jews in anticolonial struggles, Slabodsky seeks to relocate "the basis for a potential epistemological alliance"[133] among those whom Europe renders "barbarians" via the colonial gaze. Recognizing that this process would require cross-fertilization with the legacies and intellectual resources of the Global South, he likewise highlights the need to scrutinize Jewish intellectual history of the emboldened assimilation of Jews into the "west" in its "civilizational" fight against Muslim "barbarians." In the post-9/11 era, Slabodsky observes, the assimilation of (white) Jews into the civilizational discourse is yet again repositioned within "a new narrative of barbarism." The latter depicts and authorizes violence against Muslims who not only ostensibly inhabit incompatible civilizational values—as in the late Harvard political scientist Samuel Huntington's unfortunate "clash of civilizations" thesis, which was dominant in policymaking circles and the popular imagination in the 1990s—but who supposedly lack the marks of civilization altogether. Israeli and Jewish mechanisms actively participate in coauthoring this variation of the civilizational discourse.[134] Accordingly, Israel's survival symbolizes "the survival of coloniality" and "civilization" itself.[135] Inversely, "an attack against Israel represented not simply an attack against all Jewry, but an attack against the whole West."[136] JVP's Network Against Islamophobia (NAI) attempts to undo the discursive force of this narrative. However, a more robust account of antisemitism and Eurocentricity, which attends to the construction of Jews as white, is necessary in the process of reclaiming the public imagination. In so doing, such an account moves beyond a reliance on structural critiques of power, on the one hand, and civilizational outlooks, on the other. Such a discursive challenge provides analytic clarity on how Islamophobia (and Arabophobia) and antisemitism constitute two sides of the same coin.

Gil Anidjar's work clarifies the historical and theo-philosophical interconnections between these two cases of bigotry alluded to in the above discussion of Bouteldja's positing of the Jews' functionality as a "buffer community" enabling the *other*-ing of Muslims from Europe. He shows that deorientalizing the sociological spaces of Palestine and Israel requires examining the role of Europe and its enduring Christian legacy,[137] not only in colonization and the construction of blood- and land-centric Zionist interpretations of Jewishness, but also in dichotomies between Arabs and Jews. This dichotomization, of course, has its own history, which betrays the confusion, racialization, and conflation of ethnic, religious, and national indices. Anidjar's genealogy of the category "Semite," which comes to subsume both "Jews" and "Muslims,"[138] takes him to Hegel, who synthesizes Kant's construal of Judaism and "Mohammedanism" as "religions of the sublime" with Montesquieu's account of Muslim despotism. Hegel then conflates Montesquieu's "Muslims," who are portrayed as weak and slavish, with the Jews, juxtaposing both with Christianity's purportedly non-slavish qualities. This conflation—which gained traction in the nineteenth century, along with race theories—is most (in)visibly embodied in the Muselmann of the Nazi death camps, Anidjar argues. "Muselmann" *is* the word "Muslim," and it is no accident that it was the word deployed to describe the living dead in the Holocaust death camps. This European discursivity prompted secular, European, political Zionists to cultivate a Zionist teleology; they became firmly convinced, as Theodor Herzl did during the Dreyfus trial, that Europe needed to be free of Jews. Jews, accordingly, were expected to mimic—as Daniel Boyarin argues—a normative Aryan masculinity in order to overcome their "degenerate" and "effeminate" passivity, by gaining power over their own nation.[139] This, of course, reflects an internalization of the antisemitic discourse, whose negative imagery contributed to the construction of blood- and land-centric Jewishness. However, as the above genealogy suggests, antisemitism as hatred of Jews is not unrelated to Europe's other *other*: its "Muslim question." "Israel, as a theologico-political project," Anidjar asserts, "is the clear continuation of Western Christendom's relation to Islam," which has challenged Christian theological supersessionism and has been marked by a sustained history of both internal and external Muslim "threats" since the seventh century. "To ignore ['the Muslim question']," Anidjar continues, "is to renew and increase the invisibility of the Christian role in the pre-history and the history of colonialism and post-colonialism."[140] Hence, deorientalizing[141] would mean unsettling the enduring logic of Europe as a theo-political and ideological project and that project's role within the Zionist discourse. Both Muslims (employed interchangeably with "Arabs") and Jews function as the others of Christian Europe as a political project. Thus, while the "Arab" and the "Jew" are dichotomized, their construction as antonymous, like the construction of Jews as white, has deep roots in the history of modern Christian Europe. In both instances, such constructs deny hybridities exemplified by Arab Jews and JOC. The latter embody the possibility of pathways for decolonizing and deorientalizing Jewish history and identity.

JOCSM activists strive to articulate such connections among liberationist struggles and "racial justice issues in the United States, Palestine, Israel, and beyond."[142] They are co-participants in socioeconomic, anticolonial critiques and converge with groups such as JFREJ, which likewise identifies JOCSM as bridge builders for Jewish participation in a "'grassroots internationalist' vision for a just world."[143] Their objective is "mutual solidarity" among "'front line' communities around the world who are suffering from the effects of oppressive global systems." These "front line" communities are the "barbarians." When Jewish Palestine solidarity activists express that Jewish liberation is interlinked with others' liberation and struggles (including those of queer, transgender, and gender nonconforming people), this insight demands that

they decolonize their Jewishness. JFREJ recognizes, as does the JOCSM Caucus, that emboldening the praxis of mutual solidarity necessitates "centering
the vision of Jews who are ourselves on the local and global 'front lines' of
resistance to racism, colonization, displacement, and erasure, namely Jews
of Color and Mizrahi and Sephardi Jews."[144] The name of JOCSM's official
blog, *Unruly*, intentionally evokes the label of the "savage" historically imposed on JOCSM by Ashkenazi hegemony and POC communities in general.
Specifically, this is how JOCSM were framed "in Israeli and white-dominated
Jewish society."[145] *Unruly* intends to provide a platform for co-resistance that
first identifies the sites where Palestinian and JOCSM intersect and how they
further relate to other POC and indigenous communities. In addition to articulating JVP's support of MBL's platform, the JOCSM Caucus expresses its
support for other endeavors, such as the hunger strike of 1,500 Palestinian
prisoners in the summer of 2017,[146] critical investigations into the construction of Jews as white in the US, and constructive reclamation of Sephardi and
Arab Jewish meanings and practices.[147] JOCSM present themselves, therefore,
as especially well situated to play "a unique role in fighting state-sponsored
racism in both the U.S. and Israel."[148] They are located "at the intersections of
transnational white supremacy, zionism, and antisemitism where [they] have
been marginalized, exploited, sexualized, erased, tokenized, silenced, oth-
ered, oppressed, patronized, and infantilized."[149] This intersection becomes
an entry point for deeper critical caretaking, self-interrogation, and reimagining Jewishness along complex and multipronged sites of interlocking structures and ideologies. This process demands reapproaching tradition, texts,
rituals, and liturgy through a historically embedded and embodied decolonizing lens. Lived experiences of Jews in borderlands and hybrid locations
themselves become sources integral for prophetic critical caretaking and reimagining Jewishness. Rereading Jewishness through a "non-Constantinian"
lens is a historical process that requires more than a selective retrieval of
textual motifs and bracketing or dismissing departures from such motifs as
"inauthentic" forms of Jewish practice.[150] Analyzing the operation of power
(including biopolitics) necessitates the tools of social and critical theory.
Indeed, the intentionally non-Zionist communal rescripting of Jewishness
we have observed thus far recognizes intersectional solidarity with "barbarians" as pivotal to liberationist praxis. The process of what Paolo Freire
calls "conscientization"—the cultivation of a critical lens through praxis, or
transformative action—requires decolonizing Jewishness. Such decolonization, in turn, entails interrogating Jews' participation in whiteness as well as
blood- and land-centric Zionism and its interlacing (even if non-reductively)
with colonial and racist legacies. It also entails foregrounding marginalized

Jews as a means of recovering barbarity and participation in geographies of liberation.[151]

Furthermore, highlighting the experiences of JOCSM illuminates the integral role an analysis of black-Jewish relations in the US plays in reimagining Jewishness and in grappling with (Jewish) white privilege, complicity, and their multiple implications for Palestinians. This intersection is evident in the opposition of black-Palestine solidarity activists to both Islamophobia and the racialization of Muslims in the US. Davis, for instance, stresses the need "to look at the way in which anti-Muslim racism has really thrived on the foundation of anti-Black racism,"[152] arguing that "anti-Muslim racism . . . is perhaps the most virulent form of racism today."[153] Likewise, she underscores, together with Jewish Palestine solidarity activists, that the war on terror and its reliance on orientalist and civilizational narratives simultaneously augment anti-Muslim racism in the US and support for the occupation of Palestine.[154] Hence, they must be opposed in tandem. But the discursive terrain makes it difficult to draw intricate connections between Islamophobia, antisemitism, and the colonial legacies of Western Christianity. Recovering Jewish "barbarity" as a tool of antiracism and anticoloniality requires undoing whiteness as a moral choice. For Jewish activists, this choice typically plays out in terms of activism against Islamophobia, an activism that is intricately linked to a critique of the Israeli occupation of Palestinians.

As Slabodsky has shown, post-Holocaust Zionist discourse has hindered Jews from reclaiming barbarity and has served to retrench the repositioning of Jews as "civilizational" within the new narrative of barbarity. This dynamic reveals the complex intersections between Islamophobia, antisemitism, and the Global South's critical anticoloniality. While Slabodsky locates the potential for subverting epistemological certainties in the work of Jewish intellectuals, I argue that the Jewish Palestine solidarity activists themselves constitute an engine of reframing and subversion through a prophetic and intersectional grassroots social movement. These challenges reinforce the need to expose the discursive logic underpinning the connections between antisemitism, Islamophobia, and racism, and their relevance to the struggle for Palestinian rights. This interpretive process likewise demands an examination and recovery of the connections, not disjunctures, between European colonialism and its totalitarian and genocidal practices against its own citizens during WWII as well as the enduring struggles of decolonization. As Rothberg demonstrates, relinquishing hegemonic claims to Jewish experiences of suffering and destruction—language that resonates with the religiously inflected discussion of "chosenness" in the previous chapter—can unlock the potential for constructive multidirectional memory.

Multidirectional Memory

For Rothberg, "the model of multidirectional memory posits collective memory as partially disengaged from exclusive versions of cultural identity and acknowledges how remembrance both cuts across and binds together diverse spatial, temporal, and cultural sites."[155] Consistent with the aforementioned works in genocide studies, he challenges modes of zero-sum remembrance where one narrative of communal destruction cannot coexist with another's without each undermining the other. Consequently, employing a strategy akin to Slabodsky's, he recovers an intellectual counter-tradition that offers resources for challenging the "zero-sum struggle"[156] of interpreting collective memories. The suggestion that memory may be competitive or multidirectional is significant for analyzing the connections between identity construction, violence, and peacebuilding. To conceive of memory as multidirectional foregrounds "the presence of widespread Holocaust consciousness" as a prism through which the narratives of American racism can be augmented.[157] To this extent, multidirectional memory can be cultivated through a form of intersectionality grounded in the assumption that the relation between memory and identity is always interpretive and can generate "new forms of solidarity and new visions of justice."[158] Furthermore, Rothberg's unlocking of multidirectional memory challenges competitive memory's presumption that "the public sphere [is] a pregiven, limited space in which already established groups engage in a life-and-death struggle."[159] Instead, much like Butler's view of religion as a "discursive matrix,"[160] Rothberg understands the public sphere "as a malleable discursive space in which groups do not simply articulate established positions but actually come into being through their dialogical interactions with others; both the subjects and spaces of the public are open to continual reconstruction."[161] These intellectual efforts to rearticulate Jews and Jewish memories as participants in efforts to decolonize and remember the silenced narratives of "barbarians" are echoed in the grassroots intersectional Palestine social movement, where the analytic force of intersectionality actively produces a malleable multidirectional discursive space generative for refiguring identities and imagining their potentiality to partake in Bouteldja's conception of the "us." Reimagining Jewishness through grassroots social movement dynamics, as I observed in earlier chapters, involves dialogic and emergenist processes of semiotic innovations that disrupt ontological and epistemological barriers for such potentiality.

Once again, narrativity is a key tool for peacebuilding work when used to critique ethnoreligious-centric conceptions of identity and memory and to cultivate multidirectional memory, a process that involves hermeneutical critical caretaking. The critique is necessary for Jews to reimagine themselves as participants in the "community of barbarians," not just as allies who see themselves as "white" and who are thus able to bracket anti-Jewish oppression from the broader spectrum of intersectionality within which Palestine's liberation is linked with other sites of social justice activism. Multidirectional memory allows for the constructive malleability and reimagining of collective identities and intersectional solidarities. The social movement of Jews, as activists within the broader Palestine solidarity movement, needed to contend with the competitive and teleological remembering of the Holocaust in order both to participate effectively, as Jews, in Palestine solidarity, and to reimagine their own Jewishness and commitments to decolonization. Increasingly, simply rejecting the equation of critique of Israeli policies with antisemitism has proved insufficient as a tactic for Jewish solidarity in the decolonization of Palestine. Multidirectional memory is crucial both for resisting competitive and hegemonic memory and for reimagining, through social movement contentions and elastic discursivity, deepened conceptions of justice and Jewishness that do not dismiss the legacy of antisemitism and anti-Jewish oppression. The deepening of the engagement with antisemitism and the movement's effort to decolonize and deorientalize its discursive force demonstrates the elastic causality of an intersectional social movement's analysis. The movement, in other words, plays a role in decolonizing and deorientalizing Jewishness and its operative core memories. This decolonization is pivotal in refiguring a Jewish political ethics that emphasizes a transposable understanding of the victim's position[162] and encourages potential pathways for reimagining Jewish alliance with socioeconomic, cultural, and racial justice work in the US, even while recognizing the global circuits of racism and the legacy of Euro-America. This chapter demonstrated, therefore, why historically embedded comparative critical race theory and intersectionality constitute tools for ethical interrogation and critical caretaking. The next chapter further examines the intricacies of decolonizing and deorientalizing antisemitism and Holocaust memory as it relates to constructively reimagining Jewish conceptions of identity.

8

Decolonizing Antisemitism

> Talking about antisemitism isn't easy. We at JVP dragged our feet on taking up this
> project in large part because it felt too fraught and frustrating. Fraught because defining
> antisemitism elicits strong feelings and multiple analyses that felt daunting to reconcile
> with one another. Frustrating because while we always address the isolated incidents of
> real antisemitism when they do arise in our movement, we need to focus on strategies
> for ending the occupation that more urgently need our attention. We put it off for too
> long. . . . Ultimately, we realized that we were leaving our movement partners in the
> lurch through our reluctance to tackle this question. And being part of a movement
> means doing what is needed by the collective, not just what is comfortable for us.[1]

This chapter examines the critical contesting and scrutinizing of antisemitism within the social movement of critical Jews, a process that ultimately
leads to decolonizing and deorientalizing the discourse, through centering
Mizrahi, Sephardi, and Jews of Color's (JOCSM) tools of analysis and lived
experiences. Decolonizing and deorientalizing the uses and meanings of antisemitism becomes necessary for articulating Jewish Palestine solidarity and
alliance with antiracism and other social justice struggles because of how
constitutive Palestine and Zion/Israel are for articulating the meanings of
race in the US.[2] This discursive undertaking, as the previous chapter showed,
requires interrogating the relations between white supremacy, antisemitism,
and Jews' participation in US race history. This chapter engages this complexity further by examining the fragility of Jewish whiteness in light of the
resurgence of white supremacy and neo-Nazis in the US during the 2016
presidential election and subsequent administration of Donald Trump. As
many voices throughout the previous chapters have expressed, the Trump
moment offers a moral clarity that destabilizes chauvinistic modes of solidarity. Broadening and reshaping the meanings of antisemitism through an
intersectional analysis contributes to deconstructing Jewish "whiteness" and
with it the complicity and alliances of some Jews with white supremacy, racism, and settler colonialism. These alliances are of relatively recent history.
Thus, denaturalizing their logic can help relocate Jews to the anti-oppression
camp of "barbarians." Yet even within this camp, enduring patterns of antisemitism must be challenged. Reinterpreting antisemitism and transcending
the right-wing monopoly over the concept is crucial to articulating a critique

of the occupation capable of resisting intra-Jewish silencing tactics and connecting the Jewish struggle against blatant American antisemitism to an intersectional movement against multiple sites of systemic injustice.

Additionally, the moral shock produced by blatant and increasing antisemitism in the US has led Jewish activists in the movement for social, racial, economic, and cultural justice to deepen, not abandon, their unlearning of whiteness and continue grappling with their multipronged complicity with white supremacy. However, in the face of open antisemitism, they have increasingly demanded that their allies and partners in the movement likewise undergo a critical process of unlearning their antisemitism and acknowledging the need to struggle against its various manifestations within the movement for collective liberation. Multiple statements, panel discussions, workshops, and protest actions have consolidated Jewish activists' efforts to fight against white supremacy, without pushing the fight against antisemitism under the proverbial bus. The movement has also expanded the scope of its analysis by producing learning tools for allies and partners in the broad struggle for collective justice. The effort to understand antisemitism *for* the movement has involved not only discursive tools, but also interreligious mechanisms that challenge the forces that work to differentiate antisemitism from all other bigotries and forms of racism and distract the Left from its otherwise intersectional critical edge.

An Intersectional and Holistic Assessment of Antisemitism

Judith Butler speaks of "fugitive antisemitism" to describe the presumption that criticisms of Israel, at the level of human rights for instance, are actually "fueled by antisemitic hatred."[3] Such fugitive forms allow, as chapter 1 observed, accusations of antisemitism to "operate as a form of power . . . to censor a point of view . . . [and] to delegitimize the criticism."[4] As this book has shown, more and more American Jews resist the instrumentalization of the Holocaust and the legacy of antisemitism to authorize actions that contradict what they contend is the upshot of the Holocaust.[5] The growth from a few marginalized intellectuals to an expanding grassroots movement suggests that the effectiveness of fugitive antisemitism has increasingly diminished as a muzzling technique. However, simply showing up to Palestine solidarity actions visibly as Jews is not sufficient to demonstrate that criticism of Zionism and Israel is not the same as antisemitism.

The epigraph is drawn from Alissa Wise's contribution to JVP's *On Antisemitism: Solidarity and the Struggle for Justice*, a book debuted at JVP's 2017 National Membership Meeting (NMM). The book resulted from a recognition that simply rejecting the equation of anti-Zionism with antisemitism is ultimately detrimental to the Palestine solidarity and global social justice movements. Also needed is a robust intersectional and relational examination of antisemitism that highlights interconnections among sites of racism and struggles for liberation.[6] Hence, moving beyond earlier efforts to debunk and deflate fugitive antisemitism,[7] JVP conceived the book as "a holistic assessment" of antisemitism by all those affected, directly and indirectly. The book accordingly conveys the perspectives of Muslims, Christians, Jews, Israelis, Palestinians, Jews of Color, scholars, activists, and others to underscore the multidirectional impact of oppression. In response to the movement's grassroots demand for a rigorous analysis of antisemitism, the book foregrounds the tools of discursive critique. But it also shows how foundational constructive reframing is for refiguring the reliance of Jewishness on narratives of antisemitism and the zero-sum memory of the Holocaust. An intersectional engagement with these narratives, I show below, exposes a multiplicity of blind spots and facilitates the capacity for cultivating multidirectional memory through scrutiny of the complex connections between antisemitism, Jewish whiteness, and white supremacy.

This intersectional lens does not permit bracketing Jewish complicity in the occupation of Palestinians (and a broader discourse of settler colonialism) from Jewish cosmopolitanism. Nor does it allow for claiming that antisemitism is irrelevant to the struggle for justice in Israel and Palestine. But before turning to intra-Jewish attempts at decolonizing and deorientalizing antisemitism, let us sketch how American Jewish activists, informed by processes of unlearning, navigated the discursive hold of fugitive antisemitism in their effort to expose Jewish complicity with Islamophobia and thus show up as Jews by engaging with Christian efforts to disentangle fears of fugitive antisemitism from ethical commitments to Palestinians.

What Does It Mean to Show Up as Jews?

American Jewish Palestine solidarity activists have vigorously contributed to the deliberations of various Christian churches about divestment from companies profiting from the Israeli occupation. Notably, the Presbyterian Church USA (PC-USA) voted narrowly in favor of selective divestment in June 2013.[8] This was the second time such a vote had come before their General Assembly (GA). The resolution's passage involved layers of intertraditional discursive work. Present during a long week of deliberations at the GA meeting of the PC-USA in Detroit in the summer of 2013, activists from JVP and other smaller Jewish groups encouraged delegates to overcome their fears of challenging the taboo against criticizing Israel. The Jewish activists who spent the week with the Presbyterians wore t-shirts that read "Another Jew Supporting Divestment," and engaged in vigils and discussions of Christian anti-Judaism and what grappling with that legacy means for commitments to justice in the post-Holocaust era (see figure 8.1).

Susanna Nachenberg, a JVP organizer who has focused on interfaith engagements, described her dismay at how the Jewish establishment handled the Presbyterian vote: "The institutional Jewish community . . . opposed divestment by saying it would ruin Jewish-Christian relations, and even offered a meeting with Prime Minister Netanyahu if the church voted no on divestment."[9] Another Jewish activist told me that the contrast of the deep relationships formed among Jewish activists and Presbyterian commissioners during the weeklong assembly with the last-minute appearance of Jewish challengers made a difference in the minds of the commissioners, who found the Jewish establishment's threats disingenuous. The process of reaching a churchwide decision—articulated in terms of peace and justice—entailed years of research, consultation, deliberation, and grassroots interfaith work of the kind that Nachenberg and other mostly young Jewish activists engaged in. Notably, Nachenberg stresses, the decision to divest was articulated in a constructive tone (not often recognized by its critics) that sought "positive investment, an affirmation of Israel's right to exist, support for a two-state solution and a commitment to interfaith partnership." She describes a moment

FIGURE 8.1. Inaugural Open Hillel conference at Harvard, 2014 [Photo credit: Gili Getz]

during the hours leading to the divestment vote when "our group of Jews and Presbyterians joined hands to pray. We started to sing, 'peace, salaam, shalom.' The mood was solemn but hopeful. Some commissioners joined us, while anti-divestment Jews watched from afar. A young seminary student from the Presbyterian Peace Fellowship led us in prayer, as we lowered to a soft hum." The prayer called for justice to guide the pending decision. For Nachenberg, "this powerful circle encapsulated a moment in history." "I felt," she concludes, "the amazing power of interfaith partnership."

The PC-USA resolution's passage followed a sustained study of the Israeli-Palestinian conflict, including the logic and scope of Israeli occupation, and an effort to grapple with classical Christian antisemitism. The substantive deliberations resulted in a congregational study guide titled *Zionism Unsettled*, the culmination of work by the Israel/Palestine Mission Network, the Presbyterian Peace Fellowship, and Mission Responsibility through Investment (MRTI). The study guide generated some controversy and anger from the Jewish establishment and was ultimately withdrawn from circulation.[10] The text engaged the Christian legacy of antisemitism and post-Holocaust theology that has been complicit with Israeli militarism. In a section titled "Constantinian Religion," the authors draw on several Jewish thinkers who criticize the harnessing of Judaism in the service of power, including Martin Buber, Marc Ellis, and Brant Rosen.[11] Ellis offered his by-now-familiar articulation of Jewish non-Orthodox resistance to Zionism. He framed Jewish critique in rather Christian terms, taking the "Constantinian" complicity of Christianity in cultivating empire as a paradigm for describing the perversion of Judaism by Zionism. Additionally, his critique of what he termed "the ecumenical deal" invited historically embedded wrestling with the legacy of the Holocaust and Christian antisemitism. The "ecumenical deal" refers to the post-Holocaust moment when Christian support of Israel was accepted as a form of repentance of Christian complicity with the atrocities of anti-semitism in return for "Christian silence on Palestinian suffering." In other words, "any Christian dissent on Israeli policies toward Palestinians would be seen by Jews as a Christian return to anti-Semitism."[12]

This logic reveals the myopias of the reparative moment in Jewish-Christian relations. As Shaul Magid argues in his critique of Peter Ochs's engagement with John Howard Yoder's anti-Zionist Christian theology, interfaith engagement cannot simply ignore or bracket the suffering caused by Zionism. Indeed, Magid argues, it can be deepened (without self-destructing) by placing external critics such as Yoder in conversation with internal critics of Zionism. Doing so paves the way for a non-Constantinian lens for rereading tradition historically through deep contextuality rather than signaling a dyadic supersessionism or rereading Judaism *as* Christianity as Yoder had done.[13] In the context of divestment deliberation in churches, the reparative process is fully expanded to include intra-Christian interrogation of the myopias and grappling with the suffering of Palestinians. The ecumenical deal, of course, is rooted in orientalism and colonialism, which together render Palestinian lives ungrievable. Therefore, one goal of grassroots discursive intertraditional work must be the dissolution of the deal's logic through decolonization, deorientalization, and hermeneutical critical caretaking.

Such discursive interfaith work presents itself as a critical peacebuilding mechanism through religiously grounded support for the broader BDS campaigns. Similarly, the 2017 resolution in the Mennonite Church USA (which had also failed in its first attempt in 2015) passed with a resounding majority of 98% of the vote after years of careful work that likewise involved relationship building with Jews, Palestinians, and Christians of Color.[14] Addressing the issues that emerged during the failed process of 2015,[15] BDS advocates gave tours of Israel and Palestine to over one hundred leaders of the Mennonite Church USA and produced a video-based tour of American Jewish and Palestinian peacebuilders for congregations.[16] These mechanisms for raising awareness and cultivating relationship represent undertheorized facets of "interfaith" work, which emphasize the undoing of reigning discourses through relationships with subversive and marginalized sectors of a religious community. The resolution's authors deployed a restorative justice lens in order to engage self-reflexively with Christian antisemitism, historic harms to Jews, and how these relate to harms against Palestinians. The presence during the drafting, outreach, and deliberation processes of "Jewish folks who cared about Palestinian human rights" was critical.[17] This refiguration of Jewish-Christian relations is not merely the upshot of an introspective journey, but depends on audacious grassroots prophetic intervention that paves the way for rescripting collective meanings intersectionally and collaboratively.[18]

This hermeneutical focus on the prophetic legacy and Jewish histories of resistance, commitment to the underdog, and *being* the underdog become the primary idiom for critical Jews in conversing with Christian "faith-based" interlocutors who represent potential participants in the broader Palestine solidarity movement through BDS tactics. The emphasis on the prophetic also resonates strongly with Palestinian liberation theology, where it grounds critiques of Zionist ethnocentricity and helps cultivate theological tools for Christian Palestinians, who obviously cannot draw upon the paradigmatic Exodus narrative of Christian liberation theologies because they represent the indigenous populations displaced and exterminated when the Israelites arrived in the Promised Land.[19] Appeals to the prophetic as means of critiquing power and national chauvinism, however, are not without their ambiguities, especially if underscoring the prophetic as a more authentic mode of Jewishness entails implicit complicity with Christian supersessionism.[20] Indeed, the relationship building with progressive Christian churches requires undoing the hold of the ecumenical deal, which relies on an orientalist and colonialist prism that renders Palestinian lives ungrievable and mutes their suffering in order to atone for Christian crimes against Jews. The resort to the prophetic Jewish tradition, however, converges with and echoes the Christian supersessionist derision of "ethnic" and particularistic threads of Jewishness. In thus rereading Judaism *as* Christianity, this strategy authorizes the dismissal of Zionism (and Zion) as not authentically Jewish. This disaggregation of terms itself allows for creeping antisemitism on the Left, as we will see below.

Another key site where American Jewish activists "show up as Jews" is in solidarity with Muslims and Arabs fighting both Islamo- and Arabophobia and the resurgence of neo-Nazi symbols, rhetoric, and explicit violence associated with Trump's rise to power.[21] Jewish Palestine solidarity activists participate explicitly in intersectional analysis and in efforts to form or recognize cross-movements for inter-communal co-resistance. They have been especially instrumental in exposing the connections between Islamo- and Arabophobia at home and the enduring strength of the narrative that has, for decades, authorized Israeli atrocities and suppressed an entire population. One level of activism involves, for example, exposing the direct connections between anti-Arab and anti-Muslim propaganda as it relates to the "war on terrorism" and Zionist networks, interest groups, and organizations. JVP's Network Against Islamophobia (NAI) documents links among US Islamophobia, Israeli politics, and anti-Arab racism in the US. For example, the network mounted a strong counterprotest when the courts ruled in favor of Pamela Geller's 2014 anti-Muslim campaign featuring ads on public buses that read "Killing Jews is worship that draws us close to Allah." As Rosalind Petchesky from JVP-New York notes, the issue is not only the bigotry of one person such as Geller, but rather a deeper, more systemic bigotry underpinning the "discriminatory surveillance of the Muslim community." Recognizing these realities, Petchesky stresses, is what underlies the commitment to work intersectionally with Muslim groups.[22] Geller's ads visually connect Islamophobic tropes with Palestinians, drawing visceral parallels between "Muslim threats" in Israel and the US. One way of challenging this discourse is by highlighting the deep interconnections between antisemitism and Islamophobia, thereby destabilizing the association of Islamophobia with pro-Israel sentiments and thus with a rejection of antisemitism. Anti-Muslim and anti-Jewish policies and sentiments share common roots in European and Christian history.[23] The mainstreaming of white supremacy during the Trump era further clarifies the interconnections among these bigotries as well as pathways for reimagining solidarities and coalitions.

Jewish organizing typically focuses on publicly resisting Islamophobia, as manifest, for instance, in the so-called "litmus test" (that good Muslims support Israel), surveillance and securitizing of Muslims, and other forms of harassment that harm the dignity of Muslim persons. NAI expands the discursive level of solidarity to tracing the historicity of Israel's construal of Muslims as the "enemy," identifying patterns of money flows from the Israel lobby to Islamophobic campaigns, and challenging the binary of "good Muslim vs. bad Muslim."[24] The Saturday following Trump's election, I joined a broad inter-communal coalition in Chicago to canvass local businesses and ask them to post on their storefronts signs rejecting the profiling of Muslims. The brief Shabbat rally attracted more people than anticipated. JVP activists walked around with "Stop Profiling Muslims!" t-shirts with a clear understanding that this was what they needed to do that Saturday. They had to show up. Walking from store to store in a Chicago neighborhood, they recognized, was critical to their participation in the struggle for Palestinian rights. Through a complex process of analysis, unlearning, and the various mechanisms of politicization, anti-occupation Jews have come to recognize that their activism must be intersectional and tackle discursive complexities such as Islamophobia and the ecumenical deal and how white supremacy is threaded into both. Tackling discursive and epistemological violence requires discursive as well as hermeneutical interpretive tools.

What does it mean, then, for Jews to show up *as* Jews and resist the dominant narrative? In part, it entails discursive work resulting from processes of unlearning and ethical outrage at the heart of Palestine solidarity. Showing up as Jews involves explicating and exposing Jewish complicity with systemic orientalism and Islamophobia (globally and locally) and helping Christian churches grapple with the force of the ecumenical pact and the Christian legacy of antisemitism. It also translates into intersectional work with Muslim, Christian, and other communities resisting white supremacy in the US. Hence, it contributes to undoing Europe as a theopolitical and ideological project. Without a robust analysis of colonialism and the intricate relations between Israel, Jews, and antisemitism, the discursive insistence on rigid distinctions between Israelism and Judaism can provide a cover for real antisemitism.[25]

Antisemitism and the Left

Butler points out a profound irony: "The current Jewish critique of Israel is often portrayed as insensitive to Jewish suffering, past as well as present, yet its ethic is based on the experience of suffering, in order that suffering might stop."[26] This insight about Israel's monopoly on the legacy of Jewish suffering explains the indignant reactions to the MBL platform. However, the attunement by Jewish critics to Palestinian suffering, rooted in the ethical experience of indignation and deepened through an intersectional analytic and activist lens, does pose a certain risk. It risks discounting the problem of antisemitism, as though the phenomenon, which has manifested religiously, politically, and socially across centuries, dissipated magically at the end of WWII, and as though fighting it were not a major concern of social justice activism and the formation of alliances across struggles against racism. However, in addition to the relinking of the Holocaust to a critique of modernity and coloniality, as examined in the previous chapter, the inclination to discount antisemitism is mitigated through a focus on JOCSM's capacity to confront whiteness from a Jewish marginal perspective. Accordingly, the intersectional embeddedness of Jewish Palestine solidarity pushes the movement to come to terms with and then negotiate Jewish diversity, a process that unsettles the reliance on white privilege as the source and instrument of Jewish ethical action against the occupation. The examination of Jewish whiteness is intricately connected to confronting antisemitism in the way Wise suggests, intersectionally and collaboratively, by asking discursively who is affected how and why.

When I asked activists about real antisemitism (or anti-Jewish oppression) understood minimally as expressions (verbal or otherwise) of hatred, discrimination, and assigning of blame to Jews qua Jews, usually through activation of conspiracy theories and classical anti-Jewish tropes from Christian Europe, rather than its fugitive manifestations, they all conceded that antisemitism still exists. Indeed, it does, in various explicitly and implicitly religious forms and under various guises, and it emerges within the circles of the Palestine solidarity movement, under the broader veneer of human rights discourse.[27] Social media in particular allows for antisemitic expressions to unfold regularly, often through subtle semantics, "by replacing the word 'Jew' with 'Zionist.' It's now 'Zionists control the media' or 'Zionists already decided who the next US president will be' instead of 'the Jews.'"[28] Such semantic play, used also by neo-Nazis,[29] allows for an ostensible defense against accusations of antisemitism, responding that "real Jews" reject Zionism.[30]

Many activists, prior to the Trump moment and the moral clarity it afforded, may have recognized persistent antisemitism, but underscored its non-institutionalized form (unlike institutional anti-black racism) and preferred to bracket it as a nuisance and altogether a distraction from the objectives of Palestinian liberation. Indeed, my interviewees immediately offered a disclaimer that antisemitism is merely a peripheral phenomenon overblown by the American Jewish establishment, committed to Israeli advocacy. Even in cases of undisputed antisemitism, the respondents agreed that the establishment's support of the occupation and militancy is not the answer. Yuda, for instance, did not dismiss anti-Jewish motifs and their occasional incorporation into Palestine solidarity, but contextualized them, highlighting nuances: "I hear rhetoric about antisemitism in the Palestine liberation movement. . . . There is antisemitism across the spectrum, but the antisemitism that is *really* dangerous for Jews is the Christian-Zionist type. Yes. I am aware of caricatures and so forth in Islamist and other contexts, but if you take a caricature as a shorthand 'yes,' this is antisemitic, but I don't view it as a danger. If Palestinians have anti-Jewish feelings, this is different [from Jewish] hatred of a German neo-Nazi." It is different, according to Yuda, because Palestinians experience Jews as occupiers, as soldiers at checkpoints, invaders of their homes at night, demolishers, and bombers. "I personally was embraced as a Jew by Palestinians, working in solidarity with them," Yuda concluded.[31] Once again, these remarks highlight that many Jewish Palestine solidarity activists are propelled into activism because of their perception of themselves as benefiting from white privilege. This self-perception allows Yuda to downplay the severity of both the so-called new antisemitism manifesting on the Left and the Islamist propaganda that employs classical Christian antisemitic tropes to depict Zionism or Israel. He recognizes antisemitism's enduring interpretive force, nonetheless, by first highlighting its Christian and European roots, thus exposing several factors: Christian restorationist theologies' complicity with political Jewish Zionism,[32] the popular traction of Christian Zionist sentiments rooted in the sense of cultural affinity between Israel and the US and the construction of Islamophobia,[33] and the recognition that Christian Zionist "love" of Zion is as antisemitic as hate and resentment of Jews because it relies on the same supersessionist logic that undergirded classical antisemitism and spells the eventual, eschatological annihilation of Jews.

Such "love" of Zionism is also a feature of the white ethnonationalism— euphemistically called "the Alt-Right"—that gained momentum with the ascent of Trump. But here it is accompanied by an explicit antisemitism directed against Jewish diasporas. Hence, the resurgence of white nationalism in the US serves to clarify antisemitic Christian Zionism. When I spoke to Yuda before neo-Nazism made its terrifying display in daylight in the US in

2017, he felt compelled to address the Muslim and Arab antisemitism that is often associated with creeping antisemitism on the Left. The surfacing of explicitly antisemitic images in Islamic and Arab contexts is nothing but a symptom, for Yuda, of the broader story about Christian European colonialism and its exportation of such antisemitic tropes and its ideological and theological participation in the formation of Jewish Zionism. Decolonization, therefore, constitutes a key mechanism for confronting the broad nets of anti- and philo-semitism.

Leah, another activist with a background in the Reconstructionist movement, recognized the enduring, often unintentional antisemitism she encounters as part of her work with Christians. She also acknowledges antisemitism in Palestine solidarity and the inclination of other Jewish activists to diminish its significance. Yet she underscores her own position of "whiteness" and security.[34]

However, "Being white and privileged as an American Jew," Abigail (a college student from Florida) told me, does not translate globally because French Jews, for instance, "are under attack."[35] "Antisemitism creates more Zionists," she concluded regretfully. Echoing this recognition, another interviewee—whose grandparents came to the US from Russia and Romania in the 1920s and 1940s but lost their respective families during the Holocaust—identifies Israeli policies as a major culprit in antisemitism. However, she is hardly blind to antisemitism: "What I have seen in [the] pro-Palestine movement in and outside Palestine . . . is an increased antisemitism; it's about identifying something inherent about Jewish culture that allows for the occupation. I don't see a lot of traditional antisemitism, but [I do see] an increased look at Jewish texts supposedly in order to show chauvinistic exclusiveness. I do think that the 'chosen people' stuff is problematic and has effects on the politics of Israel. But I don't like the simplicity of anti-Jewish language. . . . I think it is a mistake to avoid addressing this issue internally within the movement. We don't need to call it 'antisemitism,' but we do need to recognize this trend within the Palestine solidarity movement."[36]

This activist affirms the worry expressed above about a creeping antisemitism within the global Palestine solidarity movement but adds that the problem involves negative assessments of Jewish culture and religion to account for the evils of Zionism. Christian and Jewish Palestinian liberation theology is sometimes complicit in such an approach. An elective affinity between universalizing political liberal discourse embedded nonetheless in the theological, philosophical, historical, and colonial specificities of Europe and a supersessionist reading of the Hebrew Bible is conducive for the flirtation of rights-based solidarity with antisemitism.[37] This slippage conveys the need to integrate analysis of antisemitism into the broader critique against racism, colonialism, and orientalism as well as unsettling the binary of Zionism versus diasporism, a binary that assimilates Jewishness onto Christian and modernist categories of religiosity. The latter allows for framing the prophetic strands of the Hebrew Bible as anticipating the spiritualization of Judaism in Christianity as well as the framing of religion as a set of values disarticulated from Zion. It therefore amounts to reading Judaism *as* Christianity, a re-reading that ultimately works against the kind of restorative justice outcome sought by the Mennonite Church's approach to divestment.

Regardless of the willingness to acknowledge antisemitism on the Left, activists in the pre-Trump era preferred to bracket it as relevant only insofar as they focused on undoing its hold on the dominant discourse. This is what Wise meant when she described a reluctance within the movement to tackle such complexities due to discomfort. However, this discomfort is no longer good for the movement. JVP's *On Antisemitism* thus represents a snapshot in time of the movement's grappling with antisemitism as it manifests historically in its multidirectionality. This is in line with April Rosenblum's widely circulated pamphlet on antisemitism and the Left.[38] Therein, she writes that the bracketing of antisemitism or anti-Jewish oppression is detrimental to the Left's capacity to base its strategies and alliances on an analysis that engages with the root causes of injustice. The Left's reluctance to take on this issue leaves a vacuum for the Right to play the role of "defenders of Israel and the Jews,"[39] which in Trump's America are not interchangeable: Zionism and antisemitism go hand in hand for white nationalists. In Rosenblum's view, antisemitism has traditionally functioned to distract disaffected and marginalized sectors from a critique of capitalism. This is especially effective considering that the phenomenon operates in such a way where the oppression of (white) Jews does not look the same as others'. Though there were historical moments when it did quite clearly manifest as oppression, antisemitism no longer comes in the form of poverty, mass incarceration, or other obvious forms of structural violence. Yet it persists in harder-to-identify forms where the existence of a few powerful Jews who apparently embody the very opposite of oppression is in fact symptomatic of the traditional logic of antisemitism that built on the perceived (and often invisible) strength of Jews. It is harder to identify especially when it comes in the form of *doxa* or "common sense," offering a wide array of culturally embedded conspiratorial plots to employ as explanatory frames in hard economic times. Rosenblum, therefore, worries that antisemitism diminishes the capacity of the Left to advance a critique of capitalism.[40] The issue, for Rosenblum, is not the small number of explicit antisemites on the global Left, but rather the inability to integrate the concern with anti-Jewish oppression centrally into coalition building. The Jewish activists I spoke to about antisemitism resonate with this disaggregation because of their apparent worry that any discussion of antisemitism will allow bypassing their focus on the wrongs done in the name of Jews to the Palestinians. The unease is also symptomatic of the Jewish establishment's disaggregation of antisemitism from the broader struggle against racism—as chapter 7 examined—because, for the establishment, Zionism became the incontestable answer to antisemitism in ways that contradicted the African American anticolonial critique of Israel and resulting affinity with Palestinians. Further, by actively endorsing Islamophobia, the Zionist solution is grounded in an ethnocentric form of solidarity that exhibits a monodirectional and competitive memory of pain and victimization and remains blind to its intersections with other memories and experiences. It circumscribes the transnational and global semiotic exchanges that, as we saw in the previous chapter, connect genealogies of modern antisemitism, orientalism, and anti-black racism and locate them in coloniality and their undoing in decolonialization. Jewish Zionism and its narrative of antisemitism, in other words, prevents the possibility of cultivating a strong radical Jewish Left.[41] Groups such as JFREJ, by definition, imagine justice struggles intersectionally, by decentering and even rejecting Zionist framing of Jewish history, identity, and memory.[42]

Israel's practices, however, allow Jewish activists to highlight significant cracks in its self-branding as the defender of Jews against antisemitism because such branding proved deeply paradoxical. The more explicit antisemitism rears its ugly head in a number of countries steeped in xenophobia, Islamophobia, and neoliberal forms of structural violence, the more the moral clarity of activists deepens. In this climate of moral clarity, the ironies present themselves with a striking transparency. Israel is willing to muzzle critical Jews and non-Jews in American colleges by invoking fugitive antisemitism, a form of censorship that grew into an explicit travel ban targeting Jews and non-Jews active in BDS campaigns.[43] Yet at the same time, Israel condones actual antisemitism of powerful political machineries when it appears to be consistent with Israeli military and occupation objectives.[44]

For instance, a curious closeness between the Israeli hardened right-wing government and the populist governments, politicians, and groups in Europe and the US explains why the Israeli government's officials retracted their initial outcry against an explicitly antisemitic campaign in Hungary and across Central Europe that targeted the Hungarian-born Jewish billionaire and Holocaust survivor George Soros. Soros, accused for promoting, through his Open Society Foundations, "liberal values, including support for refugees," provides a classic trope.[45] Underlying the Israeli right-wing government's condoning of the anti-Soros campaign regardless of its explicit antisemitic tones employed by leaders in Russia, Poland, Hungary, and other countries is Israeli officials' convergence with European and American populist leaders, including the Alt-Right, with its anti-Muslim and other racist, homophobic, and sexist sentiments.[46] Indeed, it was during the wave of exclusionary anti-Muslim nationalist discourses in the US and Europe that the Knesset, despite strong urging from American Jewish leaders to reconsider the ramifications,[47] passed in the summer of 2018 its nation-state Basic Law, enshrining its departure from a nominal commitment to equality extended to non-Jews and thereby solidifying the choice between "democratic" or "Jewish" and "owning" the apartheid analogy ever so precisely and unabashedly.[48] The choice of a radicalized government was unsurprisingly hailed by self-proclaimed "white nationalists" as a path to emulate.[49] It also came in short proximity to Netanyahu's condoning the Polish Holocaust Law intended to promote a whitewashed narrative about Polish complicity with the extermination of Jews during WWII, a move decried by Yad Vashem,[50] the Israeli museum tasked for remembering the Holocaust. The nation-state law and the betrayal of Jewish safety through shielding antisemitism came with an array of interrelated assaults such as on the status of the Arabic language, the rights of same-sex couples and LGBTQI individuals, as well as non-Orthodox religious currents practicing in Israel.[51] As one commentator wrote, "United around a shared hate of Arabs and Muslims, radical European right-wingers provided for certain Israeli politicians and activists a way out of their isolation in the international arena. In return, Israeli counterparts provided kosher certificates attesting that the foreign hardliners are not the anti-Semites they seem to be."[52] For the American Jewish establishment, the official departure from the pretense of the possibility of upholding the label of "a Jewish and democratic" state (despite its apparent contradictions of terms) and the Israeli concurrent attacks on Conservative and Reform currents and flirtation with antisemites begin to elucidate what the Jewish critics of the occupation have articulated through their grassroots indignation and critique. Indeed, INN highlighted the Soros affair to denote the disintegration of the mythology underpinning the diasporic Jewish requirement to defend and support Israel to maintain it as a safe haven against the recurrence of antisemitic threats. Its social media postings clearly stated that "the Israeli right turns its back on diaspora Jews and our safety."[53] Here, Jewish activists employ the evidence of Israeli support of unambiguous antisemitism to augment the moral shocks conducive for rescripting Jewishness in ways that transvalue Zionist values. While the history of Zionism has deep roots in leveraging antisemitic sentiments,[54] the

Soros affair illumines the need to expose the intersection between antisemitism, Islamophobia, and other manifestations of racism through further deconstructing Jews' whiteness and alliance with the civilizational narrative as well as scrutinizing antisemitism's centrality in white nationalist ideologies.

Antisemitism, Jewish Whiteness, and White Supremacy

Trump's election, the evident rise of emboldened antisemitism, white nationalism, and white supremacy in the US associated with it,[55] as well as his association with explicitly anti-Jewish and antisemitic figures, presented activists in the Jewish social movement with profound challenges to their own claims to whiteness and privilege in the US. The challenges to Jewish Palestine solidarity reside also in what echoes from the conclusion of one activist cited above that actual forms of antisemitism create more Zionists, presuming the intelligibility of the Zionist narrative. A simple assumption that the apparent absence of antisemitism that many of my interviewees experienced as privileged "white" American Jews (and according to a Pew survey, over 90% of American Jews define themselves as "white"[56]) is all that is needed to dismiss fugitive antisemitism, and that this will fall apart in the face of actual antisemitism (even if not systemic), proves inadequate. The manifestation of explicit antisemitism in Trump's America, however, demands delving into the construction of Jews as white in the US. Thus, attention to explicit antisemitism converges with the movement's work—detailed in the previous chapter—to understand Jewish alliance with African Americans and black-Palestinian solidarity. If a lack of overt antisemitism signals the whiteness of Jews, then do explicit forms of antisemitism revoke this privilege? A more nuanced analysis to avoid such simple proposals is operative in the movement where three-quarters of American Jews voted against the populist white nationalism of Trump and his networks.

Indeed, Trump's ascendancy demonstrates that Zionism is "the face of white nationalism" in the US, as antisemitic white nationalists herald Israel as a model for the white ethno-state to which they aspire,[57] even while espousing antisemitic views and political and ideological designs that would cleanse white societies of diaspora Jews.[58] As the previous chapter noted, Richard Spencer, a "suit-and-tie"[59] white supremacist and the popularizer of the euphemism "Alt-Right," has expressed admiration for Theodor Herzl's idea of an ethnonational state and Jewish non-assimilationist mechanisms, calling his own movement "white Zionism."[60] His ironic admiration of Zionism comes nevertheless with traditional antisemitic tropes about Jewish control of power and support of Holocaust denial and its "de-Judaification" by the

Trump Administration. It also shares elective affinities with traditional forms of Christian Zionism.

The Alt-Right's longing for an ethnic state analogous to Israel (where whites can live securely) is, in effect, entirely consistent with modern antisemitism. It reflects a rearticulation of the "Ein Volk, Ein Reich" Nazi principle and the aspiration to relocate the Jewish diaspora away from the sites of white European societies where they supposedly, activating familiar antisemitic tropes, masterminded the decay and collapse of white supremacy and masculinity, traditional heterosexual and patriarchal values, and forms of authority.[61] Hence, understanding Zionism as the face of white nationalism conveys a shift from the old guard of American white supremacy's anti-Zionist stances. David Duke, for instance, depicted Israeli leaders with familiar antisemitic tropes of blood libel, conveying a form of antisemitic anti-Zionism which, Ben Lorber underscores, is distinctly different from "the principled anti-Zionism of the Left, which views Israel's oppression of Palestinians not as a 'Jewish problem' but through the structural lens of settler colonialism, apartheid and white supremacy."[62] The antisemitism of the Trump era may be Zionist, but it is still antisemitic, wrapped up in scholarly theorizing and stamps of scientific approval in the same way that the older forms of Nazism and fascism were.[63] The historical moment exposes both Jewish and Israeli institutional complicity with these forms of Zionist antisemitism[64] and an opportunity to identify the connections between multiple sites of oppression and racism. Jews, clearly, ought to be in the anti-Nazi and anti-fascist camp with other Americans, along with undocumented and marginalized communities. This is the inexorable conclusion of Jewish Palestine solidarity activists and other Jewish critics of Israel in the face of emboldened white supremacy in the US.

This became clear on August 12, 2017. Only eight months into the Trump Administration, a violent white supremacy and neo-Nazi riot in Charlottesville, VA, to protest the removal of a Confederate memorial also interweaved explicit Nazi antisemitism and targeted Jews. This hateful display exposed the enduring interconnection of the struggle against anti-Jewish oppression with the struggle against all forms of structural injustice. The heavily militarized and torch-carrying white supremacists wore Nazi symbols, adorned with quotes from Adolf Hitler, and chanted Nazi slogans such as "blood and soil" (*Blut und Boden*) and "Jews will not replace us." The riot signaled the centrality of antisemitism to white supremacist and white nationalist ideology. "Antisemitism," claims Eric K. Ward, "forms the theoretical core of White nationalism."[65] Ward, an African American and longtime researcher for the Southern Poverty Law Center, explains that antisemitism fuels anti-black racism and other xenophobic and racist sentiments along with misogyny and homophobia. White nationalists narrate their sense of loss due to the social movements of the 1960s as the outcome of the work of a brainstorming diabolical Jewish cabal controlling entertainment (Hollywood), Wall Street, and Washington, DC, who orchestrated a takeover of the humanities and social sciences.[66] Here, Jews function classically as they did in "The Protocols of the Elders of Zion"—a Czarist-fabricated piece of propaganda adapted to the American context and popularized by Henry Ford in the 1920s as "The International Jew" or the "globalist." Ward explains that concurrent with the construction of Jews as white, "antisemitism has become integral to the architecture of American racism."[67] Hence, the question of a Jewish-black alliance capable of grappling with Jewish complicity with, but also victimization by, Europe as a religiocultural and theo-political project entangled in multiple genocidal legacies (not just the Holocaust) becomes pivotal for consolidating an intersectional movement.

While some Jewish commentators took the display of antisemitism in Charlottesville as a vindicating sign that discussion of Jewish whiteness needs to be put on hold in order to fight exclusively for Jewish survival,[68] the intersectional lens recognizes that the overt manifestation of antisemitism and its centrality to white nationalism's racism invites a multidirectional interrogation of Jews' whiteness and participation in antiracism in a way that does not revert to an exclusionary narrative of liberation and Zionist tropes about security. Indeed, the threat to Jewish safety is reinforced by the Jewish establishment's failure to condemn actual antisemites as long as they convey their support of Zionist Israeli objectives.[69] Spencer's avowal of "white Zionism" likewise exposes the incongruity, dissonance, and estrangement Jewish critics experience when they recognize the implications of Israeli ethnocracy and its inconsistency with progressive conceptions of inclusion.[70] As Naomi Dann wrote, "Richard Spencer, whose racist views are rightfully abhorred by the majority of the Jewish community, is holding a mirror up to Zionism and the reflection isn't pretty."[71] In particular, Dann refers to Spencer's explication, on Israeli TV, of his analogy between white nationalism and Zionism: "I care about my people. I want us to have a secure homeland for us and ourselves, just like you want a secure homeland in Israel."[72] Like right-wing Zionism, his nationalist ideology cannot sustain "radical inclusion."[73] Clearly, as Dann notes, white supremacy's perception of existential threat can be neither substantiated with evidence of white privilege nor equated with Jewish historical experiences of actual discrimination and existential threat underpinning Herzl's political Zionism. Nonetheless, Spencer's "white Zionism" does highlight similarities with Israel's "privileging of one group, and all too often perpetuating the erasure and displacement of another [as well as] an obsession with demographics and the maintenance of an ethnic majority."[74] Those constitute human rights violations that Jewish critics experience as violations, done in their name and under a narrative about safety (from antisemitism), of their own Jewish values. The alliance of convenience between white and Jewish Zionists unfolds through a manipulation of Islamo- and Arabophobia and antisemitism and undoing it, Jewish critics conclude, requires participation in the broader movement against racism and against the Israeli occupation of Palestinians.[75] This moral clarity in the aftermath of the violence in Charlottesville animated the group of INN activists' participation in protest marches against white supremacy from Charlottesville to Washington, DC, where they repeatedly shamed the organized Jewish community for its failures to stand on the right side of history and reaffirmed their commitment to broad-based grassroots solidarity.[76] This failure became lucidly apparent when the Zionist Organization of America (ZOA) hosted Stephen Bannon and Sebastian Gorka (among other known antisemites, Holocaust deniers, and white nationalists) at its annual gala in 2017, exemplifying not only how Jewish safety and support of Israel are not synonymous but also, by honoring these individuals, ZOA's endorsement of bigotry across the board.[77] The mostly young protesters outside the gala called out their communal leaders and elders, demanding, "Which side are you on?" (figure 8.2).

FIGURE 8.2. A guest of ZOA's 2017 gala in New York City faced by Jewish protest [Photo credit: Gili Getz]

This historical moment does not call for reverting to an affirmation of narrow ethnocentric forms of solidarity. The lesson of the Holocaust means to stand united in both fights—against antisemitism and white supremacy— concurrently. This finally entails, for the Jewish anti-occupation activists, reimagining Jewish-black alliances through a multidirectional prism that does not pretend to stand solely on the presumption of a Jewish legacy of powerlessness, but also involves struggling with the histories of Jewish power and complicity with whiteness. This reimagining entails undoing Europe as a set of discursive projects of domination by exposing that blood- and land-centric conceptions of Jewish history and identity cohere not with Black Power but with White Power, particularly in its longing for an ethnocentric self-actualization and its trafficking in explicit antisemitism.[78] As Amy Goodman, host of Democracy Now, said in her opening remarks to a panel on antisemitism she moderated at the New School in New York City in late November 2017: "The horrific scene that played out in Charlottesville, VA . . . when hundreds of young white men walked across the campus of the University of Virginia . . . many of them carrying torches and chanting 'blood and soil' and 'Jews will not replace us' . . . they were teaching us certainly about intersectionality . . . [racism, antisemitism, and Islamophobia]. *They* put it all together for us."[79] These words convey the moral clarity that only enhanced the Jewish anti-occupation movement and deepened its turn to intersectional social justice activism. In a protest against white supremacy shortly after Charlottesville, one young INN activist told the story of her grandmother, who escaped Prague to Ellis Island all alone and would never see her family again:

> How could this be real. How could I look at my 97-year-old grandma . . . and tell her that last week I fought Nazis. . . . How can I tell her that after everything she lost that there are white supremacists in our streets and our president isn't doing anything to stop it our president is even sympathizing with them? . . . In the same time, another wave of emotion was hitting me and it was a wave of intense gratitude that I am not facing this alone. I imagined my grandmother arriving in America, completely alone not speaking a word of the language and I thought about how fu**ing tough she has been her entire life. . . . She didn't get a chance to fully process what happened to her. She didn't get a chance to fully heal, and that's why I am here today. I am here to do the healing work that my grandmother . . . wasn't able to do. I am here to be a part of a community that recognizes that our safety and our liberation is bound up with the safety and liberation of all other people. . . . I am here because this is how our community moves forward.[80]

The moral clarity gained by an explicit antisemitism, in other words, does not result for this activist in a relinquishing of her responsibility to interrogate her white privilege as an Ashkenazi American Jew but rather a chance to directly confront the challenge posed by Leslie Williams, an African American Jew: "I confess to a certain discomfort in the many appeals to recognize the twin evils of antisemitism and anti-black racism in Charlottesville," she wrote. Her discomfort resides in a profound realization: "For Jews, Nazi symbols evoke a terrifying, traumatic past. For African Americans, they evoke a terrifying, traumatic, *unending* present. . . . Black people did not need to be reminded by hoods and swastikas that we live in a dangerously racist society."[81] This strong statement captures once again the requirement for multidirectional narrativity about the genocides of modernity as a key resource for reimagining Jewishness through a broad lens and intersectional conception of liberation. The resurgence of white nationalism illuminated the interconnections among anti-black racism, Islamophobia, and antisemitism and clarified for activists the complex interconnections between Israeli nationalists, the American Jewish establishment, and antisemitic Christian and white Zionists. A rise in actual antisemitism and ethno-white nationalism, therefore, demands a more rigorous scrutiny of Jews' whiteness and how it relates to the analysis of white supremacy and structural power in the US as well as antisemitism. The simple deflation of the equation upon which fugitive antisemitism relies is not a sufficient narrative frame around which to generate collective actions, especially when evidence is mounting to confirm actual antisemitic trends. What is required in order to move beyond such logic is a multidirectional interrogation that, while echoing some of the insights of Slabodsky and Rothberg's intellectual counter-histories, is distinct. Here, grassroots processes and intersectional and dialogic social movement dynamics constitute the primary vehicle for decolonizing and deorientalizing the discourse of antisemitism.

A Moral Choice

The intricacies of the debate about whiteness are important here, given how such dialogical interrogation advances communal redefinition—through semiotic innovations—in the broader social movement of Jewish activists. The movement's awareness of JOCSM's perspectives and analytic tools (epistemologies from the margins) is heightened by internal pushes for consistency on antiracism and demands on JVP and other Jewish organizing to be self-aware about internal Jewish pluralities and divergent experiences of privilege. For instance, Mark Tseng-Putterman, a writer and organizer active in Asian American and Jewish leftist spaces and a member of the JOCSM Caucus, argued that scholars and analysts—most of whom are white Ashkenazi—try to

interpret the phenomenon of antisemitism in the context of white supremacy in its most extreme form (Stephen Bannon, Richard Spencer, and other
neo-Nazis), without scrutinizing the founding pillars of white settler colonialism and racism of which the neo-Nazi type of supremacy is an extreme
symptom.[82] "It's clear that white Jews have no place in neo-Nazis' imagined
white America. But grounding our understanding of whiteness in neo-Nazi
ideology belies the fact that 'white nationalism' isn't just the domain of the
alt-right fringe; it is the guiding logic of our nation's narrative." Ashkenazi
white Jews were invited into whiteness, an invitation that is hardwired into legal and social institutions in the US. Tseng-Putterman, therefore, challenges
Karen Brodkin, who famously located the construction of Jews as white in the
US in the aftermath of World War II and the diminishing traction of eugen-
ics and race theories.[83] Instead, Tseng-Putterman, channeling James Baldwin's analysis of Jewish whiteness and resonating with the insights of Houria
Bouteldja,[84] points to how whiteness as a US legal category did not necessarily
exclude Jews from the institutions of slavery (as per Virginia's Slave Codes
of 1705), citizenship (the 1790 Naturalization Act), or marriage (while mis-
cegenation with Christians was surely unpopular, anti-miscegenation laws
such as Virginia's 1924 Racial Integrity Act did not explicitly forbid European
Jews from marrying "other Caucasians"). Here, he traces an entanglement of
Jews and whiteness in the US context and therefore Euro-Jewish participation in structural violence, even while antisemitism was manifest in terms
of immigration, residential, and other laws. As a result, "In these three sites
of legal whiteness, well before WWII Euro Jews enjoyed benefits of whiteness that Native Ams [Americans], Blacks, & Asians didn't."[85] This historical
exposition is necessary in order to complexify claims to white privilege that
if unaware of their long entanglements with white supremacy can be abandoned in moments such as those presented by the ascent and reappearance
of blatant racism and antisemitism in the seat of power.[86]

However, as Eric Goldstein cautions in *The Price of Whiteness: Jews, Race,
and American Identity*, narratives about how Jews embraced whiteness betray
little engagement with "how Jews *negotiated* their place in a complex racial
world where Jewishness, whiteness, and blackness have all made significant
claims on them."[87] Focusing on the period between 1875 and 1950, Goldstein
provides a historically sensitive account of the ambivalence American Jews
experienced in a context defined rigidly by blackness and whiteness as the cri-
teria for communal self-definition.[88] In this context, the Jewish community
in its geographical diversity (Southern Jews were different from Northern
Jews) and other internal pluralities (gender, for instance) had to navigate the
forces of inclusion but also an aspiration to maintain Jewish distinctiveness.

What was distinctly Jewish was therefore negotiated within and through the broader prism of a racialized discourse. The language of race, with its similarities to ethnicity and thus "peoplehood," enculturated Jews to American racial taxonomies even while American Jews expressed discomfort with the predicament of African Americans, with whom they felt affinity. In the late 1960s, as the previous chapter discussed, this enculturation took the shape of Zionism as pivot of Jewish identity and advocacy, operating in parallel to black struggles within a landscape of identity politics that facilitated the cultivation of difference. Goldstein's account, therefore, reveals that the assimilation of Jews into whiteness in the US was gradual, entangled with the aspiration for communal self-definition, and refracted through a racial discourse. Hence, to return to the contemporary Jewish critics of the occupation and American Jewish Israelism, disentangling Jewishness from Israelism is interwoven with a process of a communal redefinition that once again orbits centrally around the question of whiteness, but also on undoing Zionism, which itself is assimilated into a broader critique of white supremacy. This time, this process is multipronged. It involves grappling with the sins of participating in white privilege in the US, including the silencing of JOCSM experiences and voices. It also entails a global analysis of whiteness through a critique of the enduring legacies of colonialism, orientalism, and exploitative capitalism and how (white) Jews are specifically implicated in these legacies in the US and Israel. Thus, grappling with the embrace of whiteness includes confronting and atoning for the even deeper sin of endorsing Ashkenazi supremacy in Israel, and with it the European project of displacement, domination, and exploitation.

For American Jewish activists who are "woke" and immersed in struggles for racial and social justice, this multifocal interrogation constitutes no mere academic abstraction. It is a very real dimension of their process of communal refashioning, as they ask again, *Who are we?* in and through a movement that is intersectional and demands a multifocal lens. The activists cannot ask Rabbi Hillel's first question: *If I am not for myself, who will be for me?* without also asking: *Who am I?* This question, as we saw, is foundational for articulating alliances and solidarities. Nor can they avoid the question *Which side am I on?* Lamenting and atoning for Jews' whiteness, therefore, is front and center for the activists I engaged. Whiteness, critically, is not an ontology, even if Jews in the movement own up to their complicity with its systems of domination and privilege.

Drawing explicitly on Baldwin's discussion of black antisemitism and Jewish whiteness,[89] Tseng-Putterman understands whiteness as a moral choice individuals make (to own slaves, which European Jews did in the American

South and North). Thus, the Trump era may signal an opportunity to disengage from whiteness as a "psychological construction" within which "European Jews have made political [and] moral choice to participate." This disengagement process would require a moral choice rooted in analysis of white supremacy, colonialism, and racism and decolonizing interpretive lenses.

Deorientalizing and Decolonizing Antisemitism

Examining the experiences and lived critiques of JOCSM, therefore, becomes pivotal for reimagining Jewishness and for articulating collective action frames within the grassroots movement of Jews.[90] Undoing Jewish participation in the civilizational discourse requires reclaiming Jews' location with the "barbarians." Consequently, American race analysis permeates the intra-movement interrogation of antisemitism in the populist moment of white nationalism.

The framing of discussions in the 2017 NMM navigated the relation of antisemitism to white supremacy and Jewish "whiteness" by recognizing the threat of antisemitism as an outcome of the Zionist discourse and its tactics as well as classical antisemitism that nobody denied was still in circulation. In addition, the parallels drawn between white supremacy here and there were amplified by Mizrahi and Ethiopian Israeli speakers who described the atrocities committed by the Ashkenazi hegemonic system, understood as relying on (white Ashkenazi) settler colonial and orientalist discourses, against both the Ethiopian and Mizrahi communities in Israel. They are the "blacks" of Israel who were then assimilated into a broader analysis of interlocking systems of oppression explicated by the many representatives from MBL who partook in the conference. Whiteness was altogether under scrutiny in this NMM, which followed a full-day meeting of the JOCSM Caucus and involved explicit programming on the Israeli Black Panthers (featuring Mizrahi activists) and reflections of JOCSM.

The gradual problematizing of the whiteness of Jews, including the perspectives of JOCSM, demonstrates the social movement's contestability and identity construction. Debates over the interrelations between white supremacy and antisemitism occupy pivotal loci in articulating Jewish Palestine solidarity and refiguring Jewishness as a moral choice. Hence, the movement's category of "privilege" and its commitment to "being an ally"—typical words employed in Millennial-dominated circles of social justice activism[91]—where individual activists see themselves as leveraging their privilege to support a variety of actors from whom they take directives as to the nature of the support. Words I heard repeatedly in my interviews and participant observation work in the West Bank come into sharp relief with efforts to embolden activists' grasp of the meanings of privilege as constituting not only some sort of an individual accessory but also a category with deep structural, political, and ethical histories. Problematizing whiteness, therefore, demands scrutiny of antisemitism in collaborative and intersectional ways. The two spaces are interrelated in the process of reimagining Jewishness through solidarity and social movement dynamics.

JVP acknowledges this need in *On Antisemitism*. The volume reflects a process to reshape the discussion of antisemitism in a way that directly confronts the realities of the Israeli occupation as well as challenges the Eurocentric lens through which Jewish history has been narrated by bringing to the fore the perspectives of JOCSM and Palestinian allies.[92] To this extent, even while exhibiting internal disagreements among the authors, *On Antisemitism* embodies the relationality and intersectionality through which Jewish Palestine solidarity activists and critics of Israeli policies refigure their Jewishness and their public narratives dialogically. The volume underscores the need to examine antisemitism and decolonization in tandem. Hence, one of the main products of the volume was a statement capturing JVP's internal contestation and broadening of the horizons of the discussion of antisemitism in the ways described above. The statement recognizes that antisemitism "does not impact all of us who identify as Jewish in the same way,"[93] and that the struggle against antisemitism, even if currently not manifesting itself structurally through state institutions in the US, needs to be linked to the fights against "Islamophobia, sexism, classism, and homophobia, as well as anti-Arab, anti-black, and other forms of racism, as part of the work of dismantling all systems of oppression."[94] By pointing to these interconnections, JVP seeks to integrate the fight against antisemitism into an intersectional movement involving a political Left that has too often either bracketed or dismissed antisemitism as lying outside its scope, thus allowing the Right and the Jewish establishment to control the discourse surrounding the issue.

JVP is not alone in this fight. In 2017, JFREJ published its own guide and analysis of antisemitism, envisioning it as a relevant tool to the intersectional movement.[95] The moral shock of experiencing "neo-Nazis marching in Charlottesville, swastikas spray-painted on playgrounds, hate speech hurled at Jews in public, cemeteries desecrated, and bomb threats targeting Jewish congregations and community centers," the report reads, generated confusion within the Left (including the Jewish Left) about how to incorporate antisemitism "into the matrix of oppressions alongside those that we are more familiar with, such as anti-Black racism or Islamophobia."[96] Reflecting the dialogic dynamics of social movement analysis, JFREJ's scrutiny of antisemitism, a product of collaboration among "multi-racial, multi-ethnic, intergenerational team including Black, Mizrahi and white Ashkenazi Jews" that is also diverse along gender and class indicators, grounds itself on the premise that "antisemitism is real. It is antithetical to collective liberation; it hurts Jews and it also undermines, weakens and derails all of our movements for social justice."[97]

JFREJ insists that antisemitism is hardwired into the various manifestations of "Alt-Right" white nationalism and that "there is no getting free without ending antisemitism."[98] The organization seeks to disseminate this message to the broader circles of non-Jewish allies and partners in the movement, stressing that the Trump era offers a moral shock so profound, it dispels any confusion about whether antisemitism should be included in the movement's analysis of mutually reinforcing oppressions. In so doing, they see themselves as decolonizing the discourse. In earlier chapters, I discuss how gender (and especially LGBTQI) activism generates semiotic tensions. For instance, when JVP disrupted acts that it deemed to pinkwash the occupation, others framed this disruption as both homophobic and antisemitic (or self-hating). JFREJ's analysis of antisemitism locates this anti-Jewish oppression as yet another legacy of European Christianity,[99] thereby differentiating the experiences of Arab-Jews who inhabited contexts not specifically beholden to "anti-Jewish ideology."[100] The report, however, recognizes that "the Arab and Muslim world was deeply transformed by European Christian colonization and impacted by white supremacy and the ideology of antisemitism that came with it."[101] Hence, non-European (including black) antisemitism would need to be refracted through a critical anticolonial lens, a mode of critique relevant for the movement broadly. Antisemitism in Islamic and Arab contexts, as Magid notes, also conveys an intricate entanglement with anti-Israel sentiments. This cannot easily be disentangled without "a robust engagement with alternative Jewishness"[102] which, as I showed in earlier chapters, rescripts itself as non-Zionist, diasporist, nonviolent, and not chosen.

The moral shock of real and increasing antisemitism during the Trump era[103] results in an affirmation, like that of the young INN activist's story about her grandmother, that collective liberation, not Zion, is the answer to antisemitism. This emancipatory process, as does reimagining Jewish-black alliances, necessitates exposing the common roots of anti-black racism, Islamophobia, and antisemitism in Europe as a discursive hegemony. JFREJ likewise follows Rosenblum's scrutiny as to how antisemitism has functioned to distract the Left from its socioeconomic critique and away from its vision of collective liberation, including as transpired in the case of the Ocean Hill–Brownsville Schools Crisis of the 1960s.[104] "Capitalism isn't oppressive because Jews are ruining it," the report stresses, "capitalism is oppressive because capitalism is oppressive."[105] The ability to resist the ways in which historically antisemitism "has sown division within the poor and working-classes" will spell the difference in terms of enabling rather than "preventing the emergence of multi-class, multi-racial and multi-ethnic mass movements."[106]

For many activists in the movement, therefore, antisemitism can no longer be bracketed but must be integrated within the struggle. This realization allows Jews to finally disengage from Zionism and its monopoly over the narrative about Jewish safety and survival. JFREJ's "Understanding Antisemitism" argues that white Jews can own up to how they benefit from their white privilege while nonetheless understanding the "contextual and conditional" aspects of their whiteness and fight against the enduring manifestations and long-term ramifications of Christian and European antisemitism. With this consciencization, they could act like Baldwin's and Bouteldja's revolutionary lovers to end a "racial nightmare" as it also and constitutively relates to global and transnational circuits of racialization and coloniality.[107] However, to reiterate a crucial point, the experiences and hybridity of JOCSM particularly expose an intersectional potential.[108] The cover page of the report, depicting Muslims forming a protective circle around Jews praying at a synagogue in Oslo, Norway, in 2015, communicates the message that Arabo- and Islamophobia are interrelated with antisemitism and that both are "deeply rooted in the same systems of white supremacy and Christian hegemony that have also driven ongoing genocide against indigenous people, and bigotry toward non-Christians from other parts of the world."[109] JOCSM are simultaneously targeted for their Arabness or blackness as well as Jewishness and thus are instrumental in undoing the assimilation of (white) Jews into the civilizational discourse. Their hybridity, similarly, "offers a window into what a powerful, de-assimilated future looks like for all Jews who are committed to a liberatory cross-racial struggle to dismantle white supremacy and live beyond its spiritual prison."[110] The various efforts to reflect on antisemitism in light of the Trump era reveals activists' deepening critical engagement with Europe as a set of discourses that have long worked to colonize commonsense assumptions and balkanize struggles for justice. Such critical engagement amounts to the decolonization and deorientalization of antisemitism through discursive interfaith work, as we saw in the story of divestment processes, but also through an intersectional relocation of this form of oppression outside its "contextual and conditional" whiteness that seeks to mobilize Jews to co-resist the system of white supremacy.

In her contribution to the JVP volume on antisemitism, Chanda Prescod-Weinstein, an Ashkenazi and African American Jewish activist with JOCSM, exemplifies the deepening intersectional decolonization of the discourse of antisemitism. She reflects on Baldwin's "Negroes Are Anti-Semitic Because They're Anti-White," in which he calls for black and white Jews to resist all forms of supremacy, "whether it is white, Jewish, or anti-Jewish."[111] "Defending Black people," she notes, "eventually came to be at odds with defending the newfound residency in the 'tent of whiteness' of most American Jews."[112] This moral choice left "a legacy of white Jews both participating and profiting from anti-Blackness" and explains the roots of African American solidarity with Palestinians.[113] Prescod-Weinstein worries about related black anti-Jewish prejudice, but suggests that Jewish alliance with African American struggles can help address anti-Jewish sentiments within black communities.[114] Such alliance will challenge, from the grassroots, the discursive forces that facilitate African American antisemitism and obscure the connections between modernity's genocides that underpin black-Palestinian solidarity. This analysis allows for reintegrating, as well as enhancing, the discursive "interreligious" labor around divestment of Christian churches from the occupation, an analysis of colonialism and antisemitism at the heart of Jewish Palestine solidarity, and other intersecting forms of social justice work. The relevance of an analysis of black antisemitism is not merely an abstract matter but rather a concrete dimension of the broader movement for social and racial justice in the time of mobilization of collective liberation, a movement that often invokes Palestine metaphorically as a paradigm of oppression and perpetual liberation struggle.[115] In the same way in which protests against pinkwashing the occupation generated semiotic ambiguities, black antisemitism—or activists' failure to condemn it—emerges as a site of the movement's contention and growth, also reflected in JFREJ and JVP's concentrated efforts to provide clear statements to allies and partners about what antisemitism is and why fighting it is indispensable for the movement for liberation from Ferguson to Palestine.

One example that exposed what is at stake was when in 2018 Tamika Mallory, one of the co-chairs of the national Women's March organization, "publicly attended a Nation of Islam event in which its leader, Louis Farrakhan, spewed hateful and indefensible rhetoric against Jews, women, trans and queer people."[116] Mallory and the Women's March, the largest organizing platform against the outcome of the 2016 elections, were slow in reacting to the criticism. JFREJ and other Jewish organizations, including INN, immediately condemned Farrakhan's "antisemitic, homophobic, transphobic, and misogynistic statements and worldviews" as "antithetical to any project of collective liberation"[117] and also expressed regret and disappointment that the Women's March did not offer a firmer and quicker response. "Some of us feel hurt, outraged, or even betrayed that one of our allies sat through a profoundly antisemitic speech, amplified her participation on social media, and did not offer a public objection." "We will not," JFREJ's statement continues, "dismiss or minimize these feelings—they're real and we honor them."[118] However, even while expressing their outrage and condemning black antisemitism, JFREJ contextualizes Mallory's connection to the NOI (recognizing that the NOI also resonates for many black people as "facilitators of black dignity and prison rehabilitation"[119]) and affirms JFREJ's own commitment to work harder and deepen the meaning of an intersectional coalition and the critical transformative work it requires. It involves cross-(un)learning, as outlined in its "Understanding Antisemitism," designed to reach out to "people who may still be learning about Jews and our histories, as well as about the danger antisemitism poses to us directly and to the effort to dismantle white supremacy more broadly."

INN similarly stated: "The leaders of the Women's March have erred. But we can name that error without writing them off. Our fight for collective justice requires strong relationships between allied groups who will sometimes hurt one another."[120] For JFREJ, as for INN, it is important to navigate carefully a landscape prone to fugitive antisemitism, which undermines the agenda of collective liberation, while nonetheless insisting that the fight against antisemitism is crucial to the Left. Being part of a broad intersectional movement requires, therefore, cross-(un)learning and sensitization of activists: "The Jewish community must have faith in the ability of our allies on the Left to grow, knowing that just as white Jews have to unlearn racism, non-Jews have to unlearn antisemitism."[121] To underscore this point, INN draws upon the Jewish meaning of *teshuvah*, "the process of apology, correction, and moving forward." *Teshuvah* captures for the critical Jewish activists I have engaged their own process of grappling with their communal sins and their transformative resolve to stand again in front of the "burning bush" and commit to collective liberation and structural transformation. The Mallory episode clarifies that reaching that reinterpreted burning bush involves relationship building and cross-(un)learning in the broader intersectional movement. Here, unlearning means decolonizing and deorientalizing antisemitism.

Other authors and scholar activists featured in *On Antisemitism* take up the question of antisemitism from Mizrahi perspectives. An Atlanta-based scholar and JVP leader criticizes the Eurocentricity of the discourse of antisemitism, suggesting it renders Sephardi and Mizrahi Jews invisible by imposing myopias and bypassing an analysis of the reliance of antisemitism on other oppressions, including orientalism.[122] For this author, her marginalization within the dominant Ashkenazi narrative (and its own orientalism) "gave [her] insight and a feeling of connection with Palestinians who resist and struggle against discrimination and oppression. Sephardi/Mizrahi Jews continue to be targeted in visible and invisible ways by both antisemitism and Orientalism/racism."[123] Witnessing the racism, marginalization, and socioeconomic disparities between Mizrahi (and Ethiopian) and Ashkenazi sectors in Israel led this activist to challenge the construction of Israel as her "home" and as the supposed solution to antisemitism. "Having witnessed Israeli racism," she writes, "I felt intense grief about *my home*, this 'Jewish' state, with its unjust economic and social policies fueled by feelings of superiority over others: Jews over Palestinians, Ashkenazi over Sephardi/Mizrahi Jews, secular over religious."[124] Like Prescod-Weinstein, this activist argues for privileging JOCSM's standpoint, and focusing on antiracism, including tackling orientalism. "Being vigilant about racism," she stresses, "is a critical component of addressing antisemitism," and it ought to include white Christians coming to terms with "their historical and current role in antisemitism and Orientalism and how these ideologies simultaneously target European Jewish and Arab and Middle Eastern bodies."[125] In other words, echoing the discursive interreligious work on divestment, white Christians' participation in Palestine solidarity will need to involve their "refusal to participate in and align with" both orientalism and antisemitism because, "when white Christians are working in solidarity with Palestinians and against Islamophobia, antisemitism can sometimes emerge."[126] Likewise, "Christians of color . . . don't necessarily address the problematics of European-based Christian supremacy."[127] Still, this activist's commitment to Palestine solidarity is sound because her Mizrahiness taught her, through the lived experiences of her family in Arab and Muslim contexts, that "addressing the injustices toward Palestinians" does not constitute an existential threat to Jews. On the contrary, this is the entry point to "ending antisemitism and racism, colonization, imperialism, and all forms of domination."[128]

Similarly, Tallie Ben Daniel, another Mizrahi participating in the leadership of JVP, wrote in her contribution that the operative definition of antisemitism in "leftist organizing" is often complicit with "Mizrahi erasure."[129] Foregrounding the requirement to dismantle white supremacy and racism within Jewish communities, including in Israel, she nonetheless exposes the problematic ways in which some Mizrahi activists themselves perpetuate racism in the US by subsuming their claims to indigeneity in the Middle East to the dominant Israeli discourse.[130] Such Mizrahi-washing (or "brownwashing"[131]) entails leveraging claims to indigeneity in the Middle East to dispel categorizing Zionism as a form of white settler colonialism, and to derail complicity with the Nakba and the 1967 occupation and the massive waves of Palestinian refugees (supposedly canceled out by the waves of Jewish refugees from the MENA region). Like pinkwashing, brownwashing "cynically use[s] marginalized identities . . . to promote anti-Palestinian aims," and just as in the case of subverting pinkwashing by Jewish queer activists, so must "Mizrahi Jews and Jews of color . . . take collective action, and work to produce an analysis and a language to address our heritage, histories, and inheritance in ways that fight back against the exploitation of Palestinians."[132] For Ben Daniel, this process entails refiguring the meanings of antisemitism and its manifestation through an intersectional prism that always pivots around the plight of Palestinians.

Conclusion: Antisemitism Redefined through an Intersectional Lens

Unlearning whiteness through solidarity with Palestinians is a key entry point for the critical Jews I have engaged, for whom the process of *teshuvah* and participation in a broader intersectional movement is also deeply personal and relational. Confronted by the daily realities of Palestinians, they unlearn whiteness not only in abstraction, but through grappling with the specific manifestations of Jewish power and Ashkenazi hegemony. Their unlearning of whiteness and their resolve to make a different moral choice involves reimagining Jewishness as non-Zionist, nonviolent, and diasporist and reimagining the fight against antisemitism through an intersectional movement rather than through an ethnoreligious national discourse. Both *On Antisemitism* and "Understanding Antisemitism," as well as multiple panel discussions and Jewish demonstrations and other public actions against white supremacy after the neo-Nazi display in Charlottesville in 2017, convey the movement's effort to rescript antisemitism and relocate it as integral to the struggle for collective liberation. Zionism itself, understood as an emancipatory narrative, remains incongruous with the struggle because of its reliance on Europe's ills of orientalism and colonialism and its embodiment of Jewish Constantinianism. Identifying the project of Europe as a pivot for discursive analysis as well as constructive and restorative outcomes thus requires not only hermeneutical tools, but grassroots prophetic interventions. Jewish activists used to show up to Palestine solidarity actions and certify with their bodies that anti-Zionism is not antisemitism and proclaim with their t-shirts that occupation was not *their* Judaism. However, the current intensification of antisemitism in the US and the reexamination of antisemitism through an intersectional and collaborative lens illuminates the reimagining of Jewishness from the margins not only as non-Zionist, diasporist, and nonviolent (anti-Constantinian) but also as multi-ethnic, multiracial, gender-fluid, feminist, and oriented by the quest for social and economic justice and collective liberation. The moral shock of overt antisemitism and the rise of white nationalism and its form of antisemitic "white Zionism" facilitated the final disengagement from the Zionist monopoly over the narrative of Jewish survival. In fact, Israel's silence on white nationalism and its implicit or explicit condoning of antisemitic Zionists decidedly clarify for American Jewish activists that Israel is making them less safe. Instead, Jewish anti-occupation activists highlight survival as an intersectional process of co-resistance against the structures and ideologies of white supremacy. This, to return to Goldstein's analysis of the complex negotiation of Jewish whiteness in the US, signals a chapter where Jews dis-assimilate from whiteness as a moral choice. They do so by defying exclusionary and essentializing boundaries of racial taxonomies while nevertheless inhabiting multiple hybridities: Jews are black, white, brown, transgender, non-binary, and all of these combined. Through these hybridities, Jewishness is rescripting itself while also interrogating through *teshuvah* its image in the mirror provided to it by "white Zionism." Jewish activists likewise can concurrently grapple with their complicity with whiteness while nevertheless reinserting themselves through cross-unlearning and discursive interfaith work into the movement not merely as (white) allies and partners, but also distinctly as Jewish people fighting antisemitism in tandem with other forms of bigotry and violence including exploitative capitalism. The intersectional scrutiny of antisemitism, through critical tools of decolonization and deorientalization, shows how movement dynamics and contentions participate dialogically in reimagining Jewishness as multiple, internally pluralistic, and multivocal.

Deorientalizing is closely related to decolonizing because the activist focus is on undoing the orientalism of domination that produced the "west" as a hegemon. Like Edward Said, such activists seek to de-Europeanize the postcolonial subject without becoming overwhelmed by the anti-humanist inclinations to which a full embrace of Foucault might lead. This entails an enduring commitment to progressive human rights–oriented politics through democratic criticism. "I . . . still believe," Said writes, "that it is possible to be critical of humanism in the name of humanism and that, schooled in its abuses by the experience of Eurocentrism and empire, one could fashion a different kind of humanism that was cosmopolitan and text-and-language-bound in ways that absorbed the great lessons of the past . . . and still remain attuned to the emergent voices and currents of the present, many of them exilic, extraterritorial, and unhoused."[133] More precisely, the activist commitment to progressive politics must navigate what Hamid Dabashi views as the paralyzing conclusions of Gayatri Chakravorty Spivak's "Can the Subaltern Speak?" In Dabashi's reading, Spivak's subaltern is robbed of her agency because even when she does speak, "[she] speak[s] the language of the oppressor, share[s] the metaphors of his imagination, invoke[s] the sovereignty of his subject—by virtue of the hegemony he has already consolidated in the universe of meaning within which a speech—even the colonial's anti-colonial speech—is understood."[134] In contrast, Said's humanism, already apparent in his *Orientalism*, aspires to decolonize without diminishing human agency and its imaginative and subversive force. This is the hermeneutical, meaning-making, transformative agency through social movement's progressive politics, projective imagination, and critical caretaking that I have highlighted throughout this book.[135] In examining the conceptual contribution of social movement theory, we observed how norms are rewritten by grassroots modes of transformative agency and the dialogic semiotic turn. The intention was to illuminate both the operation of critique and agentic reimagining rooted in the "great lessons of the past" and the "emergent voices and currents of the present," which—for Said, as it is within the movement—are often found in the margins and in exile.

Deorientalizing and decolonizing antisemitism by foregrounding JOCSM as well as—in the case of discursive interfaith work—subversive constituents of religious publics is crucial to deepening the grassroots process of refiguring Jewishness and Jewish ethical commitments. But so is recognizing the complex operation of anti-Jewish oppression and the critique of the progressive Left's failure to intersect antisemitism with its broader struggles. In particular, the analysis of antisemitism brings to the fore race—in the American binaries of whiteness and blackness—suggesting that black-Palestinian solidarity and the symbolic force of Palestine are critical for Jews' own grappling with their white privilege and complicity with the occupation. This deconstructive lens facilitates a multipronged scrutiny of colonialism, racism, and orientalism as they relate to the construction of Jews as white and as co-participants in civilizational discourses that underpin multiple sites of oppression. However, such deconstruction, by interpreting Zionism solely as a form of oppression linked to the legacy of Europe, fails to respond adequately to the pointed question the Ethiopian Israeli Efrat Yerday raised during JVP's 2017 NMM, where she drew creatively on Baldwin's engagement with blackness to interpret her own marginality and pain as an Ethiopian Israeli: What about Ethiopian Jews' yearning for Zion?[136] This yearning persists and reminds us of the problematic supersessionist tendency to read Judaism *as* Christianity. The forcefulness of the parallels and the interconnections among African Americans and Ethiopian Jews in Israel and the structures and ideologies of domination that sustain their respective oppression clearly has its limits. The concluding chapter will address these limits through a broader examination of the study of religion, violence, and peacebuilding.

9

Decolonizing Peacebuilding

Approaches to Religion and Peacebuilding

In *Days of Awe*, I have traced the processes and examined the mechanisms that have contributed to a reimagination of the American Jewish public narrative through social movement dynamics and dialogic contestations. Rewriting a public narrative entails not only pursuing some conceptions of the "good" but also actively redefining them through an analysis of power.[1] Crucially, it also involves tapping into resources outside a reductive conception of power. Jewishness is reimagined now through intersectional movement spaces and through the cross- unlearning process they afford. Accordingly, (white) Jewish activists can atone for their participation in whiteness but also make a different moral choice because, as they have come to see, their whiteness is not an ontology but the outcome of a global semiotics of coloniality and a local historical process of negotiating Jewishness in a racialized American landscape. Making a different moral choice and finally dis-assimilating from American whiteness entails critical caretaking from the margins and the grassroots that disrupts and destabilizes Zionist ontological and epistemological claims and embodies, often through what I termed prophetic pastiche, possibilities for deeper alliances with other groups who resist the structures and ideological formations of white supremacy. Hearing and epistemologically privileging the voices of JOCSM—but also rereading tradition and Jewish histories through a particular lens—all work to consolidate American Jewishness that is multi-ethnic, multiracial, multi-gender, and diverse along other indices.

Likewise, the emerging public narrative of Jewishness is decidedly anti- or non-Zionist. This is because the activists interpret Zionism as a chauvinistic, masculine, heteronormative, homophobic, militant emancipatory narrative that simply does not cohere with the broader movement's intersectional

analysis of collective liberation and justice, for which Palestine has historically served as its metaphor. In fact, the employment of Zion as a metaphor
by white ethnonationalists to describe their own unambiguously antisemitic
White Power and the curious alliances between them and Jewish Zionists
and the Israeli official echelon in the Trump era clarify Zionism as a focus
for the resistance rather than itself amounting to an emancipatory paradigm.
The shift to intersectionality, away from the landscape of identity politics,
has propelled activists to interrogate Europe as an enduring hegemonic set
of discourses and exploitative practices. Witnessing the rise of "white Zionist" antisemitism facilitates, for the movement of critical Jews, reclaiming the
fight against antisemitism for the Left, and with this resolving the conflict
between Jewish particularism and a commitment to progressive politics by
theorizing, through the decolonial turn, blood- and land-based conceptions
of Jewishness out of existence.

Indeed, this signals the erosion of Israelism as a pivot of American Jewishness. American Jews' processes of ethical outrage, unlearning, and grappling
with sinfulness through engagement with Palestinian narratives (as they intersect with Mizrahi and Ethiopian and other marginalized communities)
and the moral shocks they generate embolden their disengagement from Zionism which, to them, is bundled up with their dis-assimilation from whiteness. As earlier chapters have suggested, the self-critique and interrogation
so pivotal for the experience of moral shocks also produce through acts of
solidarity with various allies and partners, and mutually reinforcing mechanisms of moral batteries, a sense of self-worth and approval. By their own
accounts, the Jewish activists I encountered certainly project and experience
an enhanced sense of self-approval and self-love as they prefigure their alternative communal spaces through their activist engagements.[2] They display it
in their joyous singing of Hebrew and Jewish songs during protests, in their
employment of Jewish rituals and holy days in their resistance actions, and
in multiple accounts of their indignant anger with their elders and the Jewish establishment for failing to teach them about the occupation. Reclaiming
Jewish joyfulness is itself a subversive act, disrupting the hold of a narrative
of Jewish history that underscores tragedy as a definitional Jewish experience. The activists' sense of self-approval is captured in Tzedek Chicago's
articulation of its values and normative boundaries and in various hashtags
such as #WeWillBeTheGeneration to end the moral calamity that is the occupation. The enhanced sense of self-approval thus dispels their labeling as
"self-hating" Jews. Indeed, their self-approval conveys self-love, but not of
the idolatrous kind Hannah Arendt worried about in her embrace of her lack
of *ahavat yisrael*.[3] Their shift in affective loyalties from Zion (Israelis) to Pal-

estine (Palestinians), however, does illuminate love in Baldwin's articulation as a mechanism of decolonization of identity and self-transformation with a potential of becoming open to the possibilities (through acting "like lovers" with others) of social and structural transformations.[4] The activists and critics I examine in this book, it is clear, have undergone a process of reimagining communal meanings, religiosity, and identity, with reclaiming religiosity itself constituting often an act of resistance.[5] Their journey is connected to questions of violence and peace, and the deeper the journey persists, the deeper the grappling with race and racialization reveals itself as a primary semiotic field. What makes the contemporary moment unique is the relational component of the interrogation of what it means to be Jewish at a time when Jews are so implicated in violence, even while connecting to and drawing upon a long tradition of Jewish progressivism. The movement of anti-occupation Jews exemplifies why our analysis of violence must be expansive and include discursive, symbolic, cultural, and epistemic forms.

Accordingly, before further examining some of the limitations of American Jewish Palestine solidarity's peacebuilding outcomes, this concluding chapter seeks to move the discussion beyond the particular case of Jewish Palestine solidarity activism in the US to its implications for theorizing about religion and violence and the practice of peacebuilding. The subfield of religion, violence, and peacebuilding (RVP) emerged as a significant area of research and practice around the turn of the last century.[6] It signaled a renewed interest in religion emerging from the claws of a secularism thesis that rendered religion a politically insignificant variable or, inversely, a primary cause of violence, intolerance, and divisiveness whose overcoming was pivotal for the emergence of modern tolerance, pluralism, and a human rights–oriented politics.[7] RVP's systematic and mostly inductive approach to religion and peacebuilding counters and supplements a comparable scholarship on religion and violence.[8] Likewise, it emphasized the role of religion in international relations, especially focusing on security, terrorism, and counter-terrorism.[9] By contrast, the literature in religion and peacebuilding (RPB), which emphasized peacebuilding and development, focused on identifying, cultivating, and emboldening religious actors who explicitly promote peace or resist overt violence and are amenable to development agendas such as reducing child marriage and food insecurity.[10] This "post-secular" recognition that "religion" mattered to politics led to criticisms of what is derogatively labeled the "religion and" industry. Critics of this trend are concerned with how the "good religion" industry exerts Western hegemony through a discourse of religious freedom, thus undermining or overlooking other forms of solidarity.[11] Such critics suggest that the "good religion" industry in fact precipitates violence and conflict through its claims to define who counts as "religious" and what counts as "religion," thereby reinstating colonial and orientalist dynamics and a logic of Western hegemonic governmentality.[12] Indeed, the critics are partly vindicated by evidence indicating that the language of religious freedom is, in fact, manipulated in the service of various stakeholders' religiocultural agendas.[13] But there are also significant limitations to such criticisms.[14] Hence, *Days of Awe* has broadened the scope of RPB and RVP to attend to discursive and epistemological violence, social movement production of transformative collective identities, and the interconnections among religion and gender, race, and nationalist discourses. It illuminated global and transnational processes of unlearning ideology while reimagining alternative collective boundaries. Indeed, its scrutiny of the decolonization and deorientalization of Jewishness as transformative mechanisms also gestures to the need to decolonize and deorientalize the assumptions underpinning RVP and RPB themselves.[15]

I suggest that decolonizing and deorientalizing RVP and RPB requires rejecting the enduring inclination to posit the "religious" as a separate variable that can be studied in isolation from gender, ethnicity, race, nationality, and other sites of contention. Isolating the "religious" as a distinct sphere of praxis and analysis reproduces the way racial and colonial discourses generated and deployed the categories "religion" and "religions." That the construction of "religion" as a comparative category in the nineteenth century was closely tied to imperialism, nationalism, and race theories has become standard in the academic study of religion.[16] This insight has informed this book's investigation of how reimagining Jewishness as a peacebuilding process requires grassroots efforts to decolonize and deorientalize tradition and modern Jewish history. The analysis carries lessons, I contend, for RVP and RPB broadly. "Religion" within these subfields cannot be simply deployed in abstraction from its genealogical entanglements with race produced and reproduced through coloniality. I have highlighted how politicization on critical race theory, economic justice, gender, and sexuality often functioned as mechanisms for transformative politicization on the issue of Palestine. Prophetic grassroots critical caretaking, in turn, also enhanced alliance with multiple sites of marginality in the US, further deepening the decolonizing of Jewishness beyond the more immediate objective of advancing the physical decolonization of Palestine.

Foregrounding the relevance of examining "religion" alongside "race" and "gender" does not entail a reductive approach to tradition. On the contrary, this book has shown, especially in chapters 4–6, grassroots critical hermeneutics and the cultivation of religious and historical literacy as a distinct mechanism of protest and reimagining collective meanings. What Jewish Palestine activism and layers of critique indicate is that undoing ideological terrains requires an intersectional lens. At stake are not only interpretations of Jewish resources, the competitive memory of the Holocaust, and retrievals of traditional rabbinic approaches to the possibility of return to the land. Also at stake are the modernist construction of Judaism as a religion within the context of emerging nationalist and racialized discourses; the Eurocentric, orientalist, capitalist, and colonialist underpinnings operative in Zionism; the subversion of Jewish masculinity; the assimilation of some Jews into whiteness; and the inaudibility of JOCSM. An intersectional approach to RVP and RPB sheds light on an epistemology from the margins that likewise intersects with and is enhanced by indigenous, feminist, and queer methodologies and critical race and economic lenses. Jewish Palestine solidarity activism resonates with contemporary retrievals of the Bundist secular Jewish socialist tradition in the mutual recognition that imagining alternative Jewishness demands reconnecting to leftist critiques of colonialism and neoliberalism as part of an intersectional theory and praxis. Such intersectionality animates American Jewish non- and post-Zionist peacebuilding through the practice of solidarity and demobilizing the traction of multiple layers of occupation-enabling narratives. *Days of Awe*, therefore, has focused on narratives as key sites of peacebuilding and conflict transformation, asking at every turn what "religion" has to do with reproducing, demystifying, and resignifying such narratives.

This book thus shows why isolating the "religious" from a wider examination of race, gender, and nationalism, and treating "religious peacebuilding" as a distinct sphere of activism and theorizing, overlooks the potential for subversive, innovative, and critical dimensions of religious peacebuilding. Conversations on religion—whether these emphasize peacebuilding, diplomacy, and international relations, or development, relief, and emergency actions—tend to isolate "religion" and "religious" actors in order to assess their unique instrumentality for tackling the situation at hand. In terms of policy and praxis, such efforts may be necessary for immediately addressing a conflict zone or a disaster area or even for long-term efforts to redress food insecurity or increase child literacy. Often such efforts become the basis for knowledge production in the form of book chapters, policy and other reports, and evidence-based assessments of development and peace indices in different contexts. This passes as scholarship and indeed constitutes reference points for reflective practitioners. Yet, much of this literature takes the shape of reporting and aggregating case studies into patterned accounts rather than offering interpretive analysis.[17] Hence, scrutinizing how religio-cultural meanings are rearticulated through social movement framing and contentions opens up new sites for theory and praxis. My study explores processes of refiguring collective meanings through grassroots agentic critical caretaking. The Jewishness that is prefigured is articulated, as we saw in chapter 6, along the values of non-Zionism, nonviolence, and solidarity as well as through a critique of Jewish whiteness (chapters 7 and 8). But to what degree might post- and non-Zionist Jewishness, articulated relationally and intersectionally, count as "religious" and thus fall under the purview of RVP and RPB scholarship?

Is Jewish Palestine Solidarity Work "Religious"?

Indeed, the case of Jewish Palestine solidarity broadens the scope of religion and the practice of peacebuilding. But this claim requires some nuance. First, it is important to highlight how Jewish Palestine solidarity looks beyond narrow conceptions of violence. The case of Jewish grassroots activism highlights the critical importance of hermeneutical work in denaturalizing violent narratives that operate in complex ways to authorize violent systems. It also illuminates relational and intersectional processes and analyses that deepen questions about race and coloniality operative in enduring discursive violence. Hence, the case study broadens the foci of RVP to include structural, cultural, symbolic, and epistemic forms of violence. This expansion necessitates the tools of critical theory and—in the case of Jewish Palestine solidarity work—the relational and intersectional dynamics of social movement activism, which themselves produce new modes of imagining religiosity and communal identity. In other words, this case study shows "religion" as a product and resource of meaning-making agents operating from the grassroots in a multivocal way constructing prophetic pastiche that challenges simplistic rendering of their agency as "religious."

A multifaceted conception of religious agency takes into account multiple layers of politicization on race, gender, feminism, militarism, and other issues. The case of Jewish Palestine solidarity activism exposes the fallacy of RPB and RVP studies' extrication of the religious from interrogation of race, gender, and nationalism. *Days of Awe* has examined the legacies of colonialism, racism, homophobia, antisemitism, and Islamophobia that constitute key components of the discursive zones for critical caretaking. What are the implications for RVP and RPB? Politicization in the race/gender nexus is relevant to politicization in the religion/nationalism nexus, and vice versa. We have traced activists' profound systemic and discursive critiques and innovative grassroots critical caretaking. Such processes bear upon the scope and possibilities of peacebuilding, whether through diminishing the support of the occupation by American Jewish institutions, or through on-the-ground actions of civil disobedience against the occupation.

Activists grapple with the violence of scripture and the direct forms of violence done in their names. In particular, chapters 1–3 addressed the ethical outrage born out of recognizing the suffering of Palestinians due to Israeli policies and claims to act in the name of all Jews. Chapters 4–6 examined the lens of critical caretaking and mechanisms for confronting violence in traditional resources as well as historical practices and reshaping their meanings through protest, grassroots hermeneutical refashioning, and prophetic pastiche. The latter, in particular, destabilizes conceptions of religious agency, motivation, and causal powers as beholden to *sui generis* conceptions of religion. Chapters 7 and 8 examined processes of decolonization and deorientalization as indispensable for demystifying hegemonies and ideological formations, stressing the interrelation of race, religion, and nation as a critical site of research for RPB and RVP. *Days of Awe*, therefore, exemplifies the often-overlooked relevance of engaging with discursive violence for scholarship in RVP and RPB.

Jewish Palestine solidarity distinguishes itself as a movement by attending to global multipronged operations of discursive violence and the processes of unlearning and cross-unlearning with allies and partners. These processes have emboldened the articulation of Jewishness as anti- or non-Zionist, with the imagining of collective liberation as its telos, and have equated the moral choice of Zionism with that of whiteness. Without such attention, the violence of the occupation is not self-evident, but normalized and authorized through particular appeals to Jewish narratives and memories and a reliance on segmentation of moral discourses to geopolitical demarcations of nation-states. The activists and critics are properly described as "religious" because this category is always articulated communally and in embedded ways. Therefore, the task of RVP is not to bracket, reify, or highlight self-identified instrumental religious actors. Such bracketing disarticulates the "religious" from its participation in discursive violence. Decolonized RPB, in this case, amounts to interrogating this complicity and engaging with how such a process of unlearning ideology and hegemony requires also an intersectional interrogation along lines of gender and race.

This book has conveyed the relevance of religion to the study of ideology, often manifesting through nationalist discourses that thrive on notions of authenticity, existential threats, and conceptions of peoplehood portrayed with religious markers. Hence, Jewish Palestine solidarity activism is "religious" to the degree that it targets ideology and discourse. It is "religious" in grappling with the religious meanings of peoplehood and with its own Jewishness.

It is likewise "religious" in its producing through movement activism and dialogic identity contestations religious innovations, informed by inter- and intra-tradition critical caretaking, prophetic pastiche, as well as the ethical forces of human rights.

The multivocality of Jewish Palestine solidarity work exposes the complex ways in which religiosity enters peacebuilding, thus suggesting a need to broaden our assumptions about the spaces where religious peacebuilding happens. One key category within RVP and RPB is leadership. Even while critiquing leadership for traditional hierarchy and androcentrism, RVP and RPB nonetheless conceive of change as mono-directional (top-down), focusing on leaders who might influence their communities in constructive and conducive ways. *Days of Awe* unsettled the enduring top-down approach to "religious" leadership by examining movement dialogic and semiotic dynamics, framing, and repertoire of protest to demonstrate the grassroots critical prophetic transformation—the outcome of reinforcing feedback loops between politicization on gender and race and unlearning Zionism through solidarity and alliances. Alternative religiocultural imaginations emerge through social movement as well as new interpretive authorities.

Critique of the "religion and" industry for reproducing gender and institutional hierarchies has led practitioners of RPB in various agencies to intentionally identify non-obvious leaders (women, youth) and patterns of lived religiosity outside official frames and spokespersons.[18] This amounts to an important broadening of the scope of theory and praxis and attests to the elasticity of this subfield. Yet RPB's reliance on traditional conceptions of religious leadership still discloses a conservative approach to what counts as "religious." The mechanisms of the JVP Rabbinical and Artistic Councils, for instance, cultivate new authorities and liturgies. But so do grassroots acts of nonviolent civil disobedience and protest, as well as activists' own interrogations of Jewish texts, histories, and practices in a time of a deepening crisis of authority. RPB is not concerned with such processes of religious innovation through protest and critique, but more with conceptions of religiosity as conducive to peacebuilding or development objectives. The latter often exhibit a myopic relation to discursive and epistemic legacies of violence and coloniality.

The focus on social movement grassroots prophetic critical caretaking thus broadens assumptions about directionality of RPB or conflict transformation. The logic of change does not move from abstract visions of cohabitation that might then serve to frame actions. Rather, the very horizons envisioned are produced through grassroots broad-based coalition building and intersectional analysis within the movement. Decolonizing and deorientalizing Jewishness as we encountered it has accelerated due to the need to elucidate the reasons for alliance with MBL and other marginalized groups, especially given the destabilizing of the construction of Jews as white during the Trump era. The following section further explores how Jewish Palestine solidarity exemplifies how social movement activism, human rights–oriented solidarity, and discursivity help reimagine the relationship between collective identities and religiosity.

Discursive Peacebuilding

The study of solidarity—and with it the processes of dialogic resignification as discussed in chapter 2—remains an undertheorized area for RVP and RPB. Jewish Palestine solidarity and anti-occupation activism demonstrate a gradually expansive engagement with discursive forces controlling the narrative about Israel and Palestine and about their own self-definition. In the initial stages of the movement of American Jews against the Israeli occupation, their discursive aims were directed primarily toward dismantling the Zionist logic that equated critique of Israel with antisemitism, along with an interrelated orientalism determining the myopia of the US public. Their tactics amounted mostly to showing up as Jews in support of BDS, certifying the broader Palestine solidarity movement against accusations of antisemitism, or explicitly challenging discursive formations that contribute to skewed and silencing narrations of the predicament and histories of Palestinians. Later, and through a deepening intersectional systemic analysis of interlocking ideologies of domination, reimagining Jewishness demanded further destabilizing of white Ashkenazi hegemony even within the movement itself. This process involved drawing on lived Jewish experiences in the margins, and intersections between blackness and Mizrahiness (as well as gender nonconformity and feminism) as resources for decolonizing and reimagining Jewishness outside Islamophobic and orientalist civilizational narratives, as chapters 7 and 8 emphasized. It also demanded moving beyond simply challenging the Zionist monopoly over antisemitism to grappling—via the tools of comparative race theory—with its deeper significance, and it required identifying the phenomenon as one of the oppressive ills (along with Zionism) against which an intersectional movement for collective liberation must struggle.

Days of Awe thus illuminates discursivity as a pivotal zone for prophetic grassroots interfaith and inter-traditional work that engages in intra-group change and transformation rather than conservative entrenchment through inter-traditional dialogue. The spaces of painful dialogue in the context of Christian churches' deliberations about divestment, as we observed in chapter 8, exemplify this transformative and self-scrutinizing process of discursive "interfaith" work that undoes, through relationship building, the naturalness of the discourse that renders Palestinians ungrievable.

Hence, intersectionality entails discursively sensitive and self-scrutinizing inter-tradition work, in contrast to conventional understandings and outcomes of "interfaith" work that—while building bridges and cultivating familiarities across differences—often functions more to conserve (often male-elite) interpretations of tradition rather than to innovate and interrogate the tradition relationally, intersectionally, and reparatively. The case of Jewish Palestine solidarity demonstrates that inter-traditional work within the context of a social movement can result in introspective scrutiny and a critical prophetic reimagining of tradition.

The interrogation of Jewish whiteness and the white supremacy internal to the movement—which connects to an intersectional struggle (co-resistance) against white supremacy—foregrounds this particular case of Jewish peacebuilding as directly confronting not only Zionist orthodoxy's violent manifestation in the form of the occupation, but also the *doxa* or discursivity that has authorized it. Discursive action is therefore pivotal for exposing the multiple root causes and layers of occupation-enabling violence that are not necessarily contained in the geopolitical space of the occupation. The discursive angle opens up the analysis to global semiotic examination of enabling narratives. The task of scholarship in RVP and RPB, consistent with a social semiotic perspective (as I discuss in chapter 2), is also to examine how religious and cultural meanings coalesce in producing conceptions of grievability and ungrievability. Likewise, decolonizing and deorientalizing Jewish conceptualizations of the Holocaust and antisemitism convey the relevance of critical theoretical tools to peacebuilding work involving narrativity and meanings.

Because RVP has focused primarily on how religion relates to deadly violence, the subfield has rarely engaged with critique as a means of expanding the moral imagination and for generating moral indignation.[19] The preceding analysis shows how activists' processes of pre-politicization on issues of gender, feminism, antiracism, and antimilitarism play pivotal roles in their ethical outrage and formation within the space of Palestine solidarity. Their refiguring (via deorientalizing and decolonizing) of the narratives that inform their self-understanding involves critical caretaking, drawing upon extra-traditional ethical resources but also constructive hermeneutical work within the tradition. Importantly, interfaith or inter-tradition intersectional work such as the anti-Islamophobia campaigns unfolds through the framing of human rights–oriented solidarity and thus subversively operates in co-resistance to discursive formations.

When Israeli authorities requested that certain participants of an interfaith delegation to the West Bank, including a rabbi, be refused entry to Israel, religious peacebuilders displayed the disruptive, prophetic, and subversive dynamics of religion. This was not the isolated prophetic voice crying in the wilderness and speaking truth to power. Nor was it an instrumentalized and domesticated "good" religious puppet of Western hegemony. On the contrary, this was a grassroots movement that also involved emerging religious authorities and prefigurative transformed Jewish communities, as we examined in chapters 5 and 6. There, we saw that ethical refiguring is an outcome of what Miller understands as "good" solidarity, motivated by indignation in the face of injustice and empathy. This book has explored such solidarity through the language of relationality, of constant confrontation, in the process of reimagining Jewishness, of Palestinian experiences of Jews and Judaism. Hence, reimagining Jewishness involves grappling with violent scriptural traditions as well as with the violence of Zionist and colonial histories and the underpinning discourses that pertain to marginalized JOCSM. Such deeper discursive engagement, however, is precluded by the standard RVP approach, which attends primarily to deadly violence and assumes traditional conceptions of the "religious," where it is located, and how it might be employed to attain various objectives. *Days of Awe*, by contrast, showed how crucial such discursive engagement is for thinking of Jewish Palestine solidarity activists as peacebuilders, agents operating in complex processes of conflict transformation, involving ethical outrage, unlearning, and refashioning Jewishness in and through intersectional social movement. Indeed, the discursive attention to ideology as a site of scholarship in RVP and RPB requires a more robust focus on nationalism,[20] which in turn invites integrating engagement with race (and its close connection to ethnicity) and gender. This focus clarifies that one task of RVP is to examine the threading of religious meanings into the construction of sociocultural and political identities and how such meanings relate to the capacity to negotiate plurality nonviolently and to the capacity of symbols and rituals to operate transformatively.[21]

Geneviève Zubrzycki, for instance, shows that examining visual and material culture opens up possibilities for empirical tracking of "conflicts about, and changes in, political visions of the nation."[22] In particular, she draws on anthropologist Webb Keane's theory of "bundling" that highlights objects' materiality and (potential context-specific) significations that are (might be) different than the abstract ones initially assigned to them. Keane's theory sug-

gests "the semiotic *potential* of an object at a given moment," which constitutes a departure from a totemic view of symbols.[23] This semiotic potential
carries implications for the repertoire of social and political actions and thus
is relevant for a robust study of religion, violence, and the practice of peacebuilding. Chapters 5 and 6 in particular explored the reclaiming of Jewish
ritual objects such as the sukkah, the Passover Seder plate, and the menorah
not just as protest instruments but as the very mechanisms for transforming identity through social movement frame transformation, which in turn
serves to reinforce the traction of the reinterpreted Jewish symbols and ritual
objects. Hence, the appropriation of the menorah and Hanukkah, for example, to denote JVP's resistance to colonialism, neoliberalism, and racism
in all its forms not only reflects the movement's principles; the very act of
protest and such marking of the Jewish holiday is itself transformative. Such
transformation was especially evident when Jewish Palestine solidarity activists told me that they finally felt at home within a Jewish space whose norms
they themselves construct and prefigure through social movement and critical caretaking. Likewise, the Rabbinic Council of JVP and the integration of
Jewish rituals and liturgy into the protest repertoire, as we saw in chapter 6,
constitute no mere instruments of social movement. They also produce new
religiosity and conceptions of community that, in this case, correspond to
the values Tzedek Chicago articulates of a postnationalist, postethnic, antimilitarist, pluralistically intersectional, and social justice–oriented Judaism.
Tzedek's Jewishness is highly consistent with the social movement of critics'
decolonization and deorientalization of antisemitism, a process, to reiterate,
that allows interpreting Zionism in terms of a broader analysis of racism,
whiteness, and white supremacy.

   In particular, the transformative and contested power of symbols is evident in analyzing the critical occasions when pinkwashing (the manipulative
use of freedom as a tool of state violence) was challenged in various public
manifestations of gay pride, where the Jewish symbol of the Star of David featured on the Israeli flag became the focus of a heated debate about who owned
the symbol and whether it could represent Jewish identity not linked necessarily to Israel. These contestations challenged Jewish Palestine solidarity and
the broader Jewish community for consistency along social fields and commitments. Whereas Zubrzycki examines the productive power of symbols in
effecting a reimagination of nationalist discourse, *Days of Awe* has provided
insights into how nationalist discourse is challenged and how religiosity itself
is reimagined through contesting national narratives and their interpretation
of Jewish meanings and symbols. Hence, a visual and material sociology of
nationalism and religion as well as social movement theory—especially in its

turn to a social semiotic perspective—emerge as areas of study integral to, even if not yet integrated in, RVP and RPB. This book's contribution to the subfield, therefore, is precisely in highlighting the complex intersectional and relational processes and grassroots agentic signification and critical theory that underpin transformations of identity and solidarity.

The concept and practice of ethically desired solidarity is one of the main ethical characteristics that distinguishes the diasporist anti- and non-Zionist religiocultural meaning (re)making from post-Zionist land theologies that emerged from certain sectors in the West Bank. Examining settler post-Zionism allows further reflection on how Israel features or could feature in the diasporic imagination. It also highlights some of the limitations of diasporic disengagement from Zionism and Israel for the tasks of peacebuilding and conflict transformation.

Diasporist Solidarity vs. Settler Post-Zionism?

Rabbi Menachem Froman, who served in the settlement of Tekoa in the West Bank (a location associated with the prophet Amos), saw himself as a peacebuilder. This self-perception was reinforced by expert scholars of religion,[24] even while he resided in an illegal settlement and vehemently articulated his right to reside there. He was known for his antimilitarism, his willingness to meet with foes or friends alike, and his actual meetings with Shaykh Ahmed Yassin (the spiritual leader of the Hamas movement), Yasser Arafat (the founding leader of the PLO and first president of the Palestinian Authority), and others.[25] While Froman subscribed to a form of spiritual nativism, affirming the rights of Jews to inhabit all places in the land, he also acknowledged indigenous Palestinian connections to the land. He interpreted the spiritual goals of Judaism as inclusivist and fostering human flourishing. Whenever spirituality translates into destructiveness, he insisted, it overextends itself and must be negated in order to be recharged.

Shaul Magid characterizes Froman's position as a form of "settler post-Zionism."[26] This category helps nuance some of the intricacies and internal pluralities within the settler population and the Jewish Israeli public more broadly. Such post-Zionism must be situated within the deeper context of religious Zionism dating back to Rav Abraham Isaac Kook (1865–1935). Kook laid the foundations for a Hegelian reading of secular Zionism. Accordingly, while Zionism serves to broaden and deepen the spiritual purpose of Judaism, it lacks any intrinsic value. In Froman's thought (influenced by Kook's theology), religious Zionism may have reached the historical limits of its usefulness. For Froman, Zionism had lost its essential spiritual role in bringing human freedom to fruition. In fact, it had become "an emblem of un-freedom" because of its use to dominate other people. Indeed, Froman spent years learning the Quran and Sunnah and, after in-depth conversations with Yassin and other Palestinian leaders, came to empathize with the Islamist critique of the "West" and its rendering of Zionist Israel as the "near devil," with America being the far one. He described the sense of moral injury ex-perienced by "Islam" and stressed that as long as politicians fail to attend to religious people and their narratives, peace will not be possible.[27] Unsurpris-ingly, Froman's empathy with Islamist critique of radical individualism and other "western" social ills leads him to think of such a critique as a meeting place of religious people (in their own converging struggles for conservative societal transformations), regardless of their ethnoreligious and national par-ticularities. Of course, rendering Israel as the "West" is a highly problematic proposition that reflects Froman's own embeddedness within Euro-Zionist ideological constructs (despite his otherwise critical attitudes toward them), where the normative Israeli is "Western" and Ashkenazi. Nevertheless, his concentrated effort to cultivate neighborly relations with Palestinians and his public willingness to assume Palestinian citizenship,[28] if geopolitical rear-rangement would call for it, does signal a turn to settler post-Zionism, one not normally acknowledged in conventional secularist approaches to peace-building and remapping of the possibilities of cohabitation. Froman's model constitutes a diasporic-nativist hybrid in that he was willing to accept po-litical diaspora by carrying a Palestinian citizenship card, while nonetheless connecting physically to the biblical landscape and its religious meanings.[29]

The Hegelian Kookist framework of Froman's thought, therefore, allows for cultivating an alternative, religiously grounded, post-Zionist articulation of identity as it relates to the land's topography and political and religious meanings. Hence, the supposed religious "spoiler" (the assumption that "irrational" religiosity constitutes a "spoiler" in peacebuilding) is, in fact, a potential peacebuilder,[30] operating with an Islamist counterpart within a contiguous and indivisible territory. Ironically, this is more consistent with the "one-state solution" than with the dominant (but increasingly eroding) "peace" formula of the "two-state solution" and its ethnoreligious and na-tionalist presumptions of homogeneity, thus challenging the assumption that peacebuilding falls under the purview of the secular.

Another post-Zionist settler, Rav Shimon Rosenberg (known as HaRav Shagar), who founded a yeshiva in the settlement of Efrat, diverged from Froman's reliance on Kookist modernist dialectic. He was one of the first rab-bis to introduce Hasidic teachings into the curriculum of religious Zionist yeshivas. He subsequently grounded his explicitly postmodern land theology in the thought of Rebbe Nachman of Breslov, whose mystical articulation of divine absence as the cornerstone of Hasidic spirituality resonates with Butler's interpretation of critique, discussed in chapter 4, as a virtuous practice of self-fashioning through destabilizing certainties. The resonance revolves around Shagar's postmodern relinquishing of truth claims as well as his critique of state violence as the condition of un-freedom. This form of Jewish postmodernity, therefore, shifts from religious Zionism's dialectical statism to an embrace of "mystical piety without truth," residing comfortably in a notion of *ayin* (nothingness) that cultivates possibilities of cohabitating with multiple truths as a way of living out radical neo-Hasidic spirituality. This neo-Hasidism shares elective affinities with Froman's nativist spirituality, and both denote a significant departure from Zionist theologies of land.[31]

Settler post-Zionism demonstrates that intimacy with the land is not the same as love of the political state, as had been the case for the founding generation of the settlement movement in the late 1960s and 1970s.[32] Following the evacuation of some illegal settlements in 2005 by the Israeli government, the internal discourse on land theology and statist Zionism shifted away from valorizing the institutions of the modern Israeli state, and thus closer to the aim of Shagar and Froman to cultivate cohabitation outside modernist nationalist Zionist frames.[33] For Shagar, the shift denotes a turn from modernist reliance on absolute claims to an embrace of divine absence as allowing for radical openness to cohabitation. The emphasis on intimacy with the land, in contrast to military control over its other inhabitants, opens the possibility for inter-group peacebuilding.[34] Like American anti- and non-Zionists, Shagar was concerned with how exertion of force over other populations harms the fabric of the Jewish soul, and like them he interpreted Jewish identity through a postmodernist prism. Yet these various departures from Zionism are distinct in their approaches to the land. For American non-Zionists, the religious significance of the biblical landscape is diminished by a reclaimed and reinterpreted lens of *doikayt* (hereness) diasporism and metaphorization of Zion qua liberation. Another important distinction is that American non-Zionist religiosity typically involves multiple zones of unlearning grounded not in mystical conceptions of divine absence but rather through humanistic frames that uphold the modernist language of unalienable rights and seek to overcome particularistic attachments to Zion or the land of Palestine. Furthermore, embracing the peace potential of ostensibly religious spoilers does not necessarily align with the demands for gender[35] or racial and economic justice as it does for an American Jewish Palestine solidarity movement committed to intersectional justice. Yes, Butler stresses, progressive politics need not foreclose alliances with conservative forces, highlighting sexual politics (e.g., pinkwashing) and the rhetoric of freedom as a tool of state violence that needs to be the focus of broad coalitions resisting rhetoric of religiocultural difference.[36] Another distinguishing characteristic of American Jewish anti- and non-Zionism is that the reclaiming of a "Jewish soul" through interrogation of communal sinfulness unfolds relationally and intersectionally through ethically desirable solidarity and *other*-centered empathy (not a personal quest for spiritual renewal or a nativist desire to inhabit the land) as the lens through which Jewishness is reimagined, even if the negation of Israelism does involve regenerating Jewishness and a sense of self-affirmation.

Nevertheless, analysis of Jewish Palestine solidarity in the US ultimately reveals its tendency to rely on secularist presumptions that distill a purist interpretation of authentic Judaism as diasporic and unsullied by any complicity with power, as we have seen in the recurrent appeal to "Constantinian Judaism." Such appeals, I argue, risk rereading Judaism *as* Christianity and thus severing the land of Zion from the movement's focus on rewriting Jewishness. Moreover, the complex ways in which Zion and Palestine operate within the semiotic field structuring race relations in the US illuminate how changing affective loyalties from Israelis to Palestinians and the intensifying traction of Palestine as a metaphor finally facilitates or operates through a feedback loop with American Jews' dis-assimilation from whiteness. This dis-assimilation through consciencization, decolonization, *other*-centric solidarity, and coalition work maps perfectly with rewriting Jewishness as most authentically diasporic and generates pathways for reimagining American Jewishness as multiracial, multiethnic, and non-binary in other multiple ways. This mode of imagination, however, demands a reliance on a Zion-diasporism binary. The moral choice to disengage from and disrupt Jewish whiteness necessitates, as chapters 7 and 8 show, an unequivocal disengagement from Zion(ism) partly reliant on how Palestine has featured into black antiracism struggles in the US and partly through the decolonization of Zionist narratives of Jewishness and Jewish history. This reimagined Jewishness is consequential for peacebuilding primarily through shaming the Jewish establishment's investment in the occupation and the discourses enabling it. However, its interpretation of the moral choice to decolonize Jewishness and partake in the multipronged and intersectional struggles against racism and interrelated exploitative ideologies (such as Zionism) and structures precludes engagement with intra-Jewish reparative potential. It also precludes confronting the ways in which the binarism of Zion-diasporism itself may be subject to decolonization and to interrogation of the ways in which Zion's multiple Jewish meanings diminish through the apparent simplicity of the moral choice.

An openness to the insights of post-settler neo-Hasidim and native spiri-

tuality and the critique these currents pose to Zionism through their engagement with Palestinian suffering and connection to the land offers reparative
connections that break the force of the Zion-diaspora binary and their mutual
negation.[37] An inability to move beyond the forcefulness of this binary and
its conceptions of authenticity prevents American Jewish Palestine solidarity
from offering constructive intervention in the Israel-Palestine context that is
ultimately distinct from broader Palestine solidarity work. As my interviews
with more than one hundred Jewish and non-Jewish Palestine solidarity activists showed, the two groups articulated identical visions of an "optimal"
solution to the conflict/occupation grounded in human rights language
rather than a Jewishly articulated refiguring of the meanings of Zion. Hence,
a focus on Mizrahi or non-Ashkenazi peace frames would once again shed
light on why epistemologically privileging marginalized standpoints can offer
creative openings for reimagining Jewishness outside the diasporist-Zionist
binary. This reimagining entails critical caretaking that rearticulates Jewish
ways of transforming relations between space, identity, and narrative through
an intersectional social movement framework, activism on the ground of Israel and Palestine, and intellectual counter-discourse.

"A Villa in the Jungle"

Anthropologist Smadar Lavie highlights how Mizrahi and other marginalized women inhabit a form of quotidian intersectionality, standing in the
welfare lines as battered, single, and poor. Drawing on Gloria Anzaldúa's thesis in *Borderlands/La Frontera*, Lavie identifies the potentiality of "South/
South coalitions of knowledge and activism between Mizrahim and Palestinians."[38] Accordingly, she ponders how welfare mothers from the margins
of society who desperately navigate the channels of Israeli bureaucracy are
forced into South/South sisterhood as a matter of "situational friendships"
while standing in line. A deep and ethically grounded, crosscutting, intersectional potential, however, is not actualized. Lavie observes that situational
friendships occur even when Mizrahi women hold on to their anti-Arab sentiments and Palestinian women continue to subsume Mizrahi women under
the label "Jews," thereby "indicating they [do] not distinguish between Ashkenazi and Mizrahi Jews."[39] The difficulty of translating quotidian intersectionality into a social movement that could transcend nationalist discourse
does not prevent Mizrahi feminism from being an engine of intersectionality.
That Mizrahi feminists have had difficulties asserting their emancipatory critique within the Ashkenazi-dominated feminist activist sphere[40] illuminates
the underlying misconception of Mizrahi as "anti-peace" and emphasizes

that intersectional feminist critique is pivotal for imagining alternatives to an orientalized discourse of Ashkenazi peace. The plight of Mizrahi single mothers has exposed the possibility of South/South feminist coalitions not necessarily, as in Anzaldúa's work, dependent upon white feminist mediation. It inhabits a fluid borderland or a "third country," a forced condition that nonetheless has potential for intersectional action and outlook. Indeed, in a CJNV session on Mizrahiyut held in Bethlehem in May 2017, Mizrahi social justice activists working on issues including fair housing, welfare, minimum wage, and education affirmed the critical relevance of a social justice agenda for Palestinian-Israeli peacebuilding and the bridging roles Mizrahi and other marginalized people could play in reimagining cohabitation in the region.[41] Many in the delegation embraced the presentation on Mizrahiness as a challenge to their uncomplicated feelings of estrangement from Israeli society, a call to a more nuanced engagement with its internal plurality, and an invitation from potential partners in the struggle against interconnected sites of injustice. This complexity, however, seemed to dissipate once we were again with our Palestinian partners, observing their struggle and the daily violence they face. After all, we were there to lend our bodies and "privilege" to resist the occupation in solidarity with them. The binary animating the moral choice "Whose side are you on?" overwhelmed. After a brief follow-up excursion of a small group among us to the periphery, one participant, an African American Jew, concluded that it might be beneficial to consider a Jewish diasporic delegation that crosses the Green Line in support of the Mizrahi/ Ethiopian communities to engage in solidarity work around their struggles against police brutality, public housing, health, and education. This is not to distract from the core mission of ending the occupation, but strengthening marginalized voices within Israel may be the key to imagining new ways of cohabitation beyond occupation.

Indeed, a feminist lens highlights such crosscutting and intersectional socioeconomic analysis. This potential, however, is difficult to unlock in the heavily ideological nationalist terrain that seeks to create a binary between Jews and Arabs.[42] Lavie argues that the failure of Ashkenazi feminists to recognize the intersection of the "Palestine Question" with the disenfranchisement and grievances of Mizrahi men and women and to operate within the cultural and demographic landscapes of the Middle East was detrimental to the possibility of a non-hegemonic peace agenda, which would have drawn upon shared cultural and linguistic resources rather than a cultural binary (i.e., Arabs vs. Jews).[43] The issue was about how privileged Ashkenazi ("white") feminists erased distinctive experiences of marginalization and cultural formations, including struggles born out of poverty, lack of access to education for children, unemployment, and deepening disparities resulting from Israel's turn to neoliberalism in the 1990s.[44] Mizrahi feminists, therefore, criticized Ashkenazi blindness to their own privileged position and promoted Mizrahi narratives that destabilized the Eurocentricity of the Zionist and Israeli discourse.

Mizrahi activists such as those associated with Achoti (literally "Sista," established in 2000), as well as other feminist (not necessarily Mizrahi-identified) organizations,[45] recognize the force of aggregating and intersecting the experiences of marginalized people in Israel (including Ethiopians and African asylum seekers). The challenge remains to translate quotidian friendships into an intersectional politics that embodies a "third country" of South/South feminist coalitions not constrained or predetermined by the reigning national discourses. Certainly, to highlight the limits of intersectionality as practiced does not preclude our ability to argue that both Mizrahi critique and activism challenge culturalist claims, which suggests a Mizrahi antithetical attitude to rights discourses.[46]

The emergence of the Mizrahi-Palestinian Partnership offers a contemporary example of a substantive challenge to the ideological barriers to intersectional analysis and coalitional activism. The Mizrahi-Palestinian Partnership was consolidated with the emergence of the Joint Arab List (2015) under the leadership of Ayman Ouda, who sought equality and recognition of Palestinian grievances. The Partnership was explicitly conceived as a space that would allow for the desired intersection of Mizrahi, Palestinian, class, feminist, and other struggles.[47] Its mission statement subsequently moves from the intellectual labor of intersectional counter-knowledge production to a platform of co-resistance against, for example, the disproportionate incarceration of Mizrahi and Palestinian citizens, a discriminating educational system, the erasure of cultural and historical inheritances, police brutality, domestic violence, and the effects of neoliberalism on Mizrahi and Palestinian populations.

However, the mission statement underscores that intersectionality does not mean erasing identity and difference. As Almog Bahar (a key figure in the Partnership and in broader Mizrahi-Palestinian intersectional initiatives) explains, the Partnership cannot afford to ignore the layered history of Jewish-Muslim exchanges and relationships in the region, and would do well to appreciate religiosity, even while seeking to decolonize Judaism from the hold of the Zionist discourse that has been translated into a political system of Jewish privilege and has prevented Mizrahi-Palestinian intersectionality from gaining traction. Such decolonization, consistent with the critique of intersectionality's overemphasis on structures that we encountered in chapter 7, would also involve reclaiming historical and religious Jewish-Arab experiences as well as legacies of Jewish-Muslim cooperation and cohabitation in the region. It would further entail dismantling the hierarchy of oppression grounded in a colonialist compound, "an [imagined] villa in the jungle."[48] The Partnership articulates its platform of co-resistance as operating intersectionally on gender, national, and ethnic modalities of inequality. "Fascism," its mission statement reads, "percolates through multiple relations in the common public space; the urban and peripheral the neighborly and intimate, often even onto the family's interpersonal realm. Those injured are mostly women and children."

The Partnership's mission statement unsurprisingly foregrounds the insights of feminist documentarian Simone Biton, who in 1996 recognized that the Mizrahi social justice struggle needed to be both intersectional and feminist in an agentic, emancipatory manner. She said, at the first Mizrahi feminist conference, that "we know oppression from all directions and all its hues . . . therefore, on the day when we will truly begin to fight domination, both the one we are complicit with and benefiting from and the one we endure as victims, this will be the most progressive and revolutionary platform in this land. We cannot save kids from the vocational track just to ensure that they will excel as occupiers, our own subjugation will not end till we resolve not to subordinate others."[49] The Partnership aspires to translate this intersectional insight into action—to both decolonize and deorientalize the peace and nationalist discourse and reshape the democratic domain in such a way that will not pretend that the Green Line represents a normative boundary where "democracy" ends and the occupation begins.[50] The Partnership thereby points to the pivotal need to decolonize Jewishness and, with it, to unsettle Zionism's participation in the signification of Jews as "white" and Israel as the civilized "West"—the metaphorical villa in the jungle.[51] Such resignification through deorientalization differs from American Jews' process of dis-assimilation from whiteness because Israeli Mizrahim are embedded in and confined to the Middle East, and specifically to Israel and Palestine.

For Bahar, whose artistic expressions circulate in Middle Eastern literary markets, a deeper understanding of Mizrahi literature and its rootedness in the region and its languages "offers an alternative to the hard-dichotomous separations between Arabs and Jews, religious and secular, and rich and poor." "In all spheres—the political, socioeconomic, cultural, and traditional," he underscores in an interview, "Mizrahiness has important things to offer in comprehending Jewish culture as also embedded in Arab-Jewish culture; and in comprehending that there is a connection between the 'conflict' and . . . [Mizrahi] and Arab memory of Ashkenazi repression."[52] At the heart of linking sites of injustice, regardless of national and/or religious categories, is identifying ways of liberating the cultural interconnections between Mizrahi and Middle Eastern landscapes and histories. For Bahar, Mizrahiness and the mainstreaming of Arabic language and art would constitute the main mechanisms for Jews to become indigenous (but non-hegemonic) to the region again.[53]

Beyond the linguistic register, Bahar recovers the need to contend with Mizrahi traditional and theological resources that take seriously Jewish-Muslim cohabitation throughout the centuries. He tells one interviewer that any opportunity to challenge the Ashkenazi normative constructions of history, literature, gender, and religion can only result in deepening the traction of alternative narratives.[54] The task is to reclaim and reimagine alternative Jewish meanings for inhabiting the land.[55] This entails a constructive hermeneutical process that interprets identity as not only "a site of oppression,"[56] but also one that offers resources for positive ethical, cultural, and political projects—encompassing religious terrains, memories, symbols, and practices—integral for decolonizing and deorientalizing identity and tradition. Unlike American Jewish critics' own processes of reimagining, rather than imagining Jewishness through the lens of diasporism, Bahar and other Mizrahi feminists stress decolonization and deorientalization as critical mechanisms for reimagining (through critical caretaking) Jewish modes of inhabiting the Middle East. Both sites of interrogation and reimagining, however, exemplify why decolonization and deorientalization as peacebuilding methodologies are pivotal for RVP. Identifying peace-conducive land theologies—even when these appear to have reparative potential and incorporate Palestinians—remains in itself insufficient as a site of post- or non-Zionist analysis because doing so neglects also to grapple with coloniality, heteronormativity, and patriarchy—in the way that Mizrahi feminists do, for example. However, both Mizrahi-Palestinian intersectionality and settler post-Zionism offer a challenge to diasporic anti- and non-Zionism: the latter diminishes the Jewish significance of being in the land, while the former engages in resignifying what it means Jewishly as a practice of non-hegemonic indigeneity.

Conclusion: Overcoming Zion?

Critical caretaking through decolonization and deorientalization, as well as through cultivating hermeneutical retrievals and innovations, illuminates the movement of American Jews as spiritual and audacious as Abraham Joshua Heschel was when he marched in Selma. Its intervention in Jewish meaning-making and collective reimagining thus constitutes a site for broadening our understanding of where and how religiosity intersects with demystifying ideological certainties as mechanisms for conflict transformation and peacebuilding. Froman and Shagar offer one obvious space where religious remaking destabilizes the dominant narrative about political sovereignty and thus promises innovative paths for reconfiguring debates about cohabitation in the land to which they are intimately connected. On a different front, as Bahar's Mizrahi queer and feminist outlook suggests, reshaping Jewish meanings in the Middle East entails hermeneutical retrievals of historical, cultural, and religious memories as well as a feminist intersectional epistemology from the margins. But for American anti- and non-Zionists, Zion is overcome differently. Solidarity itself is a spiritual action and a form of moral agency that embraces the struggles against racism, Islamophobia, homophobia, militarism, and antisemitism, as these are interlinked.

For the activists and critics I encountered, solidarity through critical caretaking amounts to a form of spirituality that negates Zion by reclaiming diasporism in ways that echo supersessionist rereadings of Judaism *as* Christianity. It also forecloses the potential of an intersectional Mizrahi critical lens as well as radical neo-Hasidic conceptions of cohabitation and nativist spirituality that coexist with diasporist expressions of Jewishness. Valorizing the diasporic as most authentically Jewish further diminishes the capacity to reimagine the meanings of the relations between Jews and the land in a non-hegemonic manner that offers a penetrating critique of modern statism, Israel, and modern Zionist history, as these are embedded in Europe as a discursive formation, while nonetheless recognizing spiritual, theological, and historical connections to the land. Inclusion in the intersectional movement not merely as (white) allies but also as Jews resisting antisemitism and Zionism concurrently has required challenging multiple binaries, save the one of Zion versus diaspora(s). Here, the Ethiopian Jewish Israeli social justice activist Efrat Yerday's remark about the Zion to which her ancestors in Ethiopia longed to return[57] is especially relevant. The proper response to Yerday is not a movement that wishes to assimilate her blackness while ignoring her grappling with the Jewish meanings of Zion outside the discursive hold of Euro-Zionism. The intersectional lens, as noted, tends to overemphasize interlocking structures of oppression while underemphasizing the insight of standpoint feminism that identity is a source of positive and constructive reimagining of political and ethical projects. The activists I engaged, however, are so overwhelmed by their own complicity with Jewish power and violence, and their own desire to dis-assimilate from their complicity with whiteness, that Zion becomes tolerable only as a metaphor. *Days of Awe*'s emphasis on solidarity shows how acknowledging the grievability of the ungrievable, and recognition of their pain, constitutes an engine for articulating a non-Zionist Jewishness of ethical solidarity, not a redirection of political sovereignty from humans to the divine (Froman) or an embrace of nothingness as a source of openness to cohabitation (Shagar). Attunement to the many realities of pain, suffering, and injustice lies at the heart of reimagining Jewishness through moral batteries, prophetic pastiche, and re-articulated public narratives. But so does the recovery and reinterpretation of joyous diasporism. Praying really happens through marching against police brutality in the US and occupation policies in Palestine, or sitting in front of AIPAC's conference with the message "Occupation Is Not My Judaism," or blocking the path of a violent Flag Parade through the Muslim Quarter of the Old City, or by forming a human shield, or by clearing caves in the Southern Hills of Hebron.

This spiritual audacity is not a given, contained in the writings of some rabbis, but rather is actively reimagined through critical caretaking and *other*-centered analytic lenses. It is, to return to Scout Bratt's powerful Kol Nidrei 5778/2017 sermon with which the book opens, the relentless Days of Awe, "the liminal space [where] creation happens and transformation occurs. Out of our comfort zones, out of our privileged standpoints of knowing . . . we create new understanding."

Notes

A Note about Spelling and Acronyms

1. I follow here Jewish Voice for Peace, *On Antisemitism: Solidarity and the Struggle for Justice* (Chicago: Haymarket Books, 2017), xv; and Yehouda Bauer, "In Search of a Definition of Anti-semitism," in *Approaches to Antisemitism: Context and Curriculum,* ed. Michael Brown (New York: American Jewish Committee, 1994), 22–24.

Living the Days of Awe, Relentlessly

1. Scout Bratt, "Kol Nidrei All Our Vows," a sermon delivered on Yom Kippur 5778/2017 at Tzedek Chicago Synagogue, September 29, 2017.

2. Larry Rubin, remarks on May 16, 2017, in Bethlehem, Palestine.

3. The themes of grievability and ungrievability are the overarching themes in Judith Butler, *Frames of War: When Is Life Grievable?* (London: Verso, 2016).

4. Judith Butler, "Sexual Politics, Torture, and Secular Time," in *Frames of War,* 101–36 (122).

5. For example, see Michael N. Barnett, *The Star and the Stripes: A History of the Foreign Policies of American Jews* (Princeton, NJ: Princeton University Press, 2016).

6. While I heard it used elsewhere as well, I borrow the phrase "do-goodism" from Cornel West, "Spiritual Blackout, Imperial Meltdown, Prophetic Fightback," August 29, 2017, https://hds.harvard.edu/news/2017/08/30/video-convocation-2017%E2%80%94spiritual-blackout-imperial-meltdown-prophetic-fightback. I discuss West's insightful speech in chapter 2.

7. Dov Waxman, *Trouble in the Tribe: The American Jewish Conflict over Israel* (Princeton, NJ: Princeton University Press, 2016).

8. Shaul Magid, *American Post-Judaism: Identity and Renewal in a Postethnic Society* (Indianapolis: Indiana University Press, 2013).

9. bell hooks, *Ain't I a Woman: Black Women and Feminism* (Boston: South End Press, 1981); Audre Lorde, *Sister Outsider: Essays and Speeches* (Freedom, CA: Crossing Press, 1984); Nira Yuval-Davis, *Gender & Nation.* London: Sage Publications, 1997); Yuval-Davis, "Intersectionality and Feminist Politics," *European Journal of Women's Studies* 13, no. 3 (2006): 193–209; Lynn Weber, "A Conceptual Framework for Understanding Race, Class, Gender, and Sexuality," in *Feminist Perspectives on Social Research,* ed. Sharlene Nagy Hesse-Biber and Michelle Yaisier

(New York: Oxford University Press, 2004), 121–39; Chandra Talpade Mohanty, "Under Western Eyes: Feminist Scholarship and Colonial Discourse," in *Third World Women and the Politics of Feminism*, ed. Chandra Talpade Mohanty, Ann Russo, and Lourdes Torres (Bloomington: University of Indiana Press, 1991), 51–80; Patricia Hill Collins and Sirma Bilge, *Intersectionality* (Cambridge: Polity, 2016); and Patricia Hill Collins, "Sharpening Intersectionality's Critical Edges," keynote address at the Intersectional Inquiries and Collaborative Action: Gender and Race Conference, University of Notre Dame, March 2, 2017.

10. Collins, "Sharpening Intersectionality's Critical Edges."

11. For an important critique of the turn of intersectionality studies to an overemphasis on structures rather than identity as a positive source for ethical and political imaginations, see Jakeet Singh, "Religious Agency and the Limits of Intersectionality," *Hypatia* 30, no. 4 (Fall 2015): 657–74.

12. I conducted seventy semi-structured interviews with American Jews who are Palestine solidarity activists and/or critics of Israeli policies and thirty with non-Jewish Palestine solidarity actors in the US.

13. James Baldwin, "On Being White . . . And Other Lies," *Essence* (1984), http://www.cwsworkshop.org/pdfs/CARC/Family_Herstories/2_On_Being_White.PDF. See also chapters 7 and 8 on ways that Baldwin and other African American thinkers have grappled with Jews' assimilation into whiteness.

14. Michael Rothberg, *Multidirectional Memory: Remembering the Holocaust in the Age of Decolonization* (Stanford, CA: Stanford University Press, 2009).

Chapter One

1. Miller, *Friends and Other Strangers: Studies in Religion, Ethics, and Culture* (New York: Columbia University Press, 2016), 138.

2. Here, Miller focuses specifically on Pope John Paul II and Richard Rorty, whose respective accounts of solidarity, though distinct, converge in key ways. Ibid., 138–40.

3. Ibid., 140; Walzer, *Politics and Passion: Toward a More Egalitarian Liberalism* (New Haven, CT: Yale University Press, 2005).

4. Miller, *Friends and Other Strangers*, 140.

5. Ibid.

6. Ibid., 140–41.

7. Ibid., 142. Here, Miller draws on Peter F. Strawson, "Freedom and Resentment," in *Proceedings of the British Academy* 48 (1962): 1–25.

8. Pew Research Center, "A Portrait of Jewish Americans: Findings from a Pew Research Center Survey of U.S. Jews," Pew Research Center, October 1, 2013, 7, http://assets.pewresearch.org/wp-content/uploads/sites/11/2013/10/jewish-american-full-report-for-web.pdf.

9. Ibid., 7–8. Pew's findings on intergenerational divides and declining religiosity in the under-30 demographic were confirmed by a Public Religion Research Institute study in 2017 that demonstrated that less than half (47%) of American Jews identify religiously as Jewish, and only one in five of American Jews view observance of halakhic law as essential to being Jewish. Likewise, only one in four Jews voted for Donald Trump in 2016 despite his laudatory attitude toward Benjamin Netanyahu, the Israeli prime minister at the time. See Eugene Scott, "Religion Is Increasingly Less of a Focus for America's Jewish Community. What Does That Mean for Its Political Influence?," *Washington Post*, September 21, 2017, https://www.washingtonpost.com/news/the-fix/wp/2017/09/21/religion-is-increasingly-less-of-a-focus-for-americas-jewish-community-what-does-that-mean-for-its-political-influence/.

10. Pew Research Center, "A Portrait of Jewish Americans," 9–10.

11. The breakdown of my interviewees in terms of affiliation is as follows: 40% Reform, 20% Conservative, 27% Reconstructionist, 3% Religious Zionist, 3% Hasidic, and 7% conversion to (Reconstructionist) Judaism.

12. See chapter 4 on "denominational" currents of American Judaism and their relation to Zionism.

13. Pew Research Center, "A Portrait of Jewish Americans," 82.

14. Ibid., 8.

15. This process has not happened in a vacuum. Indeed, young people in the US exhibit greater proclivity, in the second decade of the twenty-first century, toward socialism, with groups such as the Democratic Socialists of America exponentially increasing in membership. See "Harvard IOP Spring 2016 Poll," *Harvard IOP @ The Kennedy School*, April 25, 2016, http://iop.harvard.edu/youth-poll/past/harvard-iop-spring-2016-poll; Anna Heyward, "Since Trump's Victory, Democratic Socialists of America Has Become a Budding Political Force," *The Nation*, December 21, 2017, https://www.thenation.com/article/in-the-year-since-trumps -victory-democratic-socialists-of-america-has-become-a-budding-political-force/; and Michael Robin, "American Jews Have Never Needed Israel," *Forward*, February 21, 2018, https://forward.com/opinion/394903/american-jews-have-never-needed-israel/.

16. This and all other names are pseudonymous in order to protect my interviewees' identities.

17. Interview #18.

18. Interview #25.

19. Shaul Magid, *American Post-Judaism: Identity and Renewal in a Postethnic Society* (Bloomington: Indiana University Press, 2013), especially chapter 8, analyzes the competing and changing currents of post-Holocaust theology in the US.

20. For accounts tracing the changing dynamics of American Jews, see Barnett, *The Star and the Stripes*; and Waxman, *Trouble in the Tribe*.

21. See chapter 4 on the changing attitudes of American Jews.

22. This development is classically presented by Will Herberg, *Protestant, Catholic, Jew: An Essay in American Religious Sociology* (Chicago: University of Chicago Press, [1955] 1983).

23. See Jerold S. Auerbach, *Rabbis and Lawyers: The Journey from Torah to Constitution* (Bloomington: Indiana University Press, 1999).

24. See Ofira Seliktar, *Divided We Stand: American Jews, Israel, and the Peace Process* (Westport, CT: Praeger, 2002), 5–7.

25. On the ethos of the negation of exile, see Idith Zertal, *Israel's Holocaust and the Politics of Nationhood* (Cambridge: Cambridge University Press, 2010); and Baruch Kimmerling, *The Invention and Decline of Israeliness: State, Society, and the Military* (Los Angeles: University of California Press, 2005).

26. Seliktar, *Divided We Stand*, 9.

27. Waxman, *Trouble in the Tribe*, 51.

28. Ibid., 50–54, for example.

29. Bourdieu, *Outline of a Theory of Practice* (Cambridge: Cambridge University Press, 1977), 164.

30. Geertz, *The Interpretation of Cultures: Selected Essays* (New York: Basic Books, 1973).

31. Bourdieu, *Outline of a Theory of Practice*, 164.

32. Ibid., 166.

33. Ibid., 164.

34. Ibid., 168–69.

35. Ibid., 169.

36. For an analysis of AIPAC's shift to right-wing Israeli positions and alignment with the Republican Party, see John B. Judis, "Zionist Movement: How AIPAC Is Severing Its Historical Roots—and Weakening Its Influence," *Foreign Policy* 205 (2014): 16.

37. Comprehending religiocultural affinities requires analyzing the roots and trajectories of Christian Zionism and Restorationism in Europe and the US and the deep cultural roots of such theologies in the US and UK, in particular. On the relevance of Christian Zionism to the history of Jewish Zionism, and on the continuous American and other Christian support of Israeli policies, see Goran Gunner and Robert O. Smith, eds., *Comprehending Christian Zionism: Perspectives in Comparison* (Minneapolis: Augsburg Fortress Publishers, 2014); Yaakov S. Ariel, *On Behalf of Israel: American Fundamentalist Attitudes toward Jews, Judaism, and Zionism, 1865–1945* (Brooklyn, NY: Carlson, 1991); Paul C. Merkley, *Christian Attitudes towards the State of Israel* (Montreal: McGill–Queen's University Press, 2001); Merkley, *The Politics of Christian Zionism 1891–1948* (Portland, OR: Frank Cass Publishers, 1998); James Carroll, *Jerusalem, Jerusalem: How the Ancient City Ignited our Modern World* (Boston: Mariner Books, 2011); and John J. Mearsheimer and Stephen M. Walt, *The Israel Lobby and U.S. Foreign Policy* (New York: Farrar, Straus & Giroux, 2007).

38. Douglas Hartman, Xuefeng Zhang, and William Wischstadt, "One (Multicultural) Nation under God? Changing Uses and Meanings of the Term 'Judeo-Christian' in the American Media," *Journal of Media and Religion* 4, no. 4 (2005): 207–34; Jacob Neusner, *Jews and Christians: The Myth of a Common Tradition* (New York and London: Trinity Press International and SCM Press, 1990); Arthur Cohen, *The Myth of the Judeo-Christian Tradition* (New York: Harper & Row, 1970); Deborah Dash Moore, "Jewish GIS and the Creation of the Judeo-Christian Tradition," *Religion and American Culture: A Journal of Interpretation* 8, no. 1 (1998): 31–53; and Herberg, *Protestant, Catholic, Jew.*

39. Douglas Little, *American Orientalism: The United States and the Middle East Since 1945,* 3rd ed. (Chapel Hill: University of North Carolina Press, 2008); Melani McAlister, *Epic Encounters: Culture, Media, and U.S. Interests in the Middle East Since 1945* (Los Angeles: University of California Press, [2001] 2005); and Elizabeth Shakman Hurd, *The Politics of Secularism in International Relations* (Princeton, NJ: Princeton University Press, 2008).

40. A brief visit to AIPAC's website will substantiate this argument. See, for example, a video titled "Security," accessed September 27, 2017, http://www.aipac.org/about/mission. A critique of this approach, on the part of American foreign policymakers, comes not only from left-leaning activists but also from political realists. See, for example, Mearsheimer and Walt, *The Israel Lobby and U.S. Foreign Policy.*

41. Power, "U.S. Ambassador to the U.N. Samantha Power Remarks at AIPAC Policy Conference," C-SPAN, March 2, 2015, http://www.c-span.org/video/?c4529792/us-ambassador-un-samantha-power-remarks-aipac-policy-conference.

42. The annual conference is always an occasion for a show of force and cultural capital. In 2015, for example, speakers included: US senators Ben Cardin (D-MD), Lindsey Graham (R-SC), Robert Menendez (D-NJ), and Mitch McConnell (R-KY); Samantha Power; Czech Republic president Milos Zeman; former Spanish president Jose Maria Aznar; former US national security adviser Susan Rice; Conference of Presidents of Major American Jewish Organizations chairman Bob Sugarman; and Israeli prime minister Benjamin Netanyahu. The conference also has a strong presence from conservative think tanks such as the American Enterprise Institute

and the Hudson Institute. See Jeffrey Goldberg, "The Problem with the AIPAC Conference," *The Atlantic*, March 21, 2010, http://www.theatlantic.com/international/archive/2010/03/the-problem-with-the-aipac-conference/37732/.

43. A significant moment was Benjamin Netanyahu's speech to Congress on March 3, 2015, against the Iran deal championed by the Obama Administration. See Netanyahu, "Transcript of Netanyahu's Speech to Congress," *New York Times*, March 3, 2015, http://www.nytimes.com/2015/03/04/us/politics/transcript-of-netanyahus-remarks-to-congress.html. On Barack Obama's signaling of his administration's change of course, see Philip Weiss, "Obama Tells Americans It Is 'Abrogation of My Constitutional Duty' to Defer to Israel on Iran Deal," *Mondoweiss*, August 5, 2015, http://mondoweiss.net/2015/08/americans-abrogation-constitutional; and Julie Hirschfeld Davis, "Fears of Lasting Rift as Obama Battles Pro-Israel Group on Iran," *New York Times*, August 7, 2015, http://www.nytimes.com/2015/08/08/world/middleeast/fears-of-lasting-rift-as-obama-battles-pro-israel-group-on-iran.html. On American Jewish support of the Iran deal (larger than that of the broader American population), see Scott Clement, "Jewish Americans Support the Iran Nuclear Deal," *Washington Post*, July 27, 2015, http://www.washingtonpost.com/news/the-fix/wp/2015/07/27/jewish-americans-support-the-iran-nuclear-deal/; and JTA, "26 Former American Jewish Leaders Back Iran Deal," *Jerusalem Post*, August 20, 2015, http://www.jpost.com/Middle-East/Iran/26-former-American-Jewish-leaders-back-Iran-deal-412740. For the claim that different opinions about a deal with Iran do not necessarily indicate a change in narrative, see Connie Bruck, "Friends of Israel," *New Yorker*, September 1, 2014, http://www.newyorker.com/magazine/2014/09/01/friends-israel.

44. For analyses of the growing abyss between Israeli officials and Democrats during the Obama era, see Jeffrey Goldberg, "The Crisis in U.S.-Israel Relations Is Officially Here," *The Atlantic*, October 28, 2014, http://www.theatlantic.com/international/archive/2014/10/the-crisis-in-us-israel-relations-is-officially-here/382031/; and Marissa Newman, "Revelation of Nuke Talks Details by Netanyahu Would Be 'Betrayal,' US Warns," *Times of Israel*, March 2, 2015, http://www.timesofisrael.com/revelation-of-nuke-talks-details-by-netanyahu-would-be-betrayal-us-warns/. For historical perspective, see Bernie Becker, "I Barred Netanyahu from State Dept., Baker Says," *The Hill*, November 2, 2014, http://thehill.com/policy/defense/222577-james-baker-i-barred-netanyahu-from-state-dept.

45. Cited in Bruck, "Friends of Israel."

46. Cited in ibid. A Gallup poll from July 2014 also indicated that most Americans still deemed Israel's actions against Hamas as justified. In 2002, 44% of Americans indicated that Israeli actions against Palestinians were justified, compared with 42% in 2014 who indicated that Israeli actions against Hamas were justified. (The 2014 poll reflects a distinction in wording from the 2002 poll, where the generic "Palestinians" was used.) In February 2015, 70% of Americans still rated Israel "mostly favorably," compared with 17% who rated the Palestinian Authority in the same way. Likewise, 62% of Americans in 2015 indicated sympathizing "more with the Israelis," compared with the 16% who sided "more with the Palestinians." While these data suggest strong support for Israeli militancy, the generational divide is statistically significant. For analysis of the 2012 findings, see Elizabeth Mendes, "Americans Continue to Tilt Pro-Israel," *Gallup Politics*, March 2, 2012, http://www.gallup.com/poll/153092/Americans-Continue-Tilt-Pro-Israel.aspx. See also Frank Newport, "Rank-and-File Partisans Reflect Their Leaders' Views on Israel and Netanyahu," *Gallup News*, March 3, 2015, http://news.gallup.com/opinion/polling-matters/181802/rank-file-partisans-reflect-leaders-views-israel-netanyahu.aspx.

47. One telling moment of such distancing surrounded the release in the US of Michael

Oren, *Ally: My Journey across the American-Israeli Divide* (New York: Random House, 2015). See Jane Eisner, "Michael Oren, You Hardly Know Us at All," *Forward*, June 24, 2015, http://forward .com /opinion /editorial /310749/michael-oren-you-hardly-know-us /.

48. For coverage of AIPAC's flying of representatives to Israel in advance of the vote in Congress on the Iran deal of July 2015, see Ben Norton, "AIPAC Taking All but 3 Freshmen Congresspeople to Israel in Effort to Sabotage Iran Deal," *Mondoweiss*, August 3, 2015, http://mondoweiss .net /2015/08/freshmen-congresspeople-sabotage. See also Catherine Ho and Karoun Demirjian, "Lawmakers Take Well-Timed Israel Trip Paid for by AIPAC Charitable Arm," *Washington Post*, August 5, 2015, http://www.washingtonpost.com /news /powerpost /wp /2015/08/05/ lawmakers-take-well-timed-aipac-sponsored-trip-to-israel /. An AIPAC official quoted in this piece says that "the regular trip was planned before there was an expected vote on the nuclear deal, and that no lobbying of lawmakers will take place." The last time the foundation sponsored travel to Israel, in August 2013, it paid for twenty-four House Republicans and thirty-six Democrats, which cost about $1 million, roughly $18,000 per member, according to LegiStorm, which tracks congressional travel. On the exchange between the representatives invited to Israel in preparation for their vote on the Iran deal, see Barak Ravid, "Netanyahu to Democratic Congressmen: I Won't Tell You How to Vote on Iran Deal," *Haaretz*, August 10, 2015, http://www .haaretz.com /israel-news /.premium-1.670533; and Mark Landler, "Netanyahu and Trump Skip AIPAC Meeting," *New York Times*, March 27, 2017, https://www.nytimes.com /2017/03/27/ world/middleeast /netanyahu-and-trump-skip-aipac-meeting.html.

49. The protest was countered by violence from the extremist right-wing Jewish Defense League. The unfortunate target of the violence was a Palestinian man. For one analysis of this event, see Samuel Molnar, "AIPAC Protests Showed American-Jewish Activism at a Crossroads," *+972 Magazine*, March 31, 2017, https://972mag.com /aipac-protests-showed-american -jewish-activism-at-a-crossroads /126318/.

50. Shavit, *My Promised Land: The Triumph and Tragedy of Israel* (New York: Spiegel & Grau, 2013), 106.

51. Ibid., 108.

52. For an important critique of Shavit, see Nathan Thrall, "Feeling Good about Feeling Bad," *London Review of Books* 36, no. 19 (October 9, 2014): 29–34.

53. Avri Gilad's vitriolic interrogation of Breaking the Silence activist Yuli Novak inspired many and varied responses. See, for example, Odeh Birshrat, "An Israeli TV Host Presents: A Blood Price List," *Haaretz*, June 28, 2015, http://www.haaretz.com /opinion /.premium-1 .663418. For a defense of Gilad's remarks, see Benny Ziffer, "The Problem with Breaking the Silence," *Haaretz*, June 26, 2015, http://www.haaretz.com /news /israel /.premium-1.662860. See also Herb Keinon, "Hotovely Calls for Action against Swiss Exhibit by 'Breaking the Silence,'" *Jerusalem Post*, June 2, 2015, http://www.jpost.com /Israel-News /Politics-And-Diplomacy/ Deputy-FM-mulls-ways-to-stop-Breaking-the-Silence-exhibit-in-Zurich-404801; Yonah Jeremy Bob, "Breaking the Silence and Israeli Government Cut a Deal," *Jerusalem Post*, March 1, 2017, http://www.jpost.com /Israel-News /Politics-And-Diplomacy/Breaking-the-Silence-and -Israeli-Government-cut-a-deal-482909; Udi Shaham, "Government Assesses Bill Against Breaking the Silence," *Jerusalem Post*, January 7, 2017, http://www.jpost.com /Israel-News / Vote -on-Breaking-the-Silence-bill-set-for-coming-week-477719; and Yehuda Shaul, "Netanyahu Wants to Repress My Group, Breaking the Silence. May, Don't Help Him," *The Guardian*, February 8, 2017, https://www.theguardian.com /commentisfree /2017/feb /08/netanyahu-breaking -the-silence-israel-theresa-may. For Amnesty International's statement, see "Israeli Government

Must Cease Intimidation of Human Rights Defenders, Protect Them from Attacks," *Amnesty International*, April 12, 2016, https://www.amnestyusa.org/press-releases/israeli-government-must-cease-intimidation-of-human-rights-defenders-protect-them-from-attacks/.

54. See Ashley Bohrer, "Against the Pinkwashing of Israel: Why Supporting Palestinians Is a Queer and Feminist Issue," *Al Jazeera*, August 9, 2014, http://www.aljazeera.com/indepth/opinion/2014/08/against-pinkwashing-israel-201489104543430313.html; Sarah Schulman, "Israel and 'Pinkwashing,'" *New York Times*, November 22, 2011, http://www.nytimes.com/2011/11/23/opinion/pinkwashing-and-israels-use-of-gays-as-a-messaging-tool.html; Schulman, *Israel/Palestine and the Queer International* (Durham, NC: Duke University Press, 2012); and Aeyal Gross, "Pinkwashing Debate/Gay Rights in Israel Are Being Appropriated for Propaganda Value — Opinion," *Haaretz*, June 10, 2015, http://www.haaretz.com/opinion/.premium-1.660349.

55. Important tensions lie between this rebranding and the discriminatory realities LGBTQI communities face. See, for example, Andrew Tobin, "Gay Israeli Celebs Decry State Opposition to Same-Sex Adoption," *Jewish Telegraphic Agency*, July 19, 2017, https://www.jta.org/2017/07/19/news-opinion/israel-middle-east/gay-israeli-celebs-decry-state-opposition-to-same-sex-adoption.

56. See Schulman, *Israel/Palestine and the Queer International*.

57. The kind of sexual politics that posits Israel as a site of values-based power crumbles, of course, when increasingly conservative political leaders deploy misogynistic and homophobic rhetoric to reject egalitarian prayer spaces at the Western Wall or gay adoption and parenting. See, for example, Lee Yaron, "Israel Tells Top Court It Opposes Adoptions by Same-Sex Couples," *Haaretz*, July 16, 2017, http://www.haaretz.com/israel-news/1.801629. See also chapter 4's discussion of the Kotel (Western Wall) controversy.

58. Beinart, *The Crisis of Zionism* (New York: Times Books, 2012); Beinart, "The American Jewish Cocoon," *New York Review of Books*, September 26, 2013, http://www.nybooks.com/articles/2013/09/26/american-jewish-cocoon; and Beinart, "The Failure of the American Jewish Establishment," *New York Review of Books*, June 10, 2010, http://www.nybooks.com/articles/archives/2010/jun/10/failure-american-jewish-establishment/.

59. Beinart, "The Era of Iran Is Over; the Age of BDS begins," *Haaretz*, June 4, 2015, http://peterbeinart.net/haaretz-the-era-of-iran-is-over-the-age-of-bds-begins/. See also Dan Fishback, "Trauma Club: Unpacking the Disconnect Between Liberal Zionism and the Anti-Zionist Movement," *Jewschool: Progressive Jews and Views*, February 4, 2016, http://jewschool.com/2016/02/39106/trauma-club-unpacking-disconnect-liberal-zionism-anti-zionist-movement/. Here, Fishback explains pinkwashing and the risks of queer activism's (often unaware) complicity with the Israeli occupation of Palestine and with Jewish ethnocracy more broadly.

60. This was especially aided by the published opinions of Israeli security specialists and other scientists who underscored their support of the Iran deal. See William J. Broad, "29 U.S. Scientists Praise Iran Nuclear Deal in Letter to Obama," *New York Times*, August 8, 2015, http://www.nytimes.com/2015/08/09/world/29-us-scientists-praise-iran-nuclear-deal-in-letter-to-obama.html; and Justin Salhani, "Former Israeli Security Heads Support Iran Deal," *Think-Progress*, July 23, 2015, http://thinkprogress.org/world/2015/07/23/3683546/former-israeli-security-heads-support-iran-deal/.

61. Omar Bargouti, *BDS: Boycott, Divestment, Sanctions: The Global Struggle for Palestinian Rights* (Chicago: Haymarket Books, 2011); and Maia Carter Hallward, *Transnational Activism and the Israeli–Palestinian Conflict* (New York: Palgrave Macmillan, 2013).

62. Palestinian Civil Society, "Call for BDS," accessed September 27, 2017, http://bdsmovement.net/call.

63. Interview #3.

64. Hallward, *Transnational Activism*, esp. chapters 1 and 2.

65. Reut Institute, "Building a Political Firewall against Israel's Delegitimization: Conceptual Framework," March 2010, http://reut-institute.org/data/uploads/PDFVer/20100310%20Delegitimacy%20Eng.pdf. Joseph Lieberman mandated that his entire diplomatic team be briefed by the Institute's scholars, affiliates, and researchers.

66. Ben Lynfield, "Israel's Far Right Seeks to Cripple Human Rights Groups Which Monitor Government and Army Abuses in Occupied Territories," *The Independent*, June 24, 2015, http://www.independent.co.uk/news/world/middle-east/israels-far-right-seeks-to-cripple-human-rights-groups-which-monitor-government-and-army-abuses-in-the-occupied-territories-10343512.html; and Avshalom Halutz, "The Oppression of Israeli Culture Begins with the Occupation," *Haaretz*, June 25, 2015, http://www.haaretz.com/opinion/.premium-1.662810.

67. Tamara Zieve, "Israel-Diaspora Enterprise to Spend $66M. On College Campuses Globally," *Jerusalem Post*, August 12, 2016, http://www.jpost.com/Diaspora/Mosaic-United-seeks-to-unify-Jewish-people-463958.

68. Josh Nathan-Kazis, "Center for Jewish History Chief Comes Under Fierce Attack by Right-Wingers," *Forward*, September 6, 2017, http://forward.com/news/382014/center-for-jewish-history-chief-comes-under-fierce-attack-by-right-wingers/; and Zohar Segev, "This Is How to Distance American Jews," *Haaretz*, October 14, 2017, https://www.haaretz.com/opinion/.premium-how-were-distancing-american-jews-1.5457964. Many distinguished academics and other public figures, including the Center for Jewish History, came out in strong defense of Myers. See Oren Peleg, "Right-Wing Activists Target David Myers," *Jewish Journal*, September 8, 2017, http://jewishjournal.com/news/nation/224206/right-wing-activists-target-david-myers/; Josh Nathan-Kazis, "David Myers Wins Support of 500 Jewish Studies Professors Amid Attack," *Forward*, September 7, 2017, http://forward.com/fast-forward/382102/petition-backing-cjh-head-amid-right-wing-attack-draws-signatures-of-500-je/; and Shaul Magid, "How the New Israel Litmus Test Turns Jews into Christian Zionists," *Forward*, October 16, 2017, http://forward.com/opinion/israel/385046/how-the-new-israel-litmus-test-turns-jews-into-christian-zionists/.

69. Talal Asad, *Formations of the Secular: Christianity, Islam, Modernity* (Stanford, CA: Stanford University Press, 2003), 185.

70. See Jewish Voice for Peace, *Stifling Dissent: How Israel's Defenders Use False Charges of Anti-Semitism to Limit the Debate over Israel on Campus*, Fall 2015, https://jewishvoiceforpeace.org/wp-content/uploads/2015/09/JVP_Stifling_Dissent_Full_Report_Key_90745869.pdf.

71. See Gillian Rose, "Athens and Jerusalem: A Tale of Three Cities" and "Beginnings of the Day: Fascism and Representation," in *Mourning Becomes the Law: Philosophy and Representation* (Cambridge: Cambridge University Press, 1996), 15–62; and Stef Craps and Gert Buelens, "Traumatic Mirrorings: Holocaust and Colonial Trauma in Michael Chabon's *The Final Solution*," *Criticism* 53, no. 4 (2011): 569–86.

72. California Legislative Information, "House Resolution No. 35," August 29, 2012, http://leginfo.legislature.ca.gov/faces/billTextClient.xhtml?bill_id=201120120HR35.

73. Glen Greenwald and Ryan Grim, "U.S. Lawmakers Seek to Criminally Outlaw Support for Boycott Campaign Against Israel," *The Intercept*, July 19, 2017, https://theintercept.com/2017/07/19/u-s-lawmakers-seek-to-criminally-outlaw-support-for-boycott-campaign-against-israel/.

74. A series of articles coauthored by Elly Bulkin and Donna Nevel exposes the connections between Islamophobia and the dominant pro-Israel Jewish lobby. See Bulkin and Nevel, "How the Jewish Establishment's Litmus Test on Israel Fuels Anti-Muslim Bigotry," *AlterNet*, September 7, 2012, http://www.alternet.org/how-jewish-establishments-litmus-test-israel-fuels -anti-muslim-bigotry; and Mahmood Mamdani, *Good Muslim, Bad Muslim: America, the Cold War, and the Roots of Terror* (New York: Pantheon Books, 2004).

75. See, for instance, Ali Gharib and Eli Clifton, "Meet the Donors behind the Clarion Fund's Islamophobic Documentary 'The Third Jihad,'" *ThinkProgress*, January 24, 2012, http:// thinkprogress.org/security/2012/01/24/410003/donors-clarion-fund-third-jihad.

76. See chapters 7 and 8 for a detailed discussion of Islamophobia, antisemitism, and anti-black racism in the US.

77. Ben White, "Israel Lobby Uses Discredited Anti-Semitism Definition to Muzzle Debate," *Electronic Intifada*, September 28, 2012, http://electronicintifada.net/content/israel-lobby -uses-discredited-anti-semitism-definition-muzzle-debate/11716.

78. Ibid. See also ADL, "Profile: Students for Justice in Palestine," March 10, 2015, http:// www.adl.org/assets/pdf/israel-international/sjp-2015-backgrounder.pdf. The report generally describes the tactics of SJP while providing very little rebuttal or commentary. However, it occasionally interjects that the organization is "anti-Israel," accusing the organization of sensationalist tactics.

79. Ibid.

80. See Nora Barrows-Friedman, "Victory for Campus Free Speech as US Dep. of Education Throws Out 'Anti-Semitism' Complaints," *Electronic Intifada*, August 28, 2013, https:// electronicintifada.net/blogs/nora-barrows-friedman/victory-campus-free-speech-us-dept -education-throws-out-anti-semitism. For the conversations surrounding AMCHA's employment of Article VI, see "Statement by Jewish Studies Professors in North America Regarding the Amcha Initiative," *Forward*, October 1, 2014, http://forward.com/news/israel/206629/ statement-by-jewish-studies-professors-in-north-am/; AMCHA Initiative, "Antisemitic Activity and Anti-Israel Bias at the Center for Near East Studies, University of California at Los Angeles: 2010–2013," accessed September 27, 2017, http://www.amchainitiative.org/wp-content/ uploads/2014/09/CNES-Report.pdf; Louis D. Brandeis Center for Human Rights Under Law, "The Morass of Middle East Studies: Title VI of the Higher Education Act and Federally Funded Area Studies," September 1, 2014, https://brandeiscenter.com/the-morass-of-middle-east -studies-title-vi-of-the-higher-education-act-and-federally-funded-area-studies/; Middle East Research and Information Project, "Title VI and Middle East Studies: What You Should Know," November 14, 2014, http://www.merip.org/title-vi-middle-east-studies-what-you-should-know; and AMCHA Initiative, "Founder of Amcha Initiative Demanding U.S. Department of Education Reopen Title VI Complaint," October 23, 2013, http://www.amchainitiative.org/founder-of -amcha-initiative-demanding-u-s-department-of-education-reopen-title-vi-complaint/.

81. Barrows-Friedman, "Victory for Campus Free Speech." The Department of Education rejected the complaint filed against UC Berkeley by Zionist students in 2012 as unfounded. See the statement by Chancellor Nicholas Dirks, Public Affairs, "Department of Education Dismisses Complaint Alleging Anti-Semitism at Berkeley," *Berkeley News*, August 27, 2012, http:// news.berkeley.edu/2013/08/27/doe-dismisses-anti-semitism-complaint/.

82. See Faiz Shakir, "ACLU Letter to the Senate Opposing Israel Anti-Boycott Act," *American Civil Liberties Union*, July 17, 2017, https://www.aclu.org/letter/aclu-letter-senate-opposing -israel-anti-boycott-act. The ACLU has taken several actions against those who disqualify potential employees for supporting BDS. See, for instance, ACLU, "Complaint for Declaratory and

Injunctive Relief," October 11, 2017, https://www.aclu.org/sites/default/files/field_document/koontz_v._watson_complaint.pdf.

83. Nora Barrows-Friedman, "Irvine 11 Appeals Filed: Defense Lawyers Say Convictions Were Unconstitutional, Cite Trial Errors," *Electronic Intifada*, January 24, 2013, http://electronicintifada.net/blogs/nora/irvine-11-appeals-filed-defense-lawyers-say-convictions-were-unconstitutional-cite-trial. Another high-profile case involved the firing of Professor Steven Salaita by the University of Illinois at Urbana-Champaign in 2014. See Steven Lubet, "Steven Salaita's Exile from Academia: 'I Refuse to Tolerate the Indignities of a Blacklist,'" *Chicago Tribune*, July 27, 2017, http://www.chicagotribune.com/news/opinion/commentary/ct-steve-salaita-academia-exit-perspec-0728-jm-20170727-story.html; and Michael Rothberg, "Antisemitism and Salaita," *Academe Blog*, August 17, 2014, http://academeblog.org/2014/08/20/antisemitism-and-salaita/. For the critical effort to acknowledge and analyze the connections between Gaza and the University of Illinois at Urbana-Champaign, see Rothberg, "The Salaita Case, One Year Later," *Inside Higher Ed*, July 31, 2015, https://www.insidehighered.com/views/2015/07/31/essay-salaita-controversy-after-one-year-and-continuing-concerns-about-academic.

84. Nora Barrow-Friedman, "Bogus Allegations of 'Anti-Semitism' Create Real Climate of Fear for Arab, Muslim Students in U.S.," *Electronic Intifada*, August 8, 2012, https://electronicintifada.net/content/bogus-allegations-anti-semitism-create-real-climate-fear-arab-muslim-students-us/11563. The ADL's legacy came under clearer scrutiny after Donald Trump's election, which precipitated overt manifestations of anti-Jewish symbols and reinforced explicitly antisemitic views. In this tense atmosphere, the ADL nevertheless led a concentrated attack on Antifa, rather than on the white nationalists Antifa opposed. See, for example, Jewish Solidarity Caucus, "The ADL Collaborates with the Enemy," *Medium*, September 14, 2017, https://medium.com/jewish-socialism/the-adl-collaborates-with-the-enemy-89a8dc4dae97.

85. The Maccabee Task Force (launched in 2015) offers some degree of tactical diversity in its anti-BDS activism on campuses. See Ron Kampeas, "Sheldon Adelson Group Changes How It's Selling Israel on Campus," *JTA*, October 3, 2017, https://www.jta.org/2017/10/03/news-opinion/united-states/sheldon-adelson-group-changes-how-its-selling-israel-on-campus.

86. Cecilie Surasky, "JVP Asks UC President to Table Biased Report on Jewish Life on Campus," *Berkeley Daily Planet*, July 27, 2012, http://www.berkeleydailyplanet.com/issue/2012-07-27/article/40051.

87. Ari Y. Kelman, Abiya Ahmed, Ilana Horwitz, Jeremiah Lockwood, Marva Shalev Marom, and Maja Zuckerman, "Safe and on the Sidelines: Jewish Students and the Israel-Palestine Conflict on Campus" *Stanford University*, https://stanford.app.box.com/v/SafeandontheSidelinesReport.

88. Ibid., 2–3.

89. Taglit Birthright Israel, "Our Achievements," accessed November 7, 2017, https://www.birthrightisrael.com/about_us_inner/52?scroll=art_3.

90. Quoted in Ellie Shechet, "'No Brainwashing!' A Skeptic Goes on Birthright," *Jezebel*, June 15, 2015, http://jezebel.com/no-brainwashing-a-skeptic-goes-on-birthright-1710098507.

91. Stephanie Butnick, "Sheldon Adelson Doubles Down on Birthright," *Tablet*, February 12, 2015, http://www.tabletmag.com/scroll/188906/sheldon-adelson-doubles-down-on-birthright.

92. Shechet, "No Brainwashing!"

93. Kiera Feldman, "The Romance of Birthright Israel," *The Nation*, June 15, 2011, http://www.thenation.com/article/romance-birthright-israel/.

94. Shechet, "No Brainwashing!"

95. In November 2017, Birthright even announced its suspension of scheduled encounters with Palestinian citizens of Israel. See Judy Maltz, "Birthright Orders Trip Providers to End Meet-Ups with Israeli Arabs," *Haaretz*, November 2, 2017, https://www.haaretz.com/israel -news/.premium-1.820506.

96. JVP, "Reject Birthright Israel: Manifesto," accessed September 27, 2017, https://jewish voiceforpeace.org/returnthebirthright/#1503600634512–7c5eee0a-7f36.

97. The campaign #YouNeverToldMe was launched on September 7, 2017, in a *Jewschool* piece by Adina Cooper, an INN activist and a graduate of the Solomon Schechter Jewish school in New York City. See Cooper, "What They Didn't Teach Me at Solomon Schechter," *Jewschool*, https://jewschool.com/2017/09/80218/younevertoldme-solomon-schechter/.

98. Aiden Pink, "They Walked Out on Birthright to See Palestinians—And Created Their Own Conflict," *Forward*, June 28, 2018, https://forward.com/news/israel/404329/birthright -walkout-sees-debate-over-occupation-education-extend-to-israel/; Nir Hasson, "For the Second Time in Two Weeks: U.S. Jews Walk Off Birthright Trip to Join Anti-Occupation Activity," *Haaretz*, July 15, 2018, https://www.haaretz.com/israel-news/.premium-young-jews-walk-off -birthright-trip-to-join-anti-occupation-activity-1.6271943.

99. See Batya Ungar-Sargon, "The Real Reason People Are Upset About Birthright Walk-outs," *Forward*, July 18, 2018, https://forward.com/opinion/406002/the-real-reason-people-are -upset-about-birthright-walkouts/.

100. David Brennan, "Trouble at Birthright: Why Young Jews Are Rebelling on Israeli Heritage Trips," *Newsweek*, July 20, 2018, https://www.newsweek.com/death-birthright-why -young-jews-are-abandoning-israeli-heritage-trips-1034020. For efforts to disrupt Conservative's summer camps' Israel education's lack of attention to the occupation, see Ben Sales, "Conservative Camps Respond after Some Counselors Take Left-Wing Course on Israel," *Jewish Telegraphic Agency*, June 8, 2018, https://www.jta.org/2018/06/08/top-headlines/conservative -camps-respond-counselors-take-left-wing-course-israel; and Aiden Pink, "Camp Ramah Says No Way to IfNotNow's Harsh Criticism of Israel," *Forward*, June 13, 2018, https://forward.com/ news/national/403027/camp-ramah-says-no-way-to-ifnotnows-harsh-criticism-of-israel/. For gesturing to anticipated revisions to Israel curriculum within the Reform current, see Rick Jacobs, "Rabbi Rick Jacobs: Israel Turning Away BDS Supporter Ariel Gold Was 'Disgraceful,'" *Forward*, July 26, 2018, https://forward.com/scribe/406757/rabbi-rick-jacobs-israel-turning -away-bds-supporter-ariel-gold-was/?utm_source=facebook&utm_medium=social&utm _campaign=sumome_share.

101. Further discussions of the Jewish nation-state Basic Law and the anti-BDS "travel ban" can be found especially in chapters 8 and 4, respectively.

102. See Eric Lichtblau, "Divergent Path on Israel Helps Lobby Group Grow," *New York Times*, May 31, 2012, http://www.nytimes.com/2012/05/31/us/politics/j-street-a-lobbying -group-is-being-heard-as-moderate-voice-on-israel.html; and James Traub, "The New Israel Lobby," *New York Times*, September 12, 2009, http://www.nytimes.com/2009/09/13/magazine/ 13JStreet-t.html.

103. J Street website, "About Us," accessed September 27, 2017, http://jstreet.org/about-us.

104. Ibid.

105. Ibid.

106. Shortly after its emergence, J Street had become ubiquitous on university campuses. By 2017, J Street U was present on over 60 campuses in the US.

107. For J Street's positioning itself as a counter-voice to AIPAC in its support of the Iran deal in 2015, see Jacob Kornbluh, "J Street Launches Website to Counter Opposition to Iran

Deal," *Jewish Political News & Updates*, June 23, 2015, http://jpupdates.com/2015/06/23/j-street
-launches-website-to-counter-opposition-to-iran-deal/ (site discontinued). AIPAC's location
as the "right wing" organization is, however, threatened by Sheldon Adelson's bankrolling of
the even more hardline Israeli-American Council (IAC). See Josh Nathan-Kazis, "Breaking with
Script, Adelson Portrays IAC as a Hardline AIPAC Alternative," *Forward*, November 5, 2017,
http://forward.com/news/386949/breaking-with-scrip-adelson-says-iac-is-a-hardline-aipac
-alternative/.

108. See, for instance, the panel "Building an Effective Alternative to the Israeli Right" in
J Street's Annual Conference on February 25–28, 2017. Proceedings can be accessed at http://
jstreet.org/conference-highlights/#.Wo83qK6nGpo. The panel featured emerging "progressive
leadership" to highlight alternatives to extremist right-wing politics.

109. See also Nicholas Confessore and Maggie Haberman, "G.O.P. Hawks Upset with Bush
after Baker Speech on Israel," *New York Times*, March 27, 2015, http://www.nytimes.com/
politics/first-draft/2015/03/27/g-o-p-hawks-upset-with-bush-after-baker-speech-on-israel/.

110. Since the campaign, Sanders has continued to oppose the occupation. See, for instance,
Aaron Magid, "Bernie Sanders Sponsors Event Supporting Palestinian Village of Susiya," *Jewish Journal*, September 13, 2017, https://jewishjournal.com/news/nation/224335/bernie-sanders
-sponsors-event-palestinian-village-susiya/; Amir Tibon, "Bernie Sanders Meets with Prominent Palestinian Activist Targeted by Israel and Abbas," *Haaretz*, September 28, 2017, https://
www.haaretz.com/amp/middle-east-news/palestinians/1.814892.

111. The need to criticize Israeli policies, or at least to refrain from any critique of conventional support of Israeli narratives and practices, emerged during the 2016 Democratic
primary: Hillary Clinton highlighted her support of the Jewish establishment, while Sanders
offered a much more critical view that also explicitly recognized the moral claims of Palestinians. See, for instance, Samantha Lachman, "Bernie Sanders Suspends Staffer for Being as
Tough on Israel as He Is," *Huffington Post*, April 15, 2016, http://www.huffingtonpost.com/
entry/bernie-sanders-simone-zimmerman_us_57106cc3e4b0018f9cb9a71e. See also Carol
Giacomo, "Straight Talk from Bernie Sanders on the Israeli-Palestinian Conflict," *New York
Times*, March 22, 2016, https://takingnote.blogs.nytimes.com/2016/03/22/straight-talk-from
-bernie-sanders-on-the-israeli-palestinian-conflict/. The piece states that there were "18,000
AIPAC supporters" present at the annual conference in 2016, including all major presidential
candidates except Sanders.

112. Cited in Lachman, "Bernie Sanders Suspends Staffer." See also Zack Beauchamp,
"How Bernie Sanders's Jewish outreach coordinator started a major controversy over Israel," *Vox*, April 21, 2016, https://www.vox.com/2016/4/21/11438700/bernie-sanders-simone
-zimmerman; Editorial, "The Dilemma of Simone Zimmerman," *Jewish Exponent*, April 20,
2016, http://jewishexponent.com/2016/04/20/the-dilemma-of-simone-zimmerman/; Jason
Horowitz, "First Draft: Bernie Sanders Campaign Suspends Jewish Outreach Coordinator for
Vulgar Remarks About Netanyahu," *New York Times*, April 14, 2016, https://www.nytimes.com/
politics/first-draft/2016/04/14/bernie-sanders-suspends-jewish-outreach-coordinator-after
-reports-of-her-criticisms-of-israel/; and Isaac Luria, "'There's a Vicious Fight in Our Community': Simone Zimmerman Talks Bernie," *+972 Magazine*, July 25, 2016, https://972mag
.com/theres-a-vicious-fight-in-our-community-simone-zimmerman-talks-bernie-for-the
-first-time/120888/.

113. J Street executive director Jeremy Ben-Ami, "J Street Statement on Israel-Hamas Cease-
fire," J Street website, December 18, 2008, http://jstreet.org/press-releases/j-street-statement-on
-israel-hamas-ceasefire/.

114. Rabbi Eric Yoffi (at the time, president of the Union for Reform Judaism), cited in Nathan-Kazis, "Support Wins 'Moderate' Praise but Alienates Some Backers," *Forward*, July 30, 2014, http://forward.com/news/israel/203111/j-streets-gaza-war-support-wins-moderate-praise/.

115. For an account of J Street's moderation as part of its campaign for membership in the Conference of Presidents, see Michael Paulson, "Jewish Groups Consider Including J Street," *New York Times*, April 29, 2014, https://www.nytimes.com/2014/04/30/us/jewish-groups -consider-including-j-street.html. However, J Street later resisted AIPAC's rejection of the Iran deal and a counternarrative about the racism that marked the Israeli elections of 2015. See Nathan Guttman, "J Street, Newly Combative, Takes On the Jewish Establishment," *Forward*, March 25, 2015, http://forward.com/news/israel/217456/j-street-newly-combative-takes-on -the-jewish-estab/.

116. Nathan-Kazis, "Support Wins 'Moderate' Praise."

117. Eva Borgwardt, opening address on a plenary panel titled "Rising to the Challenge: American Jewish Leadership in the Trump Era," *Highlights of J Street's 2017 National Confer-ence: Defending Our Values, Fighting For Our Future*, February 25–28, 2017, http://jstreet.org/ conference-highlights/.

118. For an analysis that deploys the concept of ethnocracy in the case of Israel and Palestine, see Oren Yiftachel, *Ethnocracy: Land and Identity Politics in Israel/Palestine* (Philadelphia: Uni-versity of Pennsylvania Press, 2006).

119. J Street's defense of the two-state solution can be located at J Street, "Our Policy," ac-cessed February 23, 2018, http://jstreet.org/policy/the-two-state-solution/.

120. See "Henry Siegman, Leading U.S. Jewish Voice for Peace: 'Give Up on Netanyahu, Go to the United Nations,'" interview, *Democracy Now*, August 13, 2015, http://www.democracynow .org/2015/8/13/henry_siegman_leading_us_jewish_voice.

121. For an analysis of INN's tactical decision to omit a commitment to an explicit em-brace of BDS, see Abraham Riesman, "The Jewish Revolt: Can the Young Activists of IfNotNow Change the Conversation about Israel and the Palestinians, or Will Their Contradictions Hold Them Back?," *New York Magazine*, July 12, 2018, http://nymag.com/daily/intelligencer/2018/07/ ifnotnow-birthright-ramah-bds-israel.html.

Chapter Two

1. Liana Petruzzi, "Grappling With 50 Years in a Trump Era: A Reflection for #50Days-50Years," *IfNotNow* (blog), June 5, 2017, https://medium.com/ifnotnoworg/grappling-with-50 -years-in-a-trump-era-a-reflection-for-50days50years-6378fad1c359.

2. The coalition's partners included the Popular Committees of the South Hebron Hills, Holy Land Trust, Combatants for Peace, All That's Left: Anti-Occupation Collective, and the Center for Jewish Nonviolence.

3. In the summer of 2016, forty diaspora Jews of diverse ages and ideological locations spent ten days in the West Bank, engaging in acts of solidarity with local Palestinians (from whom they took cues and directives), including rebuilding demolished structures (later to be demolished again by the IDF) and clearing land to build a cinema on Tel Rumeida, a highly violent spot near Hebron—an act that resulted in arrests of some Jewish activists. This was the first expedition of American Jews explicitly under the banner "Occupation Is Not Our Judaism" (see figures 2.3 and 2.4). On the confrontation of diaspora Jews with Israeli anti-occupation actors, see A. Dan-iel Roth, "Cinema Hebron: A Photo Essay from the 'Occupation Is Not Our Judaism' Actions," *Jewschool*, July 22, 2016, https://jewschool.com/2016/07/77071/cinema-hebron/.

4. Cognitive dissonance is a concept and theory in psychology that entails a contradiction of beliefs and attitudes and is often overcome through a variety of mechanisms and tactics that reconcile the inconsistencies or through shifts in beliefs. See, for a classic formulation, Leon Festinger, *A Theory of Cognitive Dissonance* (Stanford, CA: Stanford University Press, 1957). For a more recent engagement, see Joel M. Cooper, *Cognitive Dissonance: 50 Years of a Classic Theory* (London: Sage Publications, 2007).

5. Smith, *Disruptive Religion: The Force of Faith in Social Movement Activism* (London: Routledge, 1996), 1–25.

6. James M. Jasper, "Emotions and Social Movements: Twenty Years of Theory and Research," *Annual Review of Sociology* 37 (2011): 285–303 (296).

7. Alberto Melucci, *Challenging Codes: Collective Action in the Information Age* (Cambridge: Cambridge University Press, 1996), 169.

8. Ibid., 171.

9. Ibid. See also Helena Flam, "Emotions' Map: A Research Agenda," in Helena Flam and Debra King, *Emotions and Social Movements* (London: Routledge, 2005), 1–40.

10. See, for instance, Durkheim, *The Elementary Forms of Religious Life*, trans. Joseph Ward Swain (New York: Free Press, [1912] 1995), 162.

11. Jasper, "Emotions and Social Movements," 291.

12. Barnett, *The Star and the Stripes: A History of the Foreign Policies of American Jews* (Princeton, NJ: Princeton University Press, 2016). See also Christian Smith, *Religion: What It Is, How It Works and Why It Matters* (Princeton, NJ: Princeton University Press, 2017), chapter 2, for helpful analysis of the causal powers religions possess to make things happen in the world. I further address this point in chapter 6.

13. See West, "Spiritual Blackout, Imperial Meltdown, Prophetic Fightback," 2017 Convocation Address at Harvard Divinity School, August 29, 2017, https://hds.harvard.edu/news/2017/08/30/video-convocation-2017%E2%80%94spiritual-blackout-imperial-meltdown-prophetic-fightback.

14. Jasper, "Emotions and Social Movements," 289.

15. Ibid.

16. See, for example, Judy Maltz, "Jewish Agency Pulls Funding from Israel Experience Program over West Bank Activism," *Haaretz*, September 19, 2017, http://www.haaretz.com/israel-news/1.812995.

17. The academic year following the events in Gaza in the summer of 2014 saw a dramatic increase in protests against Israeli policies on American campuses. AMCHA cites fifteen approved resolutions for divestment by university student bodies in 2014–2015, two more than the previous year. AMCHA (the watchdog initiative self-described as "protecting Jewish students") stated that between 2012 and 2016, fifty-three divestment resolutions passed, and fifty-nine resolutions failed. Likewise, fifty-six individual campuses had divestment activity and three university systems had similar activity. See AMCHA Initiative Protecting Jewish Students, "Antisemitic Divestment from Israeli Initiatives Scorecard on U.S. Campuses 2012–2017," updated September 6, 2017, https://amchainitiative.org/israel-divestment-vote-scorecard/.

18. Chapter 1 discusses these tactics.

19. Nathan Guttman, "Students for Justice in Palestine Builds Support with In-Your-Face Push," *Forward*, May 20, 2015, http://forward.com/news/israel/308236/the-guerilla-political-warriors-on-campus/.

20. See my discussion of Bourdieu in chapter 1.

21. For Open Hillel's chronology, see Open Hillel, "Open Hillel Highlights," accessed Sep-

tember 27, 2017, http://www.openhillel.org/history. For the early call from Harvard students for Hillel International to change its ideological standards, see Sasha Johnson-Freyd, Emily Unger, and Rachel Sandalow-Ash, "Opinion: An Open Hillel," *Harvard Crimson*, November 16, 2012, http://www.thecrimson.com/article/2012/11/16/hillel-pja/. On the Swarthmore split, see Elisheva Goldberg, "Swarthmore Hillel Breaks from Guidelines over Ban on 'Anti-Zionist' Speakers," *Daily Beast*, December 10, 2013, http://www.thedailybeast.com/articles/2013/12/10/swarthmore-hillel-breaks-from-guidelines-over-ban-on-anti-zionist-speakers.html.

22. See Open Hillel, "Academic Council: Statement," January 2016, http://www.openhillel.org/academic-council/. For press coverage discussing the academic council, see JTA, "Peter Beinart, 54 Other Academics Demand Hillel Open Up Israel Dialogue," *Jewish Telegraphic Agency*, January 27, 2016, http://www.jta.org/2016/01/07/news-opinion/united-states/open-hillel-movement-establishes-council-of-55-academic-backers; Aaron W. Hughes, "Why I Joined Open Hillel's Academic Council along with 45 Other Leading Jewish Academics," *Jewschool*, January 8, 2016, https://jewschool.com/2016/01/38854/why-i-joined-open-hillels-academic-advisory-council/; and Debra Nussbaum Cohen, "Top U.S. Professors Back Call for Hillel to Be More Inclusive on Israel Debate," *Haaretz,* January 13, 2016, http://www.haaretz.com/jewish/.premium-1.696813.

23. See Stefan Knieger, "Hillel International's Shameful Retreat Behind the Barricades on Israel and Palestine," *Haaretz*, January 18, 2016, https://www.haaretz.com/opinion/.premium-hillel-s-retreat-behind-barricades-on-israel-1.5392335.

24. Rachel Brustein, "Dialogue Doesn't Cost Money: A Call for a Non-Zionist Jewish Space at Goucher," *Quindecim*, December 10, 2015, https://thequindecim.wordpress.com/2015/12/10/dialogue-doesnt-cost-money-a-call-for-a-non-zionist-jewish-space-at-goucher/.

25. Judy Maltz, "Progressive Jewish Students to Protest Hillel Partnership with Israeli Minister Naftali Bennett," *Haaretz*, January 19, 2017, http://www.haaretz.com/israel-news/.premium-1.765932.

26. Open Hillel, "Hillel International: End Your Partnership with Mosaic United and Affirm Your Commitment to Pluralism," accessed September 27, 2017, http://www.openhillel.org/petition-1/.

27. If Not Now, When?, "Letter to the Conference of Presidents," July 28, 2014, https://ifnotnowmovement.org/letter-to-the-conference-of-presidents/.

28. Marshall Ganz, "Public Narrative, Collective Action, and Power," in *Accountability through Public Opinion: From Inertia to Public Action*, ed. Sina Odugbemi and Taeku Lee (Washington, DC: World Bank, 2011), 273–89 (274).

29. See Francesca Polletta, *It Was Like a Fever: Storytelling in Protest and Politics* (Chicago: University of Chicago Press, 2006); Roberto Franzosi, "Narrative Analysis—Why (and How) Sociologists Should Be Interested in Narrative," *Annual Review of Sociology* 24 (1998): 517–54; Peter Abell, "Narrative Explanation: An Alternative to Variable Centered Explanation?," *Annual Review of Sociology* 30 (2004): 287–310; Donileen R. Loseke, "The Study of Identity as Cultural, Institutional, Organizational, and Personal Narrative: Theoretical and Empirical Integrations," *Sociological Quarterly* 18, no. 4 (2007): 661–88; and Francesca Polletta, Pang Ching Bobby Chen, Beth Gharrity Gardner, and Alice Motes, "The Sociology of Storytelling," *Annual Review of Sociology* 37 (2011): 109–30. For the use of storytelling for mobilization, see Ronald Jacobs, "The Narrative Integration of Personal and Collective Identity in Social Movements," in *Narrative Impact: Social and Cognitive Foundations*, ed. M. C. Green, J. J. Strange, and T. C. Brock (Mahwah, NJ: Lawrence Erlbaum, 2002), 205–28; Robert A. Benford, "Controlling Narratives and Narratives as Control within Social Movements," in *Stories of Change: Narrative and Social*

Movements, ed. Joseph E. Davis (Albany: State University of New York Press, 2002), 53–75; and Patricia Ewick and Susan Silbey, "Narrating Social Structure: Stories of Resistance to Legal Authority," *American Journal of Sociology* 108, no. 6 (2003): 1328–72.

30. Polletta et al., "The Sociology of Storytelling," 111. See also Elinor Ochs and Lisa Capps, *Living Narrative: Creating Lives in Everyday Storytelling* (Cambridge, MA: Harvard University Press, 2001).

31. For the complex impossibility of such a task, see Judith Butler, *Giving an Account of Oneself* (New York: Fordham University Press, 2005).

32. Ibid., 118. This also resonates with the concept of "poaching" in Michel de Certeau and Henry Jenkins's work. See Jenkins, *Textual Poachers: Television Fans and Participatory Culture* (New York: Routledge, 2013); and de Certeau, *The Practice of Everyday Life,* trans. Steven Rendall (Los Angeles: University of California Press, 1984).

33. Philip Smith, *Why War? The Cultural Logic of Iraq, the Gulf War, and Suez* (Chicago: University of Chicago Press, 2005); Polletta, *It Was Like a Fever;* William A. Gamson, "How Storytelling Can Be Empowering," in *Culture in Mind: Toward a Sociology of Culture and Cognition,* ed. Karen A. Cerulo (New York: Routledge, 2001), 187–98.

34. Maurice Halbwach, "On Collective Memory," ed. Lewis A. Coser (Chicago: University of Chicago, 1992); Jeffrey K. Olick, *The Politics of Regret: On Collective Memory and Historical Responsibility* (New York: Routledge, 2007); and Astrid Erll, *Memory in Culture,* trans. Sara B. Young (New York: Palgrave Macmillan, 2011).

35. Polletta et al., "The Sociology of Storytelling," 122. See also Jacobs, "The Narrative Integration"; Lyn Spillman, "When Do Collective Memories Last? Founding Moments in the United States and Australia," in *States of Memory: Continuities, Conflicts, and Transformation in National Retrospection,* ed. Jeffrey Olick (Durham, NC: Duke University Press, 2003), 161–92; and Robin Wagner-Pacifici and Barry Schwartz, "The Vietnam Veteran Memorial: Commemorating a Difficult Past," *American Journal of Sociology* 97 (1991): 376–420.

36. See the discussion of Shavit's *My Promised Land* in chapter 1.

37. If Not Now, When?, "Letter to the Conference of Presidents."

38. This is the conference in which J Street sought membership. See chapter 1.

39. Rachel Leider, testimonial about B'nai B'rith Youth Organization (BBYO), *YouNever ToldMe,* accessed September 27, 2017, https://younevertoldme.org/stories/2017/9/6/9n6vdm0m 3tnxb2cy5wmx1gqw8a8qr0.

40. Shaina, testimonial about Union of Reform Judaism (URJ) Camp, *YouNeverToldMe,* accessed September 27, 2017, https://younevertoldme.org/stories/2017/9/6/wvjnq2xqiduem xao2upgji4rsabsit.

41. Max Broad, "Why I Ran from Judaism—Until Recently: A Reflection For #50DAYS-50YEARS," *IfNotNow,* June 13, 2017, https://medium.com/ifnotnoworg/why-i-ran-from -judaism-until-recently-b9237b135a72.

42. Ibid.

43. Tenara Calem, "Holding Complexity: A Reflection For #50DAYS50YEARS," *IfNotNow,* June 10, 2017, https://medium.com/ifnotnoworg/50-years-too-many-4f5ec953279.

44. Ibid.

45. Maiya Zwerling, "This Is Not My Judaism: A Reflection For #50DAYS50YEARS," *IfNotNow* video, June 8, 2017, http://50days50years.com/stories/2017/6/8/this-is-not-my -judaism-a-reflection-for-50days50years (site discontinued).

46. See also Abraham Riesman, "The Jewish Revolt: Can the Young Activists of IfNotNow Change the Conversation about Israel and the Palestinians, or Will Their Contradictions Hold

Them Back?," *New York Magazine*, July 12, 2018, http://nymag.com/daily/intelligencer/2018/07/ifnotnow-birthright-ramah-bds-israel.html.

47. Sumka, "Punched, Dismantled, Unbowed: How Diaspora Jews Are Unsettling the Occupation," *Haaretz*, May 29, 2017, http://www.haaretz.com/opinion/.premium-1.792576.

48. Ibid.

49. Ibid.

50. Ibid.

51. Ibid.

52. The pipeline protests garnered steam in April 2016, and at their peak attracted about 10,000 protesters (or water defenders) who joined the Standing Rock Sioux tribe to resist the Dakota Access Pipeline to be constructed under a lake near the indigenous reservation. The encampment was dismantled after Donald Trump took office in 2017.

53. Ilana Sumka, "Punched, Dismantled, Unbowed: How Diaspora Jews Are Unsettling the Occupation," *Haaretz*, May 29, 2017, https://www.haaretz.com/misc/haaretzcomsmartphoneapp/.premium-1.792576.

54. Brammer-Shlay, "Israeli Police Broke My Arm, But They Can't Stop Me from Resisting—Or Speaking Out," *Forward*, May 30, 2017, http://forward.com/scribe/373377/exclusive-israeli-police-broke-my-arm-but-they-cant-stop-me-from-resisting/.

55. All That's Left, "About," accessed September 27, 2017, http://www.allthatsleftcollective.com/about/.

56. Robin Levy, "From Thought to Action," *All That's Left* (blog), April 13, 2016, http://www.allthatsleftcollective.com/blog/2016/4/13/from-thought-to-action (site discontinued).

57. Ibid.

58. Honi ha-M'agel (or Circle Maker) was a Jewish scholar and miracle worker thought to have lived during the first century BCE. Honi was noted for his ability to pray for rain. According to legend, he drew a circle around himself during a time of drought, demanding God to bring rain. See Mishnah Ta'anit 3:8, http://www.mechon-mamre.org/b/h/h29.htm.

59. Anonymous participant in Nonviolence in Action, October 2015, *Center for Jewish Nonviolence*, accessed September 27, 2017, https://centerforjewishnonviolence.org/jewish-nonviolence/.

60. These strategies are reproduced in the program of the 2017 meeting. See Jewish Voice for Peace, "2017 National Member Meeting" (program), 3, https://nmm.jewishvoiceforpeace.org/wp-content/uploads/2016/09/NMM-2017-Program-Book-Digital-3.20.pdf.

61. Ibid.

62. Ibid., 4. In 2017, JVP launched a member-wide discussion (through webinars, online curricula, and coordinated chapter meetings), hoping to arrive at a clear position on the question of Zionism by January 2018. The discussion involved at least seven planned meetings intentionally prioritizing the narratives of Palestinians, Mizrahi, Sephardi, and Jews of color. See Jewish Voice for Peace, "Zionism Policy Discussion Group—FAQ," September 1, 2017, https://org.salsalabs.com/o/301/images/Zionism_Discussion_Group_FAQ_Sept1Final (site discontinued).

63. Chapter 7 offers an extensive discussion of the relevance of American race history to Jewish Palestine solidarity.

64. See, for example, T'ruah (The Rabbinic Call for Human Rights), "Statement on Black Lives Matter Platform," August 4, 2016, http://www.truah.org/press/statement-on-black-lives-matter-platform/.

65. JVP tweeted on August 4, 2016: "JVP endorses the #Vision4BlackLives platform in its entirety, without reservation," and IfNotNow issued a statement the following day: "The Jewish

Community Needs to Support the Movement for Black Lives," https://ifnotnowmovement.org/2016/08/05/statement-the-jewish-community-needs-to-support-the-movement-for-black-lives/. JVP's statement can be found in Jewish Voice for Peace, "JVP Response to the Movement for Black Lives Policy Platform," August 4, 2016, https://jewishvoiceforpeace.org/jvp4bl/.

66. Jews of Color, Sephardim, and Mizrahim (JOCSM), "Jews of Color Caucus Statement in Solidarity with the Movement for Black Lives," August 5, 2016, http://jocsm.org/jews-of-color-caucus-statement-in-solidarity-with-the-movement-for-black-lives-matter/.

67. Jews for Racial & Economic Justice, "Our Strategic Vision," accessed September 27, 2017, http://jfrej.org/wp-content/uploads/2015/06/JFREJ-Strategic-Vision-2015.pdf.

68. See, in particular, Smith, *Disruptive Religion*, 9–22; Ron Aminzade and Elizabeth J. Perry, "The Sacred, Religious, and Secular in Contentious Politics: Blurring Boundaries," in *Silence and Voice in the Study of Contentious Politics*, ed. Ronald R. Aminzade, Jack A. Goldstone, Doug McAdam, Elizabeth J. Perry, William H. Sewer Jr., Sidney Tarrow, and Charles Tilly (Cambridge: University of Cambridge Press, 2001), 155–78; and Mayer N. Zald and John McCarthy, "Religious Groups as Crucibles of Social Movements," *Social Movements in an Organized Society: Collected Essays*, ed. Zald and McCarthy (London: Transaction Publishers, 1987), 67–95.

69. See chapter 9 for further analysis of this point.

70. Tarrow, *Power in Movement: Social Movements, Collective Action and Politics* (Cambridge: Cambridge University Press, 1994), 4. See also Donatella Della Porta and Sidney Tarrow, *Transnational Protest and Global Activism* (Lanham, MD: Rowman & Littlefield, 2005).

71. Tilly, *Social Movements, 1768–2004* (Boulder, CO: Paradigm Publishers, 2004).

72. James and van Seeters, *Globalization and Politics, Vol. 2: Global Social Movements and Global Civil Society* (London: Sage Publications, 2014), xi.

73. See David Couzens Hoy, *Critical Resistance: From Poststructuralism to Post-Critique* (Cambridge, MA: MIT Press, [2004] 2005), 79.

74. Bourdieu, *Logic of Practice* (Stanford, CA: Stanford University Press, 1990), 53, cited in Landy, *Jewish Identity & Palestinian Rights: Diaspora Jewish Opposition to Israel* (London: Zed Books, 2011), 28.

75. Bourdieu, *Practical Reason: On the Theory of Action*, trans. Randal Johnson et al. (Stanford, CA: Stanford University Press, 1998).

76. See chapter 1 for a discussion of Bourdieu's categories of *doxa*, orthodoxy, heterodoxy, and the logic of social reproduction. See also Bourdieu, *Outline of a Theory of Practice*, 1982; and Bourdieu, *Pascalian Meditations* (Cambridge: Polity Press, 2000), 51. For an analysis of Bourdieu's concept of *illusio*, which refers to participants' willing engagement with and valuation of the game or field, see Carl-Göran Heidegren and Henrik Lundberg, "Towards a Sociology of Philosophy," *Acta Sociologica* 53, no. 1 (2010): 3–18. They explain that, for Bourdieu, "illusio is an illusion only to those outside the field" (12).

77. Here, Landy follows Nick Crossley's revision of Bourdieu's account of transformative systemic change. See Crossley, "From Reproduction to Transformation: Social Movement Fields and the Radical Habitus," *Theory Culture & Society* 20, no. 6 (2003): 43–68.

78. Here, it is useful to look at sociological efforts to mediate Bourdieu's conception of symbolic domination and Antonio Gramsci's hegemony. For example, see Michael Burawoy (2008), "Durable Domination: Gramsci Meets Bourdieu," available at http://burawoy.berkeley.edu/Bourdieu/Lecture%202.pdf.

79. Chapters 7 and 8 explore the complexity of these terms as they relate to the movement of critical Jewish Palestine solidarity.

80. Martha Nussbaum, *Upheavals of Thought: The Intelligence of Emotions* (New York: Oxford University Press, 2001).

81. See Louis Althusser, "Ideology and Ideological State Apparatuses (Notes Towards an Investigation)," in *Lenin and Philosophy and Other Essays*, trans. Ben Brewster (New York: Monthly Review Press, 1971).

82. For Nietzsche's influence on poststructuralist critique and accounts of resistance, see Hoy, *Critical Resistance*, esp. 46–56.

83. Emirbayer and Mische, "What Is Agency?," *American Journal of Sociology* 103, no. 4 (January 1998), 962–1023 (989).

84. Marc W. Steinberg, "The Talk and Back Talk of Collective Action: A Dialogic Analysis of Repertoires of Discourse among Nineteenth-Century English Cotton Spinners," *American Journal of Sociology* 105, no. 3 (November 1999): 736–80. See also Patricia Ewick and Marc W. Steinberg, "The Dilemmas of Social Movement Identity and the Case of the Voice of the Faithful," *Mobilization: An International Quarterly* 19, no. 2 (2014): 209–27. The dialogic turn in social movement theory offers a critique of the theoretical concept of framing.

85. For example, see Francesca Polletta and James Jasper, "Collective Identity and Social Movements," *Annual Review of Sociology* 27 (2001): 283–305; and Sharon Erickson Nepstad, "Creating Transnational Solidarity: The Use of Narrative in the U.S.-Central America Peace Movement," in *Globalization and Resistance: Transnational Dimensions of Social Movement*, ed. Jackie Smith and Hank Johnston (Lanham, MD: Rowman & Littlefield, 2002), 133–49.

86. For prominent examples of this approach, see David Snow, Burke Rochford, Steven Worden, and Robert Benford, "Frame Alignment Processes, Micromobilization, and Movement Participation," *American Sociological Review* 51, no. 4 (1986): 464–81; Erving Goffman, *Frame Analysis: An Essay on the Organization of Experience* (New York: Harper & Row, 1974); Robert D. Benford and David A. Snow, "Framing Processes and Social Movements: An Overview and Assessment," *Annual Review of Sociology* 26 (2000): 611–39; and Doug McAdam, Sidney Tarrow, and Charles Tilly, *Dynamics of Contention* (Cambridge: Cambridge University Press, 2001).

87. Benford and Snow, "Framing Processes and Social Movements."

88. Ibid., 614.

89. Ibid.

90. Ibid.

91. See Hank Johnston and Bert Klandermans, eds., *Social Movements and Culture* (Minneapolis: University of Minnesota Press, 1995); Tarrow, *Power in Movement*; Mitch Berbier, "'Half the Battle': Cultural Resonance, Framing Processes, and Ethnic Affections in Contemporary White Separatist Rhetoric," *Social Problems* 45 (1998): 431–50; Sharon Erickson Nepstad, "The Process of Cognitive Liberation: Cultural Synapses, Links, and Frame Contradictions in the U.S.-Central America Peace Movement," *Social Inquiry* 67 (1997): 470–87; Nepstad, "Creating Transnational Solidarity"; Alford A. Young, "New Life for an Old Concept: Frame Analysis and the Reinvigoration of Studies in Culture and Poverty," *Annals of the American Academy of Political and Social Science* 629 (2010): 53–74; M. Eugenia Deerman, "Transporting Movement Ideology into Popular Culture: Right-Wing Think Tanks and the Case of 'Virgin Chic,'" *Sociological Spectrum* 32, no. 2 (2012): 95–113; Francesca Polletta and M. Kai Ho, "Frames and Their Consequences," in *The Oxford Handbook of Contextual Political Analysis*, ed. Robert E. Goodin and Charles Tilly (Oxford: Oxford University Press, 2006), 187–209; David Snow, "Framing Processes, Ideology, and Discursive Fields," in *The Blackwell Companion to Social Movements*, ed. David A. Snow, Sarah A. Soule, and Hanspeter Kriesi (Walden, MA: Blackwell, 2004), 380–

412; and David L. Westby, "Strategic Imperative, Ideology, and Frame," *Mobilization* 7 (2002): 287–304.

92. A critical caretaker bears a critical relationship to her particular religious tradition, but engages constructively with its histories, symbols, traditions, and so on. I develop this lens more fully in chapter 4. See also two earlier works: Atalia Omer, *When Peace Is Not Enough: How the Israeli Peace Camp Thinks About Religion, Nationalism, and Justice* (Chicago: Chicago University Press, 2013); and Omer, "Can a Critic Be a Caretaker Too? Religion, Conflict, and Conflict Transformation," *Journal of the American Academy of Religion* 79, no. 2 (June 2011): 459–96.

93. Cited in Hoy, *Critical Resistance*, 100. See also Butler, "What Is Critique? An Essay on Foucault's Virtue," in *The Political*, ed. David Ingram (Boston: Blackwell, 2002); and Michel Foucault, "What Is Critique?," in *The Political.*

94. Steinberg, "The Talk and Back Talk of Collective Action," 739. The dialogic and social semiotic approach extends a Bakhtinian perspective articulated in Mikhail M. Bakhtin, *The Dialogic Imagination: Four Essays*, trans. Caryl Emerson and Michael Holquist, ed. Michael Holquist (Austin: University of Texas Press, 1981). Still, the framing literature and adjacent conversations do include some important reflections on meanings and narratives. For instance, see Walter Fisher, "Narration as a Human Communication Paradigm: The Case of Public Moral Argument," *Communication Monographs* 51 (1984): 1–23; and Rita K. Noonan, "Women Against the State: Political Opportunities and Collective Action Frames in Chile's Transition to Democracy," *Sociological Forum* 10, no. 1 (1995): 81–111. For critiques of the framing literature's theorizing of culture, see, for instance, Ann Swidler, "Cultural Power and Social Movements," in *Social Movements and Culture* (Minneapolis: University of Minneapolis Press, 1995), 25–40; James Jasper, *The Art of Moral Protest* (Chicago: University of Chicago Press, 1997); Jeff Goodwin and James Jasper, "Caught in a Winding, Snarling Vine: The Structural Bias of Political Process Theory," *Social Forum* 14 (1999): 27–54; Jeff Goodwin, James Jasper, and Francesca Polletta, *Passionate Politics: Emotions and Social Movements* (Chicago: University of Chicago Press, 2001); and Benford and Snow, "Framing Processes and Social Movements," 629. The critics mainly highlight a problematic inclination to reify culture and cultural resources.

95. Steinberg, "The Talk and Back Talk of Collective Action," 740.

96. Ibid., 737–43.

97. Ibid., 747.

98. Ibid., 748–49. See also Lyn Spillman, "Culture, Social Structures and Discursive Fields," *Current Perspectives in Social Theory* 15 (1995): 129–54.

99. Tarrow, "Mentalities, Political Cultures, and Collective Action Frames: Constructing Meaning through Action," in *Social Movement Theory*, ed. Aldon D. Morris and Carol M. Mueller (New Haven, CT: Yale University Press, 1992), 189; also cited in Benford and Snow, "Framing Processes and Social Movements," 629. See also Snow and Byrd, "Ideology, Framing Processes, and Islamic Terrorist Movements," *Mobilization: An International Quarterly Review* 12, no. 1 (2007): 119–36.

100. Smith, "Correcting a Curious Neglect, or Bringing Religion Back In," in *Disruptive Religion: The Force of Faith in Social Movement Activism* (London: Routledge 1996), 1–25, for instance.

101. Snow and Byrd, "Ideology, Framing Processes, and Islamic Terrorist Movements," 123.

102. Ibid.

103. For an analysis from a psychosocial perspective of religion's relevance to social meaning-making processes and boundary construction, see Janine Dahinden and Tania Zit-

toun, "Religion in Meaning Making and Boundary Work: Theoretical Explorations," *Integrative Psychological and Behavioral Science* 47, no. 2 (2013): 185–206.

104. See Benford and Snow, "Framing Processes and Social Movements"; David Snow and Doug McAdam, "Identity Work Processes in the Context of Social Movements: Clarifying the Identity/Movement Nexus," in *Self, Identity, and Social Movements*, ed. Sheldon Stryker, Timothy Joseph Owens, and Robert W. White (Minneapolis: University of Minnesota Press, 2000); and Hunt, Benford, and Snow, "Identity Fields: Framing Processes and the Social Construction of Movement Identities," in *New Social Movements: From Ideology to Identity*, ed. Enrique Laraña, Hank Johnston, and Joseph R. Gusfield (Philadelphia: Temple University Press, 1994), 185–208.

105. See the discussion above of Mische and Emirbayer.

106. Steinberg, "The Talk and Back Talk of Collective Action," 216. For other sociological analyses of a complex relational and interactionist collective identity construction in movement, see Verta Taylor and Nancy E. Whittier, "Collective Identity in Social Movement Communities: Lesbian Feminist Mobilization," in *Frontiers in Social Movement Theory*, ed. Aldon D. Morris and Carol McClurg Mueller (New Haven, CT: Yale University Press, 1992), 104–29; Paul Lichterman, "Talking Identity in the Public Sphere: Broad Visions and Small Spaces in Sexual Identity Politics," *Theory and Society* 28 (1999): 101–41; David S. Meyer, Nancy Whittier, and Belinda Robnett, eds., *Social Movements: Identity, Culture and the State* (New York: Oxford University Press, 2002); Sheldon Stryker, Timothy J. Owens, and Robert W. White, eds., *Self, Identity, and Social Movements* (Minneapolis: University of Minnesota Press, 2000); and Jo Reger, Daniel J. Myers, Rachel L. Einwohner, eds., *Identity Work in Social Movements* (Minneapolis: University of Minnesota Press, 2008).

107. For example, see Almond Gabriel, Scott Appleby, and Emmanuel Sivan, *Strong Religion: The Rise of Fundamentalisms around the World* (Chicago: University of Chicago Press, 2002); and Geneviève Boudreau, "Radicalization of the Settlers' Youth: Hebron as a Hub for Jewish Extremism," *Global Media Journal–Canadian Edition* 7, no. 1 (2014): 69–85.

108. Consider, for instance, the debate surrounding the publication of Graeme Wood, "What ISIS Really Wants," *The Atlantic*, March 2015, http://www.theatlantic.com/magazine/archive/2015/03/what-isis-really-wants/384980/. Critics challenged Wood's presumption of "authority" and that of his scholarly sources in narrating the way Da'esh (or ISIS/ISIL) interprets the resources of Islam and Muslim history, overriding Muslim challengers and hermeneutical work within the tradition, which has always been internally plural, contested, and contextually specific. For two such critiques, see Robert Wright, "The Clash of Civilizations That Isn't," *New Yorker*, February 25, 2015, http://www.newyorker.com/news/news-desk/clash-civilizations-isnt; and Ross Douthat, "In Defense of Islam," *New York Times*, February 18, 2015, http://douthat.blogs.nytimes.com/2015/02/18/in-defense-of-islam/.

109. Benford and Snow, *Framing Processes and Social Movements*, 613; see also Snow and Benford, "Ideology, Frame Reference, and Participant Mobilization," *International Social Movement Research* 1, no. 1 (1988): 197–217.

Chapter Three

1. Talia Baurer, "Unlearning Zionism," in *Confronting Zionism: A Collection of Personal Stories*, ed. Jewish Voice for Peace-NYC (New York City: JVP-NYC, 2017), 7.

2. I employ the multidimensional psychological concept of cognitive dissonance because

the activists I interviewed typically describe a process of coming to recognize the inconsistency of their received narratives with their own experiences. For those I interviewed, the contradictions are simply no longer tolerable, and the psychological mechanisms of dissonance are no longer effective. For a historical overview of psychological research on cognitive dissonance, see Leon Festinger, *A Theory of Cognitive Dissonance* (Stanford, CA: Stanford University Press, 1957); Elliot Aronson, "The Theory of Cognitive Dissonance: A Current Perspective," in *Advances in Experimental Social Psychology*, ed. L. Berkowitz (New York: Academic Press, 1969), vol. 4, 1–34; and Joel M. Cooper, *Cognitive Dissonance: 50 Years of a Classic Theory* (Thousand Oaks, CA: Sage Publications, 2007).

3. Sagiv Galai, "From the Other Side of the Green Line and How I Got Here," in Jewish Voice for Peace-NYC, *Confronting Zionism*, 23.

4. Ibid.

5. Ibid.

6. Ibid., 23–24.

7. Ibid., 24.

8. James M. Jasper, "Emotions and Social Movement: Twenty Years of Theory and Research," *Annual Review of Sociology* 37 (2011): 291. See also chapter 2 for further discussion of moral batteries and shocks as well as public narrative as a social movement's mechanism.

9. Katie Miranda, "Interview with Rebecca Vilkomerson," Palestine Solidarity Telesummit, October 20, 2014, http://vimeo.com/109270156.

10. See chapter 1 for an account of J Street and its limitations as a space for renegotiating the meaning of being "pro-Israel and pro-peace."

11. See my discussion, in chapter 2, of Marshall Ganz on "public narrative."

12. The use of the word "conversion" is likely influenced by how I framed a question asking the activist to describe her shift in affective loyalties, underscoring that I did not intend "conversion" in an explicitly (or at all) religious or theological sense.

13. Interview #14.

14. This quotation was also highlighted by Tzedek Chicago's preface to the video of the Corries' Yom Kippur presentation, which can be found at Tzedek Chicago, "Craig and Cindy Corrie on Sacrifice and Solidarity," October 1, 2017, http://www.tzedekchicago.org/craig_and _cindy_corrie.

15. Interview #7. See chapter 1 for a discussion of Birthright tours.

16. Jewish Voice for Peace, "Reject Birthright Israel: Manifesto," accessed September 20, 2017, https://jewishvoiceforpeace.org/returnthebirthright/#1503600634512–7c5eee0a-7f36.

17. Daniel J. Solomon, "IfNotNow Launches #YouNeverToldMe Anti-Occupation Campaign," September 11, 2017, http://forward.com/fast-forward/382337/ifnotnow-launches-you nevertoldme-anti-occupation-campaign/.

18. Interview #21.

19. See chapter 1 on AMCHA and other organizations' efforts to muzzle debate on university campuses.

20. The Bil'in nonviolent struggle was effectively documented in the film *5 Broken Cameras*, directed by Emad Burnat and Guy Davidi (2011).

21. Interview #21.

22. "Sabra" is the iconic self-representation of Israelis as cacti: tough and resilient. The term refers specifically to a Jewish person born in Israel, who thus exhibits a masculine physicality that subverts diasporic conceptions of Jewishness as lacking in this area. Such "other-ing" of

the diasporic of course reflects the internalization of antisemitic tropes. On the issue of trans-valuation of masculinity, see Daniel Boyarin, *Unheroic Conduct: The Rise of Heterosexuality and the Invention of the Jewish Man* (Los Angeles: University of California Press, 1997); and Todd Samuel Presner, *Muscular Judaism: The Jewish Body and the Politics of Regeneration* (New York: Routledge, 2007).

23. Interview #1.

24. Interview #21.

25. Interview #26.

26. Grappling with the whiteness of Jews constitutes a central focus of chapters 7 and 8.

27. See chapters 7 and 8.

28. See Sherry Gorelick, "Peace Movement in the United States," *Jewish Women: A Comprehensive Historical Encyclopedia*, March 20, 2009, Jewish Women's Archive, http://jwa.org/encyclopedia/article/peace-movement-in-united-states.

29. Smadar Lavie, "Mizrahi Feminism and the Question of Palestine," *Journal of Middle East Women's Studies* 7, no. 2 (2011): 56–88; and Lavie, *Wrapped in the Flag of Israel: Mizrahi Single Mothers and Bureaucratic Torture* (New York: Berghahn, 2014). See also my chapter 9.

30. For a deep contextualization of Breira, see Michael E. Staub, *Torn at the Roots: The Crisis of Jewish Liberalism in Postwar America* (New York City: Columbia University Press, 2004), chapter 8. See also the discussion later in this chapter of the historical complexities of progressive intellectual and activist Jewish currents in the US as well as chapters 4, 7, and 8.

31. One Jewish activist who distinguished herself as instrumental for Code Pink's work against the US-funded occupation of Palestine is Ariel Gold. See Allison Kaplan Sommer, "Jewish Mother and BDS Activist: Code Pink's Ariel Gold vs. Israel's Travel Ban," *Haaretz*, July 11, 2017, https://www.haaretz.com/israel-news/.premium-1.800625.

32. Interview #2.

33. Ibid.

34. Ibid.

35. Interview #5.

36. Ibid.

37. Interview #19.

38. Interview #27.

39. For the complex relation of Chabad Lubavitch to modern Israel, see Norton Mezvinsky and Joshua Kolb, "Eyes upon the Land: Chabad Lubavitch on Israel," *Religious Studies and Theology* 32, no. 1 (2013): 7–21.

40. Herzl (1860–1904) is celebrated as the founder of political European Zionism. His pamphlet *Der Judenstaat* (1896) explicitly outlines a political statist program for a Jewish state.

41. Interview #7.

42. See Open Hillel Facebook page, July 1, 2015, https://www.facebook.com/openhillel/photos/a.577610768939661.1073741825.532994396734632/1001791759854891/.

43. Interview #13.

44. Interview #9. For the interviewee's choice of the word "conversion," see note 12 above.

45. Ibid.

46. Interview #17.

47. Wendy Elisheva Somerson, "The Intersection of Anti-Occupation and Queer Jewish Organizing," *Tikkun* 25, no. 4 (July/August 2010): 58–73.

48. For a background critique of the logic underlying associations between homosexuality

and conventional ideological frames and practices, with an emphasis on the concept of "homonationalism," see Puar Jasbir, *Terrorist Assemblages: Homonationalism in Queer Times* (Durham, NC: Duke University Press, 2007); and Sarah Schulman, *Israel/Palestine and the Queer International* (Durham, NC: Duke University Press, 2012).

49. Open Hillel, "Over 100 Rabbis Call on Hillel International to Reinstate Booted LGBTQ Group," *Forward*, June 22, 2017, http://forward.com/scribe/375454/over-100-rabbis-call-on-hillel-international-to-reinstate-booted-lgbtq-grou.

50. See the discussion of challenges to Hillel International in chapter 1.

51. An example of such compartmentalization can be found in a response by a senior adviser for strategic communications at Hillel International who self-identifies as a gay Jew: Matthew E. Berger, "Hillel Is Proudly LGBTQ," *Forward*, June 23, 2017, http://forward.com/scribe/375537/hillel-is-proudly-pro-lgbtq/.

52. Craig Willse, "No Apartheid in Our Name: LGBT Jewish Groups Block 'Celebrate Israel' Parade," *Truthout*, June 7, 2017, http://www.truth-out.org/opinion/item/40870-no-apartheid-in-our-name-lgbt-jewish-groups-block-celebrate-israel-parade.

53. See, for instance, Rachel Delia Benaim, "LGBT Contingent 'Infiltrated' by Protesters at Celebrate Israel Parade," *Tablet*, June 5, 2017, http://www.tabletmag.com/scroll/236292/lgbt-contingent-infiltrated-by-protesters-at-celebrate-israel-parade; and Jay Michaelson, "Shame On You, Jewish Voice for Peace, For Targeting Pro-Israel Gays," *Forward*, June 6, 2017, http://www.jaymichaelson.net/shame-on-you-jewish-voice-for-peace-for-targeting-pro-israel-gays/.

54. For the official statement by JQY, see "'Jewish Voice for Peace' Infiltrators Sabotage At-Risk LGBTQ Jewish Youth at the Celebrate Israel Parade," Jewish Queer Youth, accessed September 27, 2017, https://www.jqyouth.org/parade-statement/. For a statement by JQY's executive director, who employed mechanisms of cognitive dissonance to subvert the critique, see Mordechai Levovitz, "JVP's Targeting of LGBTQ Youth Shows 'An Unbelievable Lack of Empathy,'" *Forward*, June 9, 2017, http://forward.com/scribe/374267/jvps-targeting-of-lgbtq-youth-shows-an-unbelievable-lack-of-empathy/.

55. On another controversial event by A Wider Bridge (AWB), see Liza Behrendt, "Shutting Down a Pinkwashing Event Is a Smart, Legitimate Protest Against Israel's Occupation," *Haaretz*, January 28, 2016, https://www.haaretz.com/opinion/.premium-shutting-down-pinkwashing-is-legitimate-protest-against-occupation-1.5397068. The organization rejects the concept of pinkwashing as misdirected. See "The Myths of Pinkwashing," A Wider Bridge, accessed October 3, 2017, http://awiderbridge.org/our-work/trainings/the-myths-of-pinkwashing/. On its commitment to the state of Israel as "the most important project of Jewish people," see "About," A Wider Bridge, accessed October 3, 2017, http://awiderbridge.org/about.

56. Anna Fox, "I'm a Queer Jewish Student. Is My Acceptance in Organized Jewish Communities Conditional?," *Jewschool*, June 14, 2017, https://jewschool.com/2017/06/79786/im-queer-jewish-student-acceptance-organized-jewish-communities-conditional/. The inconsistencies between the branding of Israel as LGBTQI friendly and the realities are striking, especially when considering the strong push by the same social sectors driving Mosaic United against gay adoption in Israel and other homophobic manifestations.

57. Philip Weiss, "Israel Surveils and Blackmails Gay Palestinians to Make Them Informants," *Mondoweiss*, September 24, 2014, http://mondoweiss.net/2014/09/blackmails-palestinian-informants/; and Anshel Pfeffer, "Unit 8200 Refuseniks Shed Light on Ethics of Israel's Intel Gathering," *Haaretz*, September 15, 2014, http://www.haaretz.com/israel-news/.premium-1.615811.

58. Willse, "No Apartheid in Our Name."

59. Stephanie Skora, "Queer Jews Should Think Again before Celebrating Israel," +972 *Magazine*, June 18, 2017, https://972mag.com/queer-jews-should-think-again-before-celebrating-israel/128195/. But see also Eli Ungar-Sargon, "What Really Happened at JVP's Queer Protest at the Israel Parade: JVP, JQY, and the Weaponization of Vulnerability," *Jewschool*, June 12, 2017, https://jewschool.com/2017/06/79759/jvp-jqy-weaponization-vulnerability/.

60. Alissa Wise, "JVP: Reactions to Our Parade Protest Were 'Cruel,' 'Homophobic,' and 'Hyperbolic,'" *Forward*, June 7, 2017, http://forward.com/scribe/374055/jvp-reactions-to-our-parade-protest-were-cruel-homophobic-and-hyperbolic/.

61. Ibid.

62. Ibid.

63. One key intellectual influence on the critique of Israeli and Zionist conceptions of masculinity, often cited by activists I spoke to, is Daniel Boyarin, *Unheroic Conduct*. However, it is important to note that conceptions of Ashkenazi masculinity in Israel have shifted, as the Ashkenazi man has come to embody the peace-loving, educated, gay-friendly inverse of the uncontrolled sexuality and "savagery" assigned to the Mizrahi man. See, for example, Raz Yosef, *Beyond Flesh: Queer Masculinities and Nationalism in Israeli Cinema* (Piscataway, NJ: Rutgers University Press, 2004).

64. See chapter 8 for an exposition of the discussion around antisemitism on the Left, specifically as it manifests in Palestine solidarity work.

65. For the demands articulated by a Chicago-based trans-led coalition, see Rad Fag, "Happening Now: Trans-Led Coalition Shuts Down Chicago Pride Parade," *Radical Faggot*, June 25, 2017, https://radfag.com/2017/06/25/happening-now-trans-led-coalition-shuts-down-chicago-pride-parade/.

66. See Staub, *Torn at the Roots*.

67. Ibid., 24–25.

68. See Marc Dollinger, *Black Power, Jewish Politics: Reinventing the Alliance in the 1960s* (Waltham, MA: Brandeis University Press, 2018), 6. See also the discussion of Jewish-black relations in chapter 7.

69. Ibid., 7.

70. Ibid., 7–8.

71. See Dollinger, *Black Power, Jewish Politics*, chapter 6 in particular. Dollinger challenges prevalent accounts of the changing patterns of black-Jewish relations that attribute the breakup of the Jewish-black alliance to the emergence of Black Power's exclusionary approach and that do not quite make the connection between the mutually reinforcing emergences of Black and Jewish Power. See chapter 7 for further discussion of the implications and interconnections of black-Jewish relations with patterns of solidarity with Israel or the Palestinian liberation struggle.

72. Ibid., 11.

73. See chapter 7 for a further discussion of black-Jewish alliance as it relates to black-Palestinian solidarity.

74. For instance, see Dollinger's discussion of the Union of Jewish Students at the University of California–Berkeley and the Jewish Education Coalition in the late 1960s and 1970s, *Black Power, Jewish Politics*, 116–19; and his discussion of Jewish responses in the late 1960s to black anti-Zionism, 161–62. For a different account of the black-Jewish break associated with Black Power, see Eric J. Sundquist, *Strangers in the Land: Blacks, Jews, Post-Holocaust America* (Cambridge, MA: Belknap Press, 2005). See also chapters 7 and 8 in this book.

75. For late 1960s and early 1970s examples of reflections on this dilemma, see Sol Stern, "My Jewish Problem—and Ours: Israel, the Left, and the Jewish Establishment," *Ramparts* 10

(August 1971): 32; and M. Jay Rosenberg, "My Evolution as a Jew," *Midstream* 16 (August/September 1970): 53.

76. Quoted in Staub, *Torn at the Roots*, 303.

77. Staub, *Torn at the Roots*, 317.

78. For example, Murray Friedman, *What Went Wrong? The Creation and Collapse of the Black-Jewish Alliance* (New York: Free Press, 1995).

79. Dollinger, *Black Power, Jewish Politics*, 4–5.

80. See chapter 4 for a discussion of Hannah Arendt's critique of the requirement of the love of Israel (*ahavat yisrael*).

81. See chapters 1 and 2.

82. Interview #5.

83. This pattern of estrangement from Israeli society is also highlighted in chapter 1.

84. Baurer, *Unlearning Zionism*, 8.

85. See the discussion of MBL's platform especially in chapters 2 and 7.

86. Interview #9.

87. Interview #4.

88. The focus on unlearning became a major area of activism for JVP and other organizations. For instance, JVP launched the Nakba Education Project to create accessible curricula to dispel Zionist muting of the Nakba. Likewise, JVP launched a member-wide discussion of Zionism in late 2017. See chapter 2, note 62.

89. Created by Jill Soloway, the Amazon Prime show has gained traction especially in American Jewish circles. See Alex Tretbar, "Amazon Orders Second Season for Wildly Popular Original Series 'Transparent,'" *Digital Trends*, October 9, 2017, https://www.digitaltrends.com/home-theater/amazon-renews-original-series-transparent-for-second-season/; and Sadie Gennis, "Amazon Renews *Transparent* for Season 5," *TV Guide*, August 24, 2017, http://www.tvguide.com/news/amazon-transparent-renewed-season-5/. The lead actor, Jeffrey Tambor, was fired in 2017 due to sexual harassment accusations in the wake of the #metoo movement.

90. IfNotNow Facebook page, September 23, 2017, https://www.facebook.com/events/898668416962427/.

91. Shaul Magid's analysis in a Facebook post for the *Transparent* discussion group, October 5, 2017, https://www.facebook.com/search/top/?q=shaul%20magid%20transparent.

92. Jenny Singer, "The New Season of 'Transparent' Is Full of Palestinian Propaganda—And That's Not Necessarily a Bad Thing," *Forward*, September 38, 2017, http://forward.com/schmooze/383820/the-new-season-of-transparent-is-full-of-palestinian-propaganda-and-thats-n/.

Chapter Four

1. Interview #6.

2. See discussion in chapter 3.

3. Interview #13.

4. Jasper, "Emotions and Social Movements."

5. Foucault, "What Is Critique?," in *The Politics of Truth*, ed. Sylvère Lotringer and Lysa Hochroth (New York: Semiotext(e), 1997), 35–63. See also Foucault, "What Is Enlightenment?," in *The Foucault Reader*, ed. Paul Rabinow (New York: Pantheon, 1984), 32–50. Of course, Foucault worked within the long trajectory of the Enlightenment's tradition of engaging and conceptualizing critique, going back to Immanuel Kant's destabilization of metaphysics in his

Critique of Pure Reason, trans. and ed. Paul Guyer and Allen W. Wood (Cambridge: Cambridge University Press, 1998). See also Kant, "What Is Enlightenment?," in *What Is Enlightenment? Eighteenth-Century Answers and Twentieth-Century Questions*, ed. James Schmidt (Berkeley: University of California Press, 1996), 58–64; and Judith Butler, "Critique, Dissent, Disciplinarity," *Critical Inquiry* 35, no. 4 (2009): 773–95, where she explains enlightenment as critique and thus "a process subject to historical translation, to the recurrence of questioning the limits imposed upon the askable" (787).

6. Butler, "What Is Critique?" The essay was originally given as the Raymond Williams Lecture at Cambridge University in May 2001. It is also available at the European Institute for Progressive Cultural Politics website, http://eipcp.net/transversal/0806/butler/en. I credit Heather DuBois, a former doctoral student and now an alumna of the Kroc Institute for International Peace Studies at the University of Notre Dame, for pointing me to the self-transformative dynamics entailed by this discussion of critique in Butler's treatment of Foucault.

7. Foucault, "What Is Critique?," 199.

8. Butler, "What Is Critique?"

9. Foucault, "What Is Critique?," 32. Cited in Butler, "What Is Critique?"

10. Butler, "Critique, Dissent, Disciplinarity," 787.

11. Ibid., 790.

12. On the disaggregation of the transformative or projective dimensions of human agency, see Mustafa Emirbayer and Ann Mische, "What Is Agency?," *American Journal of Sociology* 103, no. 4 (January 1998): 962–1023.

13. Ibid., 985.

14. See Wendy Brown, "Introduction," in Talal Asad, Wendy Brown, Judith Butler, and Saba Mahmood, *Is Critique Secular? Blasphemy, Injury, and Free Speech*, 2nd ed. (New York: Fordham University Press, 2013), 1–13. Brown, Butler, and Mahmood capture this point in their "Preface" to the same volume: "Secular critique, if it is to remain critical, must be concerned with the epistemic limits on the knowable imposed by secularism itself" (xvi).

15. See interview with Rosen in Ben Murane, "Five American Jews who Fought the Occupation This Summer," *Jewschool*, August 3, 2016, https://jewschool.com/2016/08/77154/five-american-jews-who-fought-the-occupation/. I address the complex matter of Jews and whiteness in the US in chapters 6 and 7.

16. Jeffrey Stout, *Blessed Are the Organized: Grassroots Democracy in America* (Princeton, NJ: Princeton University Press, 2010), examines, in ways that resonate with the intersectional challenge that critical caretaking engages, the relations between social practice and social norms as these relations play out in community organizing, focusing specifically on religiosity's role in the organizational process and the cultivation of grassroots democracy.

17. "Why Award-Winning Author and Activist Naomi Klein Supports Jewish Voice for Peace," YouTube video, Jewish Voice for Peace, April 25, 2016, https://youtu.be/sNmLset_UW4.

18. For JVP member stories about why they feel at home in JVP, see "Stories from Our Members," Jewish Voice for Peace, accessed October 4, 2017, https://jewishvoiceforpeace.org/membership/.

19. See "Who We Are," Jewish Voice for Peace Arts and Culture, accessed October 4, 2017, http://artists.jewishvoiceforpeace.org/. The Artists and Cultural Workers Council (ACWC) involves forty artists in leadership as well as hundreds of other artists who participate in the network. They see their role as central to imagining a more just future. They write: "Art compels us to question, invites us to memory, provokes us to act. What does a pluralistic, socially just, multi-ethnic, vibrant, safe, and flourishing Israel/Palestine look like? What do the houses and

cities look like? Which books are on the shelves? What does an open, joyous, diverse, global Jewish community feel like? What do we pray about? How do our instruments sound?" The ACWC played a role in raising awareness among artists' communities who responded to the call for a cultural boycott. See, for instance, the decision by the People Artist Collective (a collective of radical Black and People of Color artists in Chicago) to boycott Israel: "Answering the Call to Boycott: Why FTP Pledges to Uphold the Academic & Cultural Boycott of Israel," *FTP Artists Collective*, March 13, 2017, http://www.forthepeoplecollective.org/answering-the-call-to-boycott/. The ACWC also focuses on assisting Palestinian artistic initiative. See, for example, *Friends of the Jenin Freedom Theatre*, accessed October 4, 2017, http://www.thefreedomtheatre.org/friends-supporters/new-york/.

20. See "Rabbinical Council," Jewish Voice for Peace, accessed October 4, 2017, https://jewishvoiceforpeace.org/jewish-community-transformation/. One prominent council member related that tensions exist between rabbis on the Council and JVP's leadership, though since about 2015, a clear understanding has emerged that the Council should be bound by JVP's campaigns, while JVP will in turn allow rabbis and emerging rabbis to have greater input in planning stages through advisory roles. The Council, according to this same interviewee, "is a great place for rabbis to talk things out, and they value the opportunity for support when the larger Jewish community is so opposed to what we're doing, [but some left] if they didn't feel that they were totally able to support the larger organization, and have their names publicly associated with it." Nonetheless, this interviewee contended, involving rabbis in a more central advisory role to the movement is beneficial. "Because rabbis work most directly with Jewish communities, we tend to be more sensitive to how those communities will respond" (email correspondence with author, August 20, 2017).

21. This point is explicitly noted by activists. For instance, echoing other activists I interviewed, one commented on JVP's website: "Since joining JVP, I've begun to reengage with Jewish ritual and community in a way that finally feels meaningful to me and consistent with my belief in honoring the humanity of all people." See "What Is Membership?," Jewish Voice for Peace, accessed October 4, 2017, https://jewishvoiceforpeace.org/membership/.

22. The work of David Ellenson is a frequent touchstone for the historical moment in which Israel has become integrated into liturgical reflections. See his "Envisioning Israel in the Liturgies of North American Liberal Judaism," in *Envisioning Israel*, ed. Allon Gal (Jerusalem and Detroit: Magnes Press & Wayne State University Press, 1996), 127–38. Variations of the "Prayer for the State of Israel" are found in various liturgical contexts in and outside Israel, depending on denominational orientations. The Reconstructionist movement's *Tefilah Limdinat Yisrael* ("prayer for the State of Israel"), for instance, reads "Strengthen the hands of those who guard our holy land. Let them inherit salvation and life. And give peace to the land, and perpetual joy to its inhabitants. Appoint for a blessing all our kindred of the house of Israel in all the lands of their dispersion. Plant in their hearts a love of Zion." The *Avoda Shebalev* in the *siddur* of the Israel Movement for Progressive Judaism reads similarly, "Our Divine Guardian, Rock and Redeemer of Israel, bless the State of Israel, the beginning of our redemption. . . . May a spark of Your spirit inspire the actions of its President, Prime Minister, officials, judges and advisors that they may follow the path of righteousness, liberty and freedom. Strengthen the hands of those who build and protect our Holy Land and grant them salvation and life. Grant peace to this land and everlasting joy to its inhabitants."

23. The Zionization of the liturgy within the Reform movement is reflected in the updated prayerbook *Gates of Prayer*, released in 1975 and deeply informed by shifts during the interwar period and WWII.

24. See, for instance, W. Gunther Plaut, *The Growth of Reform Judaism: American and European Sources* (Philadelphia: Jewish Publication Society, [1965] 2015), chapter 10.

25. Brian Walt, "Affirming a Judaism and Jewish Identity without Zionism," *The Palestinian Talmud: Blog of the Jewish Voice for Peace Rabbinical Council*, June 1, 2012, https://paltalmud.com/2012/06/01/affirming-a-judaism-and-jewish-identity-without-zionism/ (site discontinued).

26. Interview #24.

27. See Shaul Magid, "Christian Supersessionism, Zionism, and the Contemporary Scene: A Critical Reading of Peter Ochs's Reading of John Howard Yoder," *Journal of Religious Ethics* 45, no. 1 (2017): 104–41; and Peter Ochs, *Another Reformation: Postliberal Christianity and the Jews* (Grand Rapids, MI: Baker Academic, 2011).

28. Marc H. Ellis, "On the Rabbis and the Future of Jewish Life" (lecture delivered at the Montague Centre, London, to the Rabbinic Conference of the Union of Liberal & Progressive Synagogues, June 5, 2001), http://student.cs.ucc.ie/cs1064/jabowen/IPSC/articles/article0004163.txt. Ellis distinguished himself with scholarship on Jewish Palestine liberation theology. See, for another example, his *Toward a Jewish Theology of Liberation* (London: SCM Press, [1987] 2002). Other works in this genre include Dan Cohn-Sherbok, "On Earth as It Is in Heaven: Jews, Christians, and Liberation Theology" (New York: Orbis Books, 1987); and Mark Braverman, *Fatal Embrace: Christians, Jews, and the Search for Peace in the Holy Land* (New York: Beaufort Books, 2010).

29. See Daniel Boyarin and Jonathan Boyarin, "Diaspora: Generation and the Ground of Jewish Identity," *Critical Inquiry* 19, no. 4 (Summer 1993): 693–725 (715–16).

30. One prominent example of this approach is articulated in Judith Butler, *Parting Ways: Jewishness and the Critique of Zionism* (New York: Columbia University Press, 2012). For a broader overview of interlocutors in the tradition of ethical critique of Zionism, see *Prophets Outcast: A Century of Dissident Jewish Writing about Zionism and Israel*, ed. Adam Shatz (New York: Nation Books, 2004); as well as Jacqueline Rose, *The Question of Zion* (Princeton, NJ: Princeton University Press, 2005).

31. Daniel Boyarin, *A Traveling Homeland: The Babylonian Talmud as Diaspora* (Philadelphia: Pennsylvania University Press, 2015); Simon Dubnow, *Nationalism and History: Essays on Old and New Judaism*, ed. Koppel S. Pinson (Philadelphia: Jewish Publication Society, 1958); Allan Arkush, "From Diaspora Nationalism to Radical Diasporism," *Modern Judaism* 29, no. 3 (2009), 326–50; and Melanie Kaye/Kantrowitz, *The Colors of Jews: Racial Politics and Radical Diasporism* (Bloomington: Indiana University Press, 2007).

32. Boyarin, *A Traveling Homeland*, 5.

33. Boyarin and Boyarin, "Diaspora," 715.

34. Ibid.

35. Ibid., 711.

36. Ibid.

37. Ellis's use of the concept of "betrayal" was strongly criticized for its Christian supersessionist tones. See Richard L. Rubenstein, "Attacking the Jews," review of *Toward a Jewish Theology of Liberation*, by Marc H. Ellis, *Commentary* 89, no. 3 (March 1990): 70.

38. One paradigm of post-Holocaust chauvinism is the ongoing legacy of Rabbi Meir Kahane. See, for example, Shaul Magid, "Is Meir Kahane Winning? Reflections on Benjamin Netanyahu, the Hilltop Youth, and AIPAC," *Tikkun*, March 24, 2016, http://www.tikkun.org/nextgen/is-meir-kahane-winning-reflections-on-benjamin-netanyahu-the-hilltop-youth-and-aipac; and Magid, *American Post-Judaism*, chapter 8.

39. "Toward a Jewish Theology of Liberation: 30 Years Later," Brant Rosen's Facebook page, May 31, 2017, https://www.facebook.com/events/1089506887822095/permalink/1139828

286123288/. Ellis specifically criticizes so-called Jewish "Holocaust thinkers," especially Elie Wiesel and Emile Fackenheim, but also Richard Rubenstein.

40. Yoder's reputation has been terribly tarnished by multiple allegations of sexual abuse and harassment against him. See Rachel Waltner Gossen, "Mennonite Bodies, Sexual Ethics: Women Challenge John Howard Yoder," *The Mennonite*, August 11, 2016, https://themennonite.org/feature/mennonite-bodies-sexual-ethics-women-challenge-john-howard-yoder/.

41. Cited in Magid, "Christian Supersessionism," 120.

42. Ibid., 122.

43. Ibid., 125.

44. Ibid., 121.

45. Ibid., 124.

46. See chapter 2 for an extensive exposition of the dialogic approach.

47. Rosen, "A Force More Powerful: A Sermon for Tzedek Chicago's Inaugural Rosh Hashanah Service," *Gandhi's Be Magazine*, September 15, 2015, http://www.bemagazine.org/rabbi-brant-rosen-force-powerful-sermon-tzedek-chicagos-inaugural-rosh-hashanah-service/.

48. Michael Lerner, "Mourning for a Judaism Being Murdered by Israel," *Tikkun Daily*, August 4, 2014, http://www.tikkun.org/tikkundaily/2014/08/04/mourning-for-a-judaism-being-murdered-by-israel/.

49. Here, he deeply echoes Yeshayahu Leibowitz, *Judaism, Human Values, and the Jewish State*, ed. and trans. Eliezer Goldman (Cambridge, MA: Harvard University Press, 1995).

50. Lerner, however, does not remain merely in the mode of critique, instead offering constructive resources for both atoning and refiguring Jewish identity as it relates to the Israeli state. Toward the end of the article, he encourages Jews who are sympathetic to his analysis to urge their congregations to include in the High Holiday services of that year "repentance for sins of the Jewish people in giving blind support to immoral policies of the State of Israel." *Tikkun*, accordingly, compiled a workbook entitled "For Our Sins," which they made available on their website.

51. Brian Walt, "Affirming a Judaism and Jewish Identity without Zionism: A Personal Spiritual Ethical Journey," *Mondoweiss*, May 23, 2012, http://mondoweiss.net/2012/05/affirming-a-judaism-and-jewish-identity-without-zionism/.

52. Ibid.

53. See Leora Batnitzky, *How Judaism Became a Religion: An Introduction to Modern Jewish Thought* (Princeton, NJ: Princeton University Press, 2011), 36−37.

54. Ibid., 33.

55. On this dynamic, see what is by now a classic account of religion and modernity: Talal Asad, *Genealogies of Religion: Discipline and Reasons of Power in Christianity and Islam* (Baltimore: John Hopkins University Press, 1993); and Asad, *Formations of the Secular: Christianity, Islam, Modernity* (Stanford, CA: Stanford University Press, 2003). See also Saba Mahmood, *Religious Difference in a Secular Age: A Minority Report* (Princeton, NJ: Princeton University Press, 2016).

56. For instance, the 1885 Pittsburgh Platform states: "We consider ourselves no longer a nation but a religious community." The Pittsburgh Platform represents the most acute articulation of "Classical" or "radical" Reform in its underscoring of Judaism as ethical and spiritual orientation rather than toward orthopraxis. See Howard A. Berman, "New Introduction to the 50th Anniversary Edition," W. Gunther Plaut, *The Growth of Reform Judaism: American and European Sources* (Philadelphia: Jewish Publication Society, [1965] 2015), ix. Similarly, on March 4, 1919, Julius Kahn, a Jewish congressman from San Francisco, presented a letter to

President Woodrow Wilson rejecting Zionism's intention to ghettoize Jews. The letter was endorsed by 299 prominent American Jews who, in line with the broader orientation of Reform at the time, viewed Zionism's intentions to establish a "Jewish home" in Palestine as antithetical to democratic values and objected to the distillment of Jewish tradition into the message of ethical monotheism and its transformation into one other "religion" among others. This attitude was reinforced in April 20, 1922, when Rabbi David Philipson testified before the House Foreign Affairs Committee, adamantly challenging the characterization of Palestine as "the national home of the Jewish people." The Jews, he argued, "are nationals of many lands." For earlier articulations of America as the new Zion, see Gustav Poznanski (1805–1879) who, according to a report by the *Charleston Courier* on the 1841 Beth Elohim dedication of a new building, said: "This synagogue is our *temple*, this city our *Jerusalem*, this happy land our *Palestine*, and as our fathers defended with their lives *that* temple, *that* city and *that* land, so will their sons defend *this* temple, *this* city, and *this* land" (cited in ibid., 9). See also Jacob Neusner, "The Real Promised Land Is America," *International Herald Tribune*, March 10, 1987.

57. Plaut, *The Growth of Reform Judaism*, 145.

58. Cited in ibid., 145.

59. Cited in ibid., 146.

60. Berman, "New Introduction"; and Plaut, *The Growth of Reform Judaism*, ix.

61. Ibid., x.

62. Ibid., xi–xiii.

63. David Neumark, "No Zionism without Religion," cited in Plaut, *The Growth of Reform Judaism*, 148–49; and Herman Cohen, "Nationalism as Religious Fiction," cited in ibid., 149–50.

64. See the exchange between Stephen S. Wise and Israel Mattuck on the meeting of the World Union in 1926 in London. Cited in ibid., 150–52.

65. Abba Hillel Silver, "Anti-Zionism Is Paulist Judaism," in *The Growth of Reform Judaism*, 152.

66. The emergence of the Reconstructionist current is usually dated to 1968 with the founding of the Reconstructionist Rabbinical College.

67. *Pace* Beinart, *The Crisis of Zionism*, which construes it as a simple choice.

68. Mordechai Kaplan, *Judaism as a Civilization* (Philadelphia: Jewish Publications Society, 1994). See also Kaplan, *The Meaning of God in Modern Jewish Religion* (Detroit: Wayne State University Press, 1962).

69. According to the Pew survey of 2013, Orthodox Jews are more likely than self-described secular, Reform, or Conservative American Jews to oppose an independent Palestinian state, to support settlements, and to argue that Israel was promised by God. The findings are intriguing given the history of traditionalist and Orthodox Jews' rejection of Zionism. See Pew Research Center, "A Portrait of Jewish Americans: Findings from a Pew Research Center Survey of U.S. Jews," October 1, 2013, 7, http://assets.pewresearch.org/wp-content/uploads/sites/11/2013/10/jewish-american-full-report-for-web.pdf.

70. Influenced by Ahad Ha-Am, Kaplan himself supported Zionism, interpreting it as ethical nationhood and a movement to revitalize Jewish civilization and culture. The concept of "ethical nationhood" means, for Kaplan, the institutionalization of justice through a desupernaturalized and demythologized conception of public religion. His Zionism, therefore, did not entail the negation of exile, as was the key ethos for political Zionism in its earlier decades; see *Judaism as a Civilization*, 241, as well as his *Religion of Ethical Nationhood*, 132, and his *A New Zionism* (New York: Herzl Press and Jewish Reconstructionist Press, 1959). Also see the "Platform on Reconstructionism" (1986), where Zionism and *aliyah* were encouraged, but also a

1988 resolution of the Federation of Reconstructionist Congregations and havurot stressing the obligation of North American Jews to challenge ethical problems emerging from Israeli policies and the 2004 Israel Task Force Report, which called for recommitment to Zionism. See JRF Israel, "Zionism and Communal Covenant: A Reconstructionist Approach to Essential Jewish Principles," September 2004, https://www.jewishrecon.org/sites/default/files/resources/document/zionism_and_communal_covenant.pdf.

71. Rebecca Alpert, "Reconstructionism without Zionism: A Guest Post by Rabbi Rebecca Alpert," *Shalom Rav*, January 18, 2017, https://rabbibrant.com/2017/01/18/reconstructionism-without-zionism-a-guest-post-by-rabbi-rebecca-alpert/.

72. Magid, *American Post-Judaism*. He takes his inspiration from David A. Hollinger, *Postethnic America* (New York: Basic, 1995).

73. Ibid., 5.

74. Ibid.

75. Landy, *Jewish Identity*. By underscoring the process of "re-cognising," Landy deploys Ron Eyerman and Andrew Jamison's argument about knowledge production within social movements as pivotal for processes of change. See Eyerman and Jamison, *Social Movements: A Cognitive Approach* (Cambridge: Polity Press, 1991). Landy also draws on Mario Diani's definition of social movements as networked interactions revolving around a shared identity or a shared conflict. See Diani, "The Concept of Social Movement," *Sociological Review* 40, no. 1 (1992): 13.

76. For a classic discussion of the ethos of the negation of exile, see Nurit Gertz, *Myths in Israeli Culture: Captives of a Dream* (London: Valentine Mitchell, 2000). See also Alan Wolfe, *At Home in Exile: Why Diaspora Is Good for the Jews* (Boston: Beacon Press, 2014).

77. See also my discussion of Breira in chapter 3.

78. Thomas Kolsky, *Jews Against Zionism: The American Council for Judaism, 1942–1948* (Philadelphia: Temple University Press, 1992). The ACJ explicitly stresses that one of its key animating principles is "that Judaism is primarily a universal religious commitment, rather than an ethnic or nationalist identity . . . Our link to the land of Israel is a deep historic one, as the 'cradle of our faith'—but Israel is not our 'homeland.' We believe that America alone is our homeland, not only geographically, but because Jewish Biblical values of freedom, liberty and justice have helped shape the democratic tradition of the United States from the beginning." See American Council for Judaism, "American Jews and the State of Israel," accessed March 6, 2018, http://www.acjna.org/acjna/about_position.aspx.

79. Kaplan, *A New Zionism*.

80. See David N. Myers, *Between Jew and Arab: The Lost Voice of Simon Rawidowicz* (Waltham, MA: Brandeis University Press, 2008), 85. The label "cruel Zionism" was first employed by Zionist activist Avraham Sharon to denote negationist tendencies vis-à-vis Jewish diasporas (this is the early Zionist ethos of negating and devaluing the diaspora). Rawidowicz saw this cruelty as expanding to the treatment of indigenous Arab communities. Hence, he viewed the need to examine the Palestinian predicament as "an urgent moral and political necessity" (Myers, *Between Jew and Arab*, 6). See also Rawidowicz, *Bavel v'Yerushalayim* [Babylon and Jerusalem] (Waltham, MA: Ararat, 1957).

81. Hans Kohn, quoted in Anthony G. Bing, *Israeli Pacifist: The Life of Joseph Abileah* (Syracuse, NY: Syracuse University Press, 199), 69. His lament shares strong affinities with the Palestine-based attempts by other Jewish thinkers such as Martin Buber and Yehouda Magnes to organize against exclusionary interpretations of Jewish nationalism. See, for instance, my discussion of Brit Shalom in my *When Peace Is Not Enough*, 28–32.

82. Their thoughts on the occupation were variously anthologized. See, for instance, *Wrestling with Zion: Progressive Jewish-American Responses to the Israeli-Palestinian Conflict*, ed. Tony Kushner and Alisa Solomon (New York: Grove Press, 2003). See also Jacqueline Rose, *The Question of Zion* (Princeton, NJ: Princeton University Press, 2005).

83. See Richard Bernstein, *Hannah Arendt and the Jewish Question* (Cambridge, MA: MIT Press, 1996).

84. Hannah Arendt, *The Origins of Totalitarianism* (New York: A Harvest Book, [1951] 1973), 290.

85. For the specifics of this argument, see chapters 7 and 8. For Shohat's influential critique, see her "Sephardim in Israel: Zionism from the Perspective of its Jewish Victims," *Social Text* 7, nos. 19/20 (Autumn 1988): 26–29. It draws critical insights from Edward Said, "Zionism from the Standpoint of Its Victims," *Social Text*, no.1 (Winter, 1979): 7–58. Later works by Judith Butler extend this intellectual project, putting Arendt, Emmanuel Levinas, Primo Levi, Martin Buber, and Walter Benjamin in tension and in conversation with the Palestinian thinker (Said) and the poet Mahmood Darwish. Butler's effort to develop a political ethic draws on Arendt's conception of un-chosenness as a foundation for articulating conceptual frames for cohabitation. See Butler, *Parting Ways*.

86. Hannah Arendt, *The Portable Hannah Arendt*, ed. Peter Baehr, rev. ed. (New York: Penguin [2000] 2003), 392–93.

87. Ibid., 393.

88. See the discussion of Benjamin in Santiago Slabodsky, *Decolonial Judaism: Triumphal Failures of Barbaric Thinking* (New York: Palgrave Macmillan, 2014), 86.

89. One artistic project independent of JVP is the "Radical Jewish Calendar Project," managed by Jessica Rosenberg, Elissa Martel, and Ariana Katz. This project aims to offer "a celebration of Jewish culture that is intersectional, queer, feminist, anti-racist, and that challenges and builds a Judaism and Jewishness beyond Zionism," which involves severing a reliance on establishment's Jewish aesthetic. See Radical Jewish Calendar Project, "About," accessed October 4, 2017, http://radicaljewishcalendar.bigcartel.com /artists. See also Jessica Rosenberg, "#Torah-ForResistance—5778 Years of Radical Dreaming: Living in Jewish Time as an Act of Resistance," *Jewschool*, August 16, 2017, https://jewschool.com /2017/08/80098/torahfortheresistance-5778 -years-of-radical-dreaming/. Rosenberg writes: "Having a Jewish calendar put me in relationship to Jewish people and Judaism across time and place. At a time when I was also coming to learn all of the parts of Judaism and Jewish history that I hadn't learned in Hebrew School, a Jewish calendar let me live into Jewishness without reading a textbook, but by starting to align myself with the cycles of Jewish time."

90. Ben Lorber, "A Spot at the Kotel Won't Save Us: A Crisis in American Judaism," *Tikkun Daily*, September 6, 2017, http://www.tikkun.org/tikkundaily/2017/09/06/a-spot-at-the-kotel -wont-save-us-a-crisis-in-american-judaism/.

91. Ibid.

92. Brant Rosen, *Wrestling in The Daylight: A Rabbi's Path to Palestinian Solidarity* (Charlottesville, VA: Just World Books, 2012), 14.

93. Ibid., 23.

94. Ibid., 24.

95. Ibid.

96. Ibid., 26.

97. Ibid.

98. Ibid., 30.

99. Ibid., 32.

100. Ibid., 30.

101. Miller, *Friends and Other Strangers: Studies in Religion, Ethics, and Culture* (New York: Columbia University Press, 2016), 57. See also my discussion of emotions, particularly in chapter 2.

102. Magid, "Liberal Rabbis, American Judaism & Gaza," *Jewish Philosophy Place*, August 4, 2014, http://jewishphilosophyplace.wordpress.com/2014/08/04/9827/.

103. Ibid.

104. Ibid.

105. For criticism of the indignation expressed by the organized Jewish community in the aftermath of Netanyahu kowtowing to conservative religious sectors and canceling the agreement over an egalitarian prayer space in the Kotel contrasted with the lack of communal outrage pertaining the occupation, see Simone Zimmerman, "It's Only about Them: U.S. Jews' Outrage on the Wall, Silence on the Occupation Is Obscene," *Haaretz*, June 29, 2017, http://www.haaretz.com/opinion/1.798484; and Brant Rosen, "The Real Wall Problem: When Will Diaspora Jews Fight for Palestinians?," *Forward*, July 2, 2017, http://forward.com/opinion/israel/376101/diaspora-jews-palestinians-israel-western-wall-occupation/.

106. The "Rabbinic Letter against Israel's Travel Ban" can be found here: https://docs.google.com/forms/d/e/1FAIpQLSeVo6OiD9nFLWuWuaygbZTHYSPBFCZotiGps_mu7Nc3MdLVJA/viewform.

107. Laurie Zimmerman, "Why Rabbis Like Me Oppose Israel's Ban on BDS Activists," *Jewish Telegraphic Agency*, August 29, 2017, http://www.jta.org/2017/08/29/news-opinion/opinion/why-rabbis-like-me-oppose-israels-ban-on-bds-activists.

108. Ibid.

109. Susannah Heschel, "Introduction to the Perennial Classics Edition," in Abraham Joshua Heschel, *The Prophets* (New York: HarperCollins, [1962] 2001), xiv.

110. Ibid., xv.

111. Ibid., xvii.

112. Ibid., xviii. See also Heschel, *The Prophets*, 288–89.

113. Ibid., xviii.

114. Ibid., 5.

115. Susannah Heschel, "Introduction," in Abraham Joshua Heschel, *Moral Grandeur and Spiritual Audacity: Essays*, ed. Susannah Heschel (New York: Farrar, Straus & Giroux, 1996), vii–xxx (xxiv).

116. See Susannah Heschel, review of *On Earth as It Is in Heaven: Jews, Christians, and Liberation Theology*, by Dan Cohn-Sherbok, and *Toward a Jewish Theology of Liberation*, by Marc H. Ellis, *Present Tense* 15, no. 3 (1988): 52–53.

117. Ayelet Wachs Cashman, "Ki Tavo: Tochachot and White Supremacy," *Medium*, September 8, 2017, https://medium.com/ifnotnowtorah/ki-tavo-tochachot-and-white-supremacy-d38d040905ae.

118. See Magid, *American Post-Judaism*.

119. Heschel, *The Prophets*, xxii.

120. Abraham Joshua Heschel, remarks at a 1963 gathering at the Concord Hotel in New York City. A recording of these remarks in Yiddish is available (along with an English translation) in Susannah Heschel, "Praying with Their Legs: Rabbi Abraham Heschel and Rev. Martin Luther King, Jr.," YouTube video, from a lecture at Elon University on October 21, 2014, posted by Elon TLT, October 23, 2014, https://youtu.be/-HrEVfE1vKw (39:40–42:48).

121. Miller, *Friends and Other Strangers*, 147.

122. Ibid., 148.

123. "About Us," IfNotNow, accessed October 4, 2017, https://ifnotnowmovement.org/about-us/.

124. "Our Story," IfNotNow, accessed October 4, 2017, https://ifnotnowmovement.org/about-us/our-story/.

125. Albert J. Raboteau, *American Prophets: Seven Religious Radicals and Their Struggle for Social and Political Justice* (Princeton, NJ: Princeton University Press, 2016), 23. The mystical dimensions in Heschel's prophetic work share an affinity with the mystical theology of Catholic theologian Johann Baptist Metz, *Faith in History and Society: Toward a Practical Fundamental Theology*, trans. J. Matthew Ashley (New York: Herder & Herder, 2011).

126. Abraham Joshua Heschel, "The White Man on Trial," in *The Insecurity of Freedom: Essays on Human Existence* (London: Macmillan, 1963), 101–3 (103).

Chapter Five

1. Interview #7 (Hila) and interview #9 (activist from the Bay Area).

2. Interview #21.

3. Interview #5.

4. This construal of Judaism as an ethical or moral tradition is consistent with the findings of the 2013 Pew survey of US Jews discussed in chapter 1.

5. See chapter 2 for an explication of Marshall Ganz's concept of public narrative.

6. See chapter 4 for a discussion of modernity's construction of Judaism as religion and its reification of the language of "values."

7. Interview #52.

8. See chapter 3 for a discussion of identity politics and its implications for American Jewish advocacy.

9. Interview #22.

10. I spoke with this activist on April 3, 2016.

11. See chapter 3.

12. For a reflection on this conference, see Dan Fishback, "Trauma Club: Unpacking the Disconnect between Liberal Zionism and the Anti-Zionist Movement," *Jewschool*, February 4, 2016, https://jewschool.com/2016/02/39106/trauma-club-unpacking-disconnect-liberal-zionism-anti-zionist-movement/.

13. Adam Walker, Creating Change conference, "An Alternative Shabbat of Solidarity," *Pomomusings* (January 22, 2016): 3–4.

14. Samah Sabawi, "The Liberation Anthem—A Poem," *The Palestine Chronicle*, June 27, 2011, http://www.palestinechronicle.com/the-liberation-anthem-a-poem/.

15. See chapter 4 for this historical contextualization.

16. Cynthia Ozick, "Notes toward Finding the Right Question," *Lilith* 6 (1979): 19–29; and Judith Plaskow, "The Right Question Is Theological," in *The Coming of Lilith: Essays on Feminism, Judaism, and Sexual Ethics, 1972–2003* (Boston: Beacon Press, 2005), 56–64.

17. Plaskow, *Standing Again at Sinai: Judaism from a Feminist Perspective* (New York: HarperCollins, 1990).

18. Plaskow, "The Right Question," 63–64.

19. "About Us," IfNotNow, accessed March 7, 2018.

20. Ibid.

21. Plaskow, *Standing Again*, 1.

22. Ibid.

23. Ibid., 1–2.

24. Fringes: A Feminist, Non-Zionist Havurah, "Original Liturgy," accessed October 10, 2017, https://fringeshavurah.com/original-liturgy/.

25. Fringes: A Feminist, Non-Zionist Havurah, "Fringes' Founding Statement," accessed October 7, 2017, https://fringeshavurah.com/who-we-are/fringes-founding-statement/.

26. Fringes illustrates the role a feminist hermeneutic plays in this process in its decision to sing "She Carries Me" in place of the traditional, highly heteronormative, and patriarchal Adon Olam. The synagogue sings the lyrics of "She Carries Me" to the melody of Adon Olam, thus blending the innovative and new with the traditional and capturing the themes of Adon Olam without its gendered implications. See "Adon Olam/She Carries Me," Fringes: A Feminist, Non-Zionist Havurah, accessed October 7, 2017, https://fringeshavurah.com/original-liturgy/adon-olam-she-carries-me/.

27. Such public ritualizations, however, surely also constitute tools in the repertoire of the Jewish movement for Palestinian liberation. A Global Shabbat Against Demolition was framed as an urgent "call to action" to protest the scheduled demolition of homes in four Palestinian villages in August 2016. Global Jewish communities were invited to conduct a Kabbalat Shabbat protest on behalf of the Palestinian residents of these villages on August 12, 2016. This Global Shabbat Against Demolition came a month after Palestinians in Susiya (one of the threatened villages) hosted fifty Jewish activists for a Shabbat during the CJNV's solidarity trip. Endorsing the "call to action" were All That's Left: Anti-Occupation Collective, the CJNV, and T'ruah. They called for a ritualized Shabbat qua protest to target carefully selected institutions, such as the Jewish National Fund and Israeli embassies. See A. Daniel Roth, "Emergency Call to Action: Global Shabbat Against Demolition!," *Jewschool*, August 6, 2016, https://jewschool.com/2016/08/77196/emergency-call-action-global-shabbat-demolition/.

28. Interview #10.

29. Tarrow, *Power in Movement*, 118; also cited in Snow and Byrd, "Ideology, Framing Processes, and Islamic Terrorist Movements," 130. See also chapter 2's discussion of Tarrow and religious innovation.

30. "Rabbinical Council," Jewish Voice for Peace, accessed October 4, 2017, https://jewishvoiceforpeace.org/jewish-community-transformation/.

31. See chapter 7 for a discussion of inter-traditional discursive peacebuilding work.

32. This scope of activism was described by Rabbi Alissa Wise, cofounder of JVP's Rabbinical Council, at an event I attended in Chicago on June 29, 2016. See "Meet the Rabbis of Jewish Voice for Peace!," June 23, 2016, http://chicagoevents.us/meet-the-rabbis-of-jewish-voice-for-peace/79058.

33. Lizz Goldstein, "Parashat Va'Era: Marching Toward Liberation," IfNotNow, January 12, 2018, https://medium.com/ifnotnowtorah/parashat-vaera-marching-toward-liberation-8566cea5fa01.

34. Ibid.

35. Boyarin develops the concept of the diaspora as synchronic in this way in *A Traveling Homeland*. See also chapter 4.

36. Boyarin and Boyarin, "Diaspora," 715–16.

37. Boyarin, *A Traveling Homeland*, 4. See Galit Hasan-Rokem's review in *Journal of the American Academy of Religion* 84, no. 1 (March 2016): 260–84, for an important critical engagement with what she deems Boyarin's circular argument taking as a given the idea of the Talmud

as a traveling homeland. "By claiming diaspora as the child of the Talmud rather than its birth ground, Boyarin endows his preferred existential position as a diasporic Jew, ergo himself, with a respectable genealogy" (264).

38. Alana Alpert, "There Were Three Trees in the Garden: A Midrash," *Palestinian Talmud*, May 21, 2012, http://paltalmud.com/2012/05/21/there-were-three-trees-in-the-garden-a -midrash/ (site discontinued).

39. Rachel Barenblat, "Looking for Water: A Drash for Parshat Toldot," *Palestinian Talmud*, November 3, 2013, http://paltalmud.com/2013/11/03/looking-for-water-a-drash-for-parshat -toldot/ (site discontinued).

40. The Tu B'Shvat Seder is celebrated on the fifteenth day of Shvat and traditionally has underscored the celebration of nature and spring. Jews mark the "new year" of the trees by eating different kinds of fruits and planting trees. The latter practice has been foregrounded in the context of Zionism in Israel, where children plant trees to mark the date, now understood entirely through the discourse of national rebirth.

41. Brant Rosen, "New Life is Rising: A Prayer for Tu B'shvat," *Yedid Nefesh*, January 22, 2016, https://ynefesh.com/2016/01/22/new-life-is-rising-a-prayer-for-tu-bshvat/.

42. Michael Davis, "Occupying Tu Bishvat," *Palestinian Talmud*, January 15, 2014, http:// palestiniantalmud.com/2014/01/15/occupying-tu-bishvat/ (site discontinued). See https:// rabbibrant.com/2014/01/15/reclaiming-a-tu-bshvat-of-liberation/ for quote.

43. Brant Rosen, "Reclaiming a Tu B'shvat of Liberation," *Palestinian Talmud*, January 16, 2014, http://palestiniantalmud.com/2014/01/16/reclaiming-a-tu-bshvat-of-liberation/ (site discontinued).

44. Brant Rosen, "Introduction" to "New Life Is Rising: A Tu B'Shvat Haggadah," January 22, 2016, https://jewishvoiceforpeace.org/wp-content/uploads/2016/01/Tzedek-Chicago -Tu-Bshvat-Haggadah.pdf, 1.

45. Lynn Gottlieb, "Hanuka: Dedicated to Resisting Militarism through Peace Education," *Palestinian Talmud*, November 22, 2013, http://palestiniantalmud.com/2013/11/22/hanuka -dedicated-to-resisting-militarism-through-peace-education (site discontinued).

46. Ibid.

47. Davis, "Occupying Tu Bishvat."

48. Cited in Ben Murane, "#ShabbatAgainstDemolition Sweeps 15+ Cities, 5 Countries," *Jewschool*, August 13, 2016, https://jewschool.com/2016/08/77240/shabbatagainstdemolition -sweeps-fifteen-cities-five-countries/.

49. Brant Rosen, "For Tisha B'Av: A New Version of Lamentations," *Yedid Nefesh*, August 13, 2016, https://ynefesh.com/2016/08/13/for-tisha-bav-a-new-version-of-lamentations-1/. See chapter 6 for another discussion of Lamentations as a site of Jewish ethical outrage.

50. See chapter 2's discussion of agency.

51. Max Schindler, "What's Shabbat Like in a Palestinian Village?," *Jerusalem Post*, July 17, 2016, http://www.jpost.com/Arab-Israeli-Conflict/Whats-Shabbat-like-in-a-Palestinian -village-460667.

52. For coverage of this multi-city protest, see Ben Norton, "'We Will Not Be Silent': American Jews Hit the Streets during Hanukkah to Fight Islamophobia and Racism," *Salon*, December 10, 2015, http://www.salon.com/2015/12/10/we_will_not_be_silent_american_jews_hit _the_streets_during_hanukkah_to_fight_islamophobia_racial_profiling/.

53. Alissa Wise, "Light a Candle for Gaza," *Palestinian Talmud*, December 26, 2011, http:// palestiniantalmud.com/2011/12/26/light-a-candle-for-gaza/ (site discontinued).

54. Ibid.

55. Jewish Voice for Peace, "Stop Prawer Plan Sukkot Toolkit 2013," accessed October 4, 2017, http://www.scribd.com/doc/165217594/Stop-Prawer-Plan-Sukkot-Toolkit-2013-Jewish-Voice-for-Peace, 1.

56. Ibid., 2.

57. Ibid.

58. One early example is Arthur Waskow's 1969 *Freedom Seder*, which connected the story of Jewish redemption with anti-American Vietnamese resistance and struggle for liberation; see Waskow, "Judaism and Revolution Today: Malkhut Zadon M'herah T'aker," which originally appeared in *Judaism* 20, no. 4 (Fall 1971).

59. Ibid., 3.

60. Jewish Voice for Peace, *Passover Haggadah* (2016 version), accessed September 6, 2016, https://jewishvoiceforpeace.org/wp-content/uploads/2016/04/5776-Haggadah-5JVP-Digital .pdf. The 2015 and 2016 versions are no longer accessible on the JVP website, but the current version uses similar wording.

61. Immediately following the *Nizkor* prayer, the Haggadah of 2015 includes a protest song, "I Can't Breathe," which likewise underscores the universal meanings of the Seder story. The words "I can't breathe," of course, were the last words of Eric Garner as he was choked to death by the police on Staten Island on July 17, 2014.

62. Ibid., 4.

63. Jewish Voice for Peace, *Passover Haggadah*, 8.

64. See chapter 8 as well as insights from materiality studies such as Chandra Mukerji, "Space and Political Pedagogy at the Gardens of Versailles," *Public Culture* 24, no. 3 (Fall 2012): 509–34; Webb Keane, "Subjects and Objects," in *Handbook of Material Culture*, ed. Chris Tilley, Webb Keane, Susanne Küchler, Mike Rowlands, and Patricia Spyer (London: Sage Publication, 2006), 197–202; Webb Keane, "The Evidence of the Senses and the Materiality of Religion," *Journal of the Royal Anthropology Institute* 14, no. S1 (April 2008): 110–27; and Geneviève Zubrzycki, *Beheading the Saint: Nationalism, Religion, and Secularism in Quebec* (Chicago: University of Chicago Press, 2016).

65. Jewish Voice for Peace, *Passover Haggadah*, 8.

66. Ibid.

67. Ibid., 10–12.

68. Ibid., 10.

69. See chapter 4 for this discussion of Arendt's response to Scholem.

70. Jewish Voice for Peace, "Tashlich L'Tzedek 2014/5775: A Ritual of Reflection & Recommitment," July 15, 2015, https://jewishvoiceforpeace.org/wp-content/uploads/2015/07/JVP -TASHLICH-L%E2%80%99TZEDEK-20145775.pdf, 1.

71. Ibid., 2.

72. David Landy's important work primarily focuses on how the diasporist interpretation advances the objectives of Palestine solidarity and criticism of Israeli policies. See Landy, *Jewish Identity*.

73. Ganz, "Public Narrative," 274. See also chapter 2.

Chapter Six

1. Brant Rosen, "Lamentation for a New Diaspora," Jewish Voice for Peace, July 24, 2017, https://jewishvoiceforpeace.org/wp-content/uploads/2017/07/lamentation-for-a-new -diaspora.pdf.

2. Discussion of such phenomena typically describes them as "prefigurative politics." See Carl Boggs, "Revolutionary Process, Political Strategy, and the Dilemma of Power," *Theory & Society* 4, no. 3 (Fall 1977): 359–93; Sheila Rowbotham, "The Women's Movement and Organizing for Socialism," in Sheila Rowbotham, Lynne Segal, and Hilary Wainwright, *Beyond the Fragments: Feminism and the Making of Socialism* (London: Merlin Press, 1979), 21–155; Wini Breins, *Community and Organization in the New Left, 1962–1968: The Great Refusal* (New Brunswick, NJ: Rutgers University Press, 1989); and Andy Cornell, "Consensus: What It Is, What It Is Not, Where It Came From, and Where It Must Go," in *We Are Many: Reflections on Movement Strategy from Occupation to Liberation,* ed. Kate Khatib, Margaret Killjoy, and Mike McGuire (Oakland, CA: AK Press, 2012), 163–73.

3. For an engagement with counter-hegemony from a neo-Gramscian dialectic perspective, see Nicola Pratt, "Bringing Politics Back In: Examining the Link between Globalisation and Democratization," *Review of International Political Economy* 11, no. 2 (2004): 331–36.

4. See my discussion of Jewish Constantinianism in chapter 4 and below. See also Shaul Magid, "Christian Supersessionism, Zionism, and the Contemporary Scene: A Critical Reading of Peter Ochs's Reading of John Howard Yoder," *Journal of Religious Ethics* 45, no. 1 (2017): 104–41.

5. Other comparable (but not necessarily self-defined non-Zionist) intentional communities include a variety of havurot (lay-led groups) that are emerging across the US, as well as synagogues such as Nevei Kodesh in Boulder, CO; Kadima Reconstructionist Community in Seattle, WA; Makom Shalom in Chicago; Kehilla Community Synagogue in Oakland, CA; Tikkun Olam Chavurah in Philadelphia, PA; and Fringes: A Feminist, Non-Zionist Havurah, consisting primarily of women, lesbian and queer-identified (also located in Philadelphia). JVP's 2017 National Members Meeting devoted a highly attended session to such communities and their approaches to engagement with Israel/Palestine, other social justice issues, and Jewish practice.

6. Manya Brachear Pashman, "Chicago Rabbi Establishes Non-Zionist Congregation," *Chicago Tribune,* September 11, 2015, http://www.chicagotribune.com/news/ct-non-zionist -synagogue-met-20150911-story.html.

7. While a growing number of American Jews are drawn to the social justice and non-Zionist agenda of Tzedek Chicago, some express disappointment at its loose approach to liturgy and prayer, which are primarily influenced by the Reconstructionist current. See, for instance, Jonathan Paul Katz, "Can a Non-Zionist Synagogue Succeed—and Spread?," *Forward,* July 13, 2015, http://forward.com/opinion/311886/are-non-zionist-synagogues-like-tzedek -chicago-the-way-of-the-future/.

8. "Core Values," Tzedek Chicago, accessed October 7, 2017, http://www.tzedekchicago.org/ core_values.

9. Eli Ungar-Sargon, "Dystopian Lamentation: An Interview with Rabbi Brant Rosen," *Jewschool,* July 26, 2017, https://jewschool.com/2017/07/79914/dystopian-lamentation-interview -brant-rosen/.

10. Ibid.

11. Stanton, "What Will We Make Different this Year? A Guest Sermon for Erev Yom Kippur," *Shalom Rav,* September 25, 2015, https://rabbibrant.com/2015/09/24/what-will-we-make -different-this-year-a-guest-sermon-for-erev-yom-kippur-by-jay-stanton/.

12. Ibid.

13. Rosen, "On Sukkot and the Struggles over Chicago's Dyett High School and the South Side Trauma Center," *Shalom Rav,* October 2, 2015, https://rabbibrant.com/2015/10/02/ on-sukkot-and-the-struggles-over-chicagos-dyett-high-school-and-the-south-side-trauma

-center/; Ben Murane, "Rosh Hashana Petition to Rahm Emmanuel: Save Dyett High School: Solidarity Action by Rabbi Brant Rosen's New Shul," *Jewschool*, September 16, 2015, https://jewschool.com/2015/09/37781/rosh-hashana-petition-to-rahm-emmanuel-save-dyett-high-school/; and Dahleen Glanton and Dawn Rhodes, "South Side to Get Adult Trauma Center after Years of Protest," *Chicago Tribune*, September 11, 2015, http://www.chicagotribune.com/news/ct-university-of-chicago-mount-sinai-south-side-trauma-center-20150910-story.html.

14. Rosen, "On the Trayvon Martin Verdict and the 'National Conversation,'" *Shalom Rav*, July 17, 2013, https://rabbibrant.com/2013/07/17/a-post-tisha-bav-meditation-on-trayon-martin-and-the-national-conversation/.

15. Jay Stanton, "A Piyut to End Police Violence This Rosh Hashanah," *Shalom Rav*, September 23, 2017, https://rabbibrant.com/2017/09/23/guest-post-by-jay-stanton-end-police-violence-this-season-of-open-gates/.

16. Ibid.

17. Adam Gottlieb, "This Is the Year (5778)," *People Are Poets Are Prophets*, September 21, 2017, http://peoplearepoets.blogspot.com/2017/09/this-is-year-5778.html.

18. This point is further developed in chapters 7 and 8. The notion of "ungrievability" derives from Judith Butler's essays in her *Frames of War*.

19. See chapter 4 for a discussion of Heschel and the distinction between prophetic social movement and the prophetic exemplar.

20. Rosen, "The Uprooted and Unwanted: A Sermon for Tzedek Chicago's First Yom Kippur Service," *Shalom Rav*, September 25, 2015, https://rabbibrant.com/2015/09/25/the-uprooted-and-unwanted-a-sermon-for-tzedek-chicagos-first-yom-kippur-service/.

21. Ibid.

22. Ibid.

23. JFREJ itself connects to other historical manifestations of the Jewish Left and its focus on antiracism, including the students' group "the Zealots," which protested in 1964 against 250 Jewish land- or slumlords in New York City who discriminated against African Americans by delivering a letter to the New York Board of Rabbis calling their leaders to "uphold our historic standards of social justice," quoted in Marc Dollinger, *Black Power, Jewish Politics: Reinventing the Alliance in the 1960s* (Waltham, MA: Brandeis University Press, 2018), 123. Another related organization is Jews for Urban Justice, which first emerged in 1966 and immediately focused on the failures of the Jewish establishment to respond to the needs of migrant workers. See Dollinger, *Black Power, Jewish Politics*, 124.

24. See Jews for Racial & Economic Justice, "2015 Strategic Vision," accessed October 7, 2016, http://jfrej.org/wp-content/uploads/2015/06/JFREJ-Strategic-Vision-2015.pdf.

25. Ibid.

26. See chapter 4 on this analogy taken from Christian history.

27. Rosen, "Celebrating a New Jewish Diasporism: A Sermon for Rosh Hashanah 5777," *Shalom Rav*, October 4, 2016, https://rabbibrant.com/2016/10/04/celebrating-a-new-jewish-diasporism-a-sermon-for-rosh-hashanah-5777/.

28. "For I desire mercy, and not sacrifice, And the knowledge of God rather than burnt-offerings" (Hosea 6:6).

29. The rabbinic interpretive resources underpinning "Olam Chesed Yibaneh" include: Mishnah Peah 1:1, "These are the things that have no measure: The *Peah* [corner of the field that must be given to the poor], the *Bikurim* [first fruits that must be given to the *Kohen*], the appearance-sacrifice [at the Temple in Jerusalem on Pilgrimage Festivals], acts of kindness, and the study of Torah"; Mishnah Torah, Mourning 14:1, on the rabbinic commandment to "visit the

sick, comfort mourners. . . . These are deeds of kindness that one carries out with his person that have no limit"; Ruth Rabba 2:14, on the significance of lovingkindness (*hasadim*); and Kohelet Rabba 7:4, "Rabbi Yehuda said: anyone who denies the primacy of *hesed*, it is as if they deny the Holy One and all that is good." See Robyn Fryer Bodzin, "Chesed: Source Sheet," *Sefaria*, June 1, 2016, https://www.sefaria.org/sheets/35874.

30. Magid, "Christian Supersessionism," 114.

31. Ibid., 118.

32. Ibid., 119.

33. See chapter 5.

34. Melanie Kaye/Kantrowitz, *The Colors of Jews: Radical Politics and Radical Diasporism* (Bloomington: Indiana University Press, 2007). For a critique of Rosen's discussion of non-Zionism and diasporism as exclusionary and precluding deeper intra-Jewish conversation, see Mira Sucharov, "My Problem with the Idea of a 'Non-Zionist Synagogue,'" *Forward*, October 9, 2016, http://forward.com/opinion/351643/my-problem-with-the-idea-of-a-non-zionist-synagogue/. One response to Sucharov's criticism came from Jay M. Stanton, "Zionists Have Many Jewish Spaces to Call Home. Our Synagogue Needn't Be One of Them," *Forward*, October 14, 2016, http://forward.com/opinion/351972/zionists-have-many-jewish-spaces-to-call-home-our-synagogue-neednt-be-one-o/.

35. Fringes: A Feminist, Non-Zionist Havurah, "Why We Define as a Non-Zionist Havurah," accessed July 24, 2018, https://fringeshavurah.com/who-we-are/why-we-define-as-a-non-zionist-havurah/.

36. See the "Introduction" for a discussion of this sermon.

37. See Smith, "Correcting a Curious Neglect"; and my discussion in chapter 2.

38. Such podcasts include *Treyf* and *Judaism Unbound*, which often feature non-Zionist, JOCSM, and critical scholars as part of an effort to broaden conversations about the meanings and boundaries of Jewishness.

39. Interview #1.

40. See chapters 3 and 7 for further discussion.

41. Rosen, "Communal Vidui: Confession," in Tzedek Chicago's Service for Erev Yom Kippur, *Shalom Rav*, September 17, 2015, https://rabbibrant.com/2015/09/17/a-confession-of-communal-complicity-a-new-al-chet-for-yom-kippur/.

42. See Tzedek Chicago, "Core Values."

43. See Smith, "Correcting a Curious Neglect"; Ronald R. Aminzade and Elizabeth J. Perry, "The Sacred, Religious and Secular in Contentious Politics: Blurring the Boundaries," in *Silence and Voice in the Study of Contentious Politics*, ed. Ronald R. Aminzade, Jack A. Goldstone, Doug McAdam, Elizabeth J. Perry, William H. Sewer Jr., Sidney Tarrow, and Charles Tilly (Cambridge: University of Cambridge Press, 2001), 155–78; and Mayer N. Zald and John McCarthy, "Religious Groups as Crucibles of Social Movements," in *Social Movements in an Organized Society: Collected Essays*, ed. Zald and McCarthy (London: Transaction Publishers, 1987), 67–95.

44. The story is in *parashat Shemot* (Ex. 1:1–6:1). The midwives appear in 1:15.

45. According to Rashi Exodus 1:15 and Sotah 11b, Shifrah is Yocheved and Puah is Miriam. Other traditional figures (Yehudah HaChasid, 1150–1217; Don Isaac Abarbanel, 1437–1508; Samuel David Luzzatoo, 1800–1865; and a fragment of a midrash from the Cairo Genizah dated ca. 1000 CE) suggest they were Egyptian women who provided resources for the concept of righteous Gentiles. See Moshe Lavee and Shana Strauch-Schick, "The 'Egyptian' Midwives," *Projects TABS*, accessed October 7, 2017, http://thetorah.com/the-egyptian-midwives/.

46. Tzedek Chicago, "Haggadah for Passover 5777," https://d3n8a8pro7vhmx.cloudfront

.net/tzedekchicago/pages/24/attachments/original/1502906435/tzedek-haggadah-5777.pdf, 3–4.

47. Jacob Friedman, "Ki Tisa: Sinai and The Bad Parts of Torah and Activism," *If Not Now,* March 17, 2017, https://medium.com/ifnotnowtorah/ki-tisa-sinai-and-the-bad-parts-of-torah-and-activism-477a5f13ae82.

48. Michael Davis, "Mishpatim: The Covenant of Justice and Conquest," *Palestinian Talmud,* January 29, 2014, https://paltalmud.com/2014/01/29/mishpatim-the-covenant-of-justice-and-conquest/ (site discontinued).

49. The first public service of Tzedek Chicago—described in the opening vignette of this chapter—engaged this biblical passage, employing relationality and the tools of liberation theology and postcolonial theory to own the narrative and to explore its ramifications for the contemporary moment.

50. Interview #55.

51. Lynn Gottlieb, *Trail Guide to the Torah of Nonviolence* (Paris: Éditions Terre d'Espérance, 2013), 16.

52. Ibid., 39.

53. Ibid., 17.

54. Ibid., 19.

55. Jewish Voice for Peace, "We Must Hold Israel Accountable," *ActionSprout,* accessed October 24, 2017, https://actionsprout.io/F71047.

56. Ibid.

57. Rosen, "Empathy, not Vengeance: A Rabbinical View on the Recent Violence in Palestine," *Shalom Rav,* July 3, 2014, http://rabbibrant.com/2014/07/03/empathy-not-venegeance-a-rabbinical-view-on-the-recent-violence-in-israelpalestine/.

58. Miller, *Friends and Other Strangers,* 146.

59. Ibid., 146–48.

60. Judith Butler, "Sexual Politics, Torture, and Secular Time," 122.

61. Recall the epigraph to this chapter. On empathic indignation, see chapter 4.

62. Smith, *Religion,* 97.

63. Ibid., especially 78–84.

64. Ibid., 97.

65. Ibid., 92–93.

66. Ibid., 93 (emphasis in original).

67. Fredric Jameson, "Postmodernism, or The Cultural Logic of Late Capitalism," *New Left Review* 1, no. 146 (1984): 53–92 (65).

68. On pastiche as a mechanism of intertextuality, see Daniel Bowles, *The Ends of Satire: Legacies of Satire in Postwar German Writing* (Berlin: Gruyer, 2015), 161.

69. This interpretation of the prophetic is distinct from Alberto Melucci's analysis of the prophetic functions of social movement. See chapter 2 for this discussion.

70. On extending Jameson's view of the pastiche as lacking parody, see Bowles's reading of Gérard Genette in Bowles, *The Ends of Satire,* 161.

Chapter Seven

1. David Palumbo-Liu, "'It's Ugly, It's Vicious, It's Brutal': Cornel West on Israel in Palestine—and Why Gaza Is 'The Hood on Steroids,'" *Salon,* February 25, 2015, https://

www.salon.com/2015/02/25/its_ugly_it's_vicious_it's_brutal_cornel_west_on_israel_in _palestine_—_and_why_gaza_is_the_hood_on_steroids/.

2. See Alex Lubin, *Geographies of Liberation: The Making of An Afro-Arab Imaginary* (Chapel Hill: University of North Carolina Press, 2014).

3. StoptheWall Campaign, "Call for the World Social Forum Free Palestine, Nov. 2012 in Brazil," *BDS: Freedom, Justice, Equality*, January 19, 2012, http://www.bdsmovement.net/2012/call-for-the-world-social-forum-free-palestine-nov-2012-in-brazil-8603.

4. Helga Tawil-Souri, "Media, Globalization, and the (Un)Making of the Palestinian Cause," *Popular Communication* 13, no. 2 (2015): 145–57; Helga Tawil-Souri and Dina Matar, eds., *Gaza as Metaphor* (London: Hurst & Company, 2016); Atalia Omer, "'It's Nothing Personal': The Globalisation of Justice, the Transferability of Protest, and the Case of the Palestine Solidarity Movement," *Studies in Ethnicity & Nationalism* 9, no. 3 (2009): 497–518; and Omer, "Religion, Nationalism, and Solidarity Activism," in *The Oxford Handbook of Religion, Conflict, and Peacebuilding*, ed. Atalia Omer, R. Scott Appleby, and David Little (New York: Oxford University Press, 2015), 613–58.

5. Tawil-Souri, "Media, Globalization, and the (Un)Making of the Palestinian Cause."

6. Omar Bargouti, *BDS: Boycott, Divestment, Sanctions: The Global Struggle for Palestinian Rights* (Chicago: Haymarket Books, 2011). See also Maia Carter Hallward, *Transnational Activism and the Israeli-Palestinian Conflict* (New York: Palgrave Macmillan, 2013).

7. Keith P. Feldman, *A Shadow over Palestine: The Imperial Life of Race in America* (Minneapolis: University of Minnesota Press, 2015), 8.

8. Ibid.

9. Muriel Kane, "Report: Israeli Model Underlies Militarization of U.S. Police," *RawStory*, December 4, 2011, http://www.rawstory.com/rs/2011/12/report-israeli-model-underlies -militarization-of-u-s-police/.

10. Max Blumenthal, "From Occupation to 'Occupy': The Israelification of American Domestic Security," *Mondoweiss*, December 2, 2012, http://mondoweiss.net/2011/12/from -occupation-to-occupy-the-israelification-of-american-domestic-decurity. See also Sari Horwitz, "Israeli Experts Teach Police on Terrorism," *Washington Post*, June 12, 2005, http://www .washingtonpost.com/wp-dyn/content/article/2005/06/11/AR2005061100648.html.

11. See Davis, *Freedom Is a Constant Struggle: Ferguson, Palestine, and the Foundations of Movement*, ed. Frank Barat (Chicago: Haymarket Books, 2016), esp. 51–60. Feldman's discussion of black feminists' exchanges with Third World feminists and critique of American white feminists and how the liberation of Palestine became foregrounded in feminist African American political futurity sheds further light on this legacy of black feminist critical activism; see especially *A Shadow over Palestine*, chapter 5.

12. See Jewish Voice for Peace, "Deadly Exchange," accessed September 27, 2017, https:// deadlyexchange.org/.

13. Beyond the focus on police brutality and African American solidarity, Chicano solidarity also emerged surrounding analysis of the border wall with Mexico and Israeli involvement in security issues. See M.E.Ch.A., "National M.E.Ch.A. Endorses Palestinian Boycott Call against Israel," *BDS: Freedom, Justice Equality*, March 30, 2012, https:// bdsmovement.net/news/national-mecha-endorses-palestinian-boycott-call-against-israel. For coverage of Palestine solidarity activists' direct action as a form of co-resistance in "Operation Streamline," see Latino Rebels, "Developing Story: Immigration Activists in Tucson Block Deportation Buses," October 11, 2013, *Latino Rebels*, http://www.latinorebels

.com/2013/10/11/developing-story-immigration-activists-in-tucson-block-deportation
-buses/. For a debate about whether the campaign trafficked in antisemitic tropes, see Mira
Sucharov, "Jews Drive U.S. Police Brutality against People of Color? JVP Crosses over into Anti-
Semitism," *Haaretz*, July 10, 2017, http://www.haaretz.com/opinion/1.800523. The executive di-
rector of JVP, Rebecca Vilkomerson, responded with a controversial opinion piece that, because it
misquoted Sucharov, generated often vicious social-media attacks on Sucharov. See Vilkomerson,
"Own It to Fight It: Yes, We U.S. Jews Are Complicit in Violence against Palestinians and People of
Color," *Haaretz*, July 19, 2017, http://www.haaretz.com/opinion/1.802172; and Rebecca Pierce,
Twitter post, July 11, 2017, https://twitter.com/aptly_engineerd/status/884876995837837312.

14. In addition to the evidence produced by JVP's #DeadlyExchange, see also the campaign
against Israel's arms selling to Myanmar, whose ethnic cleansing targets the Muslim Rohingya
people. IfNotNow, "Help Stop Israel's Weapons Sales to Myanmar—American Jewish Leaders, It's Time to Act," accessed November 3, 2017, https://actionnetwork.org/petitions/help-stop
-israels-weapons-sales-to-myanmar-american-jewish-leaders-its-time-to-act.

15. Michelle Alexander, *The New Jim Crow: Mass Incarceration in the Age of Colorblindness*
(New York: New Press, 2011).

16. Rana Baker, "Palestinians Express 'Solidarity with the People of Ferguson' in Mike
Brown Statement," *Electronic Intifada*, August 15, 2014, https://electronicintifada.net/blogs/rana
-baker/palestinians-express-solidarity-people-ferguson-mike-brown-statement.

17. Mark Molloy and Agencies, "Palestinians Tweet Tear Gas Advice to Protesters in Ferguson," *Telegraph*, August 15, 2014, http://www.telegraph.co.uk/news/worldnews/northamerica/
usa/11036190/Palestinians-tweet-tear-gas-advice-to-protesters-in-Ferguson.html.

18. Davis, *Freedom Is a Constant Struggle*, 90.

19. Annie Robbins, "'Protest in the Form of a Prayer': Dream Defenders Demonstration in
Nazareth Makes Connections from Ferguson to Palestine," *Mondoweiss*, January 15, 2015, http://
mondoweiss.net/2015/01/demonstration-connections-palestine.

20. See, for instance, Stokely Carmichael and Charles V. Hamilton, *Black Power: The Politics of Liberation in America* (New York: Random House, 1967); Devin Fergus, *Liberalism, Black
Power, and the Making of American Politics, 1965–1980* (Athens: University of Georgia Press,
2009); and Kathleen Cleaver and George N. Katsiaficas, *Liberation, Imagination, and the Black
Panther Party: A New Look at the Panthers and Their Legacy* (New York: Routledge, 2001).

21. Later, the "N" in the name was changed to "National."

22. Marc Dollinger, *Black Power, Jewish Politics*, 159.

23. Cited in ibid., 160.

24. NOI rhetoric remains a point of contention within the contemporary intersectional
social justice movement. See chapter 8 for further discussion.

25. Quoted in Sundquist, *Strangers in the Land*, 19.

26. Ibid.

27. James Baldwin, *The Fire Next Time* (New York: Vintage, [1962] 1993).

28. Ibid., 22.

29. See, for instance, Sundquist, *Strangers in the Land*, 316; Seth Forman, *Blacks in the Jewish
Mind: A Crisis of Jewish Liberalism* (New York: New York University Press, 1998); and William
M. Phillips, *An Unillustrious Alliance: The African American and Jewish American Communities*
(New York: Greenwood Press, 1991).

30. Albert Vorspan, "Blacks and Jews," in *Black Anti-Semitism and Jewish Racism* (New York:
Schocken Books, [1970] 1972), 191–226 (208).

31. Ibid.

32. Quoted in Dollinger, *Black Power, Jewish Politics*, 157.

33. Quoted in ibid., 165.

34. Alan W. Miller, "Black Anti-Semitism—Jewish Racism," in *Black Anti-Semitism and Jewish Racism* (New York: Schocken Books, [1969] 1972), 79–114 (82).

35. See also Nat Hentoff, "Introduction" to *Black Anti-Semitism and Jewish Racism* (New York: Schocken Books, [1970] 1972), ix–xvii.

36. Miller, "Black Anti-Semitism—Jewish Racism," 93.

37. Ibid., 104, emphasis mine.

38. Ibid.

39. Ibid., 90.

40. Dollinger, *Black Power, Jewish Politics*, 157.

41. Ibid., 169.

42. See, in particular, ibid., 144–49.

43. Ibid., 146.

44. See chapter 1.

45. Feldman, *A Shadow over Palestine*, especially chapter 2.

46. Ibid., 11.

47. Ibid., 12.

48. Lubin, 7.

49. Ibid.

50. For an examination of "coloniality," see Walter D. Mignolo, *Local Histories/Global Designs: Coloniality, Subaltern Knowledges, and Border Thinking* (Princeton, NJ: Princeton University Press, 2000); and Anibal Quijano, "Coloniality of Power, Eurocentrism, and Latin America," *Nepantla: Views from South* 1, no. 3 (2000): 533–80.

51. For another prominent example of an intersectional expression of black-Palestinian solidarity, see Kristian Davis Bailey and Khury Petersen-Smith, "1,000 Black Activists, Artists, and Scholars Demand Justice for Palestine," *Ebony*, August 18, 2015, http://www.ebony.com/news-views/1000-black-activists-artists-and-scholars-demand-justice-for-palestine.

52. See also Feldman, *A Shadow over Palestine*, especially chapter 5.

53. Davis, *Freedom Is a Constant Struggle*, 48.

54. Ibid., 104.

55. Ibid.

56. Ibid.

57. Movement for Black Lives, "Invest-Divest Platform," accessed October 7, 2017, https://policy.m4bl.org/invest-divest/.

58. Wendy Elisheva Somerson, "The Twin Ghosts of Slavery and the Nakba: The Roots that Connect Ferguson and Palestine," *Tikkun*, January 23, 2015, http://www.tikkun.org/nextgen/the-twin-ghosts-of-slavery-and-the-nakba-the-roots-that-connect-ferguson-and-palestine.

59. This is not only the case for those actively pursuing Palestine solidarity, but also for those within more conventional frameworks such as J Street, who comprehend why African Americans draw connections between police brutality in the US and the military system of the occupation in Palestine. See chapter 1 for this discussion.

60. See also the discussion in chapter 6 of Tzedek Chicago's exploration of the history of race in the US and of Jewish participation in whiteness.

61. See Mitchell B. Hart, "Jews and Race: An Introductory Essay," in *Jews & Race: Writings*

on Identity & Difference, 1880–1940, ed. Mitchell B. Hart (Waltham, MA: Brandeis University Press, 2011), 9–29.

62. Ibid., 19.

63. Ibid., 20. Emphasis in original.

64. Ibid. See also the discussion below of Herzl's internalized antisemitism.

65. See the discussion in chapter 3, as well as Susan Glenn, "In the Blood? Consent, Descent, and the Ironies of Jewish Identity," *Jewish Social Studies* 8, nos. 2–3 (2002): 139–52; and David Biale, *Blood and Belief: The Circulation of a Symbol between Jews and Christians* (Berkeley: University of California Press, 2007).

66. Movement for Black Lives, "Invest-Divest Platform."

67. Ibid.

68. See, for instance, Shaw and Bartov, "The Question of Genocide in Palestine, 1948: An Exchange between Martin Shaw and Omer Bartov," *Journal of Genocide Research* 12 (2010): 243–59.

69. Zellner, "If It's Not Genocide, What Word Should We Use?," *Jewish Currents*, June 30, 2017, http://jewishcurrents.org/if-its-not-genocide-what-word-should-we-use/.

70. For another instance of support by the Jewish press, see William L. Patterson, "Genocide against the Negro People," *Jewish Life* (January 1952): 11–13.

71. Quoted in Zellner, "If It's Not Genocide."

72. The applicability of the category "genocide" is also supported by others in the human rights community. See, for instance, Center for Constitutional Rights, "The Genocide of the Palestinian People: An International Law and Human Rights Perspective," August 25, 2016, https://ccrjustice.org/genocide-palestinian-people-international-law-and-human-rights-perspective.

73. Joy James, "The Dead Zone: Stumbling at the Crossroads of Party Politics, Genocide, and Postracial Racism," *South Atlantic Quarterly: Africana Thought* 108, no. 3 (Summer 2009): 477n3, quoted in Zellner, "If It's Not Genocide."

74. Rothberg, *Multidirectional Memory: Remembering the Holocaust in the Age of Decolonization* (Stanford, CA: Stanford University Press, 2009), chapter 4.

75. Du Bois, "The Negro and the Warsaw Ghetto," *Jewish Life* (May 1952): 15, cited in Rothberg, *Multidirectional Memory*, 115–16.

76. Rothberg, *Multidirectional Memory*, 121.

77. See W. E. B. Du Bois, *The World and Africa: An Inquiry into the Part Which Africa Has Played in World History* (New York: Viking, 1947), 23.

78. Rothberg, *Multidirectional Memory*, 125.

79. Ibid., 124; and Giorgio Agamben, *Remnants of Auschwitz: The Witness and the Archive*, trans. Daniel Heller-Roazen (New York: Zone Books, 1999).

80. Rothberg, *Multidirectional Memory*, 126.

81. Ibid.

82. See also Enzo Traverso, *The Origins of Nazi Violence* (New York: New Press, 2003).

83. James P. Sterba, "Understanding Evil: American Slavery, the Holocaust, and the Conquest of the American Indians," *Ethics* 106, no. 2 (1996): 424–48. See also Laurence Mordekhai Thomas, *Vessels of Evil: American Slavery and the Holocaust* (Philadelphia: Temple University Press, 1993); and A. Dirk Moses, "Does the Holocaust Reveal or Conceal Other Genocides? The Canadian Museum of Human Rights and Grievable Suffering," in *Hidden Genocides: Power, Knowledge, and Memory*, ed. Doug Irvin, Alexander Hinton, and Tom LaPointe (New Brunswick, NJ: Rutgers University Press, 2013), 21–51.

84. See Mark Levene, *The Crisis of Genocide*, vol. 1: *Devastation: The European Rimlands,*

1912–1938; vol. 2: *Annihilation: The European Rimlands, 1939–1953* (New York: Oxford University Press, 2013); Timothy Snyder, *Bloodlands: Europe between Hitler and Stalin* (New York: Basic Books, 2012); and Caroll P. Kakel, *The Holocaust as Colonial Genocide: Hitler's "Indian Wars" in the "Wild East"* (New York: Palgrave Macmillan, 2013).

85. See David Chidester, *Empire of Religion: Imperialism and Comparative Religion* (Chicago: University of Chicago Press, 2014), for an important examination of the centrality of race in the comparative study of religion, a crucial dimension of modern colonial expansion.

86. Moses, "Conceptual Blockages and Definitional Dilemmas in the 'Racial Century': Genocides of Indigenous Peoples and the Holocaust," *Patterns of Prejudice* 36, no. 4 (2002): 7–36 (9).

87. For a classic account, see David Chidester, *Savage Systems: Colonialism and Comparative Religion in Southern Africa* (Charlottesville: University of Virginia Press, 1996).

88. Judith Butler, *Precarious Life: The Powers of Mourning and Violence* (London: Verso, 2006), 20.

89. Ibid., 33.

90. Ibid.

91. See, for instance, Adi Ophir, "On Sanctifying the Holocaust: An Anti-Theological Treatise," *Tikkun* 2, no. 1 (1987): 61–67; Steven T. Katz, *Post-Holocaust Dialogue* (New York: New York University Press, 1983); Emil Fackenheim, "Why the Holocaust Is Unique," *Judaism* 5, no. 4 (Autumn 2001): 438–47; Yehuda Bauer, "Comparison of Genocides," in *Studies in Contemporary Genocide,* ed. Levon Chorbajian and George Shirinian (New York: St Martin's Press, 1999); and Moses, "Conceptual Blockages," 10–19. For critiques of those who construe the Holocaust as unique, see David E. Stannard, "Uniqueness as Denial: The Politics of Genocide Scholarship," in *Is the Holocaust Unique? Perspectives on Comparative Genocide,* ed. Alan S. Rosenbaum (Boulder, CO: Westview Press, 2001), 245–90; and Stannard, *American Holocaust* (New York: Oxford University Press, 1992).

92. See, for instance, Patrick Wolfe, "Settler Colonialism and the Elimination of the Native," *Journal of Genocide Research* 8, no. 4 (2006): 387–409; and Lorenzo Veracini, *Settler Colonialism: A Theoretical Overview* (London: Palgrave Macmillan, 2010).

93. Moses, "Conceptual Blockages," 18.

94. Ibid., 33.

95. See the discussion of IfNotNow's logo of the burning bush in chapter 4.

96. See Dollinger, *Black Power, Jewish Politics.* See also my discussion in chapter 3.

97. Ibid.

98. Rachel Gilmer, remarks on a panel entitled "Let's Talk about Zionism," JVP's National Membership Meeting, April 1, 2017.

99. Singh, "Religious Agency and the Limits of Intersectionality," *Hypatia* 30, no. 4 (Fall 2015): 657–74. On the concept of difference within intersectional analyses, see also Nira Yuval-Davis, "Intersectionality and Feminist Politics," *European Journal of Women's Studies* 13, no. 3 (August 2006): 193–209.

100. See, for instance, Saba Mahmood, *Politics of Piety: The Islamic Revival and the Feminist Subject* (Princeton, NJ: Princeton University Press, 2005); Rachel Rinaldo, "Pious and Critical: Muslim Women Activists and the Question of Agency," *Gender & Society* 28, no. 6 (December 2014): 824–46; and Elizabeth Bucar, "Dianomy: Understanding Religious Women's Moral Agency as Creative Conformity," *Journal of the American Academy of Religion* 78, no. 3 (September 2010): 662–86.

101. Singh, "Religious Agency," 667.

102. See Kimberlé Williams Crenshaw, "Mapping the Margins: Intersectionality, Identity Politics, and Violence against Women of Color," *Stanford Law Review* 43, no. 6 (1991); and Elizabeth V. Spellman, *Inessential Women: Problems of Exclusion in Feminist Thought* (Boston: Beacon Press, 1988). For key works by Dorothy Smith, Nancy Hartsock, Hilary Rose, Patricia Hill Collins, Donna Haraway, and Sandra Harding that focus on standpoint feminist methodologies, see Sandra Harding, ed., *The Feminist Standpoint Theory Reader* (New York: Routledge, 2004).

103. Singh, "Religious Agency," 668.

104. Vincent Lloyd, "How Religious Is #BlackLivesMatter?," in *Humanism and the Challenge of Difference*, ed. Anthony Pinn (New York: Palgrave Macmillan, 2018), 215–37.

105. Judy Maltz, "Jewish Groups Respond to Movement for Black Lives Platform," *Haaretz*, August 8, 2017, https://www.haaretz.com/amp/world-news/u-s-election-2016/1.735760.

106. Feldman, *A Shadow over Palestine*, 11.

107. See Dollinger, *Black Power, Jewish Politics*, 94.

108. For some examples of explicit black antisemitism pivotal for the Jewish narrative about this phenomenon, see Joyce S. Fay, "Jackson Admits Saying 'Hymie' and Apologizes at a Synagogue," *New York Times*, February 27, 1984, https://www.nytimes.com/1984/02/27/us/jackson-admits-saying-hymie-and-apologizes-at-a-synagogue.html; and "The Nation of Islam," Anti-Defamation League, accessed March 15, 2018, www.adl.org/education/resources/profiles/the-nation-of-islam.

109. See Josh Nathan-Kazis, "Why No One Talks about Black-Jewish Relations," *Forward*, August 8, 2011, http://forward.com/news/141519/why-no-one-talks-about-black-jewish-relations/; Edward S. Shapiro, *Crown Heights: Blacks, Jews, and the 1991 Brooklyn Riot* (Waltham, MA: Brandeis University Press, 2006); and Henry Goldschmidt, *Race and Religion among the Chosen People of Crown Heights* (New Brunswick, NJ: Rutgers University Press, 2006).

110. One momentous event was the New York City teachers' strike of 1968 (to which Rabbi Alan W. Miller reacted), which revolved around the question of community control of education in a demographically changing city. In 1978, Jewish groups expressed opposition to affirmative action programs debated in the Supreme Court (*Regents of the University of California v. Baake*), a pattern of black-Jewish tension that continued beyond the 1970s.

111. Baldwin, "Negroes Are Anti-Semitic Because They're Anti-White," *New York Times*, April 9, 1967, http://www.nytimes.com/books/98/03/29/specials/baldwin-antisem.html.

112. Ibid., emphasis mine.

113. Ibid.

114. Ibid.

115. For an engagement of Baldwin's concept of love and how it mitigates Hannah Arendt's critique of love in politics, see Sean Kim Butorac, "Hannah Arendt, James Baldwin, and the Politics of Love," *Political Research Quarterly* 71, no. 3 (2018): 710–21.

116. Baldwin, *The Fire Next Time*, 105.

117. Butorac, "Hannah Arendt," 711.

118. See, for examples, James Baldwin, *No Name in the Street* and *Notes of a Native Son*, in James Baldwin, *Baldwin: Collected Essays* (New York: Literary Classics of the United States, 1998).

119. Butorac, "Hannah Arendt," 719.

120. Baldwin, "On Being 'White,'" 90–92.

121. Houria Bouteldja, *Whites, Jews, and Us: Toward a Politics of Revolutionary Love* (South Pasadena, CA: Semiotext(e), 2017). Bouteldja also drew extensively on the insights of Cyril Lio-

nel Robert James as well as Malcolm X, Jean Genet, Aimé Césaire, Audre Lorde, Frantz Fanon, and Chela Sandoval in articulating her conception of revolutionary love.

122. Ibid., 121.

123. Bouteldja formed the Indigenous of the Republic in 2005 with an open call that turned into a political movement and later into a French political party by the name of le Mouvement des Indigènes de la République. See http://indigenes-republique.fr/.

124. Bouteldja, *Whites, Jews, and Us*, 63.

125. Ibid., 57.

126. Ibid.

127. This approach is consistent with UN Resolution 3379 (adopted in 1975), which declared Zionism to be a form of racism but, combined with the earlier 1963 Declaration of the Elimination of All Forms of Racial Discrimination, stressed the complex relations of race and religion within a modernist discourse that pushes toward disembodied conceptions of religion. See also Feldman, *A Shadow over Palestine*, chapter 1.

128. See also chapters 8 and 9.

129. Slabodsky, *Decolonial Judaism*, 94.

130. Ibid., 78.

131. Slabodsky examines similar contradictions in other Jewish thinkers, such as the Tunisian Albert Memmi. See ibid., 115–44, in particular.

132. Ibid., 12 and passim.

133. Ibid., 13.

134. Ibid., 179–201. Slabodsky refers to Robert Kaplan, "The Coming Anarchy," *Atlantic Magazine*, February 1994, https://www.theatlantic.com/magazine/archive/1994/02/the-coming-anarchy/304670/.

135. Ibid., 182–83.

136. Ibid., 184.

137. See Gil Anidjar, *Blood: A Critique of Christianity* (New York City: Columbia University Press, 2014).

138. Anidjar, *The Jew, the Arab: A History of the Enemy* (Stanford, CA: Stanford University Press, 2003), 101–50.

139. Daniel Boyarin, *Unheroic Conduct*, 180.

140. See Nermeen Shaikh, "The Jew, the Arab: An Interview with Gil Anidjar," *Asia Society*, accessed October 7, 2017, http://asiasociety.org/jew-arab-interview-gil-anidjar.

141. Critically, orientalism comes in different forms. I refer here to what Hamid Dabashi calls "orientalism of domination" and its participation in the invention of "the West"; see his *Post-Orientalism Knowledge & Power in a Time of Terror* (London: Transaction Publishers, [2009] 2015), 103.

142. JOCSM, "Welcome to Unruly: A Blog by the Jews of Color Caucus," October 19, 2016, http://jocsm.org/unruly/.

143. Jews for Racial & Economic Justice, "2015 Strategic Vision," accessed October 7, 2016, http://jfrej.org/wp-content/uploads/2015/06/JFREJ-Strategic-Vision-2015.pdf.

144. Ibid.

145. JOCSM, "Welcome to Unruly."

146. JOCSM, "Jews of Color and Sephardi/Mizrahi Caucus Statement in Support of 1,500 Palestinian Prisoners on Hunger Strike," May 15, 2017, http://jocsm.org/jews-of-color-and-sephardimizrahi-caucus-statement-in-support-of-1500-palestinian-prisoners-on-hunger-strike/.

147. Danny Bryck, "This is How I Spell 'Unruly,'" *Unruly*, March 29, 2017, http://jocsm.org/this-is-how-i-spell-unruly/.

148. JOCSM, "Introducing the Jews of Color and Sephardi/Mizrahi Caucus Working in Partnership with JVP," August 4, 2016, http://jocsm.org/introducing-the-jews-of-color-caucus-working-in-partnership-with-jvp/.

149. Ibid.

150. On the employment of Constantinian Judaism in the movement of critical Jews, see chapters 4 and 5.

151. Paulo Freire, *Pedagogy of the Oppressed* (New York: Bloomsbury Academic, [1968] 2000).

152. Davis, *Freedom Is a Constant Struggle*, 39.

153. Ibid., 48.

154. Ibid., 79.

155. Rothberg, *Multidirectional Memory*, 11.

156. Ibid., 2.

157. Ibid., 3.

158. Ibid., 5.

159. Ibid.

160. See chapter 6.

161. Rothberg, *Multidirectional Memory*, 5.

162. See Judith Butler, "No, It's Not Anti-Semitic," *London Review of Books* 25, no. 16 (August 21, 2003): 19–21, http://www.lrb.co.uk/v25/n16/judith-butler/no-its-not-anti-semitic.

Chapter Eight

1. Alissa Wise, "Building toward the Next World," in *On Antisemitism: Solidarity and the Struggle for Justice*, ed. Jewish Voice for Peace (Chicago: Haymarket Books, 2017), 207–12 (207–8).

2. See chapter 7.

3. Butler, "Foreword" to *On Antisemitism*, ix. See also Judith Butler, "No, It's Not Anti-Semitic," 19–21.

4. Butler, "Foreword," xi.

5. Activists often cite works such as Norman Finkelstein, *The Holocaust Industry: Reflections on the Exploitation of Jewish Suffering* (London: Verso, 2000), as formative in their capacity to expose manipulative uses of the Holocaust.

6. Wise, "Building toward the Next World," 210.

7. For JVP's earliest efforts to systematically examine antisemitism in relation to Palestine solidarity activism, see Jewish Voice for Peace, *Reframing Anti-Semitism: Alternative Jewish Perspectives* (Oakland, CA: Jewish Voice for Peace, 2004).

8. Other churches that voted for selective divestment include the United Church of Christ (2015) and the Mennonite Church USA (2017). Those that considered but ultimately rejected such a proposal include the Evangelical Lutheran Church in America (2005) and the United Methodist Church (2012). The latter, however, passed in 2017 multiple regional resolutions to defend the right to divest.

9. "Susanna Nachenberg, Another Jew Supporting Divestment: Reflections from the Presbyterian Divestment Vote," June 24, 2014, http://sumogaza.tumblr.com/post/92874855655/another-jew-supporting-divestment-reflections (site discontinued).

10. For instance, Chris Leighton, "An Open Letter to the Presbyterian Church," Institute

for Christian and Jewish Studies, February 6, 2014, https://icjs.org/articles/2014/open-letter
-presbyterian-church.

11. Israel/Palestine Mission Network of the Presbyterian Church (U.S.A.), *Zionism Unsettled: A Congregational Study Guide* (2014).

12. Ellis, "The Mennonites and the Interfaith Ecumenical Deal," *Mondoweiss*, July 10, 2017, http://mondoweiss.net/2017/07/mennonites-interfaith-ecumenical/. Ellis's contribution in articulating a Jewish Palestine liberation theology is significant. See, for example, Ellis, *Judaism Does Not Equal Israel: The Rebirth of the Jewish Prophetic* (New York: New Press, 2010); and Ellis, *Toward a Jewish Theology of Liberation* (Baylor University Press, [1987] 2010). For a similar line, see Mark Braverman, *Fatal Embrace: Christians, Jews, and the Search for Peace in the Holy Land* (Austin, TX: Synergy Books, 2010).

13. See chapter 4 for this discussion.

14. Mennonite Church USA, "Seeking Peace in Israel and Palestine: A Resolution for Mennonite Church USA," for consideration by the Delegate Assembly at Orlando 2017, accessed November 4, 2017, http://mennoniteusa.org/wp-content/uploads/2017/01/IP-Resolution.pdf.

15. Jonathan Brenneman reported that the main objection to the failed 2015 resolution was that it appeared "one sided, non-reconciliatory, hypocritical, unfair to Israel, and anti-Semitic" (email to author, August 4, 2017). See Mennonite Church USA, "Israel-Palestine Resolution: Summary of Delegate Comments," considered and tabled by delegates, July 1, 2015, Kansas City, http://mennoniteusa.org/wp-content/uploads/2015/04/SummaryDelegateComments_Israel PalestineResolutions.pdf.

16. http://mennoniteusa.org/news/come-see-tours-enable-leaders-learn-israelpalestine/; Mennonite Church USA, "'Jewish and Palestinian Voices for Peace Tour' announced," March 17, 2017, http://mennoniteusa.org/news/jewish-palestinian-voices-peace-tour-announced/. The relationship building and awareness raising also involved a webinar entitled "A Rabbi and a Pastor Walk through a Checkpoint" featuring Amy Yoder McGloughlin (a Mennonite pastor) and Rabbi Linda Holtzman (JVP) about "relating to Jewish neighbors while working for justice in Palestine." In addition, the coordinating committee launched a speaking tour highlighting "Jewish and Palestinian Voices for Peace." The tour featured Jonathan Kuttab (a Palestinian human rights lawyer affiliated with the Mennonites), who visited at least twenty locations, where he engaged local JVP representatives who spoke, among other things, about how their own experiences of antisemitism led them to engage in justice work for Palestinians. Likewise, a video highlighted the perspectives of Mennonites of color about issues raised by the resolution. See Friends of Sabeel North America FOSNA, Facebook video, July 6, 2017, https://www.facebook .com/fosnalive/videos/1698418443520241/.

17. Email correspondence with Jonathan Brenneman, August 4, 2017.

18. See also Brant Rosen, *Wrestling in the Daylight: A Rabbi's Path to Palestinian Solidarity* (Charlottesville, VA: Just World Books, [2012] 2017), 211.

19. Key works in Christian Palestinian liberation theology include Naim Stifan Ateek, *Justice, and Only Justice: A Palestinian Theology of Liberation* (Maryknoll, NY: Orbis Books, 1989); Ateek, *A Palestinian Christian Cry for Reconciliation* (Maryknoll, NY: Orbis Books, 2008); Jean Zaru, *Occupied with Nonviolence: A Palestinian Woman Speaks*, ed. Diana Eck and Marla Schrader (Minneapolis: Fortress Press, 2008); and Laura Robson, "Palestinian Liberation Theology, Muslim-Christian Relations and the Arab-Israeli Conflict," *Islam and Christian-Muslim Relations* 21, no. 1 (2010): 39–50.

20. For an engagement with this question, see Atalia Omer, "The Cry of the Forgotten

Stones: A Palestinian Liberation Theology and the Limits of a Theology for the Oppressed as a Peacebuilding Method," *Journal of Religious Ethics* 43, no. 2 (January 2015): 369–407.

21. For examples of Jewish-Muslim-Arab co-resistance and solidarity amid anti-Muslim and antisemitic bigotry in the age of Trump, see Sofia Ali-Khan, "Other Together: American Jewish-Muslim Solidarity in the Age of Trump," *Jewschool: Progressive Jews & Views*, July 21, 2017, https://jewschool.com/2017/07/79896/jewish-and-muslim-solidarity-age-trump/; and Colby Itkowitz, "'Stand Together Against Bigotry': Another Jewish Cemetery Vandalized and Again Muslims Reach Out to Help," *Washington Post*, February 27, 2017, https://www.washingtonpost .com/news/inspired-life/wp/2017/02/27/stand-together-against-this-bigotry-another-jewish -cemetery-vandalized-and-again-muslims-reach-out-to-help/. For examples of specifically inter-communal grassroots organization, see Sisterhood of Salaam Shalom, "Who We Are," accessed November 4, 2017, https://sosspeace.org/who-we-are/sisterhood/; and NYC Muslim-Jewish Solidarity Committee, "Our Mission and Values," accessed November 4, 2017, http://nyc .muslimjewishsolidarity.org/mission/.

22. Jewish Voice for Peace, "Jewish Groups Stand in Opposition to Hate Speech and All Forms of Islamophobia," April 28, 2015, https://jewishvoiceforpeace.org/jewish-groups-stand -in-opposition-to-hate-speech-and-all-forms-of-islamophobia/.

23. See also chapter 7.

24. For an exposition of this frame, see Mahmood Mamdani, *Good Muslim, Bad Muslim: America, the Cold War, and Roots of Terror* (New York: Pantheon Books, 2004).

25. See also Shaul Magid, "On Antisemitism and Its Uses," in *On Antisemitism*, 59–69 (62).

26. Butler, "No, It's Not Anti-Semitic."

27. See, for instance, Benjamin Balthaser's discussion of overt antisemitism he experienced growing up in rural California, where the antisemitic tropes emerged clearly from local churches in sermons and other settings. Balthaser, "Lessons on Anti-Semitism from Growing Up in Rural America," *Jewschool: Progressive Jews & Views*, November 30, 2017, https://jewschool.com/2016/ 11/78215/anti-semitism-in-the-trump-era-what-i-learned-growing-up-in-rural-america/. See also Stephen Glain, "Zealots Are Trying to Turn the Military into a Religious Army, Mikey Weinstein Is Fighting Back," *The Nation*, February 10, 2011, https://www.thenation.com/article/ backward-christian-soldiers-2/; and April Rosenblum, *The Past Didn't Go Anywhere: Making Resistance to Antisemitism Part of All Our Movements* (self-pub., 2007), https://archive.org/ details/ThePastDidntGoAnywhere.

28. Gary Spedding, "We in the Palestinian Solidarity Movement Have a Problem with Anti-Semitism," *Haaretz*, July 23, 2016, https://www.haaretz.com/opinion/.premium-1.732735.

29. See, for instance, the 2005 international conference "Zionism as the Biggest Threat to Modern Civilization," co-chaired by David Duke, who later endorsed Donald Trump, whose campaign explicitly invoked antisemitic tropes. The conference's title evokes a classical trope, embedded in Christian theology and history, of the demonic, power-hungry Jew.

30. Spedding, "We in the Palestinian Solidarity Movement."

31. Interview #6.

32. Merkley, *The Politics of Christian Zionism*; Donald Wagner and Walter T. Davis, eds., *Zionism and the Quest for Justice in the Holy Land* (Eugene, OR: Wipf and Stock Publishers, 2014); Paul S. Rowe, John H. A. Dyck, and Jens Zimmerman, eds., *Christians and the Middle East Conflict* (London: Routledge, 2014); and Robert O. Smith, *More Desired Than Our Owne Salvation* (New York: Oxford University Press, 2013).

33. Stephen Specter, *Evangelicals and Israel: The Story of American Christian Zionism* (New York: Oxford University Press, 2009); and Steven Fink, "Fear Under Construction: Islamopho-

bia Within American Christian Zionism," *Islamophobia Studies Journal* 2, no. 1 (Spring 2014): 26–43.

34. Interview #47.

35. Interview #26.

36. Interview #13.

37. Omer, "Cry of the Forgotten Stones."

38. Rosenblum, *The Past Didn't Go Anywhere.*

39. Ibid., 14.

40. Ibid., 5, 10.

41. Ben Lorber, a JVP campus organizer, noted shortly after the violent eruption of white supremacy in Charlottesville, VA, on August 12, 2017, that Herzl had appealed to the widespread fear among American Jews of radical socialism to promote his Zionism. "Today," Lorber writes, "many American Jews—even many descendants of Holocaust survivors—are unwilling to join left movements against fascism, because they're convinced that leftist anti-Zionism is anti-Semitism. In fact, they're joining in right-wing efforts to bash these justice movements by falsely accusing them of antisemitism. A century later, Zionism is working exactly as it was designed—to weaken the left and isolate Jews from justice movements." Lorber, Facebook post, August 16, 2017, https://www.facebook.com/ben.lorber.1/posts/ (site discontinued).

42. See, for example, the platform of the Jewish Solidarity Caucus (an informal group of Jews organizing with Democratic Socialists of America), August 9, 2017, https://medium.com/@jewishsocialism/dsa-jewish-solidarity-caucus-a26f94f9212a. The JSC sees itself as operating within the deep roots of the Jewish socialist (and anti-Zionist) tradition.

43. In March 2017, the Israeli parliament amended the Law of Entry to prevent activists and leaders of BDS from entering the country. See Ari Paul, "Israel Criminalizes Thought by Banning BDS Supporters in Orwellian Twist," *Forward*, March 9, 2017, http://forward.com/opinion/365534/israel-criminalizes-thought-by-banning-bds-supporters-in-orwellian-twist/; Alissa Wise, "I'm the First Jew Banned from Israel for Supporting BDS," *Forward*, July 26, 2017, http://forward.com/opinion/israel/378100/im-first-pro-bds-jew-israel-banned/; and "Rabbinic Letter Against Israel's Travel Ban," signed by 234 rabbis, *Medium*, August 8, 2017, https://medium.com/@rabbisagainsttheban/rabbis-against-the-ban-17585c59c74b. This parliamentary decision resulted in issuing an extensive list of twenty anti-occupation groups active in BDS, including JVP, as prohibited entry to Israel. See Noa Landau, "Israel Publishes BDS Blacklist: These Are the 20 Groups Whose Members Will Be Denied Entry," *Haaretz*, January 7, 2018, https://www.haaretz.com/israel-news/1.833502. This decision galvanized a wave of angry reactions from American Jews across the spectrum. See David Rothkopf, "Israel Is Becoming an Illiberal Thugocracy, and I'm Running Out of Ways to Defend It," *Haaretz*, January 8, 2018, https://www.haaretz.com/opinion/1.833634; Rebecca Vilkomerson, "I'm a U.S. Jew on Israel's BDS Blacklist. I Have Family in Israel. But I Won't Be Silenced," *Haaretz*, January 7, 2018, https://www.haaretz.com/opinion/1.833516; and Mira Sucharov, "BDS Blacklist: Sadly, Now Might Be the Time for Jews to Boycott Israel," January 7, 2018, https://www.haaretz.com/opinion/.premium-1.833538.

44. For example, the Zionist Organization of America invited Stephen Bannon (a known antisemite and white nationalist) to speak at a gathering on November 9, 2017. INN activists protested the event, crying, "if you openly support the occupation, you are on Stephen Bannon's side." See IfNotNow, Facebook post, November 12, 2017, https://m.facebook.com/story.php?story_fbid=1549837565103206&id=678900828863555. See also note 77 below.

45. Associated Press, "Demonization of George Soros throughout Europe Recalls Anti-

Semitic Conspiracy Theories of Yore," *Haaretz*, July 10, 2017, https://www.haaretz.com/world-news/europe/1.789307.

46. Yair Netanyahu, son of Israel's prime minister, came under intense fire when he reproduced classical antisemitic caricature of Soros, betraying ignorance of the semiotic meanings of the images. See, for instance, Andrew Tobin, "Yair Netanyahu Exposes Israel's Own Version of the 'Alt-Right,'" *Times of Israel*, September 12, 2017, https://www.timesofisrael.com/yair-netanyahu-exposes-israels-own-version-of-the-alt-right/.

47. Allison Kaplan Sommer and Bar Peleg, "'Racist and Discriminatory': U.S. Jewish Leaders Warn Israel against Passage of Nation-State Bill," *Haaretz*, July 15, 2018, https://www.haaretz.com/israel-news/.premium-u-s-jewish-chiefs-warn-against-passage-of-racist-nation-state-bill-1.6270788.

48. Max Fisher, "Israel Picks Identity over Democracy. More Nations May Follow," *New York Times*, July 22, 2018, https://www.nytimes.com/2018/07/22/world/middleeast/israel-jewish-state-nationality-law.html.

49. *Haaretz*, "White Nationalist Richard Spencer Backs Israel's Contentious Nation-State Law," July 22, 2018, https://www.haaretz.com/israel-news/israeli-nation-state-law-backed-by-white-nationalist-richard-spencer-1.6295314.

50. Ofer Aderet and Noa Landau, "Yad Vashem Rebukes Netanyahu: Israel-Poland Holocaust Declaration Contains 'Grave Errors and Deceptions,'" *Haaretz*, July 5, 2018, https://www.haaretz.com/jewish/.premium-yad-vashem-israel-poland-declaration-is-historically-inaccurate-1.6244829.

51. David Sarna Galdi, "With New Laws, Netanyahu Is Hijacking Judaism as We Know It," *+972 Magazine*, July 22, 2018, https://972mag.com/with-new-laws-netanyahu-is-hijacking-judaism-as-we-know-it/136790/.

52. Hillel Ben-Sasson, "Attacking Soros: Israel's Unholy Covenant with Europe's Anti-Semitic Ultra-Right," *Haaretz*, July 12, 2017, https://www.haaretz.com/opinion/1.800967. On invitations extended by Zionist organizations to white nationalists and known Nazi sympathizers, see David A. Love, "Right-Wing Zionism, White Supremacy and the BDS," *Al Jazeera*, September 29, 2017, http://www.aljazeera.com/indepth/opinion/wing-zionism-white-supremacy-bds-170929071542094.html. Love contrasts the welcome shown to explicit antisemites with the millions raised to fight Jewish and non-Jewish BDS activists.

53. IfNotNow, Facebook post, July 12, 2017, https://www.facebook.com/IfNotNowOrg/posts/1431210513632579.

54. Theodor Herzl was explicit about the instrumental role of "respectable anti-Semites" in implementing political Zionism and Zionist colonization of Palestine. See, for instance, Brant Rosen, "Zionism's Marriage of Convenience to Anti-Semitism," *Shalom Rav*, February 19, 2017, https://rabbibrant.com/2017/02/19/on-zionisms-marriage-of-convenience-to-anti-semitism/. See also Ben Lorber, "Understanding Alt-Right Antisemitism," *Doikayt*, March 24, 2017, https://doikayt.com/2017/03/24/understanding-alt-right-antisemitism/.

55. For instances of antisemitic attacks and their surge around Trump's ascendancy, see Associated Press, "American Jews Alarmed By Surge in Anti-Semitism," *Fortune*, November 17, 2016, http://fortune.com/2016/11/17/anti-semitism-donald-trump-jews/; Mark Oppenheimer, "Is Anti-Semitism on the Rise? Does Anyone Care?," *Chicago Tribune*, February 19, 2017, http://www.chicagotribune.com/news/opinion/commentary/ct-antisemitism-jews-trump-alt-right-20170218-story.html; and Ashley Lisenby, "For Some Families, Pain at Finding Vandalized Headstones at University City Cemetery," *St. Louis Post-Dispatch*, February 1, 2017, http://www

.stltoday.com/news/local/crime-and-courts/for-some-families-pain-at-finding-vandalized
-headstones-at-university/article_bafef56a-6ef2–5f90-a327–0ba7fa11e50b.html.

56. Pew Research Center, "A Portrait of Jewish Americans," October 1, 2013, http://www
.pewforum.org/2013/10/01/jewish-american-beliefs-attitudes-culture-survey/, 46.

57. See, for example, Richard Spencer, "Facing the Future as a Minority," speech at the
American Renaissance Conference, April 30, 2013, Montgomery Bell State Park.

58. Greg Johnson, "White Nationalism & Jewish Nationalism," *Counter-Currents Publishing*
(blog), August 5, 2011, http://www.counter-currents.com/2011/08/white-nationalism-jewish
-nationalism/. For a critical analysis of the coalescing of antisemitism and Zionism within
American white supremacy, see Sam Kestenbaum, "The 'Alt-Right' Hates the Jews. But It Also
Loves Them—And Israel," *Forward*, January 16, 2017, http://forward.com/news/359889/the-alt
-right-hates-the-jews-but-it-also-loves-them-and-israel/.

59. Lorber, "Understanding Alt-Right Antisemitism."

60. Spencer, "Facing the Future"; *Haaretz*, "Richard Spencer Tells Israelis They 'Should
Respect' Him: 'I'm a White Zionist,'" *Haaretz*, August 16, 2017, http://www.haaretz.com/israel
-news/1.807335. By contrast, another white supremacist leader, Andrew Anglin, who runs the
neo-Nazi site *Daily Stormer*, writes: "The goal is to ethnically cleanse white nations of nonwhites
and establish an authoritarian government. Many people also believe that the Jews should be
exterminated." Anglin is critical of US-Israel relations, deeming them an expression of diabolic
Jewish power. Kestenbaum, "The 'Alt-Right' Hates the Jews."

61. Greg Johnson, "White Nationalism"; Southern Poverty Law Center, "Kevin MacDonald," accessed November 4, 2017, https://www.splcenter.org/fighting-hate/extremist-files/
individual/kevin-macdonald.

62. Lorber, "Understanding Alt-Right Antisemitism."

63. See, for example, Jared Taylor, *White Identity: Racial Consciousness in the 21st Century*
(Quezon City, Philippines: New Century Books, 2011).

64. Jay Michaelson, "Why Trump's Jewish Backers Love the Alt-Right," *Daily Beast*, August 15, 2017, http://www.thedailybeast.com/why-trumps-jewish-backers-love-the-alt-right.

65. Eric K. Ward, "Skin in the Game: How Antisemitism Animates White Nationalism,"
Political Research Associates, June 29, 2017, http://www.politicalresearch.org/2017/06/29/skin-in
-the-game-how-antisemitism-animates-white-nationalism/.

66. Ibid. On the specifics of neo-Nazi intellectualizing of these claims, see Kevin MacDonald, *The Culture of Critique* (Westport, CT: Praeger Publishers, 1998); MacDonald, "Jews and the
Civil Rights Movement," *Occidental Observer*, June 5, 2013, http://www.theoccidentalobserver
.net/2013/06/jews-and-the-civil-rights-movement/; and MacDonald, "Jewish Involvement in
Shaping American Immigration Policy, 1881–1965: A Historical Review," *Population and Environment: A Journal of Interdisciplinary Studies* 19, no. 4 (March 1998): 295–356.

67. Ward, "Skin in the Game."

68. Yair Rosenberg, "'Jews Will Not Replace Us': Why White Supremacists Go after Jews,"
Washington Post, August 14, 2017, https://www.washingtonpost.com/news/acts-of-faith/wp/
2017/08/14/jews-will-not-replace-us-why-white-supremacists-go-after-jews/.

69. During Netanyahu's first visit to the Trump White House, in response to a journalist
who probed Trump about his manifest Holocaust denial, Netanyahu said, "Nobody loves Israel
more than Donald Trump." Here, a political figure who has never missed an opportunity to
speak in the name of all Jews and raise red flags about existential danger ironically capitulates to
Holocaust denial. His son, likewise, offered a Trump-like condemnation of "all sides" involved
in neo-Nazi violence in Charlottesville, VA, in August 2017. See TOI Staff and AFP, "Yair Netan-

yahu Says Leftists More Dangerous Than Neo-Nazis," *Times of Israel*, August 16, 2017, http://www.timesofisrael.com/netanyahu-junior-says-leftists-more-dangerous-than-neo-nazis/.

70. See chapter 3 on experiences of estrangement from Israeli society.

71. Dann, "Richard Spencer Might Be the Worst Person in America But He's Right About Israel," *Forward*, August 17, 2017, http://forward.com/opinion/380384/richard-spencer-israel/.

72. *Haaertz*, "Richard Spencer Tells Israelis."

73. Josh Nathan-Kazis, "'Alt-Right' Leader Ties White Supremacy to Zionism—Leaves Rabbi Speechless," *Forward*, December 7, 2016, http://forward.com/news/356336/alt-right-leader-ties-white-supremacy-to-zionism-leaves-rabbi-speechless/.

74. Dann, "Richard Spencer."

75. Ibid. For a similar intersectional conclusion, see Michael Chabon and Ayelet Waldman, "An Open Letter to Our Fellow Jews," *Medium*, August 17, 2017, https://medium.com/@vanzorn/to-our-fellow-jews-in-the-united-states-in-israel-and-around-the-world-ff421a1d325d.

76. See also chapter 4.

77. Batya Ungar-Sargon, "ZOA Rolled Out the Red Carpet for Steve Bannon—And It Backfired," November 13, 2017, *Forward*, https://forward.com/opinion/387527/zoa-rolled-out-the-red-carpet-for-steve-bannon-and-it-backfired/; and Peter Beinart, "Bannon Is Not an Anti-Semite. He's Something Worse," *Forward*, November 22, 2017, https://forward.com/opinion/israel/388194/actually-steve-bannon-is-not-an-anti-semite-hes-something-worse/. See also note 44 above.

78. See chapter 7 as well.

79. For a recording of the event featuring Linda Sarsour (a Palestinian American Muslim social justice activist and often a target of the American Jewish mainstream media and establishment), two JOCSM—Leo Ferguson (of Jews for Racial & Economic Justice) and Lina Morales (JVP)—as well as Rebecca Vilkomerson (executive director of JVP), see *Jacobin Magazine*, "Antisemitism and the Struggle for Justice: Antisemitism Is Real and Harmful. But It's Not the Same as Criticism of Israel," November 28, 2017, https://www.facebook.com/jacobinmag/videos/vb.143021112391265/1965805270112831/.

80. IfNotNow, "LIVE IN CHICAGO: Jews and Allies Are Protesting at Trump Tower," Facebook video, August 20, 2017, https://www.facebook.com/IfNotNowOrg/videos/1471403956279901/.

81. Leslie Williams, "White Jews: Deal with Your Privilege and Call Out Jewish Support for White Supremacy," *Unruly* (blog), August 23, 2017, http://jocsm.org/white-jews-deal-with-your-privilege-and-call-out-jewish-support-for-white-supremacy/ (emphasis in original).

82. Tseng-Putterman, Twitter, January 6, 2017, https://twitter.com/tsengputterman/status/817494208034537473. The main arguments were later reproduced in a blog post format: Tseng-Putterman, "More Than a Feeling: Jews and Whiteness in Trump's America," *JOCSM*, February 23, 2017, http://jocsm.org/more-than-a-feeling-jews-and-whiteness-in-trumps-america/.

83. Tseng-Putterman, "More Than a Feeling"; and Brodkin, "How Jews Became White Folks—and May Become Nonwhite Under Trump," *Forward*, December 6, 2016, http://forward.com/opinion/356166/how-jews-became-white-folks-and-may-become-nonwhite-under-trump/. Brodkin illustrates Jews' ambivalent relation to whiteness in America—their relative whiteness in relation to blackness. She particularly highlights the post-WWII era as a turning point for Jews, especially in light of prominent Jewish intellectual emigres and the delegitimizing of Semitic racializing categories, as well as economic dynamics that enabled many Jews to transition from working class to middle class, stressing the intricate connections between race and class. Brodkin's original analysis of Jews' whiteness focused only on Ashkenazi Jews, universal-

izing their experience as though all Jews were light-skinned and of European origin. She regrets this assumption in "White Jews, Whiteness, & Anti-Semitism," *Treyf*, a podcast hosted by Sam Bick and David Zinman, January 3, 2017.

84. See chapter 7.

85. Tseng-Putterman, Twitter, January 6, 2017, https://twitter.com/tsengputterman/status/817500782929055747.

86. See "Short: Jews & Whiteness with Mark Tseng-Putterman," *Treyf*, January 18, 2017.

87. Eric L. Goldstein, *The Price of Whiteness: Jews, Race, and American Identity* (Princeton, NJ: Princeton University Press, 2006), 5.

88. Ibid., 221.

89. Baldwin, "On Being 'White.'" See also chapter 7.

90. Sigal Samuel, "For Sephardic and Mizrahi Jews, Whiteness Was a Fragile Identity Long Before Trump," *Forward*, December 6, 2016, http://forward.com/opinion/356271/for-sephardic-and-mizrahi-jews-whiteness-was-a-fragile-identity-long-before/.

91. See, for instance, Public Autonomy Project, "The Rise of the Post-New Left Political Vocabulary," January 27, 2014, https://publicautonomy.org/2014/01/27/the-rise-of-the-post-new-left-political-vocabulary/.

92. JVP, *On Antisemitism*, 3.

93. "JVP Statement on Antisemitism," in *On Antisemitism*, 213.

94. Ibid., 214.

95. JFREJ, "Understanding Antisemitism: An Offering to Our Movement: A Resource from Jews for Racial & Economic Justice," November 2017, http://jfrej.org/wp-content/uploads/2017/12/JFREJ-Understanding-Antisemitism-November-2017-v1–3.pdf.

96. Ibid., 4.

97. Ibid.

98. Ibid.

99. Ibid., 5 and 11–13, for instance. See also chapter 7.

100. Ibid., 13–14.

101. Ibid., 15.

102. Magid, "On Antisemitism," 68.

103. ADL, "2017 Audit of Anti-Semitic Incidents," accessed March 21, 2018, https://www.adl.org/resources/reports/2017-audit-of-anti-semitic-incidents.

104. JFREJ, "Understanding Antisemitism," 6.

105. Ibid., 19. See also 27.

106. Ibid., 25.

107. See chapter 7 for an exposition of Baldwin's and Bouteldja's discussion of love.

108. Ibid., 9.

109. Ibid., 21.

110. Ibid., 23.

111. Chanda Prescod-Weinstein, "Black and Palestinian Lives Matter: Black and Jewish America in the Twenty-First Century," in *On Antisemitism*, 31–41 (33).

112. Ibid., 34.

113. Ibid., 35. See my discussion in chapter 7 of black-Jewish relations in the US and their relevance to Palestine solidarity work. See also Feldman, *A Shadow over Palestine*, which examines how the Israel/Palestine complexities have influenced race dynamics in the US.

114. Prescod-Weinstein, "Black and Palestinian Lives Matter," 39.

115. See chapter 7 for this discussion.

116. JFREJ, "Living Our Values: A Letter from JFREJ Executive Director Audrey Sasson," March 16, 2018, http://jfrej.org/living-our-values-a-letter-from-jfrej-executive-director-audrey-sasson/.

117. Ibid.

118. Ibid.

119. See Terrell Jermaine Starr, "A Word About Louis Farrakhan and Tamika Mallory," *The Root*, March 9, 2018, https://www.theroot.com/a-word-about-louis-farrakhan-and-tamika-mallory-1823607435.

120. IfNotNow, "IfNotNow Statement on Louis Farrakhan, Women's March, and Antisemitism," March 9, 2018, https://medium.com/ifnotnoworg/ifnotnow-statement-on-louis-farrakhan-womens-march-and-antisemitism-509946e4b2c9.

121. Ibid.

122. Ilise Benshushan Cohen, "Intersections of Antisemitism, Racism, and Nationalism: A Sephardi/Mizrahi Perspective," in *On Antisemitism*, 43–57 (45). Pursuing the same line of analysis is Tallie Ben Daniel, "Antisemitism, Palestine, and the Mizrahi Question," in *On Antisemitism*, 71–80. The mechanism for rendering Mizrahiness invisible, Ben Daniel argues, relates to the employment of European categories and experiences to analyze Mizrahi histories, and constitutes a form of epistemic violence. See Ben Daniel, "Antisemitism," 74. Her analysis relies on the radical Mizrahi discourse developed by Ella Shohat in, for instance, "Sephardim in Israel: Zionism from the Standpoint of Its Jewish Victims," *Social Text* 19/20 (1988): 1–35; and Shohat, "The Invention of the Mizrahim," *Journal of Palestine Studies* 29, no. 1 (Autumn 1999): 5–20. See also Yehouda Shenhav, *The Arab Jews: A Postcolonial Reading of Nationalism, Religion, and Ethnicity* (Stanford, CA: Stanford University Press, 2006); Orit Bashkin, *New Babylonians: A History of Jews in Modern Iraq* (Stanford, CA: Stanford University Press, 2012); and Bashkin, *The Other Iraq: Pluralism and Culture in Hashemite Iraq* (Stanford, CA: Stanford University Press, 2008).

123. Benshushan Cohen, "Intersections of Antisemitism," 46.

124. Ibid., 46.

125. Ibid., 47.

126. Ibid.

127. Ibid.

128. Ibid., 56.

129. Ben Daniel, "Antisemitism," 75.

130. In particular she discusses the work of JIMENA (Jews Indigenous to the Middle East and North Africa). See "Antisemitism," 78–79.

131. Ibid., 79–80.

132. Ibid., 80.

133. Edward W. Said, *Humanism and Democratic Criticism* (New York: Columbia University Press, 2003), 10–11. His defense of humanism directly responds to earlier criticism of his *Orientalism* for retaining "residual humanism" despite its importation of Foucault. See James Clifford, "Review of *Orientalism*," *History and Theory* 19, no. 2 (February 1980): 204–23.

134. Dabashi, *Post-Orientalism Knowledge & Power in a Time of Terror* (London: Transaction Publishers, [2009] 2015), 162. Dabashi further argues that both Said and Spivak need to be disabused of their inclination to always posit European thought as their interlocutor. See ibid., chapters 3 and 4.

135. See chapter 4 for an exposition of Judith Butler's rereading of Foucault's "What Is Cri-

tique?" as offering a path for virtuous self-transformation. See chapter 2 for a discussion of projective imagination and transformative agency.

136. Efrat Yerday, remarks on panel "Let's Talk About Zionism," JVP National Member Meeting, April 1, 2017, Chicago, IL.

Chapter Nine

1. See the discussion of Marshall Ganz's concept of "public narrative" in chapter 2.

2. On James M. Jasper's concept of "moral batteries" in social movements, see chapter 2, as well as chapters 3 and 4.

3. See chapter 4.

4. See especially chapter 7.

5. Steven Davidson, "Progressive Jewish Millennials Are Returning to Their Roots—Thanks to Trump," *Times of Israel*, March 16, 2018, https://www.timesofisrael.com/progressive-jewish-millennials-are-returning-to-their-roots-thanks-to-trump/.

6. The subfield is also often referred to as Religion, Conflict, and Peacebuilding (RCP). See Douglas Johnston and Cynthia Sampson, *Religion, the Missing Dimension of Statecraft* (New York: Oxford University Press, 1994); R. Scott Appleby, *The Ambivalence of the Sacred: Religion, Violence, and Reconciliation* (Lanham, MD: Rowman & Littlefield, 2000); Atalia Omer, R. Scott Appleby, and David Little, eds., *The Oxford Handbook of Religion, Conflict, and Peacebuilding* (Oxford: Oxford University Press, 2015); and Harold Coward and Gordon S. Smith, eds., *Religion and Peacebuilding* (Albany, NY: SUNY Press, 2004).

7. See Atalia Omer, "Religious Peacebuilding: The Exotic, the Good, and the Theatrical," in *Oxford Handbook of Religion, Conflict, and Peacebuilding*, 3–32; and Omer, "Interreligious Action as a Driver for Social Cohesion and Development," in *Interreligious Action for Peace: Studies in Muslim-Christian Cooperation*, ed. Tom Bamat, Nell Bolton, Myla Leguro, and Atalia Omer (Baltimore: Catholic Relief Services Press, 2017), 1–20. On the secularism thesis, see William T. Cavanaugh, *The Myth of Religious Violence: Secular Ideology and the Roots of Modern Conflict* (Oxford: Oxford University Press, 2009); Mark Juergensmeyer and Jonathan VanAntwerpen, eds., *Rethinking Secularism* (Oxford: Oxford University Press, 2011); and Hurd, *The Politics of Secularism in International Relations*.

8. Martin E. Marty and R. Scott Appleby, eds., *The Fundamentalism Project*, 5 vols. (Chicago: University of Chicago Press, 1991–1995); Karen Armstrong, *Fields of Blood: Religion and the History of Violence* (New York: Alfred A. Knopf, 2014); Sudhir Kakar, *The Colors of Violence: Cultural Identities, Religion, and Conflict* (Chicago: University of Chicago Press, 1996); Jolyon Mitchell, *Promoting Peace, Inciting Violence: The Role of Religion and Media* (London: Routledge, 2012); Mark Juergensmeyer, *Terror in the Mind of God: The Global Rise of Religious Violence* (Los Angeles: University of California Press, 2003); and Mark Juergensmeyer, Margo Kitts, and Michael Jerryson, eds., *The Oxford Handbook of Religion and Violence* (Oxford: Oxford University Press, 2015).

9. Chris Seiple, Dennis R. Hoover, and Pauletta Otis, eds., *The Routledge Handbook of Religion and Security* (London: Routledge, 2013); Fabio Petito and Pavlos Hatzopoulos, eds., *Religion in International Relations: The Return from Exile* (Palgrave, 2013); and Giorgio Shani, *Religion, Identity and Human Security* (London: Routledge, 2014). For important interventions in the religion and security (and terrorism) debates, see Cecelia Lynch, "A Neo-Weberian Approach to Studying Religion and Violence," *Millennium: Journal of International Studies* 43 (September

2014): 273–90; and Luca Mavelli and Erin Wilson, eds., *The Refugee Crisis and Religion: Secularism, Security and Hospitality in Question* (Lanham, MD: Rowman & Littlefield, 2016).

10. Peter Mandaville and Melissa Nozell, "Engaging Religion and Religious Actors in Countering Violent Extremism," United States Institute of Peace Special Report 413, August 2017, https://www.usip.org/sites/default/files/SR413-Engaging-Religion-and-Religious-Actors-in -Countering-Violent-Extremism.pdf; Jeffrey Haynes, *Faith-Based Organizations at the United Nations* (London: Routledge, 2014); Jeffrey Haynes, *Religious Transnational Actors and Soft Power* (London: Routledge, 2012); Susan Hayward and Katherine Marshall, eds., *Women, Religion, and Peacebuilding* (Washington, DC: USIP Press, 2015); Patrick James, ed., *Religion, Identity, and Global Governance* (Toronto: University of Toronto Press, 2011); and Erin Wilson, *After Secularism: Rethinking Religion in Global Politics* (London: Palgrave Macmillan, 2012). For an important engagement with the secularist and modernist underpinnings of development and humanitarian work, see Cecelia Lynch and Tanya B. Schwartz, "Humanitarianism's Proselytism Problem," *International Studies Quarterly* 60, no. 4 (December 2016): 636–46.

11. For instance, see Elizabeth Shakman Hurd, *Beyond Religious Freedom: The New Global Politics of Religion* (Princeton, NJ: Princeton University Press, 2015). For my engagement with her argument there, see Omer, "When 'Good Religion' Is Good," *Journal of Religious and Political Practice* 4, no. 1 (2018): 122–36.

12. Mahmood, *Religious Difference in a Secular Age.*

13. See, for instance, Rosalind I. J. Hackett, "Regulating Religious Freedom in Africa," *Emory International Law Review* 25 no. 2 (2011): 853–79.

14. See also Omer, "When 'Good Religion' Is Good."

15. See Victoria C. Fontan, *Decolonizing Peace* (Lake Oswego, OR: Dignity Press, 2012); and Heidi Hudson, "Decolonizing The Mainstreaming of Gender in Peacebuilding: Toward an Agenda for Africa," African Peacebuilding Network Working Papers, no. 8 (July 2016), Social Science Research Council Working Papers, http://webarchive.ssrc.org/working-papers/APN _WorkingPapers_08_Hudson.pdf.

16. For example, see Tomoko Masuzawa, *The Invention of World Religions: Or, How European Universalism Was Preserved in the Language of Pluralism* (Chicago: University of Chicago Press, 2005); Donald S. Lopez Jr., *Prisoners of Shangri-La: Tibetan Buddhism and the West* (Chicago: University of Chicago Press, 1998); David Chidester, *Savage Systems: Colonialism and Comparative Religion in Southern Africa* (Charlottesville: University of Virginia Press, 1996); and his *Empire of Religion: Imperialism and Comparative Religion* (Chicago: University of Chicago Press, 2014).

17. For instance, Susan Hayward, "Religion and Peacebuilding: Reflections on Current Challenges and Future Prospect," United States Institute of Peace Special Report 313, August 2012, https://www.usip.org/sites/default/files/SR313.pdf; Sara Silvestri and James Mayall, *The Role of Religion in Conflict and Peacebuilding* (London: British Academy, 2015), https://www .britac.ac.uk/sites/default/files/Role-of-religion-in-conflict-peacebuilding_0.pdf; and Katherine Marshall, Lauren Herzog, and Wilma Mui, "Religious Dimensions of Development: Lessons at the Country Level," Berkeley Center for Religion, Peace & World Affairs: World Faiths Development Dialogue, March 29, 2017, https://s3.amazonaws.com/berkley-center/ 170329BCWFDDReligiousDimensionsDevelopmentLessonsCountryLevel.pdf.

18. For example, Hayward and Marshall, *Women, Religion, and Peacebuilding.*

19. John Paul Lederach's account of moral imagination is promising, but lacks the discursive angle and the tools of critical theory that deepen the moral imagination and conceptions of

solidarity. Lederach, *The Moral Imagination: The Art and Soul of Building Peace* (Oxford: Oxford University Press, 2010).

20. For instance, Zubrzycki, *Beheading the Saint*, is insightful in how it traces the aesthetic, embodied sociocultural practices involved in enacting secular identities in Québec and subsequently reframing Québécois identity itself as secular, a process involving reshaping the "ghosts" of religion through the language of "national heritage" and "patrimony," two key touchstones for negotiating pluralistic citizenship and multiculturalism in Québec.

21. For example, ibid., 19–21. See also Victoria Bonnell, *Iconography of Power: Soviet Political Posters under Lenin and Stalin* (Berkley: University of California Press, 1997); Robin Wagner-Pacifici, *The Art of Surrender: Decomposing Sovereignty at Conflict's End* (Chicago: University of Chicago Press, 2005); Webb Keane, "Semiotics and the Social Analysis of Material Things," *Language and Communication* 23 (2003): 403–25; Keane, "Subjects and Objects"; Keane, "The Evidence of the Senses"; Krisztina Fehérváry, *Politics of Color and Concrete: Socialist Materialities and the Middle Class in Hungary* (Bloomington: Indiana University Press, 2013); and Terence McDonnell, "Cultural Objects as Objects: Materiality, Urban Space, and the Interpretation of AIDS Campaigns in Accra, Ghana," *American Journal of Sociology* 115, no. 6 (2010): 1800–1852.

22. Zubrzycki, *Beheading the Saint*, 20.

23. Ibid., 22; and Keane, "Subjects and Objects."

24. See Tanenbaum Center for Interreligious Understanding, "Menachem Froman," accessed November 4, 2017, https://tanenbaum.org/peacemakers-in-action-network/meet-the -peacemakers/rabbi-menachem-froman/; and David Little, ed., *Peacemakers in Action: Profiles of Religion in Conflict Resolution* (Cambridge: Cambridge University Press, 2007), 341–55.

25. Larry Derfner, "Praying with the Enemy: West Bank Rabbi Seeks Common Ground with Hamas Sheiks," *Baltimore Jewish Times*, March 3, 1995, 38; and Isabel Kershner, "From an Israeli Settlement, a Rabbi's Unorthodox Plan for Peace," *New York Times*, December 5, 2008, http:// www.nytimes.com/2008/12/06/world/middleeast/06froman.html.

26. Shaul Magid, "Re-Thinking American Jewish Zionist Identity," talk at the Taube Center for Jewish Studies, Stanford University, October 8, 2015. Other scholars identified the pluralization of messianic conceptions within the settlement bloc as well as consolidation of post-Zionist interpretations of settlers' religious connection to the land. See, for example, Assaf Harel, "On Faith, Redemption, and Messianism in West Bank Settlements," *Theory and Criticism* 47 (2016): 159–80 (in Hebrew). See also Shaul Magid, "West Bank Rabbi: Menachem Froman's Zionist Post-Zionism, and What It Can Teach American Jews," *Tablet*, August 4, 2015, http://www .tabletmag.com/jewish-news-and-politics/192626/froman-zionist-post-zionism.

27. "Rabbi Froman: Complete Interview" (film), Global Oneness Project, accessed November 4, 2017, http://www.globalonenessproject.org/library/interviews/rabbi-froman-complete -interview.

28. Gershon Baskin, "Menachem Froman, the Settler Rabbi Who Wanted to Be a Palestinian Citizen," *Haaretz*, March 6, 2013, http://www.haaretz.com/opinion/menachem-froman-the -settler-rabbi-who-wanted-to-be-a-palestinian-citizen.premium-1.507631. Froman explained: "I am a citizen of the state of God. It doesn't so much matter who has political control." "Challenges of Menachem Froman," YouTube video interview posted by Harvey Stein, September 5, 2010, https://www.youtube.com/watch?v=atlc3egCacI.

29. Froman's model is distinct from Haredi (ultra-Orthodox) settlers, who constitute 30% of the settlements' population, but whose presence in the territories occupied in 1967 depends more on an ability to afford the Haredi lifestyle and less on an intimacy with the biblical land.

See Lee Cahaner, "Between Ghetto Politics and Geopolitics: Ultra-Orthodox Settlements in the West Bank," in *Normalizing Occupation: The Politics of Everyday Life in the West Bank Settlements*, ed. Marco Allegra, Ariel Handel, and Erez Maggor (Bloomington: Indiana University Press, 2017), 112–27.

30. Joyce Dalsheim, *Producing Spoilers: Peacemaking and the Production of Enmity in a Secular Age* (Oxford: Oxford University Press, 2014).

31. Froman eulogized Shagar, who died an untimely death, as the "fulfillment of the promise of Kook's teaching. He illuminated the religious world with the light of freedom—not in the intellectual sense but the deep spiritual one of freedom." Kobi Nahshoni, "He Was the Fulfillment of Rav Kook's Promise," *Ynet*, November 6, 2007.

32. See Akiva Eldar and Idith Zertal, *Lords of the Land: The War over Israel's Settlements in the Occupied Territories, 1967–2007* (New York: Nation Books, 2007).

33. On Rabbi Shagar's view, see Shagar, *Faith Shattered and Restored: Judaism in the Postmodern Era*, ed. Zohar Maor, trans. Elie Leshem (Jerusalem: Magid, 2017); and Shaul Magid, "The Settler Nakba and the Rise of Post-Modern Post-Zionist Religious Ideology on the West Bank," *Tablet*, September 19, 2017, http://www.tabletmag.com/jewish-arts-and-culture/245084/settler-nakba-post-zionist-religious-identity. On Froman, see David Little, ed., *Peacemakers in Action: Profiles of Religion in Conflict Resolution* (Cambridge: Cambridge University Press, 2007), 341–55.

34. See Marc Gopin, *Bridges Across an Impossible Divide: The Inner Lives of Arab and Jewish Peacemakers* (New York: Oxford University Press, 2012), 70.

35. According to Ilan Fuchs, Shagar identified religious potential for engaging with postmodernism. He attempted to draw on relativism as a horizon for religious renewal, arguing that engaging this conversation through the mediation of Hasidic texts prevents relativism from sliding into nihilism. This approach then led him to open up to feminist renewals of tradition and the permissibility of women to study Torah. Textual deconstruction, therefore, became a religious tool. Nonetheless, a tension between postmodernism and tradition persists. See Fuchs, "Her Voice and the Study of Torah: Rav Shimon Rosenberg and Cultural Feminism," in *Studies in Israeli Revival: Gender in Israel*, ed. Margalit Shilah and Gidon Katz (Be'er Sheva: Ben Gurion University Press, 2011), 771–89 (in Hebrew).

36. Judith Butler, "Sexual Politics, Torture, and Secular Time."

37. See also Magid, "West Bank Rabbi."

38. Smadar Lavie, "Where Is the Mizrahi-Palestinian Border Zone? Interrogating Feminist Transnationalism through the Bounds of the Lived," *Social Semiotics* 21, no. 1 (2011): 67–83; Anzaldúa, *Borderlands/La Frontera: The New Mestiza* (San Francisco: Aunt Lute Books, 1987). See also Lavie, *Wrapped in the Flag of Israel: Mizrahi Single Mothers and Bureaucratic Torture* (New York: Berghahn Books, 2014). Lavie's analysis coheres with the later work of Houria Bouteldja examined especially in chapter 7.

39. Lavie, "Where Is the Mizrahi-Palestinian Border Zone?," 79.

40. Tikva Honig-Parnas, "Reclaiming the Place of 'Black Feminism,' 'Mizrahi Feminism' and the 'Socialist Feminism,'" *MeTzad Sheni* 5–6 (1996): 34–39 (in Hebrew); Vicki Shiran, "Feminist Identity vs. Oriental Identity," in *Calling the Equality Bluff: Women in Israel*, ed. Barbara Swirski and Marilyn P. Safir (Oxford: Pergamon Press, 1991), 303–11; Shiran, "Mizrahi Women and Other Women," *MeTzad Sheni* [On the Other Hand] 5–6 (1996): 24–28 (in Hebrew); Shiran, "The Symmetrical Self-Representation: Mizrahi Women's Contribution to Israeli Feminism," in *Azut Mezach*, ed. Vardit Damari Madar (Jerusalem: Students for Social Justice,

2002), 12–19; and Pnina Motzafi-Haller, "Scholarship, Identity, and Power: Mizrahi Women in Israel," *Signs: Journal of Women in Culture and Society* 26, no. 3 (2001): 697–734.

41. CJNV's team leader—who is American Jewish Japanese Israeli and Moroccan—organized the panel in response to criticism of CJNV's delegation the previous year. The criticism highlighted the delegation's lack of attention to poor Israelis on the peripheries. See Seth J. Frantzman, "A Blind Spot of Diaspora Jews on Israel," *Jerusalem Post*, July 24, 2016, http://jpost .com/Opinion/A-blind-spot-of-Diaspora-Jews-on-Israel-462249.

42. Ella Shohat, "Sephardim in Israel: Zionism from the Standpoint of Its Jewish Victims," *Social Text* 19/20 (1988): 1–35; Yehouda Shenhav, *The Arab Jew: A Postcolonial Reading of Nationalism, Religion, and Ethnicity* (Stanford, CA: Stanford University Press, 2006); Shenhav, *Beyond the Two State Solution: A Jewish Political Essay* (London: Polity Press, 2012); and Atalia Omer, "Hitmazrehut, or Becoming of the East: Re-Orienting Israeli Social Mapping," *Critical Sociology* 43, no. 6 (2017): 949–76.

43. Lavie, "Mizrahi Feminism and the Question of Palestine," *Journal of Middle East Women's Studies* 7, no. 2 (2011): 56–88.

44. See, for example, Henriette Dahan-Kaleb, "Tensions in Israeli Feminism: The Mizrahi Ashkenazi Rift," *Women's Studies International Forum* 24, no. 6 (2001): 669–84; and Lavie, "Mizrahi Feminism."

45. See, for example, Itach-Ma'aki [Women Lawyers for Social Justice], http://www.itach .org.il/.

46. Nissim Mizrachi, "Sociology in the Garden: Beyond the Liberal Grammar of Contemporary Sociology," *Israel Studies Review* 31, no. 1 (2016): 36–65.

47. "Mizrahi Palestinian Partnership," March 17, 2016, https://mizrahipalestinianpartnership .wordpress.com/2016/03/17 (in Hebrew, translation mine).

48. Ibid.

49. Ibid.

50. Rivi Gillis also highlights how the "ethnic" dimensions of the settlements themselves are bracketed, thereby reinforcing a discourse differentiating the "ethnic" and "domestic" issue from the occupation. Gillis, "The Question of Ethnic Identity in the Israeli Settlements," *Theory and Criticism* 47 (Winter 2016): 41–63.

51. Other Mizrahi organizations are following a similar path. One such example is the meeting between Abu Mazen and representatives of Hakeshet Hademokratit Hamizrahit held in August 2015. See Sigal Harush-Yonatan, "The Democratic Rainbow meeting with Abu Mazen: The Day My Hurt Was Reopened," *Haokets*, August 13, 2015, http://www.haokets.org/2015/08/ 13/%D7%A4%D7%92%D7%99%D7%A9%D7%AA-%D7%94%D7%A7%D7%A9%D7%AA -%D7%94%D7%9E%D7%96%D7%A8%D7%97%D7%99%D7%AA-%D7%A2%D7%9D- %D7%90%D7%91%D7%95-%D7%9E%D7%90%D7%96%D7%9F-%D7%94%D7%99%D7 %95%D7%9D-%D7%91%D7%95/ (in Hebrew).

52. Carmit Sapir-Weitz, "Hebrew Is a Mizrahi Language: The Poet Who Formulates a Vision for the Jewish-Arab Culture," *Ma'ariv*, August 8, 2016, http://www.maariv.co.il/culture/ literature/Article-554982 (in Hebrew, translation mine).

53. Other artistic venues that allow for Mizrahi reimagining include Ars Poetica, the bilingual literary journal *Gerila Tarbut*, and Bahar's "New Hebrew Arabic Anthology." See Rachel Delia Benaim, "The Mizrahim Are Finding Their Voice," *The Tower* 33 (December 2015), http:// www.thetower.org/article/the-mizrahim-are-finding-their-voice/; and Almog Bahar, *An Anthology for Contemporary Young Literature 2014: "A New Hebrew Arabic Anthology"* (in Hebrew),

October 13, 2014, https://almogbehar.wordpress.com/2014/10/13/%D7%90%D7%A0%D7
%AA%D7%95%D7%9C%D7%95%D7%92%D7%99%D7%94-%D7%A2%D7%91%D7%A8
%D7%99%D7%AA-%D7%A2%D7%A8%D7%91%D7%99%D7%AA-%D7%97%D7%93
%D7%A9%D7%94-%D7%A9%D7%AA%D7%99%D7%99%D7%9D-%D8%A7%D8%AB
%D9%86.

54. See Weitz. See also Eli Eliyahu, "The poet Almog Bahar writes prose, clarifying that the Mizrahi-Ashkenazi conflictic is still far from Disappearing," *Haaretz*, June 1, 2011, https://www.haaretz.co.il/misc/1.1156502 (in Hebrew).

55. See also Ron Kakhlili, "Hamahapeha haMizrahit lo hitzliha" [The Mizrahi Revolution Failed], *Haaretz*, November 24, 2015, http://www.haaretz.co.il/opinions/.premium-1.3132357.

56. Jakeet Singh, "Religious Agency and the Limits of Intersectionality," *Hypatia* 30, no. 4 (2015): 657–74 (667).

57. See chapter 8.

Index

Page numbers followed by "f" refer to figures.